HABITATS OF EUROPE

HABITATS OF EUROPE

A Field Guide for Birders, Naturalists, and Ecologists

Dale Forbes, Iain Campbell, and Pete Morris

Special Contributors
Giselle Velastegui and Pablo Cervantes

PRINCETON UNIVERSITY PRESS
PRINCETON AND OXFORD

Published by Princeton University Press
41 William Street, Princeton, New Jersey 08540
99 Banbury Road, Oxford OX2 6JX

press.princeton.edu
GPSR Authorized Representative: Easy Access System Europe, Mustamäe tee 50, 10621 Tallinn, Estonia, gpsr.requests@easproject.com

ISBN (pbk.) 9780691245171
ISBN (e-book) 9780691245188

Library of Congress Control Number: 2025930833
British Library Cataloging-in-Publication Data is available

Editorial: Robert Kirk and Megan Mendonça
Production Editorial: Mark Bellis
Cover Design: Wanda España
Production: Steve Sears
Publicity: Matthew Taylor and Caitlyn Robson-Iszatt
Copyeditor: Amy K. Hughes
Typesetting and Design: D & N Publishing, Wiltshire, UK

Cover illustrations by Christine Elder

This book has been composed in Cambay Devanagari

Printed in China

10 9 8 7 6 5 4 3 2 1

CONTENTS

FIGURES AND SIDEBARS

FIGURES

SIDEBARS

PREFACE

GENESIS OF THE HABITATS OF THE WORLD BOOKS

This book is part of a series of seven continental books and one global book in the Habitats of the World series. The authors of all the books have had a lifelong fascination with biogeography and wildlife ecosystems. Like the vast majority of other passionate travelling naturalists, we are most interested in birds and larger mammals, while also paying some attention to reptiles, amphibians, butterflies, and other groups. We understand that anywhere an animal exists is its individual 'habitat' but also that broadly similar ecosystems with similar animal assemblages are distinct habitats. We have been frustrated by ambiguous habitat/ecosystem classifications used in most books and the complete absence of habitat information in many vertebrate field guides. To remedy this, we created the global *Habitats of the World* guide (2021), which was limited in scope, with enough space for just 189 habitats to be delineated and described. What became apparent was that at a slightly more detailed level, with around 545 habitats divided among the seven continents, we could delineate habitats at a scale that mirrored the regional level of world vegetation but reclassify them, using bird assemblages along with vegetation, and make a system that is functional for botanists, intuitive for ecologists, and accessible to naturalists. To do this required one of the series' authors to undertake a PhD to align major world vegetation mapping systems, create bird assemblages for all habitats, and test whether bird assemblages better predict habitats than vegetation mapping alone. The viability of using bird assemblages to predict habitat varies across the world, and bird assemblages work better in some regions than others. On islands, birds tend to be range restricted but generalists, so habitat prediction is more complicated than in, say, continental mountain ranges. Europe also differs from tropical environments, and even from the equivalent temperate zone of Asia, in that the birds tend to be generalists. The reasons for this are not completely clear, but it is likely that the repeated, intense glaciation (and consequent drying) of Europe during the Pleistocene (2.6 MYA to ~12,000 YA) caused numerous population bottlenecks and favoured generalist species. By contrast, regions with less glaciation, such as e. North America and e. Eurasia, have many more specialised bird species.

We present our view of European wildlife habitats (ecosystems) in this book and employ a common language that reflects a collaboration with a broader group of experts from the professional nature guiding and conservation world. We have also created online resources, such as a bird-assemblage habitat database, listing all global habitats along with the indicator bird species, which will allow people to search via birds or habitats to find and understand their relationships (www.habitatsoftheworld.org/birdassemblages).

There are innumerable lenses through which planet earth's habitats can be assessed. Geology, geography, and botany are all critically important. But we do not view any of them as the final word on habitats, and much of what these models prioritise is of little immediate relevance to travelling naturalists or ecologists. A specialist in entomology or herpetology will apply a different, and fascinating, lens to the world. Our reason for prioritising the bird (and to a lesser extent mammal) 'lens' is that we look at the world primarily through this lens, as do the vast majority of the world's travelling naturalists. Our presentation at first glance may lack the perceived clarity of a botanical approach to the world's habitats, but by using bird assemblages in conjunction with botany, we provide a truly ecological description of Europe's habitats rather than a botanical one. At the scale we present it, our classification has far greater utility to most world travellers, regional ecologists, and conservationists than any other previous perspective on habitats.

Attempting to cover the wildlife habitats of the entire continent of Europe in a single book is an ambitious undertaking in which hard decisions had to be made about what to include and exclude based on botanical and bird assemblages. We freely admit that deep oceanic habitats, and to a lesser extent, surface aquatic habitats, are worthy of far more detailed coverage using fish and invertebrate assemblages than we have given in this volume. We will fill these gaps in a global marine and aquatic volume once the terrestrial and surface habitats have been described. At this time, the habitats are almost all based on terrestrial botany and aquatic habitats as they relate to birds and mammals. Our approach is certain to alienate some, but we firmly believe it will be both enjoyable and useful to other ecologists, conservationists, and global naturalists like us.

Red-breasted Flycatcher is a specialist of Temperate Broadleaf Woodlands. © MARKUS VARESVUO, AGAMI

INTRODUCTION

AREA COVERED BY THIS BOOK

This book covers all of continental Europe, east to the Urals and including Türkiye, Armenia, Georgia, and Azerbaijan. It excludes the Canaries, as these are treated in the *Habitats of Africa* book, and Greenland, covered in the *Habitats of North America* book.

ABOUT THIS BOOK

The bulk of this book consists of habitat accounts; these are organised by biomes. While some habitats could reasonably be classified under multiple biomes, each is described only once. The introduction to each of the biomes includes a dendrogram illustrating how the European habitat relates to similar habitats within the global *Habitats of the World* book. Habitats found on multiple continents naturally have very similar descriptions across the books in the Habitats of the World (HotW) series, with some text elements being identical in two or more of the continent or world books. For much more detailed explanations of our habitat classification system and additional dendrograms, readers are referred to the Habitats of the World website (www.habitatsoftheworld.org).

Each of the habitat accounts includes the following sections and elements.

In a Nutshell: A succinct explanation of what makes the habitat distinctive and worthy of separation from other habitats.

Global Habitat Affinities: Habitats from other continents that are structurally similar, providing a cross-reference to habitats that may be familiar to you, helping you to understand the unfamiliar habitat covered.

Continental Habitat Affinities: Habitats from elsewhere in Europe that are structurally similar. For these cross-references to other habitats within this book, we drop the broad regional designation and name just the habitat; for example, we list Boggy Tundra rather than European Boggy Tundra.

Species Overlap: The habitats that have the most similar assemblages of birds (predominantly) and mammals. These are ranked from the most similar habitat to the least. The vast majority of these are habitats within the same zoogeographic region as the habitat covered. As with Continental Habitat Affinities, for habitats within Europe, we do not include the regional designation in the name.

Habitat Silhouette: These silhouettes are designed to give a quick visual snapshot of a habitat, showing some of its distinctive plant shapes and its overall height and structure. They include a human silhouette for scale.

Range Map: These are visual representations of a habitat's occurrence within a given zoogeographic region. Dark shading is used for areas where the habitat is the predominant habitat, or one of the predominant habitats. In some maps, pale shading is used to indicate areas where the habitat is found only sporadically.

Description: This section explains what makes a habitat distinctive and how it works. Some of the commonly included information is the height and composition of the various layers of vegetation, the overall 'feel' and accessibility, local temperature, and rainfall. The accompanying climate graphs are discussed in Climate Descriptions and Graphs, below. In the descriptions, we have purposefully chosen not to always include the same information or to present it in the same order. This allows us both to stress what is most important about a given habitat and to simply vary these sections to keep them interesting for readers.

Wildlife: This section may be the most interesting for a typical reader. Beyond the nuts and bolts of what makes a habitat distinctive and what makes it work, most visitors are keen to learn about and to find its wildlife. Throughout this book, when considering wildlife, larger mammals and birds are our primary focus, but in many accounts, we go well beyond this to feature a broad array of vertebrates. Species that are indicative of or restricted to a habitat are highlighted, as finding these will be the priority for many visitors.

Conservation: This section provides a quick summary of the conservation status of the habitat and major issues it is facing.

Distribution: This section and the accompanying range map indicate where the habitat occurs within a given zoogeographic region. The elevations at which it is found are sometimes mentioned, though this information may also be in the Description.

Where to See: These are places that you can visit to experience a given habitat. In general, these are the most readily or frequently visited places, in the most accessible country or countries.

Photos: Photos are included that illustrate both the habitat itself and some of its charismatic wildlife. Some photos are chosen because they effectively show both the habitat and some of its wildlife.

Sidebars

Throughout the book, there are boxes or sidebars that discuss aspects of a habitat, biome, or region—in some cases these discussions are somewhat tangential, in others more in-depth. They may be about geology, ecology, or prehistory. We have chosen to place this sort of information in sidebars to make it more accessible and relevant (rather than in long, dry introductory sections that are likely to be ignored by most readers).

WHAT DO WE COVER AS A DISTINCT HABITAT IN THIS BOOK AND HOW DID WE MAKE THE MAPS?

We evaluate habitats based on two main criteria: (1) their visual distinctiveness, which can be easily assessed by a casual observer and usually relates to the types of structures (forest vs. shrubland) and the species of plants present—a very similar approach to other ecosystem-mapping systems; and (2) their assemblage of wildlife, primarily birds—but we also consider other vertebrates, in a departure from any existing global or regional ecological mapping system. Each habitat is described with a suite of obligate and indicator bird species, available online at www.habitatsoftheworld.org/birdassemblages. An example is European Rocky Tundra, which is quite distinct in appearance from other habitats and supports a fairly distinctive set of wildlife. But in some cases, one or the other criterion is of predominant importance. Except to the eye of a trained botanist, European Maquis is not very different from other Mediterranean-climate shrublands around the world, but the bird assemblage there is very different from analogous habitats in North America or Chile, so it is considered a distinct habitat. Most examples in Europe, however, are the opposite. In stark contrast to Australia or South America, most broadleaf European habitats appear very distinctive and easily recognisable yet have similar bird assemblages to surrounding forests. Having said that, the (very valid) case can be made that if we were to use the full suite of vertebrate assemblages, including amphibians and fishes, the distinction between this habitat and surrounding ones would be more obvious. The great strength of our system of using bird assemblages to refine habitat delineation also shows its weakness, compared to what could be, and we think should be, done with the use of other vertebrate and invertebrate groups. If readers know of readily identifiable animals that we can use to make our system better, please contact us, and let's see how we can incorporate them into the algorithms we are building.

The individual habitat maps were created using a variety of sources, including FLORAVEG, EUNIS (European Nature Information System), the European Red List of Habitats, and various national mapping projects (especially for Türkiye). As with the *Habitats of North America* and *Habitats of Africa* books, we are using the regional classification as a base to search for bird-assemblage associations. In North America, South America, and Africa, we start with the International Vegetation Classification (IVC) Macrogroups. In Europe, we started with the lowest-level units in the EUNIS system and repeatedly combined them when their animal assemblages were the same or very similar. We repeated this process, moving up the crosswalk levels until neighbouring units had significantly different assemblages.

This was particularly the case with savannas and mixed systems, where EUNIS classifies the systems as either one or the other 'pure' form. The Iberian Magpie is a savanna species (Oak Dehesa) but will also use woodlands (Mediterranean Oak Forest). To consider just the forest would ignore the value of the savanna ecosystem. Some habitats have broad altitudinal and latitudinal ranges in which the animal assemblages change along a gradient. We have split these habitats when they have distinct animal assemblages (e.g., Lowland Heath vs. Montane Heath and Moorland) and combined them where the change is gradual or hard to clearly separate. In the latter case, we have described such in-habitat variations as habitat subtypes.

HOW DOES HABITATS OF THE WORLD COMPLEMENT OTHER GLOBAL HABITAT CLASSIFICATION SYSTEMS?

The understanding and correct classification of habitats is crucial to the development of useful and viable nature reserve systems, as is knowing what wildlife occurs in threatened habitats within them. The problem is that, as of now, there is no system to classify all the world's habitats at a level that is appreciable to most casual naturalists, birders, conservationists, and ecologists. There are reasons for this, such as, but not limited to, systems and typologies being overly hierarchical by design, and the challenges of trying to syncretise different national mapping systems. The Global Ecosystem Typology (GET) system, developed by the International Union for Conservation of Nature (IUCN), and the IVC, mainly developed through NatureServe, both have excellent ecosystem classifications that aim to define and protect ecological communities. These systems are extremely useful in principle, but neither works globally at a scale that conservation groups, birders, or ecologists can readily use, because they do not yet have all habitats described at a level that is convenient to use and understand (see fig. 1). However, we do use the IVC/NatureServe Group levels to build our system, with the IVC Macrogroups as a starting point. Our Habitats of the World (HotW) system works as a Rosetta Stone for applying the GET and IVC habitat classification systems at a global scale. A complete walk-through from the HotW system to the IVC and GET systems is available online at www.habitatsoftheworld.org/intotheweedstypology.

As illustrated in figure 1, the GET system jumps from 108 global (described) units at Group level to between 3000 and 3750 (undescribed) units at Regional Ecotype level. Similarly, the IVC system jumps from 76 (described) units at Division level to 1196 (often undescribed) units at Macrogroup level. Neither system describes the animals living in the habitats. It will be many years before either system has the coverage required for global use at the most detailed scale.

The HotW system has global coverage and includes c. 545 global (56 in Europe), mainly terrestrial habitats, covering the natural environments of almost all the world's birds and much of the other wildlife. At this level, it becomes much easier for the non-botanist to discern one habitat from another, understand how they differ, and develop the understanding and criteria to be able to comprehend their ecology. Consequently, the HotW approach makes it easier to incorporate habitats into conservation planning, mapping, and ecological studies.

Habitats (sometimes called 'vegetation types') are amalgamations of various species of plants and animals under specific environmental conditions with artificially human-imposed boundaries delineating them from adjacent similar habitats in what is almost always a gradual boundary at some scale. They are not taxonomic entities analogous to species of animals and plants. Organisms have distinct genetic codes and evolutionary histories that infer relatedness, which can be detailed in the form of a strict dendrogram (fig. 2). However, all the habitat classification systems use a hierarchical typology that fails to fit this rigid structure. As you will see in the breakdowns of different biomes in the Biomes of Europe section below, the dendrograms are helpful in showing relationships, but many habitats are crossovers or can easily be classified in multiple biomes. Hence, the relationships are not hierarchical but often more weblike. Examples include European Coniferous Peat Woodland, which fits in forest and in wetland biomes, and Caucasian Montane Desert Steppe, which may be described as both a desert and a grassland. These are not either/or alternatives but simultaneous both/ands.

One reason there are so many more birders than other types of naturalists is because there are a manageable number of species (~11,000, compared to 400,000 beetles), that are largely colourful

Fig. 1. Comparison of global ecosystem, habitat, and vegetation classification systems. The Habitats of the World (HotW), the International Vegetation Classification (IVC), and the IUCN's Global Ecosystem Typology (GET) are all systems for global habitat classification. The chart shows that although the GET system will be comprehensive, it is still in the very rudimentary stages, with only the 108 Groups defined. The IVC system is much more developed, with about half the 1196 Macrogroups defined and described. The HotW system is almost complete, with most of the approximately 545 regional habitats classified and described. The shaded area shows the number of units that are comprehensive enough to describe variations of the world habitats but sufficiently general to be understood and learnt for the whole planet.

GET	HotW	IVC
Wildlife not included in classification	Wildlife included in classification	Wildlife not included in classification
REALM 5		VEG/NON-VEG 2
		FORMATION CLASS 8
BIOME 25	BIOME 11	FORMATION SUBCLASS 22
GROUP 108	GLOBAL 189	DIVISION 76
	REGIONAL c. 545 Almost completely classified and described (56 in Europe)	MACROGROUP 1196 Approximately half classified and described
REGIONAL ECOTYPE 3000–3750 Mostly undescribed		GROUP c. 3500 Approximately half classified and described
GLOBAL ECOSYSTEM Unknown		ALLIANCE c. 25,000 Mostly undescribed
SUB-GLOBAL ECOSYSTEM Unknown		ASSOCIATION Unknown Mostly undescribed

GET: Global Ecosystem Typology
HotW: Habitats of the World
IVC: International Vegetation Classification

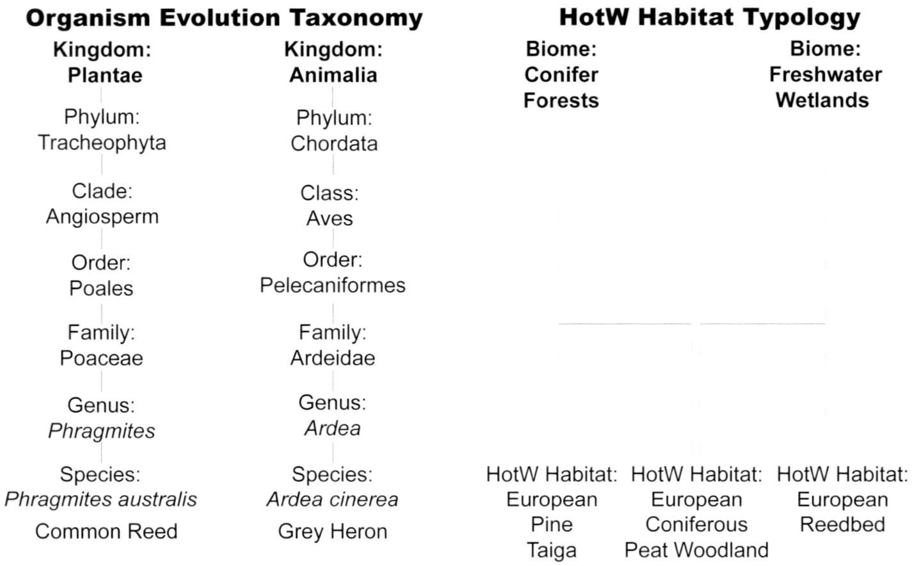

Organism Evolution Taxonomy

Kingdom: Plantae	Kingdom: Animalia
Phylum: Tracheophyta	Phylum: Chordata
Clade: Angiosperm	Class: Aves
Order: Poales	Order: Pelecaniformes
Family: Poaceae	Family: Ardeidae
Genus: *Phragmites*	Genus: *Ardea*
Species: *Phragmites australis*	Species: *Ardea cinerea*
Common Reed	Grey Heron

HotW Habitat Typology

Biome: Conifer Forests

Biome: Freshwater Wetlands

HotW Habitat: European Pine Taiga

HotW Habitat: European Coniferous Peat Woodland

HotW Habitat: European Reedbed

Fig. 2. Comparison of biota taxonomy and habitat typology. Species of flora and fauna, such as the Common Reed and the Grey Heron, have clearly defined phylogenetic taxonomic classifications, each following a hierarchical Linnaean lineage encompassing phylum, class (or clade), order, family, genus, and species. Conversely, habitats present more complexity; some habitats, like European Pine Taiga, can belong to a single biome, yet others, such as European Coniferous Peat Woodland, integrate elements from multiple biomes, something not found in plants or animals. Consequently, with multi-biome habitats and ecotones between habitats, we can create a topology of habitats, but applying a pseudo-Linnaean phylogenetic taxonomy to habitats is illogical.

and diurnal. By contrast, there are fewer species of mammals, they are typically less colourful, and they are largely crepuscular or nocturnal. It is possible to learn most of the world's bird species, to identify them, and to catalogue them (i.e., to keep lists), as so many birders are prone to doing. This then becomes a meaningful contribution to citizen-science projects like Cornell's eBird and iNaturalist, which can be used to analyse global trends in species distribution and occurrence. In its approach, the Habitats of the World system employs the 'Goldilocks principle', which makes it 'just right': detailed enough to be valuable but easy enough for anyone to understand. When trying to develop a system for understanding habitats that allows conservationists, ecologists, and planners to communicate across continents, we are left with similar problems, where the systems are either so broad as to be of little use at the birder and conservationist scale or so detailed and difficult to separate that most users, including conservationists, don't understand them.

TYPES OF HABITAT BOUNDARIES AND ECOTONES

An ecotone is a place where two or more biomes meet, usually possessing traits of both. For example, European Freshwater Marsh could be regarded as an ecotone between a water body and European Wet Grassland, while Subalpine Timberline Woodland could form an ecotone between the montane forests below and the European Alpine Tundra at higher elevations. Many locales are ecotones at some scale. We try to avoid use of this confusing term in the book and prefer to treat zones between defined habitats as boundaries, where the ends of the transitions are different habitats with different bird assemblages. Sometimes the transitions are extremely **sharp**, especially where natural forests abut anthropogenic farmlands or wetland systems in arid terrains (fig. 3). **Mosaics** have distinct patches of different habitats in one area. This type of transition is very common in coastal forests and savanna edges. In a **mélange**, distinct systems intertwine in a complex manner across a broad zone. This pattern is very common in mountainous areas with complex geomorphology and geology and complex microclimates. The fourth kind of transition is **nebulous**, where the changes are so gradual that it is difficult to determine which habitat you are in. The bird and animal assemblages mix in this type of ecotone, and it can be difficult to determine the habitat based on either plant or animal assemblages; in a finer-scale habitat typology, these nebulous transition zones might be defined as a different habitat.

There are also regions where habitats **intrude** into one another, such as moist forests that extend far into arid terrains along waterways. The opposite exists where dry and heath-type habitats can extend as **outliers** in very humid environments along ridgelines with nutrient-deficient rocks such as granites. To confuse everything further, another system exists on mountains that are high enough to become cold and/or attract orographic rainfall. Here the system flips, and wetter forests can occur on mountains, such as the deciduous rainforests of the Talish Mountains of Azerbaijan, which sit above the deserts of the Caspian coast.

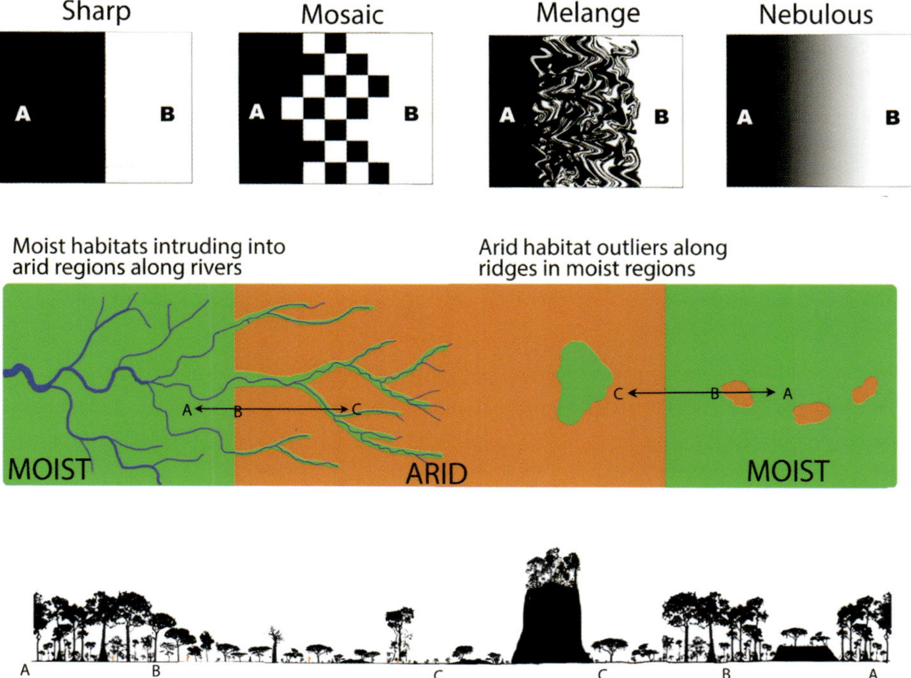

Fig. 3. Types of habitat boundaries and ecotones. Top: There are four types of habitat boundaries. In sharp and mosaic habitat boundaries, the bird assemblages between the different habitats remain separated. The habitats are separate in mélange boundaries, but the bird assemblage overlaps because the two habitats are so intertwined. Nebulous boundaries are ecotonal, where the exact change from one habitat to another is very diffuse with a clinal change in bird assemblages. Bottom: Habitats can occur as outliers in other habitats, such as where wetter habitats intrude into arid environments along rivers, or arid habitats occur in wet environments along ridgelines with poor soils.

THE KÖPPEN CLIMATE CLASSIFICATION

The Köppen climate classification system is the most widely used global method to classify and categorise different climatic regions. Each climate is assigned a simple two- or three-letter code.

The first letter denotes the average temperature (B is an exception):

A: Tropical climate, with year-round average temperatures above 18°C (64°F).
B: Arid climate with low precipitation.
C: Mid-latitude climate with mild to cool temperatures.
D: Mid-latitude climate with cold winters and mild to cool summers.
E: Polar or alpine climates with extremely cold temperatures.

The second letter denotes when most precipitation occurs:

f: Year-round rainfall pattern, with precipitation evenly distributed throughout the year.
F: Ice cap, perennial frost.
m: Monsoonal, with a pronounced wet season and a dry season.
w: Dominant dry winter season.
s: Dominant dry summer season.
T: Lacks a true summer.

The third letter denotes maximum and minimum temperatures, or hot/cold desert:

a: Hot summers, with the warmest month having an average temperature above 22°C (71.6°F).
b: Mild summers, with the warmest month averaging below 22°C (71.6°F) but above 10°C (50°F).
c: Cool summers, with the warmest month averaging below 10°C (50°F) but above 0°C (32°F).
d: Very cold winters, with the coldest month averaging below 0°C (32°F).
e: Cold summers, with the warmest month averaging below 10°C (50°F).
h: Hot desert.
k: Cold desert.

Europe encompasses a wide range of temperature zones, from the polar regions of Svalbard, Norway, through the subtropics of Türkiye. Simultaneously, there are also varying rainfall regimes, resulting in everything from polar deserts and hot deserts to very wet deciduous rainforests and pretty much everything in between. Using the Köppen system, we have assigned the environments the codes shown in figure 4. When used in conjunction with the climate graphs that accompany each habitat account (explained below), these Köppen codes can explain why most habitats occur where they do.

In figure 5, the Köppen climate for the recent past is presented against the projected Köppen climate for n. Europe (Fennoscandia) in the late 21st century. Although climate change is of great concern, it is beyond the scope of this book to predict future habitats related to these changes in Europe. What this prediction does show is that northern latitudes of Europe are going to go through a profound change, with the climate of continental Norway becoming unsuitable for tundra (e.g., European Rocky Tundra and European Boggy Tundra), and the European Spruce-Fir Taiga becoming greatly reduced.

1. Hot-summer Mediterranean climate (**Csa**): These climates occur in the Mediterranean zone from Portugal to Türkiye. They are categorised by hot, dry summers and mild, wet winters. The main habitats are EUROPEAN GARRIGUE and EUROPEAN MAQUIS.

2. Cold semi-arid climate (**Bsk**): These desert regions are characterised by extremely low annual precipitation and little vegetation. Only cold deserts, like the CAUCASIAN SHRUB DESERT, occur in Europe.

3. Temperate oceanic climate (**Cfb**): These areas have mild winters that get cold but not freezing for long periods, and mild summers that are not hot for too long. Typical habitats are EUROPEAN TEMPERATE MIXED FOREST and EUROPEAN BEECH FOREST.

4. Tundra (**ET**): In these climates, winters are long and cold, with even the warmest monthly average only just getting above freezing temperatures. Tundras are found both in the Arctic far north and above the timberline in higher mountains.

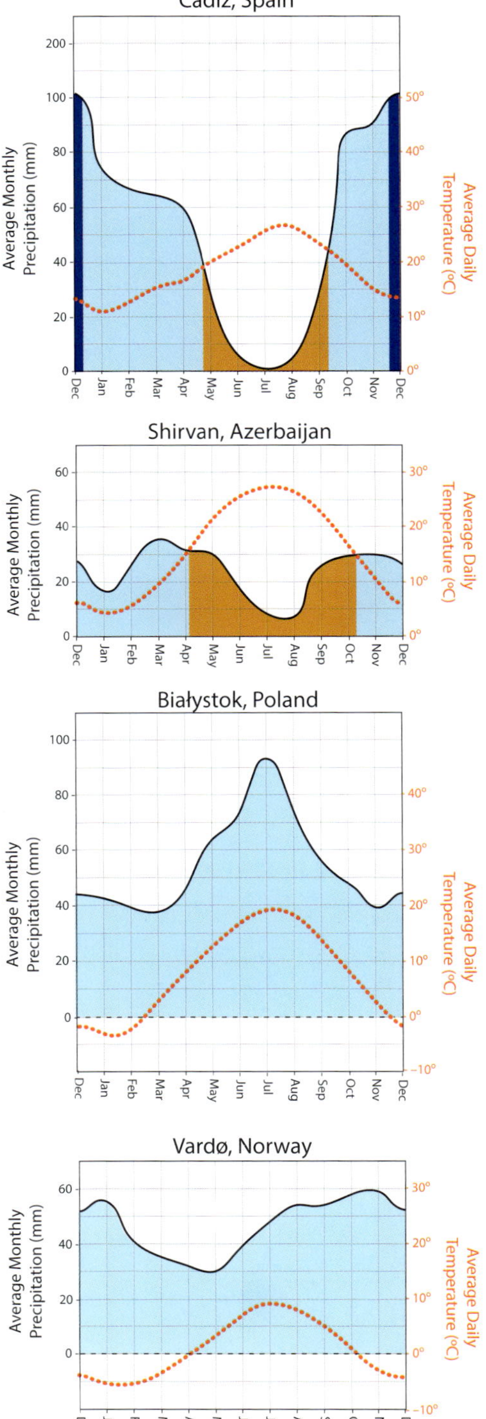

Fig. 4. Köppen codes and sample climate graphs.

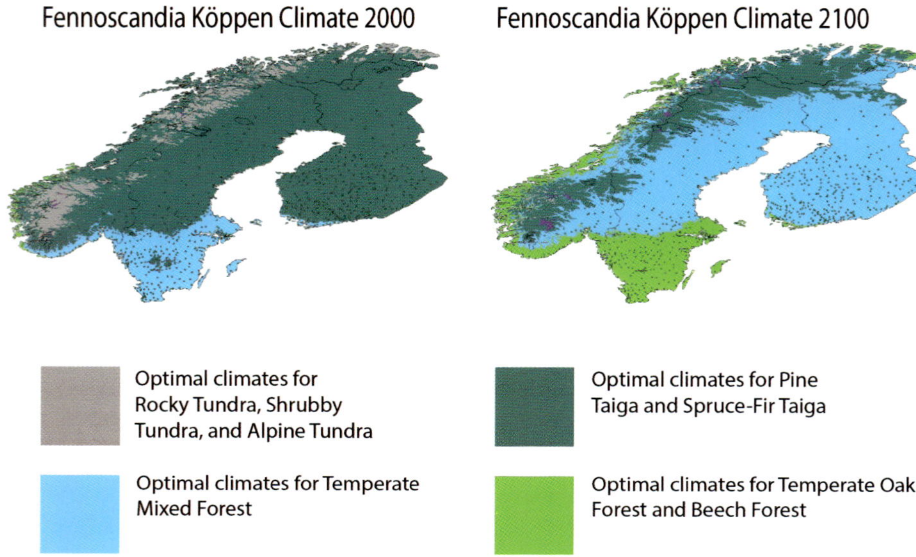

Fig. 5. Köppen climate maps for Fennoscandia in the present day (2020) and predicted for 2100. Maps show the expected change in climate types and changes of optimal growing conditions for the various HotW habitats of n. Europe. Areas with climates currently conducive to tundra habitats will likely be optimal for conifer forests (taiga); areas that now have conifers will be optimal for Temperate Mixed Forest, and much of the area that is now conifers or mixed forests will become optimal for European Temperate Oak Forest and possibly European Beech Forest. Very few places will be conducive to European Alpine Tundra, while it is unlikely either Rocky or Shrubby Tundra will survive these climate changes. H. E. BECK, N. E. ZIMMERMANN, T. R. MCVICAR, N. VERGOPOLAN, A. BERG, AND E. F. WOOD (2018), PRESENT AND FUTURE KÖPPEN-GEIGER CLIMATE CLASSIFICATION MAPS AT 1-KM RESOLUTION, SCIENTIFIC DATA 5: 180214.

CLIMATE DESCRIPTIONS AND GRAPHS

Throughout the book, each habitat description includes a brief overview of the climate with the Köppen climate code and a heavily adapted version of the Walter-Lieth climate graph, which create a powerful tool when combined. Looking at habitat distributions and their relationships to not only temperature and rainfall but also distribution of rainfall through the year, it became apparent that this annual rainfall distribution is often a more important factor in vegetation type than average precipitation alone. To help illustrate these variations through the year, we have created climate graphs for each habitat, based on the original work of Walter and Lieth, though we have heavily modified them to make them easier to read and interpret.

Reading these graphs may seem intimidating at first, but when their relevance is explained, they become more accessible (see fig. 4). When temperature and precipitation are plotted together, and where each 20 mm (0.8 in.) of precipitation is compared to each 10°C (18°F), some really interesting patterns emerge. When the precipitation plot drops below the temperature plot, the area is in a period of water stress (drought) because transpiration rates (the rate at which plants lose water) are higher than precipitation levels. In the graphs, we have coloured these drought periods in orange. When the precipitation plot lifts above the temperature line, the area has a surplus of water, and plant growth is strong; these periods are coloured light blue. However, once the precipitation exceeds 100 mm (4 in.) a month, there is an extreme surplus of water, and regardless of the temperature, most water runs off and is not used by plants; we have coloured these periods in dark blue. Because the whole method makes sense only when used with the metric system, we have included temperature only in Celsius and rainfall in millimetres on the graphs.

BIOMES OF EUROPE

Multiple biomes, or ecological communities, are described in this book. Europe falls within the Palaearctic biogeographical realm and is often referred to as the Western Palaearctic (which also includes the Sahara Desert). The Western Palaearctic is very similar to the Eastern Palaearctic and has much in common with the Nearctic of North America. While we regard the distinction between the Western Palaearctic and Eastern Palaearctic as mainly political, the birds within Europe are far more generalist than those in similar habitats in the Eastern Palaearctic for reasons that are not understood. This will become evident as you scan through the European habitats.

The broad habitat categories and subcategories used in this book are clustered by biomes, and each has been given a unique code. For example, all coniferous forests globally belong to biome 1, Conifers, and each regional habitat within that biome has its own code, such that European Tundra Taiga (Eu1A) corresponds to Nearctic Subarctic Woodland (Ne1A) in North America. Not all biomes are found in Europe; we do not have biomes 4 (Humid Forests), 5 (Tropical Dry Forests), or 9 (Sclerophyll Forests).

CONIFER FORESTS (BIOME 1): Forests made up of coniferous trees (which generally don't seasonally lose their leaves, except for larches and a few others).

Example: **European Montane Spruce-Fir Forest**

DESERTS (BIOME 2): Open arid areas with small shrubs with generally small leaves; cacti or euphorbias can be present and may be large.

Example: **Caucasian Shrub Desert**

TEMPERATE BROADLEAF WOODLANDS (BIOME 3): Broadleaf forests that lose their leaves in winter.

Example: **European Beech Forest**

SAVANNAS (BIOME 6): Habitats with an open canopy, lots of grass or shrubbery, and a strongly seasonal (usually wet summer–dry winter) climate. Most habitats in this category are heavily influenced by fire.

Example: **Middle Eastern Savanna**

GRASSLANDS AND STEPPES (BIOME 7): Habitats dominated by grasses, with or without shrubs and flowers, and with few or no trees.

Example: **Iberian Steppe**

MEDITERRANEAN SHRUBLANDS (BIOME 8): Can be either closed or open; dominated by fire and grazing. Plants are often similar to those of nearby forests.

Example: **European Maquis**

TUNDRAS (BIOME 10): Very low vegetation dominated by mosses and many lichens. Found at extreme latitudes or elevations, where temperatures, snow cover, or exposure to wind prohibit the growth of trees.

Example: **European Alpine Tundra**

FRESHWATER HABITATS (BIOME 11): Habitats whose most important aspect is their seasonal or permanent inundation with fresh water.

Example: **European Shallow Freshwater Marsh**

SALINE HABITATS (BIOME 12): Habitats where the dominant force is the presence of high levels of salt in the water or soil.

Example: **European Coastal Salt Marsh**

ANTHROPOGENIC HABITATS (BIOME 13): The primary force in shaping these habitats is the presence of humans.

Example: **European Cropland**

TAXONOMY

For birds we follow the eBird-Clements taxonomy. It is up to date, carefully maintained, and the most popular global taxonomy for birders, though we acknowledge that the IOC (International Ornithological Congress) classification is more commonly used in conservation outside the Americas. We have included the commonly used European name in parentheses where this differs significantly from the eBird-Clements name. For mammals, reptiles, amphibians, invertebrates, and plants, we follow iNaturalist. This is sure to shock some scientists and purists, but there are so many local and diverse, competing taxonomic systems through Europe that we chose to standardise to one system, accessible to all in the region and widely used by naturalists. We found iNaturalist to be largely (but not perfectly) consistent and up to date for the groups that we know intimately well, giving us confidence that other groups are covered similarly. The English dragonfly and damselfly names from *Europe's Dragonflies* (Smallshire and Swash 2020) have been appended in parentheses when these differ from those found in iNaturalist. To keep the text flowing, we use only English common names for birds and mammals but do add scientific names for all other taxa when first mentioned in a chapter. Thereafter, we use only the English common name.

USEFUL HABITAT JARGON

The following definitions will help the reader to understand some of the most important terms used in naming and defining habitats. These terms appear over and over in the book.

- **Alpine.** A life zone found in mountainous regions above the timberline but below the nival zone. Vegetation is low, and the climate is harsh (**ET**, tundra).
- **Calcareous.** Refers to alkaline soils formed from rocks rich in calcium carbonate such as limestone and marble.
- **Desert.** Very dry and either unvegetated or sparsely vegetated habitat.
- **Endemic.** Limited (i.e., native) to a specific geographic area.
- **Eutrophication.** An ecological imbalance caused by excessive nutrients (especially nitrogen and phosphorous) that results in algal blooms and the depletion of oxygen in the water. In extreme cases this can create a 'dead zone' in which fish and most water invertebrates are unable to survive.
- **Forest.** A stand of trees over 5 m (15 ft.) tall with a closed canopy of interlocking trees or an open canopy with over 70% cover.
- **Grassland.** Habitat dominated by grasses with few shrubs or trees.
- **Halophytic.** Refers to a plant or organism that can grow in highly saline environments.

- **Heath/Heathland.** Shrubland dominated by fine-leaved evergreen members of the erica family (Ericaceae).
- **Krummholz.** German for 'twisted wood', the term originally referred to the growth form of Dwarf Mountain Pine (*Pinus mugo*) and similar woody plants that naturally grow in a twisted, stunted form. Mainly used in a broader sense to describe vegetation that has been stunted and twisted through harsh climatic conditions.
- **Loess.** A wind-deposited substrate (i.e., soil) composed mostly of silt and clay particles.
- **Montane.** A life zone within mountainous regions above the lowlands and below the tree line. Often forested or with meadows.
- **Nival.** The glacial snow zone high in mountains; vegetation is sparse and low.
- **Peatland.** A wetland in which anaerobic conditions have allowed for the formation of peat (largely composed of partially decomposed sphagnum mosses).
- **Pelagic.** Referring to offshore waters, a zone also described as 'open ocean'. The transition from coastal waters to pelagic waters is usually gradual and varies from place to place, depending on factors such as underwater features (e.g., a continental shelf).
- **Rainforest.** Lush forest that receives abundant moisture.
- **Refugium** (plural: **refugia**). Area in which the habitat type and/or species assemblages were able to persist through the last glacial maximum (~20,000 YA). As the climate warmed, the habitat and animal assemblages were able to spread out from these reservoirs.
- **Riparian.** Describes water-adapted trees and other vegetation growing along the banks of a watercourse.
- **Savanna.** A lightly wooded tropical or subtropical grassland with prominent wet and dry seasons.
- **Sclerophyll.** Plant with hard, desiccation-resistant leaves; the leaves are often, but not exclusively, small.
- **Siliceous.** Refers to acidic soils formed from rocks rich in silica, especially granites and sandstones.
- **Steppe.** Vast, natural grasslands where climate, soils, or fire restrict the growth of trees.
- **Taiga.** Moist forest of spruce, pine, or fir trees that grows in harsh subarctic climates south of the tundra; also known as boreal forest.
- **Wetland.** Habitat that is frequently or permanently flooded.
- **Woodland.** Habitat with abundant trees, forming a nearly interlocking canopy, though sunlight still reaches the ground, allowing the growth of an understorey such as shrubs, grasses, or forbs.

ACKNOWLEDGMENTS

Our families have provided amazing support as we have created this book, and it would not have been possible without them. Thank you, Babsi, Leo, and Alex for giving Dale the time, space, and support on so many evenings and weekends to work on this project. Thank you, Cristina, Gabriel, and Amy for putting up with Iain's numerous outbursts when things didn't go as planned. Gabriel joined Iain for ground truthing the descriptions and maps from a non-expert perspective, and this was very helpful. Pete's wife, Nina, was amazingly supportive as ever, and Pete would like to extend special thanks to his fellow authors, Dale and Iain, for their support, patience, and encouragement during what was a busy and challenging period.

Giselle Velastegui and Pablo Cervantes were instrumental in the creation of the maps and climate graphs for the book. Thanks to Keith Barnes and Nick Athanas for giving Iain the time to work on the project, and to Angela Moles from the University of New South Wales for being Iain's PhD supervisor and guiding him through the conceptualisation of the project.

A huge thank you too to all those who helped read chapters and acted as sparring partners. Some who stand out include Jeremy Robertson, Martin Kelsey, Ramona Roach, Rick Bateman, Kate Utsi, Rob Sheldon, János Oláh, Yanina Maggiotto, Christiane Aufschnaiter, Danielle McKenney, Gerald Driessens, and Måns Karlsson. Thank you to Christopher Sands and Ariel Brunner for all of your support in this project and for providing the sidebar on the conservation of the Aquatic Warbler.

ABBREVIATIONS

Directions (north, south, east, west, central) are abbreviated only when they directly precede a geographical place name.

ac. acre
aka also known as
av. average
c. central
cm centimetre
e. east/eastern
ec. east-central
EU European Union
ft. foot/feet
g gram
ha hectare
HotW Habitats of the World book series
in. inch/inches
IUCN International Union for the Conservation of Nature
KBA key biodiversity areas
kg kilogram
km kilometre
km^2 square kilometre
lb. pound
m metre
MYA million years ago
mi. mile
mm millimetre
n. north/northern
nc. north-central
ne. northeastern
nw. northwestern
oz. ounce
s. south/southern
sc. south-central
se. southeastern
sp. species (singular)
spp. species (plural)
sq. mi. square mile
ssp. subspecies
sw. southwestern
var. variety
w. west/western
wc. west-central
YA years ago

SELECTED BIBLIOGRAPHY

Amundsen, T., ed. 2015. *Birding Varanger: The Biotope Guide to the Best Bird Sites in Arctic Norway*. Biotope AS.

Archibold, O. W. 1995. *Ecology of World Vegetation*. Chapman and Hall.

Billerman, S. M., B. K. Keeney, P. G. Rodewald, and T. S. Schulenberg, eds. 2024. *Birds of the World*. Cornell Laboratory of Ornithology. https://birdsoftheworld.org.

Bohn, Udo, N. Zazanashvili, G. Nakhutsrishvili, and N. Ketskhoveli. 2007. 'The Map of the Natural Vegetation of Europe and Its Application in the Caucasus Ecoregion'. *Bulletin of the Georgia Academy of Science* 175: 112–21. https://www.researchgate.net/publication/237396766_The_Map_of_the_Natural_Vegetation_of_Europe_and_its_application_in_the_Caucasus_Ecoregion.

Bohn, Uwe, G. Gollub, and C. Hettwer, eds. 2000. *Map of the Natural Vegetation of Europe: Explanatory Text, Legend, and Maps*. 1st ed. Federal Agency for Nature Conservation.

Bond, W. J., and J. E. Keeley. 2005. 'Fire as a Global "Herbivore": The Ecology and Evolution of Flammable Ecosystems'. *Trends in Ecology and Evolution* 20: 387–94. https://doi.org/10.1016/j.tree.2005.04.025.

Boros, E., Z. Ecsedi, and J. Oláh. 2013. *Ecology and Management of Soda Pans in the Carpathian Basin*. Hortobágy Environmental Association.

Campbell, I., K. Behrens, C. Hesse, and P. Chaon. 2021. *Habitats of the World: A Field Guide for Birders, Naturalists, and Ecologists*. Princeton University Press.

Clements, J. F., P. C. Rasmussen, T. S. Schulenberg, M. J. Iliff, T. A. Fredericks, J. A. Gerbracht, D. Lepage, A. Spencer, S. M. Billerman, B. L. Sullivan, M. Smith, and C. L. Wood. 2024. *The eBird/Clements checklist of Birds of the World*, v2024. https://www.birds.cornell.edu/clementschecklist.

Cramp, S., and K.E.L. Simmons, eds. 1983. *Handbook of the Birds of Europe, the Middle East, and North Africa: The Birds of the Western Palearctic*. Vol. 3: *Waders to Gulls*. Oxford University Press.

Dijkstra, K.-D.B., and R. Lewington. 2006. *Field Guide to the Dragonflies of Britain and Europe, Including Western Turkey and North-western Africa*. British Wildlife Publishing.

Eionet Forum. 2016. 'Reports on European Red List of Habitats: Terrestrial Habitat Fact Sheets'.

Erdős, L., D. Ambarlı, O. A. Anenkhonov, Z. Bátori, D. Cserhalmi, M. Kiss, G. Kröel-Dulay et al. 2018. 'The Edge of Two Worlds: A New Review and Synthesis on Eurasian Forest-Steppes'. *Applied Vegetation Science* 21 (3): 345–62. John Wiley.

European Environment Agency, Museum national d'Histoire naturelle (MNHN), Richard, D., Spyropoulou, R., Poncet, L. et al., *Terrestrial habitat mapping in Europe – An overview*, Spyropoulou, R.(editor) and Poncet, L.(editor), Publications Office, 2014, https://data.europa.eu/doi/10.2800/11055.

Faber-Langendoen, D., T. Keeler-Wolf, D. Meidinger, D. Tart, B. Hoagland, C. Josse, G. Navarro et al. 2014. 'EcoVeg: A New Approach to Vegetation Description and Classification'. *Ecological Monographs* 84 (4): 533–61. https://doi.org/10.6084/m9.figshare.c.3309873.v1.

Flannery, T. 2018. *Europe: A Natural History*. Penguin.

Goldstein, M. I., and D. A. DellaSala, eds. 2020. *Encyclopedia of the World's Biomes*. Elsevier.

Grove, A. T., and O. Rackham. 2003. *Nature of Mediterranean Europe: An Ecological History*. Yale University Press.

Haft, J. 2021. *Natur Nebenan: Von den Alpen bis ans Meer—Eine Entdeckungsreise durch unsere schönsten Lebensräume*. Penguin.

Hagemeijer, W.J.M., and M. J. Blair, eds. 1997. *The EBCC Atlas of European Breeding Birds: Their Distribution and Abundance*. T. and A. D. Poyser.

Heath, M. F., M. I. Evans, D. G. Hoccom, A. J. Payne, and N. B. Peet, eds. 2000. *Important Bird Areas in Europe: Priority Sites for Conservation*. BirdLife International.

Hilbers, D. 2011. *Crossbill Guides: Extremadura—Spain*. Crossbill Guides Foundation.

Hilbers, D. 2011. *Crossbill Guides: Hortobágy and Tisza River Floodplain—Hungary*. Crossbill Guides Foundation.

Hilbers, D., and J. Cantelo. 2017. *Crossbill Guides: Western Andalucía—Huelva to Málaga*. Crossbill Guides Foundation.

Hilbers, D., and B. ten Cate. 2013. *Crossbill Guides: North-east Poland*. Crossbill Guides Foundation.

iNaturalist. 2025. https://www.inaturalist.org.

Johnson, O., and D. More. 2004. *Collins Tree Guide: The Most Complete Field Guide to the Trees of Britain and Europe*. HarperCollins.

Keller, V., S. Herrando, P. Voříšek, M. Franch, M. Kipson, P. Milanesi, D. Martí et al. 2020. *European Breeding Bird Atlas 2: Distribution, Abundance and Change*. European Bird Census Council and Lynx Edicions.

Krieger, C. 2022. *Crossbill Guides: Ireland*. Crossbill Guides Foundation.

Lake, S., D. Liley, R. Still, and A. Swash. 2020. *Britain's Habitats: A Field Guide to the Wildlife Habitats of Great Britain and Ireland*. Princeton University Press.

Møller, A., P. W. Fiedler, and P. Berthold, eds. 2010. *Effects of Climate Change on Birds*. Oxford University Press.

Moss, D. 2008. *EUNIS Habitat Classification—A Guide for Users*. European Environment Agency. https://www.eea.europa.eu/data-and-maps/data/eunis-habitat-classification/documentation/eunis-habitat-classification-users-guide-v2.pdf/file.

Reisigl, H., and R. Keller. 1999. *Lebensraum Bergwald: Alpenpflanzen in Bergwald, Baumgrenze und Zwergstrauchheide*. Spektrum Akademischer.

Smallshire, D., and A. Swash. 2020. *Europe's Dragonflies: A Field Guide to the Damselflies and Dragonflies*. Princeton University Press.

Speybroeck, J., W. Beukema, B. Bok, J. van der Voort, and I. Velikov. 2016. *Field Guide to the Amphibians and Reptiles of Britain and Europe*. Bloomsbury.

Sterry, P. 2000. *Complete Mediterranean Wildlife: Photoguide*. HarperCollins.

Tolman, T., and R. Lewington. 2009. *Collins Butterfly Guide: The Most Complete Guide to the Butterflies of Britain and Europe*. HarperCollins.

Wilson, D. E., and R. A. Mittermeier, eds. 2014. *Handbook of the Mammals of the World*. Vol. 4: *Sea Mammals*. Lynx Edicions.

THE OUTSIDERS' GUIDE TO THE MANY REGIONS OF EUROPE

This description of Europe is for people who do not live here and are unfamiliar with its natural history but want an annotated index of the dominant habitats in various regions. It provides an overview of the extremely varied regions of Europe and what they have to offer. Below, each region is illustrated with a 'habitat niche' diagram; please note that these diagrams are representative of the relative niches of major habitats only—there is no space for minor habitats. Habitats that are completely azonal and occur over many climates, such as coastlines, are not represented in these diagrams. In the niche diagrams, coloured type in the names of habitats indicates the following: Blue designates a habitat that is colder relative to others because it is in a montane region (i.e., cold because of elevation rather than latitude). Red indicates a habitat that is dominated by fire and that in the absence of fire may revert to a different habitat. Yellow designates a habitat that is anthropogenic or altered by grazing and occurs in a variety of environments otherwise occupied by different habitats.

Muskox is a tundra specialist and relict of the mammoth steppe—a dry, cold grassland that was once one of the most extensive habitats on the planet. © ALAIN GHIGNONE, AGAMI

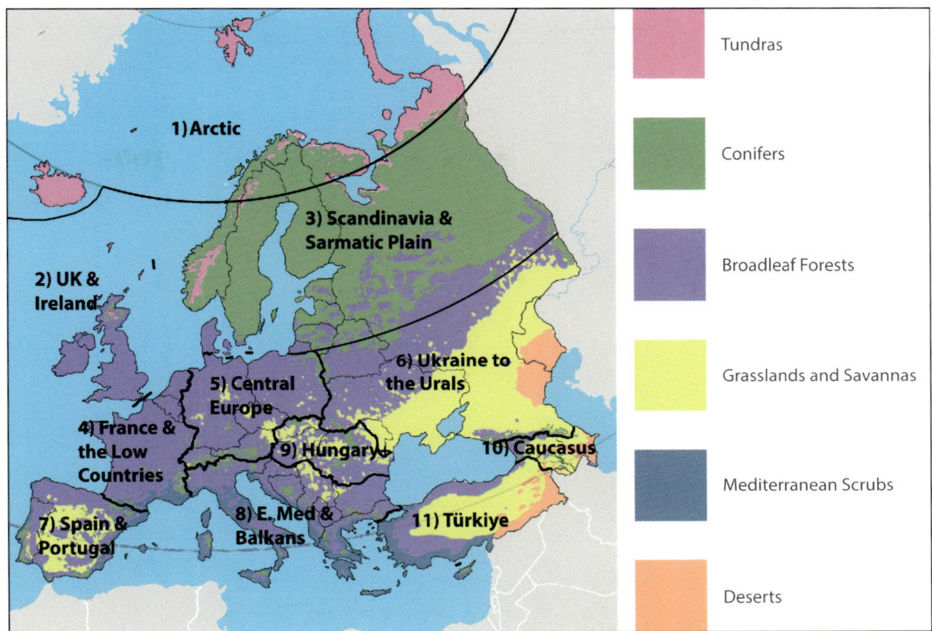

Fig. 6. Regions and biomes of Europe. The numbers on this map correspond to the regions of Europe that follow in the Outsiders' Guide.

1 THE ARCTIC

The Arctic region is defined in this book as the area of Europe above the Arctic Circle in the northernmost parts of Norway, Sweden, and Finland. It is where the conifer forests (or taiga) meet the wide-open tundras. It includes the islands north of Europe but not the Arctic part of European Russia, though that area is biogeographically related.

People visiting the Arctic in areas such as Kirkenes, in n. Norway (Köppen **Dfc**, subarctic climate), may be surprised by the extent of deciduous forest this far north. The general perception is that conifer forests are the most northerly forests, but between Kirkenes and the Varanger Peninsula, to the north, there are extensive areas of **Eu3G** EUROPEAN SUBARCTIC RIPARIAN WOODLAND. This is a low forest in the protected areas at the bases of hillsides and along valley floors. To the south of this forest is a narrow band of open taiga woodland—the **Eu1A** EUROPEAN TUNDRA TAIGA. This is the summer habitat of many Arctic breeding birds that use trees.

A little farther south, some 80 km (50 mi.) south of Kirkenes, is where the taiga proper starts. The northern taiga area is predominantly composed of Precambrian granites and gneisses, which are both quartz-rich, nutrient-poor rocks. These landscapes were significantly shaped by glacial processes during the Quaternary, particularly during the last ice age, which peaked only about 20,000 YA. Glaciers carved away the overlying rock and dumped vast amounts of unsorted material in moraines when they retreated. These moraines are massive impediments to drainage and have resulted in a vast mosaic of lakes, forming **Eu1C** EUROPEAN CONIFEROUS PEAT WOODLAND and aapa mires (see Sidebar 6: A Brief Overview of Europe's Diverse Peatlands, p.332). When the soils are too dry, or nutrient deficient, the main habitat type is **Eu1D** EUROPEAN PINE TAIGA. Wild and tough, this is the bad boy of conifer forests, where Scots Pine looks as if it will grow in just about

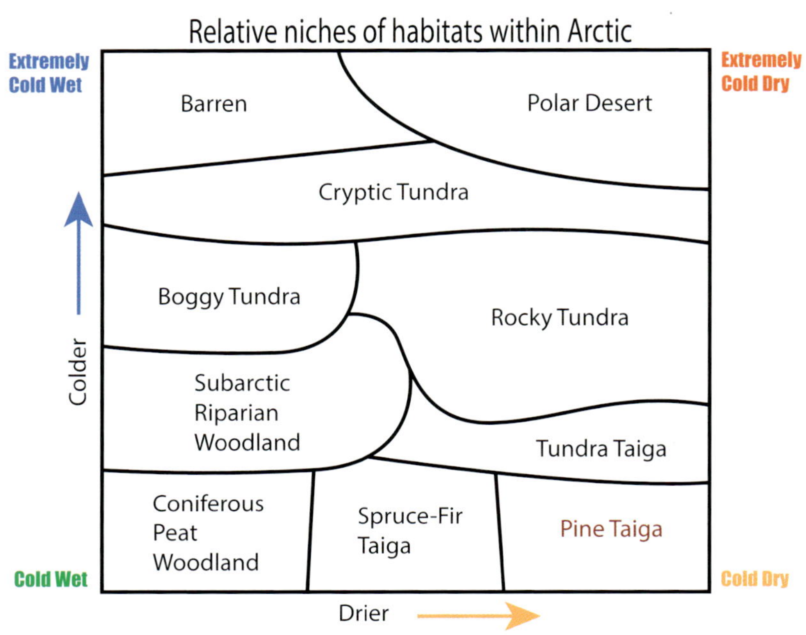

Svalbard, Norway. © PETE MORRIS

any conditions. However, if Goldilocks conditions are met, where the soil, water regime, and fire frequency are just right, the much more discerning Norway Spruce takes hold, and the dominant conifer forest is **Eu1E** EUROPEAN SPRUCE-FIR TAIGA, which has its own bird assemblage.

Conditions change when we move north from Kirkenes to the Varanger Peninsula. The climate of Båtsfjord, Norway, near the northernmost tip of the European mainland, is cold (Köppen **Cfc**, subpolar oceanic climate), but because of the moderating influence of the North Atlantic Current, it is much warmer than Utqiagvik (Barrow), Alaska. Although sitting at almost the same latitude, Utqiagvik has a tundra climate (Köppen **ET**) and summer averages 6°C (11°F) colder than Båtsfjord. The shoreline habitat here, **Eu12A** EUROPEAN ARCTIC AND TEMPERATE ROCKY COASTLINE, can be experienced with a visit to the seabird colony on the island off Vardø (Hornøya), Norway—an absolute must. The cacophony is deafening, and the flurry of activity includes dazzlingly close flybys of puffins and guillemots. However, the smell is all-pervasive, so wear plastic pants if you don't want your clothes to stink for days. The tundra around the shoreline tends to be **Eu10D** EUROPEAN SHRUBBY TUNDRA, where Ruffs lurk when not lekking.

Heading uphill, the glacial history of the Varanger Peninsula becomes obvious. During the Pleistocene, the area was repeatedly covered by ice sheets, with the last glaciation ending only around 10,000 YA this far north. At the last glacial peak, about 20,000 YA, the ice thickness was likely between 1000 and 1500 m (3300–4900 ft.), which caused a phenomenal weight on the underlying granites and gneisses. With the melting of the ice cap, the underlying rocks have risen (isostatic rebound) by 200–300 m (650–980 ft.). Sea levels rose after the ice ages, and the global rise was about 120 m (400 ft.), but because of isostatic rebound here, areas that were below sea level when the seas were at their lowest are now around 100 m (300 ft.) higher than the seas at their highest. The glaciers carved U-shaped valleys and left moraines, drumlins (small hills), and eskers (gravel ridges), resulting in elevated areas with dramatic scenery and impeded drainage. The area's tundra climate (Köppen **ET**) has allowed continued periglacial (freeze-thaw) activity, causing structures such as pingos (ice domes) and polygons to form in the various tundra habitats. In the areas with impeded drainage, it is **Eu10E** EUROPEAN BOGGY TUNDRA, while in more exposed areas, it is **Eu10C** EUROPEAN ROCKY TUNDRA. On the highest hilltops, there is a tundra normally found only on islands way to the north, **Eu10B** EUROPEAN CRYPTIC TUNDRA.

The islands to the north, such as Svalbard, are the northernmost islands in Europe. At latitude 80°N, they are separated by only 1000 km (620 mi.) of frozen ocean from the North Pole. The main terrestrial habitat on Svalbard is **Eu10B** EUROPEAN CRYPTIC TUNDRA, but just a short way upslope on these mountainous islands, the climate gets even more extreme, and the habitat changes to **Eu10A** EUROPEAN POLAR DESERT. Pretty much nothing can grow or live here.

Steller's Eider.

2 UNITED KINGDOM AND IRELAND

Most visitors to this region are heading there for the history and folklore, finding their roots, or the buzz of cities like London, Dublin, or Edinburgh. But it is not only the culture and the postcard-perfect views that people should be experiencing. An immense number of nature lovers live in the region, as attested by the 1.2 million members of the Royal Society for the Protection of Birds (RSPB). The proliferation of great wildlife guidebooks includes, in the WildGuides series alone, a suite of field guides covering the islands' habitats, birds, mammals, insects, spiders, butterflies, orchids, ferns, and even diurnal moths. If you find an unknown plant or creature in this area, there is likely to be a book to identify it.

Scotland is the northernmost country of the United Kingdom (UK). It has a much wilder feel than England or much of w. Europe, with extensive rocky coastlines and largely undeveloped highlands; the experience of vastness is not possible in other areas of the UK, Ireland, or w. Europe. Scotland's climate is predominantly maritime (Köppen **Cfb**, temperate oceanic climate), with generally mild, wet conditions across much of the country. In the Highlands and northern islands, the climate is subpolar oceanic (Köppen **Cfc**), and on a few locations, the climate transitions to tundra (Köppen **ET**). Overall, the region is much milder than the same latitudes on continental Europe because the North Atlantic Current, an extension of the Gulf Stream, moderates the temperature, making this region much milder than the comparable Labrador coastline of North America or the Kamchatka Peninsula of Asia. Farther south, the climate is also temperate oceanic (Köppen **Cfb**), but the region has milder temperatures, averaging 15–25°C (59–77°F) year-round. Rainfall is as high as 2000 mm (78 in.), often coming in drizzle rather than the torrential downpours of the tropics.

Tourist brochures advertise rugged mountain ranges, but the Scottish Highlands, which cover much of the northern and western parts of the country, are charmingly beautiful: the glens

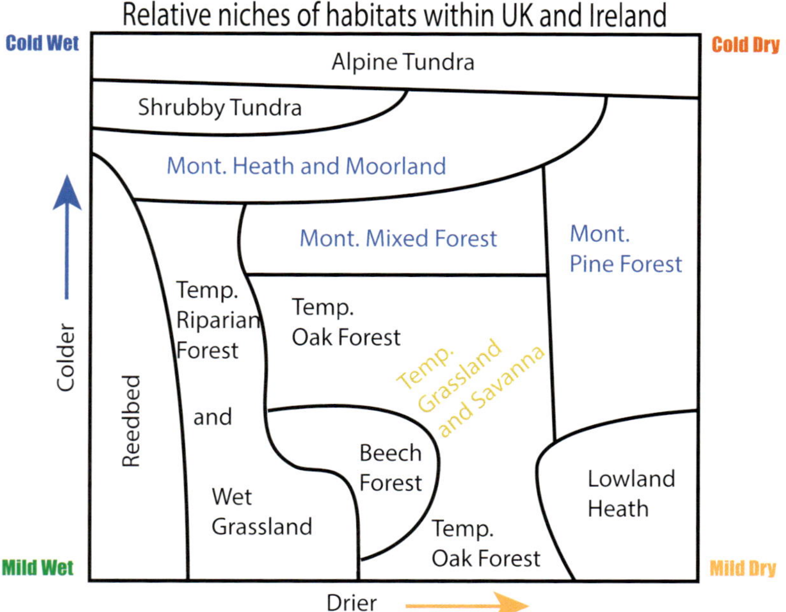

Bamburgh Castle, Northumberland, England. © BAS HAASNOOT, AGAMI

and peaks are rounded, the terrain less jagged than the rough-hewn mountains of the Alps or the Caucasus. The Highlands and the islands off Scotland were formed by glaciation of ancient Precambrian rocks during the last ice age, which formed dramatic features such as U-shaped valleys and steep fjords (called sea lochs).

Much of the Highlands was once dominated by Caledonian Forest, a subtype of **Eu1F** EUROPEAN MONTANE PINE FOREST. Unfortunately, many of these majestic pine forests were felled in the past 400 years, and most contemporary stands of Scots Pine are managed plantations that lack noteworthy bird species such as Western Capercaillie, Scottish Crossbill, and Crested Tit. The most accessible remnant of these forests is in the Abernethy Forest, which is well worth a few days' visit. Much of the Highlands has been turned into 'improved' pasture (see **Eu7B** EUROPEAN TEMPERATE GRASSLAND AND SAVANNA) with intensive grazing. This trend accelerated during the Highland Clearances (1820s–50s), when local people were forcibly removed from the land to make way for sheep. Nevertheless, large stretches of the hillsides are covered in Scotland's iconic **Eu8D** MONTANE HEATH AND MOORLAND. However, although pristine examples of this habitat still exist, most have been modified, and much of what appears to be wild heath is secondary growth after the forests were removed. Scattered through the heathlands are the various soggy bogs and fens of **Eu11D** EUROPEAN TEMPERATE PEATLAND. High in the mountains, such as in the Cairngorms, the heath changes to **Eu10F** EUROPEAN ALPINE TUNDRA. This is an important breeding ground for birds such as the Eurasian Dotterel.

The broad valleys, rolling hills, and moorlands of the Southern Uplands are in the south of Scotland. This region may lack the scenery of the Highlands, but it is a sedimentologist's dream, with both Silurian and Ordovician sedimentary rocks such as greywacke, shale, and siltstone.

Between the Scottish Highlands and the Southern Uplands are the Central Lowlands, a rift valley of relatively flat and fertile land, sharply contrasting with the surrounding uplands. The population is concentrated in these flatlands in the middle of the country, with the majority of Scotland's 5.5 million people living between Glasgow and Edinburgh. This region is much more like the rest of the UK, with its cities, intensive farming, and managed forests. Deciduous broadleaf trees dominate the many very local forests of the lowlands, some of which could arguably be regarded as temperate rainforests. However, their bird and other wildlife assemblages are indistinguishable from those of **Eu3A** EUROPEAN TEMPERATE OAK FOREST and are treated as such in this book.

Much of the lowlands of Scotland (and other parts of the British Isles) can be likened to a well-manicured garden, with neat hedgerows running through rolling hills of paddocks (see **Eu7B** EUROPEAN TEMPERATE GRASSLAND AND SAVANNA and **Eu13A** EUROPEAN CROPLAND).

Scotland's Central Lowlands originally supported forests such as **Eu3A** EUROPEAN TEMPERATE OAK FOREST in the central and colder areas and **Eu3B** EUROPEAN BEECH FOREST in the warmer, southern areas. The vast majority of these forests, however, have been cleared since medieval times. Some areas have very wet forests that could be described as rainforests, but these groves have the same bird assemblage as the other deciduous forests. Consequently, though they may be wonderful, with moss on the ground and water dripping from the trees, they do not warrant their own classification in the HotW system.

Most of Scotland's aquatic habitats have been heavily modified by human activities, so much birding today centres around artificial gravel pits, reservoirs, or canalised waterways (see **Eu11E** EUROPEAN FRESHWATER LAKES, DAMS, AND PONDS). Coastline habitats range from the typical beaches of **Eu12C** EUROPEAN SANDY SHORE AND DUNE to the cliffs of **Eu12A** EUROPEAN ARCTIC AND TEMPERATE ROCKY COASTLINE and **Eu12D** EUROPEAN COASTAL SALT MARSH. Birding the Shetland Islands means that you are never far from these coastal habitats, but it also gives you the chance to experience **Eu10D** EUROPEAN SHRUBBY TUNDRA.

In the southeast of the UK, the landscape is dominated by gently rolling hills, often underlain by chalk and limestone. This area also has heathlands, sandy soils, and saline marshes. The climate of the southeast is slightly warmer and drier, almost a warm-summer Mediterranean climate (Köppen **Csb**). In c. England and Ireland, the landscape has forest remnants, but much of the remaining forest in the southeast is **Eu3H** EUROPEAN TEMPERATE RIPARIAN FOREST, and the heathland is **Eu8C** LOWLAND HEATH. In birding hotspots such as Norfolk, England, birders tend to spend much of their time in terrestrial habitats such as **Eu7A** EUROPEAN WET GRASSLAND and aquatic habitats such as **Eu11C** EUROPEAN REEDBED and **Eu12D** EUROPEAN COASTAL SALT MARSH.

The topography of the UK and Ireland also encompasses several mountainous areas, such as the Pennines, a low mountain range in the north of England. Many visitors to Ireland are surprised by the mountains and stark karst formations formed by the chemical weathering and erosion of limestone. Wales too has some spectacular mountainous scenery, filled with legends of dragons, magicians, giants, and fairy folk. As with almost all legends to do with geomorphology and geology, the scientific truth is even more fascinating. Around 4490–390 MYA, in the late Cambrian to early Devonian, the Caledonian orogeny involved Laurentia (think North America) and Baltica (think Europe) colliding with the microcontinent of Avalon (Wales and England), which was wedged between but aligned with neither (a geological precursor to Brexit). This activity caused the uplift of these Precambrian rocks, and the Pleistocene ice age carved them into the dramatic U-shaped valleys and mountains we hike today.

The regional climate of Wales, the Pennines, and the mountains of Ireland is the same as that of the lowlands (Köppen **Cfb**, temperate oceanic). Nevertheless, the relief creates more localised conditions, such as a subpolar oceanic climate (Köppen **Cfc**) from about 600 to about 1000 m

(2000–3300 ft.). Summer average temperatures are up to 14°C (57°F), and winters are freezing. These two climates support the same basic forests in the mountains as in the lowlands, with **Eu3A** EUROPEAN TEMPERATE OAK FOREST dominating. Higher areas have **Eu8D** MONTANE HEATH AND MOORLAND, **Eu7B** EUROPEAN TEMPERATE GRASSLAND AND SAVANNA, and **Eu11B** EUROPEAN MOUNTAIN STREAMS AND RIVERS. Above about 1000 m (3300 ft.), the climate becomes tundra (Köppen **ET**), and the vegetation changes to that of **Eu10F** EUROPEAN ALPINE TUNDRA.

The Royal Society for the Protection of Birds (RSPB) and BirdWatch Ireland protect reserves and present conservation programmes throughout the region, working to ensure that future generations can enjoy the glory of nature in the region.

3 SCANDINAVIA, THE BALTIC STATES, AND THE SARMATIC PLAIN

Most first-time visitors to this part of the world expect it to be a mass of spruce or pine trees, and these habitats do abound, but mostly to the north of most of the larger cities. Flying into Copenhagen, Stockholm, or Riga (Latvia), people see a mass of deciduous trees mixed with conifers in woodlands that look a lot more like they belong in the Great Smoky Mountains (in the se. United States) than in Maine (ne. United States). This region encompasses the non-Arctic parts of Norway, Denmark, Sweden, Finland, and boreal Russia. The Baltic States of Estonia, Latvia, and Lithuania, which do not have any Arctic habitats, are also included here.

The Baltic States and the southern parts of the other countries lie within the Sarmatic mixed forests ecoregion (as classified by the World Wide Fund for Nature, or WWF), which stretches in a band from s. Norway through Moscow and across to the Ural Mountains of wc. Russia. The majority of the Sarmatic Plain is a vast landscape with little topographic relief and elevations generally ranging between 100 and 300 m (300–1000 ft.) above sea level. Although this region was covered in glaciers during the last ice age, the effect here is nowhere near as pronounced

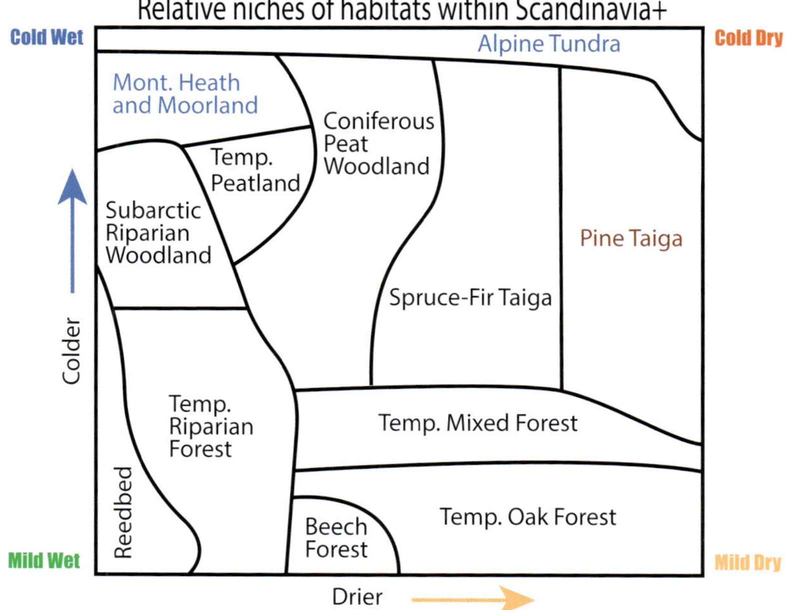

Siberian Jay. © MARKUS VARESVUO, AGAMI

as it is in the Arctic regions, and no great U-shaped valleys have been carved from the bedrock. Nevertheless, extensive moraines, drumlins, and kettle lakes clearly indicate past glacial activity, and the region is geomorphologically much like the great plains of w. Canada. Most of this southern area has a warm-summer humid continental climate (Köppen **Dfb**), with winter averages as low as −5°C (23°F) and summer averages as high as 22°C (72°F). Precipitation is moderate, with snow cover common in winter and lasting for a few months.

The Sarmatic mixed forests ecoregion is well named, because it is a mosaic, and sometimes a mélange (see fig. 3), of different forest types. Most of it is **Eu3D** EUROPEAN TEMPERATE MIXED FOREST with a wonderful, messy mix of deciduous broadleaf trees (like oaks) and conifers (like Norway Spruce). Some dominantly broadleaf forests occur, such as **Eu3A** EUROPEAN TEMPERATE OAK FOREST and very limited **Eu3B** EUROPEAN BEECH FOREST, the latter limited mainly to southernmost Sweden and n. Denmark. Along rivers and in waterlogged valleys, **Eu11C** EUROPEAN REEDBED develops, while birch, alders, and willows are common in the **Eu3H** EUROPEAN TEMPERATE RIPARIAN FOREST. Although most grasslands have been converted to intense pasture and **Eu13A** EUROPEAN CROPLAND, there are areas of **Eu7A** EUROPEAN WET GRASSLAND and scattered more natural **Eu7B** EUROPEAN TEMPERATE GRASSLAND AND SAVANNA. Some conifer forests exist, such as the southern limits of **Eu1D** EUROPEAN PINE TAIGA and **Eu1E** EUROPEAN SPRUCE-FIR TAIGA.

The subarctic taiga is on the cratonic Fennoscandian Shield, a very stable area with gneisses, granites, and greenstone over 2 billion years old. The overlying younger rocks have long since been eroded, while the older rocks were recently scoured by glaciation during the Pleistocene ice ages. Because this region was so flat prior to glaciation, it lacks dramatic landscapes and is dominated by moraines (unsorted glacial debris) and eskers (gravel ridges), which impede drainage and form many thousands of small lakes in vast areas of potholes. The north of the region has one of the most monotonous vegetation stands in Europe, a vast landscape of **Eu1D** EUROPEAN PINE TAIGA and **Eu1E** EUROPEAN SPRUCE-FIR TAIGA, most of which is managed and of uniform height and structure. Despite the tedious nature of a massive area with two main tree species, the region does offer some superb wildlife photography blinds for mammals such as Brown Bear and, even better, Wolverine. **Eu1C** EUROPEAN CONIFEROUS PEAT WOODLAND is in a much more natural state and far more interesting to birds than the managed forests. Some of the best nature-viewing is along the rivers, where there are still extensive stands of **Eu3H** EUROPEAN TEMPERATE RIPARIAN FOREST, many thousands of lakes (see **Eu11E** EUROPEAN FRESHWATER LAKES, DAMS, AND PONDS), and some interesting **Eu11C** EUROPEAN REEDBED replete with local specialties like the Azure Tit.

The Scandes (or Scandinavian) Mountains of Norway and extreme nw. Sweden and nw. Finland are an under-visited and fascinating area of n. Europe. The mountain range formed around 490–390 MYA when North America crashed into Europe, causing the Caledonian orogeny. Surprisingly, thanks to plate tectonics, these two continents are constantly combining and splitting with each other; the Caledonian was the second of four times they have had orogenies over the past 500 million years. It will happen again, but no time soon—so don't cancel any trips.

More recently, Pleistocene glaciation covered the mountains in vast ice sheets that advanced and retreated multiple times. These glaciers carved out deep U-shaped valleys and fjords, creating the dramatic topography seen today. Fjords are deep, narrow U-shaped valleys flooded with inlets of the sea by rising sea levels as the glaciers melted. Higher in the mountains, the glaciers carved cirques (rounded amphitheatres) out of the bedrock. When the glaciers retreated, they left unsorted glacial debris (moraines) and very large boulders (erratics).

Since the end of the ice ages, the climate close to the coast has been heavily influenced by the moderating North Atlantic Current, creating a subpolar oceanic climate (Köppen **Cfc**) in the north and a temperate oceanic climate (Köppen **Cfb**) in the south. These climates are similar, and both are very wet, with cold winter temperatures of −3 to 18°C (27–64°F), but the **Cfb** has summer averages above 10°C (50°F), while **Cfc** has summer averages below 10°C. The forests along the coast include the **Eu1D** EUROPEAN PINE TAIGA, **Eu1E** EUROPEAN SPRUCE-FIR TAIGA, **Eu3D** EUROPEAN TEMPERATE MIXED FOREST, and **Eu3A** EUROPEAN TEMPERATE OAK FOREST. The tree line is very low in these mountains, where the climate changes to tundra (Köppen **ET**), and the habitat is mainly **Eu10F** EUROPEAN ALPINE TUNDRA. Along the coast, the habitats are **Eu12A** EUROPEAN ARCTIC AND TEMPERATE ROCKY COASTLINE and **Eu12C** EUROPEAN SANDY SHORE AND DUNE.

BirdLife Norge (Norway), BirdLife Sverige (Sweden), BirdLife Suomi (Finland), BirdLife Denmark (DOF), BirdLife Estonia, the Latvian Ornithological Society (LOB), and the Lithuanian Ornithological Society (LOD) are some of the most important driving forces behind conservation in this region.

Red-throated Loon (Diver).
© JARI PELTOMÄKI, AGAMI

4 FRANCE AND THE LOW COUNTRIES

France is the largest country in c. and w. Europe. It offers diverse wildlife-watching opportunities, from the high mountains of the Pyrenees and Alps to the cool, oceanic climate of Brittany and the scorched heat of the Mediterranean. By contrast, the Low Countries (Belgium, the Netherlands, and Luxembourg, together refered to as Benelux) are small and very densely populated. Nevertheless, to the surprise of many first-time visitors, there is some truly phenomenal birding on offer during the early months of the year, when the Benelux wetlands are absolutely teeming with waterbirds riding out the winter before returning to the Arctic to breed.

The northern cities in the region, such as Amsterdam and Paris, are on a low-lying plain composed primarily of recent sediments overlying sedimentary rocks, especially limestone, chalk, and claystone. These chalks and sediments were deposited in a shallow sea that extended from modern-day England to Germany in what was part of the greater Tethys Sea. The chalks were derived from single-celled algae, while the limestones were created from a more complex suite of life-forms, including the algae, along with corals, bivalves, brachiopods, and foraminifera (protists). Some additional deposits came from material eroded from Scandinavia to the north and the Ardennes massif to the south. Since its formation, this region has been very stable compared to most of Europe, though there has been some gentle uplift to form the Limburg hills of the Netherlands, Belgium, and w. Germany.

The lowlands are very low, often below sea level, and are a broad series of rivers, lakes, estuaries, and palaeo-dunes and deltas that form islands and shore barriers. Traditional windmills or modern pumps keep the land relatively dry by draining the water into canals and then behind extensive dikes. The Wadden Sea, in the northern part of the Netherlands, contains vast natural expanses of **Eu12H** EUROPEAN TIDAL FLAT AND ESTUARY, giving us an idea of just how rich these areas would have been prior to reclamation. Among these landscapes with their extensive

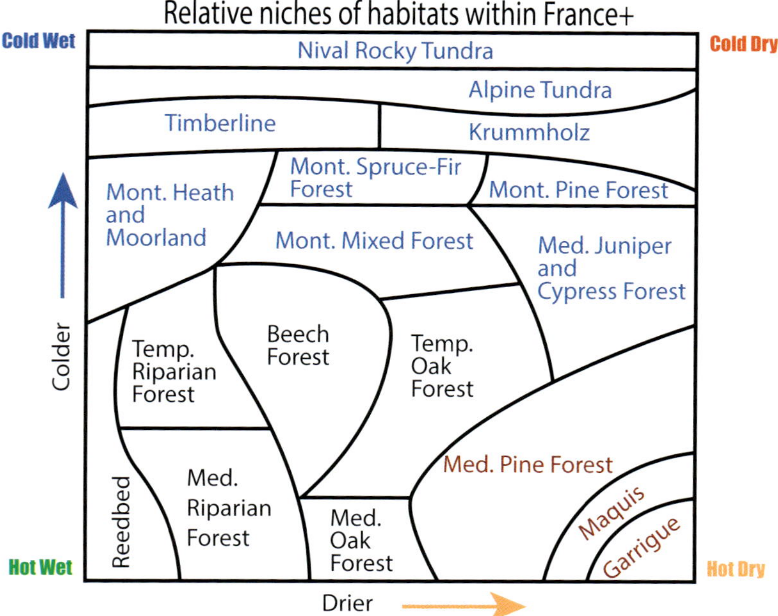

Wintery windmills, Netherlands. © MENNO VAN DUIJN, AGAMI

Eu13A EUROPEAN CROPLAND is a predictably huge human population with some of the highest densities of people in the world.

The whole north of the area has a temperate oceanic climate (Köppen **Cfb**), moderated by the Atlantic Ocean, with mild, temperate weather and summer average temperatures of 15–25°C (59–77°F). Winters are also mild, with limited snow and average temperatures typically 0–8°C (32–46°F).

The coasts are dominated by **Eu12C** EUROPEAN SANDY SHORE AND DUNE and **Eu12D** EUROPEAN COASTAL SALT MARSH, while on the other side of the dikes are the freshwater habitats **Eu11C** EUROPEAN REEDBED, **Eu11A** EUROPEAN SHALLOW FRESHWATER MARSH, and **Eu11E** EUROPEAN FRESHWATER LAKES, DAMS, AND PONDS. Some more-wooded watercourses can have reasonably natural **Eu3H** EUROPEAN TEMPERATE RIPARIAN FOREST. Very little forest remains, and it is all managed to some extent, but the natural forest here is **Eu3B** EUROPEAN BEECH FOREST and, to a much lesser extent, **Eu3A** EUROPEAN TEMPERATE OAK FOREST. Drier, open areas can have **Eu8C** LOWLAND HEATH, but the open land of **Eu7B** EUROPEAN TEMPERATE GRASSLAND AND SAVANNA and **Eu7A** EUROPEAN WET GRASSLAND is invariably used for pastures or hay meadows. With the level of farming and human population, it is little wonder that most land in this part of the world is either **Eu13A** EUROPEAN CROPLAND or **Eu13B** EUROPEAN URBAN ENVIRONMENTS.

Farther south, France's landscape is dominated by the Massif Central, a large flat range with an incongruous past. Most of this massif is an ancient crystalline basement formed around 350–300 MYA, in the Carboniferous period, when the collision of North America and Europe caused the Hercynian (Variscan) orogeny (mountain building). Pleistocene glaciation affected the Massif Central less extensively than many other European mountain ranges, but it nevertheless left behind some characteristic landforms, including cirques, U-shaped valleys, and moraines. Furthermore, during this ice age, from about 95,000 to just 8000 YA, hotspot volcanoes, caused by a plume in the mantle that kept pushing up volcanoes as the plates moved over it (much as in the Galápagos Islands and Yellowstone National Park), erupted as well. This landscape would have been a bizarre one, with intense volcanic activity under a block of ice, analogous to the Vatnajökull glacier and the Grímsvötn volcano of Iceland today. The Alpine orogeny started in the late Cretaceous (around 70 MYA) and also caused the uplift and folding of the Pyrenees as Africa crashed into Europe. Glaciation and the consequences thereof were much greater in the highest parts of the Pyrenees than in the Massif Central to the north.

The varied geomorphology of s. France has given rise to very varied climates and vegetation. The more southerly areas, such as the French Riviera and Marseille, where the summers are very hot and temperatures usually top 30°C (86°F), have what is known as a hot-summer Mediterranean climate (Köppen **Csa**). Rain is sparse, with around 1100 mm (43 in.) falling mostly in winter. The winters of the Riviera are mild, with temperatures of 5–15°C (41–59°F). In this region, **Eu8A** EUROPEAN GARRIGUE and the taller **Eu8B** EUROPEAN MAQUIS are the typical habitats of headlands and ridgelines. **Eu1G** MEDITERRANEAN PINE FOREST is widespread on the coastal plain but can also be found farther inland in a mosaic with **Eu3F** MEDITERRANEAN OAK FOREST. Extensive olive groves and **Eu13A** EUROPEAN CROPLAND of various cereals are important for open-country birds. The Mediterranean areas are dissected by many rivers with **Eu3I** MEDITERRANEAN RIPARIAN FOREST and wetlands such as **Eu11C** EUROPEAN REEDBED. **Eu12D** EUROPEAN COASTAL SALT MARSH is incredibly important for birds along France's Mediterranean coast.

Areas higher in the landscape, such as at the base of the Pyrenees and the Massif Central, also have a dry summer–wet winter Mediterranean climate (Köppen **Csb**, warm-summer Mediterranean). This climate experiences slightly milder winters than the similar **Csa**, but the differences are more obvious in the summers: temperatures are markedly milder, and highs rarely exceed 30°C (86°F). Here, the more temperate forests start to take hold, and **Eu3A** EUROPEAN TEMPERATE OAK FOREST and **Eu3B** EUROPEAN BEECH FOREST are widespread. Above about 1500 m (4900 ft.), conditions transition to a warm-summer humid continental climate (Köppen **Dfb**), which has cold winter average temperatures of −2 to 4°C (28–39°F), mild summer averages of 14–22°C (57–72°F), plenty of winter snow, and year-round precipitation of 800–1200 mm (31–47 in.). The cooler climate supports such habitats as **Eu1I** EUROPEAN MONTANE SPRUCE-FIR FOREST and **Eu3E** EUROPEAN MONTANE MIXED FOREST interwoven with the meadows and pastures of **Eu7B** EUROPEAN TEMPERATE GRASSLAND AND SAVANNA. **Eu1B** SUBALPINE TIMBERLINE WOODLAND and **Eu1J** SUBALPINE KRUMMHOLZ grow at the transition from the montane to the alpine life zones. Above about 2000 m (6500 ft.), the temperature remains cold throughout the year, and the winters have very heavy snowfalls. In this climate (Köppen **ET**, tundra), trees can no longer grow, and the vegetation is dominated by the very low shrubby or grassy **Eu10F** EUROPEAN ALPINE TUNDRA. **Eu10G** EUROPEAN NIVAL ROCKY TUNDRA is found in the glacial zone at extreme elevations, at the very edge of where plants can grow.

Conservation in the region is driven by many engaged organisations, including LPO Ligue pour la Protection des Oiseaux (France), Natagora (Belgium), Natuurpunt (Belgium), natur&ëmwelt (Luxembourg), and VBN Vogelbescherming (Netherlands).

5 CENTRAL EUROPE

Central Europe is surprisingly well forested, so a visit to Germany or Poland does not need to be only about breweries and castles. From west to east, the centre of Europe lies between the milder, oceanic climates nearer the Atlantic Ocean and the very cold continental climates of the Sarmatic Plain, which continues to the Urals. To the north are the flat lowlands of the Baltic coast, and to the south lie the high Austrian Alps.

Not much has happened on the North European Plain around Berlin and Warsaw for a few hundred million years (at least not geologically). Being part of the European Craton (the central, most stable parts of the continent), it remained stable every time Europe and North America crashed into each other and remains unaffected by the monumental pounding Europe is now getting from Africa. The older bedrock of this region is mainly Mesozoic (Triassic, Jurassic, and Cretaceous) sedimentary rocks such as sandstones, limestones, and shales. These rocks remained stable until the Pleistocene, when the glaciers of the last ice age covered the plain with 1500–2000 m (5000–6500 ft.) of ice. This caused immense pressure on the underlying rock and isostatic depression (sinking) of 100–300 m (300–1000 ft.). The glaciers scoured the underlying rock, and, with their retreat around 11,700 YA, the land began to rise with an isostatic rebound (and it still may rise for a few more thousand years). The land was covered by glacial sediments such as moraines (accumulations of glacial debris at the edges of glaciers) and tills (unsorted glacial debris). Later deposits from rivers left nutrient-rich sediments over the low-lying plains.

The uplands to the south of the North European Plain are home to many of c. Europe's most important cities, such as Luxembourg City, Frankfurt, Nuremberg, Prague, and Kraków. In contrast to the flat expanse of the North European Plain, the Central Uplands of Germany (Mittelgebirge) are a series of low to moderate mountain ranges generally lower than 1500 m (5000 ft.). The formation of the Mittelgebirge is tied to ancient tectonic processes, particularly those associated with the

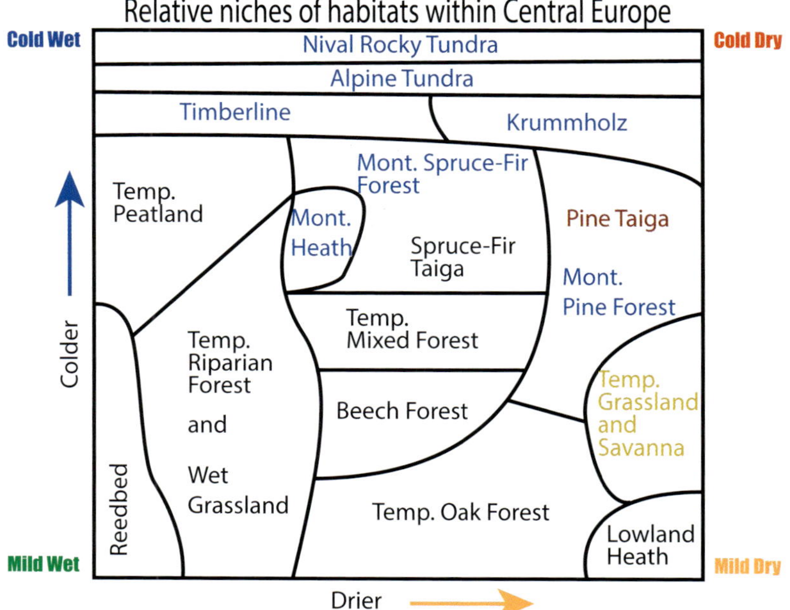

Hercynian (Variscan) orogeny, which occurred around 350–300 MYA when North America crashed into Europe. Since then, these uplands have remained fairly stable and have been eroded slowly.

The Alps were formed during the Alpine orogeny (starting around 70 MYA) when the African and Eurasian plates began colliding. This geological stress in the Alps caused tension farther north, and by the Oligocene (30 MYA), a massive block of land had slipped down between two faults (a graben). This block has continued to sink as much as 3 km (2 mi.) along the Rhine graben (named after the river that flows through it). Although it is still regarded as a proto-rift, it is possible that it could eventually develop into a true rift valley. At the same time, the subsidence of this graben forced crust upwards (horst), creating the uplands associated with the Black Forest.

In the west of the North European Plain and the Central Uplands of Germany, the climate is affected by moderating oceanic air masses associated with the North Atlantic Current. The resulting temperate oceanic climate (Köppen **Cfb**) has moderate summer temperatures of 18–25°C (65–77°F) and surprisingly mild winters, considering the high latitude (av. −2° to 5°C/28–41°F). The 570–650 mm (22–26 in.) of precipitation is evenly distributed through the year. **Eu3B** EUROPEAN BEECH FOREST and **Eu3A** EUROPEAN TEMPERATE OAK FOREST are the most common forests in the region. There is **Eu3H** EUROPEAN TEMPERATE RIPARIAN FOREST at the valley bottoms, and open areas have both **Eu8C** LOWLAND HEATH and **Eu7A** EUROPEAN WET GRASSLAND. Farther east, conditions change to a warm-summer humid continental climate (Köppen **Dfb**), with cold winters ranging from an average of −3°C (27°F) in the lower valleys to −15°C (5°F) in the higher valleys. The summers can be very warm and wet, seeing average temperatures reaching 20°C (68°F) and most of the annual 550–1500 mm (21–59 in.) of precipitation. Here in the lowlands, the forests are dominated by the **Eu3A** EUROPEAN TEMPERATE OAK FOREST and **Eu3D** EUROPEAN TEMPERATE MIXED FOREST, but **Eu3B** EUROPEAN BEECH FOREST is notably absent in the northeast. The northern areas of c. Europe touch the southern edge of the boreal forests, with stands of **Eu1E** EUROPEAN SPRUCE-FIR TAIGA and **Eu1D** EUROPEAN PINE TAIGA.

Eurasian Lynx. © SERGIO PITAMITZ, AGAMI

Bearded Vulture (Lammergeier). © RALPH MARTIN, AGAMI

Covering much of Austria and Switzerland, the Alps form the southern boundary of this region. The Alps first started to form with the collision between the African and Eurasian tectonic plates starting in the late Mesozoic, around 70 MYA, but the Alpine orogeny became much stronger later, in the Cenozoic, and is still happening today. The Alps do not have volcanic activity, suggesting that they are formed purely by orogeny (as with the Himalayas), where rocks have been buckled, folded, and faulted. (In contrast, subduction and melting are responsible for mountain ranges like the Andes of South America.) In the Pleistocene, glaciers covered the Alps, retreating only with the end of the Würm glaciation, about 11,700 YA. This glaciation caused significant erosion and an immense weight on the land. Since the end of that last ice age, the mountains have continued to grow because the Alpine orogeny is an ongoing event, though because the glaciers have all but gone, there is also an isostatic rebound, in which the earth bulges because the weight of ice has been removed. This uplift and subsequent glaciation have resulted in incredibly rugged, towering mountains with very deep valleys and a range of local climates.

Low in the Alps, the climate is similar to that of the Central Uplands (Köppen **Cfb**) and supports the same vegetation types, especially **Eu3A** EUROPEAN TEMPERATE OAK FOREST, **Eu3B** EUROPEAN BEECH FOREST, **Eu3E** EUROPEAN MONTANE MIXED FOREST, and **Eu3H** EUROPEAN TEMPERATE RIPARIAN FOREST. Nevertheless, these fertile, warmer valleys tend to be dominated by the human-influenced habitats of **Eu7B** EUROPEAN TEMPERATE GRASSLAND AND SAVANNA, **Eu13A** EUROPEAN CROPLAND, and **Eu13B** EUROPEAN URBAN ENVIRONMENTS.

The montane zone starts slightly upslope from the valley floors at about 500–1000 m (1600–3300 ft.). This might seem to be a strangely broad elevation range for the start of a climate zone, but the latitude and north–south aspect very significantly affect where the climate determines a transition to montane vegetation. The cooler montane zone has a warm-summer humid continental (Köppen **Dfb**) or subarctic (Köppen **Dfc**) climate, in which the winters are cold (av. −10 to −3°C/ 14–27°F) and summers are cool (av. highs 15–20°C/59–68°F). Precipitation of 600–1000 mm (24–40 in.), spread fairly evenly through the year, is ideal for **Eu1I** EUROPEAN MONTANE SPRUCE-FIR FOREST and **Eu3E** EUROPEAN MONTANE MIXED FOREST, interspersed with alpine meadows (see **Eu7B** EUROPEAN TEMPERATE GRASSLAND AND SAVANNA). Drier slopes develop extensive stands of **Eu1F** EUROPEAN MONTANE PINE FOREST. Nevertheless, the vast majority of these forests are heavily managed, and many are a far cry from natural forests.

The higher mountains above about 1800–2500 m (6000–8200 ft.) have a harsh alpine tundra climate (Köppen **ET**), in which the warmest month averages between 0 and 10°C (32–50°F). Summers are short and cool, and winters long and harsh with persistent snow cover and shearing winds. At these elevations, the vegetation is dominated by **Eu10F** EUROPEAN ALPINE TUNDRA. At even higher elevations, in the glacial zone, the vegetation transitions to **Eu10G** EUROPEAN NIVAL ROCKY TUNDRA with an ice cap climate (Köppen **EF**).

Conservation in the region is being led by the Nature and Biodiversity Conservation Union (NABU) (Germany), Polish Society for the Protection of Birds (OTOP), BirdLife Austria, Czech Society for Ornithology (CSO), and BirdLife Switzerland.

6 UKRAINE TO THE URALS

The vast area from w. Ukraine to the Urals and from Moscow to the Caspian Sea is a huge plain that, although under-visited by naturalists, has some very interesting habitats and is well worth exploring. Vast areas of former steppe are now Europe's wheat belt.

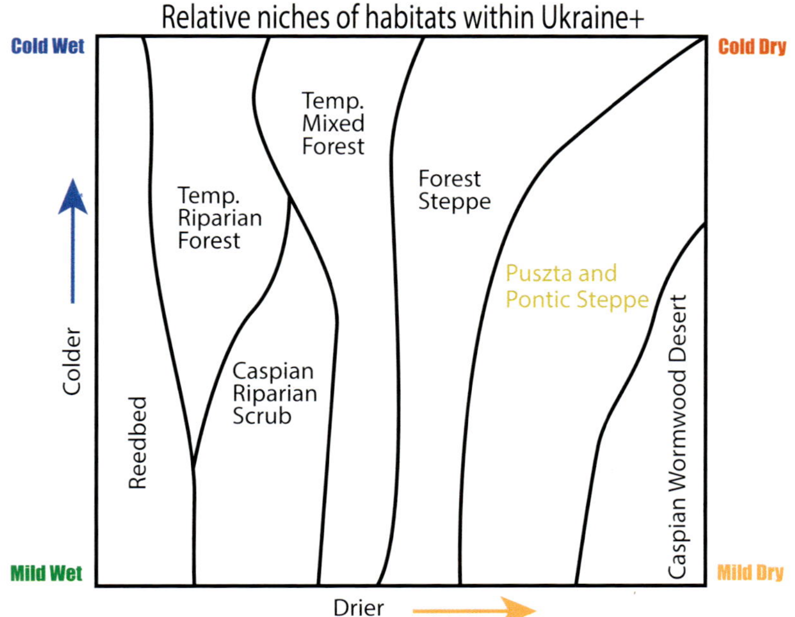

Rosy (Rose-coloured) Starling. © RALPH MARTIN, AGAMI

The most populous city in this vast region is Kyiv, at roughly the boundary between the forested zone of the north and the grasslands of the south. The region is predominantly a flat plain, maintained by a very long period of tectonic stability, in which there was very little uplift or erosion of the East European Craton. Most of this area was not glaciated, but it was, nevertheless, heavily influenced by the most recent glacial periods; strong, cold winds blew from the glaciers, moving silt and clay in clouds that resulted in large loess deposits, such as the Dnieper Upland near Kyiv. Soils formed on these deposits, but because the winds are relentless, they have been covered by loess deposits. A cross section through these deposits shows thin layers of palaeosols (preserved soil) dispersed between thick layers of fine silt.

The climate of the region's northern area is warm-summer humid continental (Köppen **Dfb**), with cold winter averages of −6 to −3°C (21–27°F), and a lot of snow is present for much of the winter. The summers are warm, with July average temperatures around 21°C (70°F) and some days exceeding 30°C (86°F). **Eu7E** EUROPEAN FOREST STEPPE develops in this zone, characterised by grasslands dotted with pockets of trees, which in the west tend to be deciduous groves, while to the east they become dominated by conifers. To the northwest of this region, the habitats are more closely associated with those of c. Europe (no. 5, above), with extensive stands of **Eu3D** EUROPEAN TEMPERATE MIXED FOREST, especially where Belarus borders Poland.

To the south and east of Kyiv, the Pontic-Caspian Plain extends from Romania, Moldova, and w. Ukraine all the way to the Ural Mountains in the east. It is hard to find a hill in this region. The climate in the west is humid subtropical (Köppen **Cfa**); winter temperatures average around freezing, and summer temperatures average 23°C (73°F). Precipitation is evenly spread throughout the year, totalling around 400 mm (16 in.). The climate in the east is humid continental (Köppen **Dfa**), with extremes in temperatures, from winter averages regularly below −10°C (14°F) to summer temperatures regularly topping 30°C (86°F). With the region's very low relief and extreme temperature gradient, there is little range for local climate variations, and hence the habitats are rather predictable. For most of the Pontic Plain, the main habitat is **Eu7C** PUSZTA AND PONTIC STEPPE with **Eu3H** EUROPEAN TEMPERATE RIPARIAN FOREST and **Eu11C** EUROPEAN REEDBED along the drainage lines. Despite trying times, the Ukrainian Society for the Protection of Birds (USPB) is working hard to try to protect birds and nature wherever possible.

The southeast of this region is where things get really interesting. The plain between the Black Sea and the Caspian Sea is flat, with a cold semi-arid climate (Köppen **Bsk**). Winters are cold and dry, with average January lows typically around −2°C (28°F). Snowfall is infrequent and does not accumulate. Summers, however, are blisteringly hot, with July averages exceeding 30°C (86°F) and temperatures occasionally topping 40°C (104°F). Most rain, which can be as low as 200 mm (8 in.) per year, occurs in the summer. The extreme climate results in the fascinating, shrubby **Eu2A** CASPIAN WORMWOOD DESERT, one of the three European desert types. Most thick vegetation is limited to ribbons of **Eu3J** CASPIAN RIPARIAN SCRUB snaking through the desert.

The far southeast borders on the Caucasus region along the Greater Caucasus Mountains. Lower elevations can have a warm-summer humid continental climate (Köppen **Dfb**), with mild summers, mild winters, and rainfall year-round. Conifer-dominated habitats such as **Eu1I** EUROPEAN MONTANE SPRUCE-FIR FOREST and broadleaf **Eu3A** EUROPEAN TEMPERATE OAK FOREST prevail. A fuller description of the Greater Caucasus Mountains is given in the Caucasus regional description (no. 10, below).

7 SPAIN AND PORTUGAL

The Iberian Peninsula is the first stop for many visitors taking a natural history vacation in Europe, and rightly so, because few areas combine superb birding with such delightful food, history, and cultural activities: **Eu8B** EUROPEAN MAQUIS in the morning, tapas for lunch, and **Eu6B** OAK DEHESA in the evening. The Iberian Peninsula is in the southwestern corner of Europe, comprising Spain and Portugal. It is geographically diverse, from the high Pyrenees mountains in the north through the rolling plains of the Meseta Central and down to magnificent coastal areas. The Mediterranean Sea lies to the east and south, the Atlantic Ocean to the west and north. A lesser-known mountain range in the southeast of the peninsula, the Sierra Nevada, has the highest peak in the region, at 3480 m (11,400 ft.). This geomorphological diversity significantly influences the climate and, consequently, the vegetation of the region.

The Iberian Peninsula is primarily underlain by ancient Precambrian and Palaeozoic rocks older than 250 million years. The mountains are much younger, formed when Africa crashed into Europe during the late Mesozoic–Cenozoic Alpine orogeny. Glaciation affected the highest parts of the Pyrenees and the Sierra Nevada during the Pleistocene (which ended only about 11,700 YA), leaving U-shaped valleys, moraines, and glacial cirques. Rock type has also affected topography; the limestone and dolomite formations in regions such as the Sierra Nevada are particularly susceptible to chemical weathering processes, forming karst, a terrain pocked with caves and sinkholes.

The southeast and central parts of the region mainly have Mediterranean climates with mild, wet winters and either warm (Köppen **Csb**) or hot (**Csa**) summers. There are even areas on the peninsula with a cold semi-arid climate (Köppen **Bsk**) of very hot summers and mild, dry winters; summer temperatures regularly exceed 35°C (95°F) in the Almería region of s. Spain, while less than 300 mm (12 in.) of rain falls annually. The south of the peninsula, with the cities of Málaga, Spain and Lisbon, Portugal, is dominated by Mediterranean habitats including the low **Eu8A** EUROPEAN

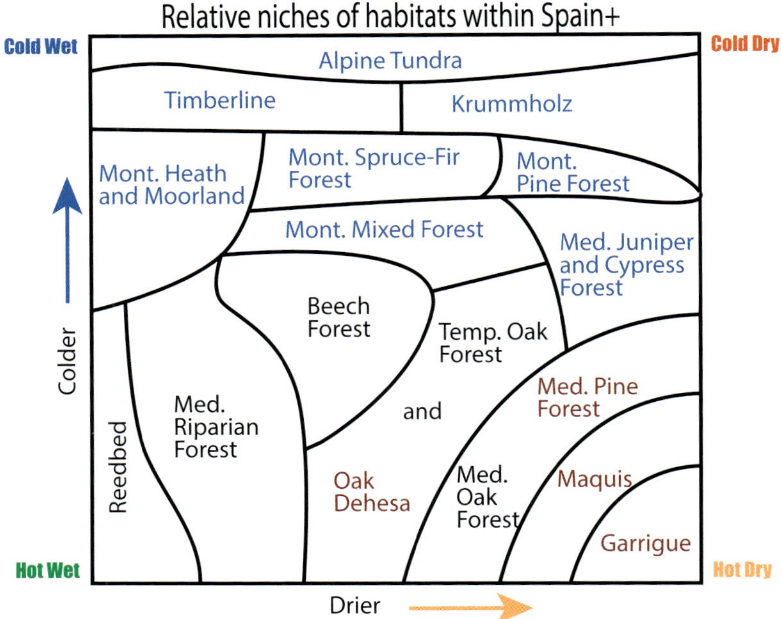

Eurasian Wryneck. © JACQUES VAN DER NEUT, AGAMI

GARRIGUE. This is the short, prickly, dry heathland you find in exposed locations and around many of the heavily visited archaeological sites. A very similar habitat in this region is **Eu8B** EUROPEAN MAQUIS, which generally grows on deeper, more fertile soils. Maquis vegetation, with small trees like Wild Olive, Tree Heath, and Strawberry Tree, is taller and denser. There are many small conifer groves in this southern region, with trees like Umbrella Pine in the **Eu1G** MEDITERRANEAN PINE FOREST and junipers in **Eu1H** MEDITERRANEAN JUNIPER AND CYPRESS FOREST. Many of these forests are managed, and the more extensive plantations can be ecological deserts devoid of all the species that make the pine forests so great for birding. Cork Oak grows naturally in communities of **Eu3F** MEDITERRANEAN OAK FOREST. To the north of this region, Madrid sits on the Meseta Central, a region offering phenomenal birding opportunities: the wide-open grasslands and

Andújar, Andalusia, Spain. © VINCENT LEGRAND, AGAMI

shrublands of **Eu7D** IBERIAN STEPPE occur in a matrix with the savannas dotted with scattered oak trees of the **Eu6B** OAK DEHESA. Iberian Steppe continues through the eastern plateau into the very dry regions of Almería. **Eu12E** EUROPEAN SODA PAN AND INLAND SALT MARSH habitat is sparsely scattered through the region, and rivers with ribbons of **Eu3I** MEDITERRANEAN RIPARIAN FOREST and **Eu11C** EUROPEAN REEDBED weave their way through the dry areas.

Eu12D EUROPEAN COASTAL SALT MARSH is found along many of the coasts behind **Eu12C** EUROPEAN SANDY SHORE AND DUNE, while a whole other world opens up offshore, with **Eu12F** MEDITERRANEAN TO CASPIAN PELAGIC WATERS in the warmer eastern waters and **Eu12G** ARCTIC AND TEMPERATE PELAGIC WATERS to the west and north.

The northern and northwestern areas, like the Basque Country of Spain and n. Portugal, have **Eu12A** EUROPEAN ARCTIC AND TEMPERATE ROCKY COASTLINE and **Eu12C** EUROPEAN SANDY SHORE AND DUNE. The climate is primarily oceanic (**Cfb**), with cool summers, mild winters, and in excess of 1200 mm (50 in.) of rain per year. Temperate broadleaf woodlands grow here, especially **Eu3A** EUROPEAN TEMPERATE OAK FOREST and **Eu3B** EUROPEAN BEECH FOREST. In mid-elevation areas of the Pyrenees and the Sierra Nevada, the climate is humid continental (Köppen **Dfb**), with cold, snowy winters, cool summers, and rainfall sometimes exceeding 1500 mm (60 in.). The Sierra Nevada has both **Eu1F** EUROPEAN MONTANE PINE FOREST and **Eu1I** EUROPEAN MONTANE SPRUCE-FIR FOREST, while the Pyrenees are dominated mainly by the latter. The Pyrenees, however, do support multiple deciduous forest types such as **Eu3A** EUROPEAN TEMPERATE OAK FOREST, **Eu3B** EUROPEAN BEECH FOREST, and **Eu3E** EUROPEAN MONTANE MIXED FOREST, with **Eu7B** EUROPEAN TEMPERATE GRASSLAND AND SAVANNA in the areas between the forests. Somewhat higher elevations have a more extreme subarctic climate (Köppen **Dfc**), leading to the development of **Eu1B** SUBALPINE TIMBERLINE WOODLAND. A tundra climate (Köppen **ET**) is found even higher in the mountains, above about 2100–2300 m (6900–7500 ft.). Temperatures remain cold throughout the year, and winters have very heavy snowfalls. At these elevations, trees can no longer grow, and the landscape is dominated by the very low, shrubby or grassy **Eu10F** EUROPEAN ALPINE TUNDRA. The glacial **Eu10G** EUROPEAN NIVAL ROCKY TUNDRA develops above about 3000 m (10,000 ft.) in the ice cap climate (Köppen **EF**).

SEO/BirdLife Spain, the Portuguese Society for the Study of Birds (SPEA), and the Gibraltar Ornithological and Natural History Society are heavily involved in bird and broader environmental conservation in the region.

8 EASTERN MEDITERRANEAN AND THE BALKANS

Millions of tourists visit the incredible monuments of Italy every year, oblivious to the subtropical wonders available to be explored off the well-worn tourist paths. The mild climate of Italy and the Mediterranean region to its east offers the keen naturalist a whole suite of birds, amphibians, reptiles, and invertebrates not found in the temperate regions farther north in Europe. It can, however, be a place of heartbreaking extremes: in spring migration, thousands of birders visit places like Lesvos to marvel at the immense migration from Africa to Europe, whereas in nearby Malta, some locals take as much pleasure in killing those same birds for absolutely no purpose other than the thrill of murder itself.

While most of Italy juts into the Mediterranean, the Alps form the country's northern border and feature environments much more typical of the c. Europe region (no. 5, p.37). The Alps started forming with the collision of the African and Eurasian tectonic plates in the late Mesozoic (around 70 MYA) but only really got cranking in the Cenozoic. In the Pleistocene (2.6 MYA–11,700 YA), these mountains were covered in glaciers, which caused significant erosion and an immense weight on the land. Since the end of the last ice age, the mountains have continued to grow through the

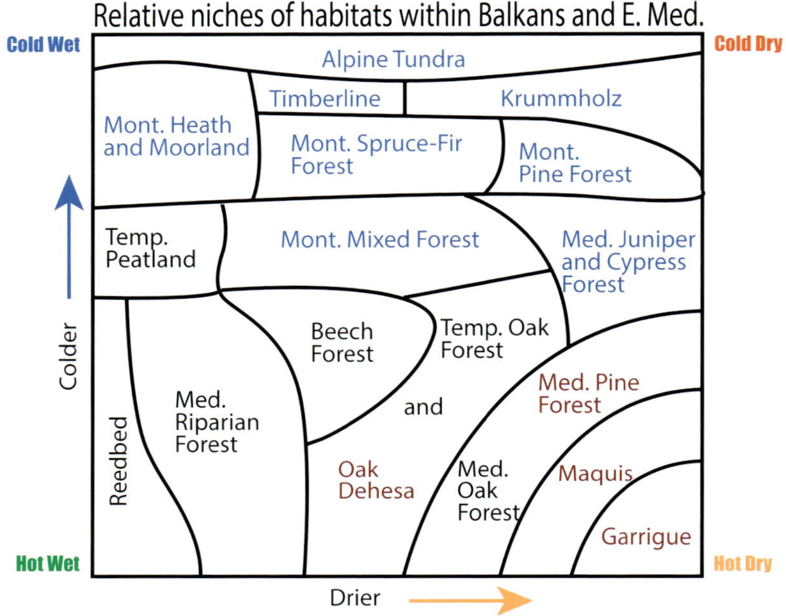

convergence of the African and Eurasian tectonic plates as well as isostatic rebound, where the earth bulges because the weight of ice has been removed. What is also fascinating about the Alps is that they do not have volcanic activity, suggesting that they were formed purely by orogeny, in which rocks have been accreted (adhered) to the mountains and buckled, folded, and faulted rather than formed by oceanic basalts and sediments being subducted and melting below the surface. This uplift and subsequent glaciation have resulted in incredibly rugged, towering mountains with very deep valleys and a range of local climates. The mountains' lower elevations—for example, around Bolzano—have a warm-summer humid continental climate (Köppen **Dfb**), and remnants of **Eu3A** EUROPEAN TEMPERATE OAK FOREST are scattered through extensive **Eu13A** EUROPEAN CROPLAND and **Eu13B** EUROPEAN URBAN ENVIRONMENTS; and areas of **Eu3H** EUROPEAN TEMPERATE RIPARIAN FOREST and **Eu7A** EUROPEAN WET GRASSLAND can be a naturalist's delight, especially in the spring. The climate changes into the montane zone (Köppen **Dfb–Dfc**), where summers are cool, with temperatures averaging between 10 and 22°C (50–72°F), and winters are snowy and cold, with averages of −3 to 3°C (27–37°F). **Eu3B** EUROPEAN BEECH FOREST, **Eu3E** EUROPEAN MONTANE MIXED FOREST, and **Eu1I** EUROPEAN MONTANE SPRUCE-FIR FOREST start to dominate at about 600 m (2000 ft.) above sea level, where they are chequered with the pastures and meadows of **Eu7B** EUROPEAN TEMPERATE GRASSLAND AND SAVANNA. The climate (Köppen **Dfc**, subarctic) turns colder with increasing elevation, and it becomes increasingly difficult for trees to grow. **Eu1B** SUBALPINE TIMBERLINE WOODLAND and **Eu1J** SUBALPINE KRUMMHOLZ establish the upper boundary above which trees are not able to grow effectively. Above this tree line, at about 1700 m (5600 ft.), the tundra climate (Köppen **ET**) allows only the shrubs and grasses of **Eu10F** EUROPEAN ALPINE TUNDRA to grow. **Eu10G** EUROPEAN NIVAL ROCKY TUNDRA is found at the most extreme of elevations and climates (Köppen **EF**, ice cap climate), typically above about 3000 m (10,000 ft.).

The Apennine Mountains run down the spine of Italy and are composed primarily of sedimentary rocks formed during the Mesozoic and Cenozoic eras, including limestone, marl, and sandstone.

Tectonic uplift from the collision of the African and Eurasian plates built this mountain range but also resulted in significant volcanism and the intrusion of magmas into the landscape. Active volcanoes like Mt. Etna and Mt. Vesuvius are very evident reminders of the geological forces at play in the region.

The mountains farther east, such as the Dinaric Alps of Slovenia to Albania, the Pindus Mountains of Greece, and the highlands of Cyprus, are made mainly of sedimentary rocks, such as shallow sea sandstone and limestones, but include deep-sea sediments such as flysch. All these Mesozoic rocks have been uplifted, folded, and faulted as Africa collides with Eurasia, resulting in a bit of the earth's mantle being smeared onto Europe (see Sidebar 1: Do You Want to See a Bit of the Mantle?, p.99).

The bases of these mountain ranges have Mediterranean climates, especially the hot-summer Mediterranean climate (Köppen **Csa**). Winters are mild and wet, while summers are dry and very hot, with temperatures soaring to 40°C (104°F) or above. Vegetation in these areas is very hardy, and **Eu8A** EUROPEAN GARRIGUE and the taller, denser **Eu8B** EUROPEAN MAQUIS are both common. Conifer groves in the lowlands of the e. Mediterranean are **Eu1G** MEDITERRANEAN PINE FOREST, with trees like Umbrella Pine, or **Eu1H** MEDITERRANEAN JUNIPER AND CYPRESS FOREST. The waterlogged valleys and rivers of the region have swaths of **Eu3I** MEDITERRANEAN RIPARIAN FOREST and **Eu11C** EUROPEAN REEDBED wetlands.

The slightly milder warm-summer Mediterranean climate (Köppen **Csb**) is found a bit higher in the landscape or on coasts with moderating winds. This environment supports habitats such as **Eu1G** MEDITERRANEAN PINE FOREST and **Eu3F** MEDITERRANEAN OAK FOREST. Low-lying seaboard can also have **Eu12D** EUROPEAN COASTAL SALT MARSH. Coastline habitats are **Eu12C** EUROPEAN SANDY SHORE AND DUNE or **Eu12B**

Above right: **Dalmatian Pelican.** © MARC GUYT, AGAMI

Right: **Lesvos, Greece.** © MARC GUYT, AGAMI

MEDITERRANEAN TO CASPIAN ROCKY COASTLINE, while extensive **Eu12F** MEDITERRANEAN TO CASPIAN PELAGIC WATERS are found offshore.

The bases of mountains in southern areas have a humid subtropical climate (Köppen **Cfa**), with hot, humid summers, mild to cool winters, and significant rainfall throughout the year. Deciduous forests such as **Eu3A** EUROPEAN TEMPERATE OAK FOREST and **Eu3B** EUROPEAN BEECH FOREST are common. Mountains in the Balkan Peninsula have a temperate oceanic climate (Köppen **Cfb**) between about 500 and 1500 m (1600–4900 ft.). The mild summers and cool, wet winters promote habitats such as the **Eu3E** EUROPEAN MONTANE MIXED FOREST. In the c. and n. Balkans, including much of Serbia and Bulgaria, the climate is warm-summer humid continental (Köppen **Dfb**), with cold, snowy winters, mild summers, and rainfall sometimes exceeding 1500 mm (60 in.). The forests are commonly coniferous, including **Eu1F** EUROPEAN MONTANE PINE FOREST and **Eu1I** EUROPEAN MONTANE SPRUCE-FIR FOREST. The higher Balkan Mountains have a subarctic climate (Köppen **Dfc**), with precipitation throughout the year and cold winters. These high slopes have **Eu1J** SUBALPINE KRUMMHOLZ interlaced with large open pastures and meadows of **Eu7B** EUROPEAN TEMPERATE GRASSLAND AND SAVANNA at somewhat lower elevations and **Eu10F** EUROPEAN ALPINE TUNDRA above the timberline. Eastern Bulgaria has a cold semi-arid climate (Köppen **Bsk**), with hot summers regularly topping 35°C (95°F) and mild, dry winters in which average January lows are typically around −2°C (28°F). Annual rainfall is typically less than 300 mm (12 in.). In addition to the Garrigue and Maquis described above, there are also extensive areas of **Eu7C** PUSZTA AND PONTIC STEPPE.

In most countries in the region, engaged and committed BirdLife International partners work tirelessly for the conservation of nature and birds, including the Lega Italiana Protezione Uccelli (LIPU) (Italy), BirdLife Slovenia (DOPPS), Association BIOM (Croatia), Centre for Protection and Research of Birds of Montenegro (CZIP), Bird Protection and Study Society of Serbia, Macedonian Ecological Society, Hellenic Ornithological Society (Greece), Protection and Preservation of Natural Environment in Albania, Bulgarian Society for the Protection of Birds, BirdLife Malta, and BirdLife Cyprus.

9 HUNGARY, SLOVAKIA, AND ROMANIA

When people visit this region, they usually spend their time in Bratislava, Slovakia; Budapest, Hungary; or Bucharest, Romania, all perched on the relatively flat plains of the Pannonian Basin, with hardly a mountain in sight. Yet this area is wrapped in the fascinating Carpathian Mountains and abutted by the captivating Transylvanian Plateau, which remain off the normal tourist or naturalist route.

The Carpathian Mountains are a prominent range that arcs through Slovakia and southeast through Romania then switchbacks to the east through s. Romania, resembling half a triangle. They are part of the Alpine–Himalayan orogenic belt, formed by the collision of the African and Eurasian tectonic plates from the late Cretaceous (~70 MYA) to the Miocene. The range comprises not only very acidic plutonic and metamorphic rocks, such as granite and gneiss, but also sedimentary rocks, such as limestone, sandstone, and shale. Adding to the complexity are significant intrusions of younger igneous rock and more recent metamorphism. During the Pleistocene, the mountains were subjected to significant glaciation and therefore have classic alpine landforms, such as cirques and steep valleys. The lower elevations and valleys of the Carpathians experience a warm-summer humid continental climate (Köppen **Dfb**), with cold winter temperatures ranging from −3°C (27°F) in the lower valleys to −15°C (5°F) in the higher valleys. The summers can be very warm and wet, seeing average temperatures reaching 20°C (68°F) and most of the annual 800–1500 mm (31–59 in.) of precipitation. The lower valleys are dominated by deciduous forests such as **Eu3A** EUROPEAN TEMPERATE OAK FOREST, **Eu3E** EUROPEAN MONTANE MIXED FOREST, and some smaller patches of **Eu3B** EUROPEAN BEECH FOREST.

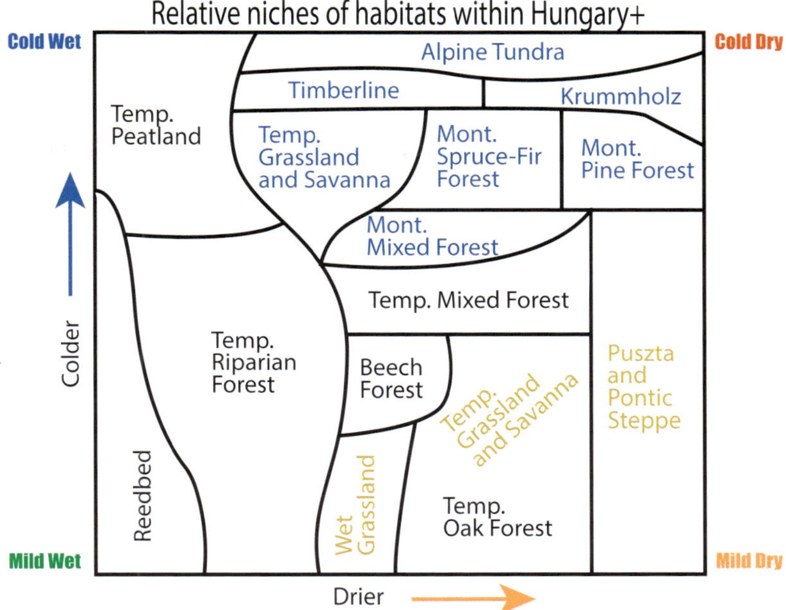

Higher upslope from the valleys, above 1500 m (4900 ft.), the climate changes to subarctic (Köppen **Dfc**), with shorter growing seasons and colder winter temperatures. The summers are very mild, with temperatures rarely exceeding 20°C (68°F), even during the peak of the season. Winters can be extreme, with heavy snows and the average temperature plummeting

Eurasian Hamster. © BENCE MÁTÉ, AGAMI

to −20°C (−4°F). The harsher climatic conditions are not conducive to deciduous forests, so the mountainsides are dominated by **Eu1I** EUROPEAN MONTANE SPRUCE-FIR FOREST and mountain pastures and meadows (**Eu7B** EUROPEAN TEMPERATE GRASSLAND AND SAVANNA), though smaller pockets of **Eu1F** EUROPEAN MONTANE PINE FOREST occur. In the higher reaches, the spruce-fir forest is replaced with **Eu1B** SUBALPINE TIMBERLINE WOODLAND and **Eu1J** SUBALPINE KRUMMHOLZ. The tundra (Köppen **ET**) climate of the higher mountains is too cold for tree growth, and **Eu10F** EUROPEAN ALPINE TUNDRA is extensive in places.

The Pannonian Basin covers much of Hungary and extends into parts of Slovakia and Romania. It can be regarded as a continuation of the Pontic Plains, which extend through Ukraine and into Russia. In the late Cretaceous, as the Carpathian Mountains were being uplifted and folding, a shallow sea was opening up through continental extension. This sea was filled with thick sequences of sedimentary rocks, primarily claystone, siltstones, and sandstones derived from the erosion of the Carpathians. Since then, while other European areas have been buckled and faulted, this region has remained very stable. Not much has happened since then. The region's geomorphology has been shaped by fluvial processes, generated particularly by the Danube River, creating extensive floodplains, alluvial plains, and low hills.

Much of the central part of the region (areas such as Budapest) has a humid subtropical climate (Köppen **Cfa**), with more extremes in weather than Bratislava in the western part of the region. The c. Pannonian Basin has mild winters, with temperatures averaging −2 to 0°C (28–32°F), and warm summers, with temperatures often exceeding 22°C (72°F). The area is considered semi-humid, with annual precipitation between 500 and 700 mm (20–28 in.). Conditions get significantly drier farther to the southeast, where there is a cold semi-arid climate (Köppen **Bsk**). In the hot summers, average temperatures can top 26°C (79°F), and in the cold winters, average temperatures are between −5 and −2°C (23–28°F). The precipitation is low, with most of the 300–500 mm (12–20 in.) falling in late spring and early summer.

The natural habitat of the wide-open plains is **Eu7C** PUSZTA AND PONTIC STEPPE peppered with **Eu12E** EUROPEAN SODA PAN. Nevertheless, much of the region has been turned over to agriculture, and **Eu13A** EUROPEAN CROPLAND abounds. Streams and rivers snake through the plains and are lined with **Eu3H** EUROPEAN TEMPERATE RIPARIAN FOREST as well as some fantastic, extensive **Eu11C** EUROPEAN REEDBED habitat. The hills rising in the salt-laden plains have deeper, more nutrient-rich soils and are blanketed in **Eu3A** EUROPEAN TEMPERATE OAK FOREST and **Eu3B** EUROPEAN BEECH FOREST.

The Transylvanian Plateau had a similar history to the Pannonian Basin during the late Cretaceous and early Cenozoic, forming limestones, sandstones, and claystones, as well as freshwater lacustrine deposits. However, it differs

Small river snaking through the Hungarian steppe. © IAIN CAMPBELL, TROPICAL BIRDING

in that during the Miocene (23–5 MYA), this area experienced intraplate volcanism, a rare form of volcanic activity that occurs within a tectonic plate rather than at plate boundaries. Here, magmas intrude along older tectonic structures, such as fault lines, rather than forming a hotspot volcano (think Hawaii) or a volcano in a subduction zone (think Mt. Fuji). The resulting uplands are now a mixture of unfolded sedimentary rocks and volcanic rocks such as basalts and andesites, which form the bedrock of nutrient-rich soils.

The climate at lower elevations on the Transylvanian Plateau is mainly temperate oceanic (Köppen **Cfb**), with mild summers and cool winters. Precipitation is evenly distributed throughout the year. This climate and the fertile soils promote **Eu3A** EUROPEAN TEMPERATE OAK FOREST and **Eu3B** EUROPEAN BEECH FOREST mixed with **Eu7B** EUROPEAN TEMPERATE GRASSLAND AND SAVANNA and **Eu7A** EUROPEAN WET GRASSLAND. At slightly higher elevations on the plateau, the forests of the warm-summer humid continental climate (Köppen **Dfb**) resemble those of the Carpathians, with extensive **Eu1I** EUROPEAN MONTANE SPRUCE-FIR FOREST, **Eu1F** EUROPEAN MONTANE PINE FOREST, and **Eu3E** EUROPEAN MONTANE MIXED FOREST.

Magyar Madártani és Természetvédelmi Egyesület (MME) (Hungary), BirdLife Romania (SOR), and BirdLife Slovakia (SOS) are some of the most important conservation organisations in the region.

10 THE CAUCASUS

The Caucasus region, encompassing Azerbaijan, Georgia, and Armenia, lies in the extreme southeast corner of Europe, where it is affected by many significant Asian elements and influences. The mélange of western and eastern habitats makes it one of the most intriguing regions in the world and a must-see for people with an interest in Eurasian biogeography.

Stretching between the Black and the Caspian Seas, this region is dominated by two parallel west–east mountain ranges: the Greater Caucasus and the Lesser Caucasus. The Greater Caucasus

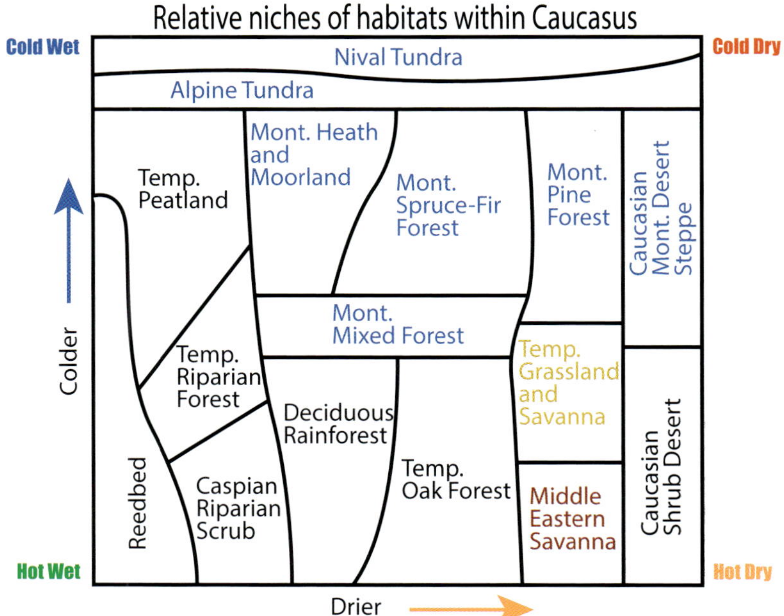

Fire-fronted Serin. © DAVID MONTICELLI, AGAMI

stretches from the Black Sea coast in Georgia to the Caspian Sea in Azerbaijan, forming a natural border with Russia. It has many of Europe's highest peaks, including Mounts Elbrus (5640 m/18,500 ft.) and Shkhara (5200 m/17,000 ft.). The Lesser Caucasus lies farther south, roughly aligning with the border between this region and Türkiye and Iran. It is much lower than the Greater Caucasus, with only a few peaks over 3700 m (12,000 ft.). These mountains have created some wildly different climates within the small area of the region. The higher mountains have tundra and ice cap climates (Köppen **ET** and **EF**), with habitats such as **Eu10F** EUROPEAN ALPINE TUNDRA and **Eu10G** EUROPEAN NIVAL ROCKY TUNDRA. These are the areas where birders search for localised species such as the Caucasian Snowcock. **Eu1B** SUBALPINE TIMBERLINE WOODLAND grows at slightly lower elevations, but the climate is still subarctic (Köppen **Dfc**), with cold winters and precipitation throughout the year. As with the other mountain ranges of Europe, lower levels can have temperate climates, with mild summers and winters and year-round precipitation (Köppen **Dfb**). This montane zone is dominated by coniferous forests, especially **Eu1I** EUROPEAN MONTANE SPRUCE-FIR FOREST.

The (relative) lowlands between the two Caucasus ranges span from the Black Sea to the Caspian Sea. The lowlands of the Rioni River valley and the bases of the ranges along the Black Sea coast in w. Georgia are dominated by fertile plains, most of which have been cleared. Nevertheless, some areas of **Eu11C** EUROPEAN REEDBED, **Eu3I** MEDITERRANEAN RIPARIAN FOREST, and patches

Mud volcano, Azerbaijan. © IAIN CAMPBELL, TROPICAL BIRDING

of other forest types remain. At the base of the Caucasus ranges, particularly the Lesser Caucasus, there is a huge amount of orographic rainfall, derived from clouds formed above the Black Sea. The very wet oceanic climate (**Cfb**) has warm summers, cold winters, and a staggering 4500 mm (175 in.) of annual rainfall in places. These conditions allow for the formation of Colchic Forest, a type of **Eu3C** EUROPEAN DECIDUOUS RAINFOREST. These forests are reminiscent of an Andean cloudforest in summer, but winters are snowy, and the trees become largely leafless. The sister rainforest habitat—Hyrcanian Forest—occurs on the Azerbaijan-Iran border at the base of the Talish Mountains. The canopies of these two forests are similar, but they have different understoreys.

Towards the Caspian Sea, the Kura-Aras valley, in sharp contrast with the westerly sloping Rioni valley, is dominated in the uplands by arid habitats such as **Eu2C** CAUCASIAN MONTANE DESERT STEPPE, much of which has been turned over to agriculture. Nevertheless, farming practices are usually artisanal, so the boundaries between the original steppe and modified habitats are not as stark as in other parts of Europe, where the steppe has been obliterated. Most visitors will be amazed at how intact the habitats appear to be. Closer to the Caspian Sea is one of the two European lowland deserts, the **Eu2B** CAUCASIAN SHRUB DESERT. Visitors can see not only Goitred Gazelle here but also fantastic petroglyphs and amazing mud volcanoes. The lowlands of Azerbaijan also have **Eu3J** CASPIAN RIPARIAN SCRUB, a habitat that continues around the Caspian Sea and along the northern side of the Tian Shan mountains all the way to Mongolia.

The Society for Nature Conservation (SABUKO) (Georgia) and the Foundation for the Preservation of Wildlife and Cultural Assets (FPWC) (Armenia) are two of the most important conservation organisations in the region.

11 TÜRKIYE

Türkiye is a must-see country for naturalists, and it is a travesty that it is not much better known. A simple north–south trip in the east of the country will span many life zones, but most people, including nature lovers, do not see beyond Istanbul, the beaches of the southwest, and a quick visit to Cappadocia.

To even attempt to understand the habitats of Türkiye, we need to take a step back and consider the geology and geomorphology of the diverse region. Türkiye is said to be the crossroads of Europe and Asia, but even this is an artificial concept (see Sidebar 3: The Illusion of Europe, p.197). Türkiye is on the Anatolian microplate, which has been a firm part of a stable Eurasia since Europe and Asia became one around 420 MYA. The recent pounding from Africa has shaped Türkiye more.

The Taurus Mountains in the south and the Pontic Mountains in the north are major orogenic belts, formed by collision and convergence as Africa crashes into Eurasia. The Taurus Mountains were uplifted mainly between the Palaeogene and Neogene (66 to ~2.6 MYA) but continue to lift today, albeit only 2.5 mm (0.1 in.) per year. As the Tethys Sea closed, the carbonate platforms were uplifted and folded, creating significant topographic relief in the south of Türkiye. At the same time, the subduction of the Tethys Sea under the Anatolian microplate pushed oceanic crust under Türkiye. This then melted, and volcanoes popped up into the Mesozoic-Cenozoic sedimentary rocks that had been accreted to (scraped onto) the Eurasian plate. This caused volcanic activity and the subsequent formation of the Pontic Mountains in n. Türkiye. The formation of the Pontic Mountains is more analogous to that of the South American Andes than Asia's Himalayas. Between the Taurus and Pontic ranges is a stable uplifted block called the Central Anatolian Plateau, a high-elevation region that is largely flat with low volcanoes.

The consequent diverse geomorphology has resulted in a variety of climates within Türkiye and a very wide range of habitats. The western parts of the country, especially around the Mediterranean

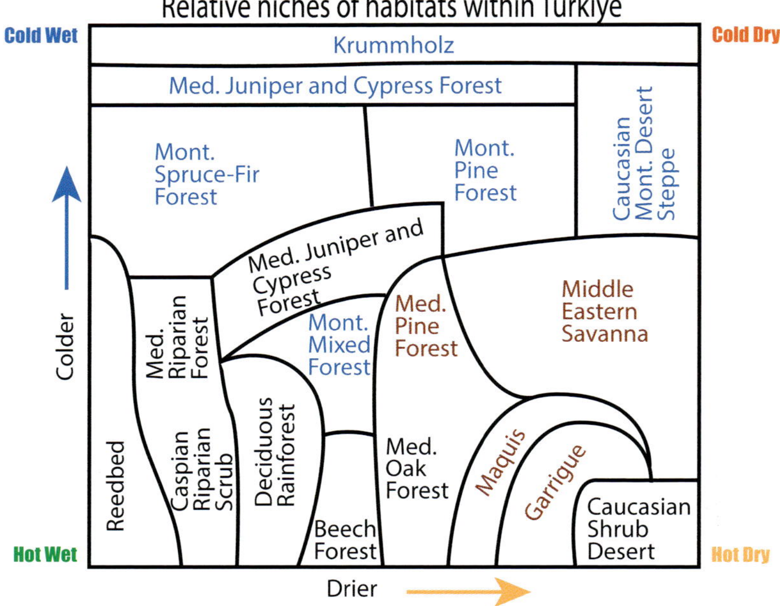

coastlines of Istanbul and Antalya, have a hot-summer Mediterranean climate (Köppen **Csa**). Summers are dry, with average temperatures exceeding 30°C (86°F). Winters are mild, usually 5–15°C (41–59°F), with annual rainfall around 1100 mm (43 in.). The widespread shrubby habitat typically encountered on the headlands and at archaeological sites is **Eu8A** EUROPEAN GARRIGUE, while the taller **Eu8B** EUROPEAN MAQUIS occurs on more protected sites. A little higher in the landscape, the climate changes to a warm-summer Mediterranean climate (Köppen **Csb**), which is similar to **Csa** but with milder summers; it tends to support habitats such as **Eu1G** MEDITERRANEAN PINE FOREST and **Eu3F** MEDITERRANEAN OAK FOREST. The Mediterranean areas are dissected by many rivers lined with **Eu3I** MEDITERRANEAN RIPARIAN FOREST and **Eu11C** EUROPEAN REEDBED.

The Pontic Mountains can receive a lot of moisture from the Black Sea, resulting in a humid subtropical climate (Köppen **Cfa**) on the coast and an oceanic climate (Köppen **Cfb**) a little higher in the mountains. Both areas have mild but very wet winters, with rainfall often

White-throated Robin. © DANIELE OCCHIATO, AGAMI

exceeding 2000 mm (80 in.), though the areas with a **Cfa** climate have hot summers, and those with **Cfb** climate have mild summers, with temperatures rarely topping 22°C (71°F). With these warm, wet climates, it is not surprising that **Eu3C** EUROPEAN DECIDUOUS RAINFOREST occurs here.

The mid-elevations of Türkiye's mountain ranges have a warm-summer humid continental climate (Köppen **Dfb**). Summers are mild, with average highs of 15–22°C (59–71.6°F), and winters snowy and cold, with temperatures regularly dropping below freezing. Farther upslope, the climate changes to subarctic (Köppen **Dfc**), with very cold winters and snow that stays for protracted periods. These regions are dominated by **Eu1I** EUROPEAN MONTANE SPRUCE-FIR FOREST and **Eu1F** EUROPEAN MONTANE PINE FOREST, although cleared areas can also have **Eu7B** EUROPEAN TEMPERATE GRASSLAND AND SAVANNA.

The vast central plains of Türkiye, including places such as Cappadocia, have a cold semi-arid climate (Köppen **Bsk**) featuring hot, dry summers and cold winters. The region gets around 300–400 mm (12–16 in.) of precipitation per year, and **Eu6A** MIDDLE EASTERN SAVANNA dominates. The climate generally gets more arid towards the east and southeast, where the drier deserts dominate: **Eu2B** CAUCASIAN SHRUB DESERT in the lowlands and **Eu2C** CAUCASIAN MONTANE DESERT STEPPE in the highlands. The arid lands are dissected by many rivers with **Eu3I** MEDITERRANEAN RIPARIAN FOREST and wetlands such as **Eu11C** EUROPEAN REEDBED.

Doğa Derneği is a Turkish organisation involved in the monitoring and conservation of a wide range of wildlife species, managing the protection of 30 key biodiversity areas (KBAs), and running environmental education programmes.

See-see Partridge. © PETE MORRIS

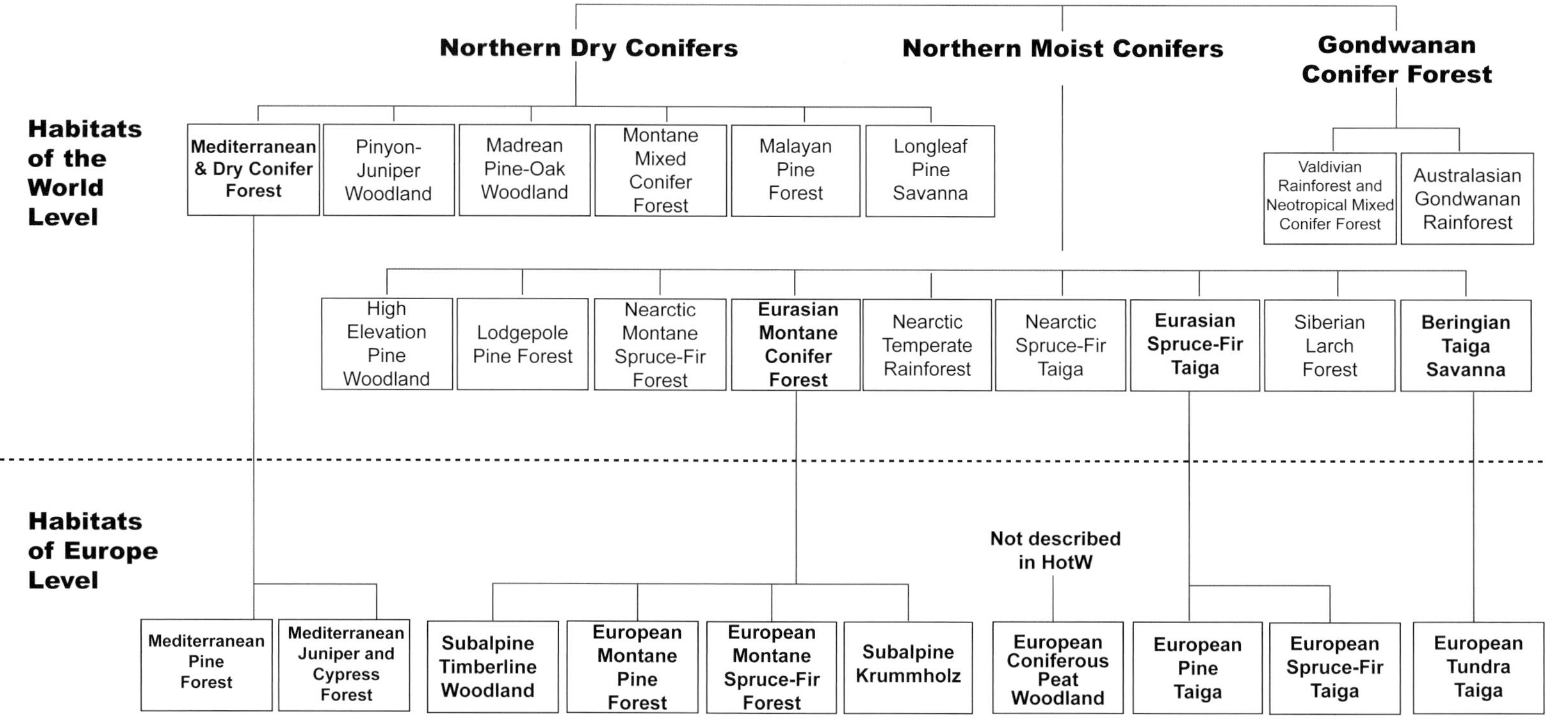
CONIFER FORESTS
Habitats of the World Level
Habitats of Europe Level
Northern Dry Conifers
Northern Moist Conifers
Gondwanan Conifer Forest
Mediterranean & Dry Conifer Forest
Pinyon-Juniper Woodland
Madrean Pine-Oak Woodland
Montane Mixed Conifer Forest
Malayan Pine Forest
Longleaf Pine Savanna
Valdivian Rainforest and Neotropical Mixed Conifer Forest
Australasian Gondwanan Rainforest
High Elevation Pine Woodland
Lodgepole Pine Forest
Nearctic Montane Spruce-Fir Forest
Eurasian Montane Conifer Forest
Nearctic Temperate Rainforest
Nearctic Spruce-Fir Taiga
Eurasian Spruce-Fir Taiga
Siberian Larch Forest
Beringian Taiga Savanna
Not described in HotW
Mediterranean Pine Forest
Mediterranean Juniper and Cypress Forest
Subalpine Timberline Woodland
European Montane Pine Forest
European Montane Spruce-Fir Forest
Subalpine Krummholz
European Coniferous Peat Woodland
European Pine Taiga
European Spruce-Fir Taiga
European Tundra Taiga

Eu1A EUROPEAN TUNDRA TAIGA

IN A NUTSHELL: This habitat, a spattering of conifers over various tundras, forms the northern tree line. **Global Habitat Affinities:** ASIAN TUNDRA TAIGA. **Continental Habitat Affinities:** Arctic equivalent of SUBALPINE TIMBERLINE WOODLAND. **Species Overlap:** SPRUCE-FIR TAIGA; CONIFEROUS PEAT WOODLAND; SHRUBBY TUNDRA.

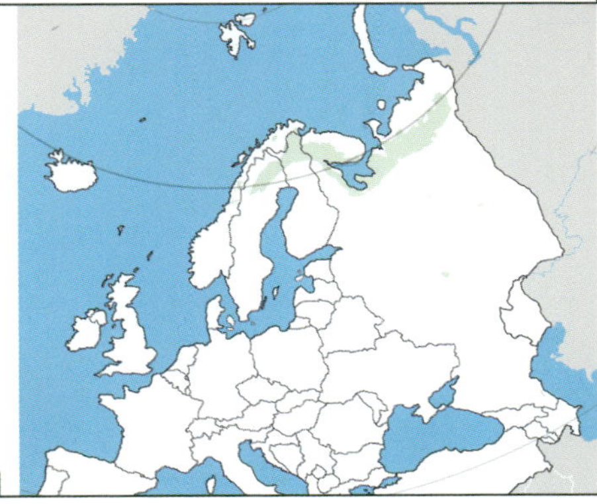

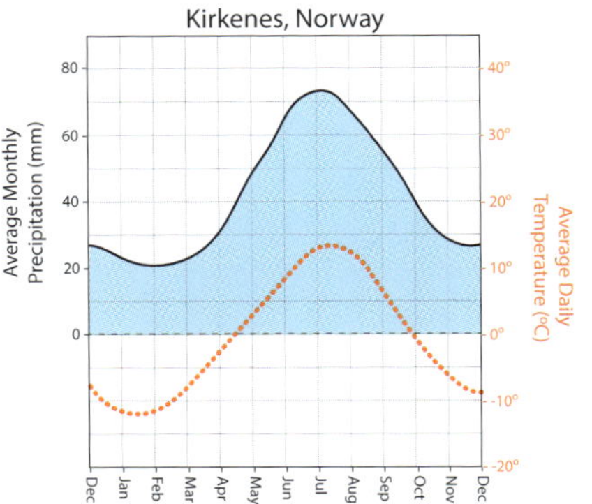

DESCRIPTION: In some areas of Arctic and subarctic Europe, the transition from tundras to PINE TAIGA is rapid. But in other regions, the transition is nebulous—this is the Tundra Taiga, a habitat in the zone between the more typical tundra and the taiga forest proper, where the tundra starts to become dotted with stunted spruces, pines, and larches.

Norway Spruce (*Picea abies*) and Scots Pine (*Pinus sylvestris*) are the dominant tree species through most of this habitat. The Norway Spruce dominates in moderately well-drained podzol (or spodosol) soils (see appendix), while the Scots Pine, being very adaptable and tolerant of most environments, including well-drained and poorly drained soils, is therefore much more widespread. Although the conifers here are the same species as those in the extensive forests to the south, their structure is very different. Small clusters of closely spaced trees can form in the Tundra Taiga, but there is often 50 m (150 ft.) between individual trees or groves, and the trees are generally short (to only 15 m/50 ft.). This is in stark contrast to the dense forests that form in optimal conditions farther south, where the trees are two to three times taller. Besides the spruce and pine, Tundra Taiga has a peppering of European Larch (*Larix decidua*), along with Least Willow (*Salix herbacea*), Downy Willow (*Salix lapponum*), Dwarf Birch (*Betula nana*), Silver Birch (*Betula pendula*), and Downy Birch (*Betula pubescens*). There is a very low shrub cover, around 30 cm (1 ft.) tall, with another gymnosperm, the Common Juniper (*Juniperus communis*), and Marsh Labrador Tea (*Rhododendron tomentosum*). In boggy areas, the ground is often covered with Red-stemmed Feather Moss (*Pleurozium schreberi*).

The average temperature through the year is −5°C (23°F), with very short summers of 8–12°C (46–54°F) and very cold winters of −24.5 to −21.5°C (−12 to −7°F). The average midsummer temperatures can be warmer than the 10°C (50°F) limit for tundra, though it is still a harsh

An open pine-dominated Tundra Taiga with scattered birches in the background, possibly transitioning to Subarctic Riparian Woodland. © IAIN CAMPBELL, TROPICAL BIRDING

(Köppen **ET**) climate. With annual precipitation ranging from 200 to 400 mm (8–16 in.), some areas could be classified as arid terrain. Nevertheless, because evapotranspiration is so low, the landscape remains humid through much of the year. Permafrost is often present in these woodlands, but the habitat can form in regions without permafrost.

Covered in ice flow throughout the ice ages, this region was only recently exposed and is still rising from isostatic rebound (the earth buckling because of a release of pressure from the thick sheets of ice). The landscape is dotted with lakes, eskers, tills, and terminal moraines—evidence of the glacial scouring—combined with permafrost features such as pingos (mounds of earth formed through expanding ice over frozen permafrost). The drainage in these areas is often impeded and rarely dendritic (the normal branching drainage pattern typical of temperate regions). This creates the conditions for many small bogs, where large hummocks of sphagnum mosses grow, with marsh grasses in the channels between them. When the bogs become larger than 15 m (50 ft.) across, the habitat is better regarded as BOGGY TUNDRA.

WILDLIFE: Tundra Taiga is very important for breeding shorebirds, in particular a wide range of species that winter in Africa and India and come here to nest. They typically arrive in late May just as the snows are melting and starting to reveal the marshy habitat below. Wood Sandpipers are

Tundra Taiga is an open savanna-like mixture of scattered trees through tundra.
© IAIN CAMPBELL, TROPICAL BIRDING

particularly common in this habitat and nest both on the ground and in abandoned passerine nests in trees. Other common breeders include Spotted and Common Redshanks, Purple Sandpiper, and Black-tailed Godwit. Rough-legged Hawk (aka Rough-legged Buzzard) hunts over the open patches of the Tundra Taiga, along with White-tailed Eagle. Short-eared Owl and Northern Hawk Owl can be in the same small area, but the Northern Hawk Owl concentrates on hunting in the forested areas, whereas the Short-eared Owl hunts more in the open spaces. Willow Ptarmigan and a variety of passerines, such as Little Bunting, Bluethroat, and Tree Pipit, are also found in the extensive SPRUCE-FIR TAIGA to the south.

Wood Sandpipers can be quite common in the Tundra Taiga, often using conifers as song posts. © MARKUS VARESVUO, AGAMI

Purple Sandpipers seem out of place when seen breeding in the Tundra Taiga, as most naturalists are more familiar with them in their rocky coastal non-breeding habitat. © MARKUS VARESVUO, AGAMI

Northern Hawk Owl is largely diurnal and likes to use prominent perches as lookouts in the Tundra Taiga. © MARKUS VARESVUO, AGAMI

The Tundra Taiga supports few mammals, but these include a number that most wildlife-watchers would love to see, such as Wolverine, Brown Bear, European Elk (Moose), and Reindeer (Caribou).

CONSERVATION: Few protection efforts are directed specifically at this habitat. With increasing world temperatures, it is migrating north into tundra habitats and, in its core range, is being replaced by thicker woodlands of the same tree species to its south, turning this very open woodland into SPRUCE-FIR TAIGA.

DISTRIBUTION: A belt of Tundra Taiga extends from Norway all the way across the top of Siberia and is wedged between the true tundra to its north and the taiga to the south. The width of the belt varies greatly, from just 5 km (3 mi.) wide in n. Finland to over 50 km (30 mi.) in c. Siberia. This habitat will likely become more widespread with global climate change as conifers and birches colonise areas dominated by ROCKY and SHRUBBY TUNDRAS.

WHERE TO SEE: Kirkenes, Norway.

The very special Wolverine is the holy grail for mammal-watchers exploring n. Europe. © JARI PELTOMÄKI, AGAMI

Eu1B SUBALPINE TIMBERLINE WOODLAND

IN A NUTSHELL: Open coniferous woodlands found above Europe's montane forests in the transition to the treeless ALPINE TUNDRA. **Global Habitat Affinities:** NEARCTIC HIGH-ELEVATION PINE WOODLAND; AFROTROPICAL MONTANE DRY MIXED WOODLAND; SUBALPINE EUCALYPT WOODLAND; HIMALAYAN SUBALPINE WOODLAND. **Continental Habitat Affinities:** SUBALPINE KRUMMHOLZ; EUROPEAN SUBARCTIC RIPARIAN WOODLAND. **Species Overlap:** ALPINE TUNDRA; MONTANE SPRUCE-FIR FOREST.

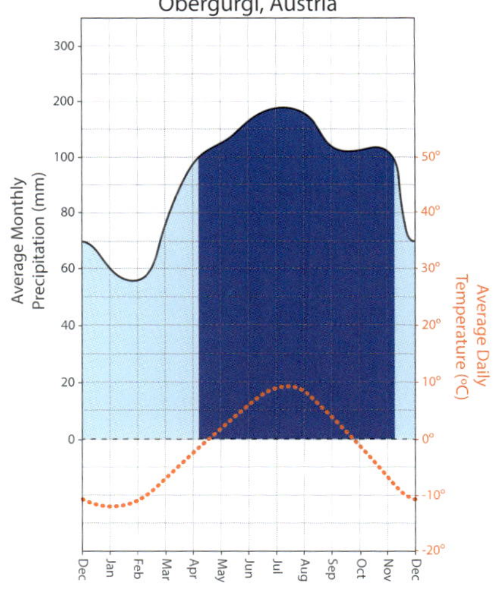

DESCRIPTION: Europe's montane forests get progressively thinner upslope as the growing conditions get tougher. Extreme cold, long periods of snow cover, high winds, high solar radiation, and a short growing season all limit plant growth. Approaching the timberline, the conditions are so harsh that forests can no longer establish and are replaced by open woodlands and species better adapted to the extreme environment (Köppen **Dfc**, subarctic). The elevation of the timberline varies from location to location and is affected by aspect, latitude, soils, local climate, wind-shearing, avalanche activity, and land management. As such, Subalpine Timberline Woodlands form a band, 50–200 m (150–650 ft.) wide, around mountains, wedged in between the lower montane forests and the higher tundras. These woodlands are higher on warmer south-facing slopes and lower on north-facing slopes where snow remains longer into spring, shortening the effective growing season. The upper limit of the Subalpine Timberline Woodland (i.e., tree line) is as high as 2500 m (8200 ft.) in some undisturbed, warmer sites in the Pyrenees, Alps, and s. Carpathians, but it is more often at about 1800 m (6000 ft.). That said, the current tree line in many European mountain areas can be much lower than the ecological tree line, with trees having been cleared either for wood or to extend pastureland, and it can be as low as 1200 m (3900 ft.) or lower in disturbed n. Carpathian locations. The slow tree growth rate means that recovery of the ecological timberline can take centuries at best and millennia if major soil erosion and degradation of the humus layer have occurred.

Above: **Open Subalpine Timberline Woodlands establish at the very limit of where trees can grow. This hiking trail weaves through scattered larches and dense Rusty-leaved Alpenrose.** © DALE FORBES

Below: **The magnificent Swiss Pine is restricted to Subalpine Timberline Woodlands, here growing alongside various grasses, Mountain Juniper, Bog Bilberry, and Dwarf Mountain Pine.** © DALE FORBES

A very short growing season means that decomposition is very slow. This leads to the development of rich humus-filled, acidic soils, with a thick peat-like layer on north-facing slopes (humo-ferric podzols) and a humic upper layer on the slightly warmer and drier south-facing slopes (brown podzols).

The open pine woodlands of the Subalpine Timberline Woodland form one of Europe's most beautiful landscapes. Conifers 25 m (80 ft.) tall are interspersed every 10–100 m (30–300 ft.) through a carpet of small shrubs and grasses, invariably with a breathtaking backdrop of mountain peaks. Despite the tough growing conditions, the magnificent Swiss Pine (*Pinus cembra*) is restricted to this environment. It is revered in the Alps for the schnapps made with its cones and for its beautifully scented wood, which many find pleasantly soothing. The cones and rock-hard seeds also form the basis of a fascinating relationship with the Northern Nutcracker. A single nutcracker

collects 50,000–100,000 seeds every year, hiding them in thousands of locations—often in little rocky nooks and crannies. Many hidden seeds are not eaten, and these semi-protected spaces are perfect for saplings to establish. This explains why many adult trees are found embracing large boulders. The Swiss Pine's deep roots reach below the upper soil layers, which freeze in winter, allowing the tree to counter the extreme transpiration by accessing groundwater all year round.

The deciduous European Larch (*Larix decidua*) deals with the extreme solar radiation in winter by dropping its needles, which first change colour, making for beautiful, blazing orange autumn landscapes. This pioneer tree species has benefitted from livestock grazing in the timberline zone, where trampling hooves expose the soil, opening it up for its saplings to establish. Treefalls, landslides, and avalanche damage can additionally open spots for European Larches to establish.

In the Alps, Subalpine Timberline Woodlands are typically at about 1700 m (5500 ft.) elevation and characterised by very open grasslands with scattered taller trees. Beneath the classic trees of this zone (Swiss Pine and European Larch) are grasses and a short shrub layer including species like Rusty-leaved Alpenrose (*Rhododendron ferrugineum*) on acid soils, Hairy Alpenrose (*Rhododendron hirsutum*) on carbonate-rich soils, Bog Bilberry (*Vaccinium uliginosum*), Lingonberry (*Vaccinium vitis-idaea*), Common Bilberry (*Vaccinium myrtillus*), and Mountain Juniper (*Juniperus communis* var. *saxatilis*). Birches (*Betula* spp.) and European Mountain Ash (*Sorbus aucuparia*) are infrequent but widespread. Subalpine Timberline Woodland will often be found in a mosaic with SUBALPINE KRUMMHOLZ, where mats of Dwarf Mountain Pine (*Pinus mugo*) come to dominate avalanche-prone and steep, calcareous slopes.

An open Swiss Pine woodland with a ground cover of Rusty-leaved Alpenrose. © DALE FORBES

Black Grouse has spectacular display grounds, known as leks, often choosing snowfields at the timberline. Many males gather to fight against each other and attempt to attract a female. © MARKUS VARESVUO, AGAMI

By contrast, European Larch and Swiss Pine are notably absent in the Pyrenees, where the tall-growing Pyrenean Mountain Pine (*Pinus uncinata*) occupies this niche. Rusty-leaved Alpenrose, Mountain Juniper, Common Bilberry, Bog Bilberry, and various grasses fill the gaps between the taller trees on cooler, moister slopes. Warmer limestone slopes tend to develop very little soil and vegetation, but some hardy species, like the beautiful Yellow Hedgehog Broom (*Echinospartum horridum*), Bearberry (*Arctostaphylos uva-ursi*), junipers (*Juniperus* spp.), and Common Lavender (*Lavandula angustifolia*), can establish and thrive.

In the Carpathians, timberline areas are often dominated by Subalpine Krummholz, but the occasional Subalpine Timberline Woodland can be found, with a varying mixture of European Larch, Norway Spruce (*Picea abies*), and Swiss Pine. These open woodlands are dominated by grasses where grazing pressure is high, with

Citril Finch prefers open forest and forest edge right up towards the tree line. © RALPH MARTIN, AGAMI

The hardy Willow Tit occupies a variety of woodlands but is particularly obvious and easiest to find at the timberline. Unusually for a tit, it excavates its own nest hole. © MARKUS VARESVUO, AGAMI

scattered bushes of Mountain Juniper and Myrtle-leaf Rhododendron (*Rhododendron myrtifolium*)—the Carpathian equivalent of the alpenroses. Farther south, Macedonian Pine (*Pinus peuce*) and Bosnian Pine (*Pinus heldreichii*) are found at the tree line.

Deciduous trees are commonly found in the subalpine zone in the Caucasus, where elfin forests of birch but also European Mountain Ash, European Beech (*Fagus sylvatica*), and oaks (*Quercus* spp.) grow in lower areas. In addition, Caucasian Pine (*Pinus sylvestris hamata*) can also reach into the subalpine zone. Grasses, Georgian Snow Rose (*Rhododendron caucasicum*), Common Bilberry, Lingonberry, and other small shrubs make up the understorey.

Subalpine Timberline Woodland does not appear to be present in the Apennines, where beech typically forms a relatively clean timberline below the grass-dominated, treeless subalpine zone.

WILDLIFE: Early on a spring morning, as the sky starts to turn blue, the Eurasian Pygmy-Owl and Boreal (Tengmalm's) Owl are still tooting as the lekking Black Grouse begin to display. Song Thrushes, Ring Ouzels, and Dunnocks sing as beautiful little Redpolls, Citril Finches, and Red Crossbills zip back and forth, and chunky Willow Tits start to look for breakfast. A reclusive Eurasian Three-toed Woodpecker works on a horizontal line in a conifer to milk the phloem sap (a third of their feeding in spring is spent on sap). But the real highlight of the morning—an icon of the Subalpine Timberline Woodland—is the Northern Nutcracker flying actively back and forth between the Swiss Pines. If you can see Northern Nutcrackers and Willow Tits, you are likely in this habitat.

If you are in the Caucasus, you are unlikely to have Northern Nutcrackers about, but you might well be treated to Mountain Chiffchaff, Fire-fronted Serin, or Caucasian Grouse.

Northern Chamois is relatively common in these woodlands, and Red Deer will gladly use them in quieter areas. Red Fox is common,

Red Fox tracks are commonly seen threading through the snow in this habitat. © ALAIN GHIGNONE, AGAMI

The Northern Nutcracker is a keystone species of Subalpine Timberline Woodland with a tight association with the Swiss Pine. © MARKUS VARESVUO, AGAMI

while Brown Bear and Grey Wolf are sporadic. The Giant Deer (aka Irish Elk) was unlikely ever to have been particularly abundant, but had it not been driven to extinction, its preference for open spruce and pine woodlands would likely have made the Subalpine Timberline Woodland its favoured habitat in c. Europe.

Reptiles are uncommon, but the Adder (*Vipera berus*) is found throughout Subalpine Timberline Woodland, while the Caucasus Subalpine Viper (*Vipera dinniki*) is a habitat specialist in the Caucasus Mountains. A wonderful diversity of interesting butterflies is found in Subalpine Timberline Woodland, including the Alpine Grayling (*Oeneis glacialis*); Eriphyle, De Prunner's, Large, and Mountain Ringlets (*Erebia eriphyle*, *E. triarius*, *E. euryale*, and *E. epiphron*); and the rare Asian Fritillary (*Euphydryas intermedia*) and Rätzer's Ringlet (*Erebia christi*).

CONSERVATION: The tough growing conditions mean that it can take centuries for the woodlands to recover once the trees have been removed at the timberline. Non-sustainable harvesting of Swiss Pine and other subalpine trees for timber, firewood, or to open up pastureland can depress the timberline dramatically. Similarly, clearing and disturbance by ski resorts and other sports venues can dramatically affect the health of this ecosystem.

DISTRIBUTION: Subalpine Timberline Woodland occurs in the subalpine zone of Europe's mountain ranges, most notably in the Pyrenees, Alps, Carpathians, and Caucasus.

WHERE TO SEE: Hohe Tauern National Park, Austria; Aigüestortes i Estany de Sant Maurici National Park, Catalonia, Spain; Stepantsminda, Mtskheta-Mtianeti, Georgia.

Eu1C EUROPEAN CONIFEROUS PEAT WOODLAND

IN A NUTSHELL: These are the boggy conifer woodlands and forests of temperate and subarctic Europe: wet underfoot and extremely difficult to walk through. **Global Habitat Affinities:** NEARCTIC BOREAL CONIFER FOREST. **Continental Habitat Affinities:** SPRUCE-FIR TAIGA; TEMPERATE PEATLAND. **Species Overlap:** SPRUCE-FIR TAIGA.

DESCRIPTION: Coniferous Peat Woodlands are azonal, being found over a variety of climatic zones from the subarctic cold, wet climate of far n. Norway (Köppen **Dfc**) to the continental wet cold-winter, warm-summer climate of s. Germany (**Dfb**) and even to alpine areas in Greece. These woodlands grow in wet conditions on acidic peat soils (histosols; see appendix), often at the edges of treeless mires (TEMPERATE PEATLAND), but also forming large tracts of forest in the boreal zone without open mires. Peat-forming mosses require a near permanently wet environment to grow. Precipitation is not high, but the cool temperatures and low evaporation mean that water builds up quickly. This is especially true in the boreal zone, where glacial deposits block drainage and create a myriad of complex landforms and an abundance of lakes and mires.

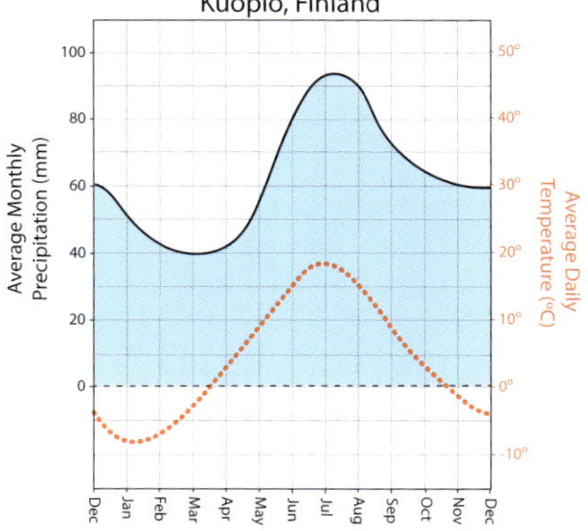

Coniferous Peat Woodlands are invariably soggy, wet places with scattered trees and an open canopy. © IAIN CAMPBELL, TROPICAL BIRDING

A Coniferous Peat Woodland dominated by Scots Pine with a diverse ground cover including bilberries, willows, and sphagnum mosses. © IAIN CAMPBELL, TROPICAL BIRDING

Coniferous Peat Woodlands also develop farther south, in the temperate zone, but here they generally form at the ecotone with TEMPERATE MIXED FOREST or where the natural hydrology of a raised bog (or other mires) has been disturbed. The draining of mires for peat extraction has allowed many of these Temperate Peatlands to become wooded and develop into Coniferous Peat Woodlands.

Although the ground plants of this habitat are similar to those of the BOGGY TUNDRA and open Temperate Peatland, the canopy cover means that the bird and other wildlife assemblages have far more in common with SPRUCE-FIR TAIGA, PINE TAIGA, and TEMPERATE RIPARIAN FOREST than they do with the tundra and other open habitats. Taiga forests typically have very uniform canopy heights, but the variety of microenvironments caused by the undulating and boggy nature of the ground surface in Coniferous Peat Woodlands means that these woodlands have very uneven canopies and forest structure. Trees are of many ages and growth forms, and even trees of the same species and age can have vastly different sizes.

Coniferous Peat Woodlands often have an open canopy but can also be closed-canopy forests. Scots Pine (*Pinus sylvestris*) or Norway Spruce (*Picea abies*) will often form a monospecific canopy when the bog water accumulates through precipitation (ombrotrophically) but rarely form uniform stands. Coniferous Peat Woodlands fed by groundwater (minerotrophically) are richer in minerals and nutrients. The tree assemblage has a greater mixture of species, but Norway Spruce, Downy Birch (*Betula pubescens*), and Alder Buckthorn (*Frangula alnus*) are invariably the most abundant in the wettest areas. By contrast, Norway Spruce and Dwarf Mountain Pine (*Pinus mugo*) are more common in the slightly drier areas.

The understorey plant assemblage varies substantially between pine-dominated and spruce-dominated peatlands. Nevertheless, the low shrub community is similar to that of TEMPERATE PEATLAND, containing Bog Bilberry (*Vaccinium uliginosum*), Bog Cranberry (*Vaccinium oxycoccos*), Marsh Labrador Tea (*Rhododendron tomentosum*), Leatherleaf (*Chamaedaphne calyculata*), Common Heather (*Calluna vulgaris*), Black Crowberry (*Empetrum nigrum*), Wild Rosemary (*Andromeda polifolia*), Twinflower (*Linnaea borealis*), and the fascinating, carnivorous Round-leaved Sundew (*Drosera rotundifolia*).

Much of the ground cover is dominated by peat-forming sphagnum mosses such as Girgensohn's Peatmoss (*Sphagnum girgensohnii*), Northern Peatmoss (*Sphagnum capillifolium*), Prairie Peatmoss (*Sphagnum palustre*), and Flat-top Bogmoss (*Sphagnum fallax*). Non-sphagnum bryophytes commonly encountered include the cosmopolitan Common Haircap Moss (*Polytrichum commune*), Bog Haircap Moss (*Polytrichum strictum*), and Ribbed Bogmoss (*Aulacomnium palustre*). Sedges include Tussock Cottongrass (*Eriophorum vaginatum*), and forbs include Arctic Starflower (*Lysimachia europaea*). The fungi include the Lichen Agaric (*Lichenomphalia* spp.).

Peat soils (histosols) have more than 30 cm (12 in.) of organic soil material in the upper 90 cm (36 in.). This has accumulated from plant remains in which excess moisture, anaerobic conditions, and acidity slowed down the decomposition process, leading to the buildup of organic matter. As with the tundras to the north, the rock type or parent material sitting below the peat deposits is unimportant to the development of peat soils, because they start developing with bryophytes (mosses and similar plants) that do not depend on roots for the uptake of nutrients from the inorganic parent material. The pioneer vascular plants that establish later, such as trees and shrubs, have root systems that use the nutrients from the breakdown of the mosses, algae, lichens, and fungi rather than nutrients from the soil below the peat.

WILDLIFE: This habitat can be seen as an ecotone between TEMPERATE PEATLAND and SPRUCE-FIR TAIGA or PINE TAIGA, and this is reflected in the bird assemblage. However, the one bird that epitomises this environment is the Eurasian Woodcock (although it is also found elsewhere). This chunky, attractive, but goofy-looking snipe spends the day hidden on the forest floor with its amazingly camouflaged plumage. During spring and early summer, males emerge at dusk to perform a unique aerial display, known as 'roding', in which they perform a linear patrolling flight just above the level of the canopy, emitting a series of nasal calls interspersed with short, high-pitched calls as they go. They also flash their white tail tips, which are brighter than any other known feather—perfect for attracting the attention of a mate in the dim light.

In the more open areas in and around boreal Coniferous Peat Woodlands, you may see migratory ground species such as the European Golden-Plover, Common Greenshank, Jack Snipe, Common Snipe, Wood Sandpiper, and Common Gull. Within the woodlands,

The cryptic Jack Snipe is usually very secretive but has an amazing aerial display. © PETE MORRIS

Above: **Willow Ptarmigan does not migrate but assumes white plumage in the winter to allow it to hide from predators in its snowy environment.** © MARKUS VARESVUO, AGAMI

Below: **Interestingly, male Bramblings acquire their attractive summer dress through abrasion rather than moult, as the pale-tipped winter feathers wear darker.** © MARKUS VARESVUO, AGAMI

there is a range of resident ground birds such as Willow Ptarmigan, Western Capercaillie, and Black Grouse, and resident canopy species include the Eurasian Three-toed Woodpecker, Siberian Jay, Grey-headed Chickadee (Siberian Tit), Willow Tit, and the widespread Great Tit. Many of the n. European owls occur here, including the Short-eared Owl and Boreal (Tengmalm's) Owl. Whooper Swan, Eurasian Wigeon, and Common Goldeneye take advantage of the habitat to breed, and Arctic Loon (Black-throated Loon or Diver) and Red-throated Loon (Diver) may be found on the larger water bodies.

In spring, the woods come alive with the calls of large numbers of thrushes, especially Fieldfare and Redwing. Other breeding migrants to this habitat include the rather drab Willow Warbler and Common Chiffchaff, along with more impressive species such as the European Pied Flycatcher, Common Redstart, Bohemian Waxwing, Common Chaffinch, Redpoll, and Brambling. The conifers are the primary haunts of the Pine Grosbeak, Parrot Crossbill, and Red Crossbill, though all these species are also found in the surrounding taiga habitats.

The birdlife in more continental Coniferous Peat Woodlands is much like that found in other coniferous forests of the region, as well as in the TEMPERATE RIPARIAN FOREST. Great Tit, Eurasian Blue Tit, and Marsh Tit are all common, and there is invariably a European Robin, Eurasian Wren, Willow Warbler, Common Chiffchaff, and Goldcrest singing somewhere. Great Spotted Woodpecker, Eurasian Treecreeper, Eurasian Bullfinch, Common Chaffinch, Eurasian Siskin, and Red Crossbill are ubiquitous. Black Grouse can still (rarely) be found in some continental Coniferous Peat Woodlands.

CONSERVATION: In the recent past, clear-felling of the forest and harvesting of peat for fuel and fertiliser destroyed vast areas of this habitat. Recent destruction in Finland has been from drainage for plantations of SPRUCE-FIR TAIGA and PINE TAIGA. In w. Europe, the active ditching and draining of the Coniferous Peat Woodlands appears to have been halted, and now the biggest threats are from eutrophication and algal blooms due to pollution. Overgrazing is resulting in a less diverse understorey, and clear-felling has resulted in a much more uniform canopy structure of secondary forests than that of the old-growth Coniferous Peat Woodlands.

DISTRIBUTION: Coniferous Peat Woodlands are widespread across Fennoscandia and Russia's boreal and subarctic regions and extend south to c. Germany and Poland. They occur as outliers in Austria and Greece, though these forests have an animal assemblage more in common with surrounding habitats than with the much colder north.

WHERE TO SEE: Øvre Pasvik National Park, Kirkenes, Norway; Kendlmühlfilzen, Bavaria, Germany.

Whooper Swan breeds on secluded ponds in Coniferous Peat Woodland. © SAVERIO GATTO, AGAMI

Eu1D EUROPEAN PINE TAIGA

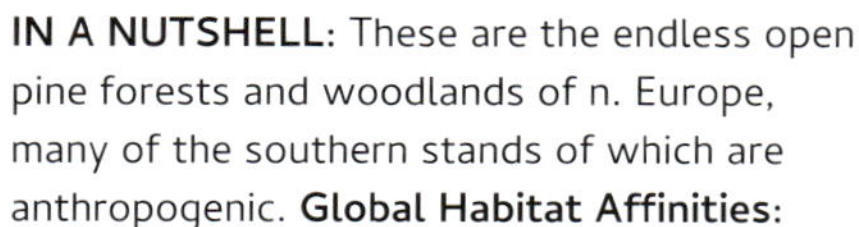

IN A NUTSHELL: These are the endless open pine forests and woodlands of n. Europe, many of the southern stands of which are anthropogenic. **Global Habitat Affinities:** NEARCTIC BOREAL CONIFER FOREST. **Continental Habitat Affinities:** SPRUCE-FIR TAIGA; MONTANE PINE FOREST. **Species Overlap:** SPRUCE-FIR TAIGA; CONIFEROUS PEAT WOODLAND.

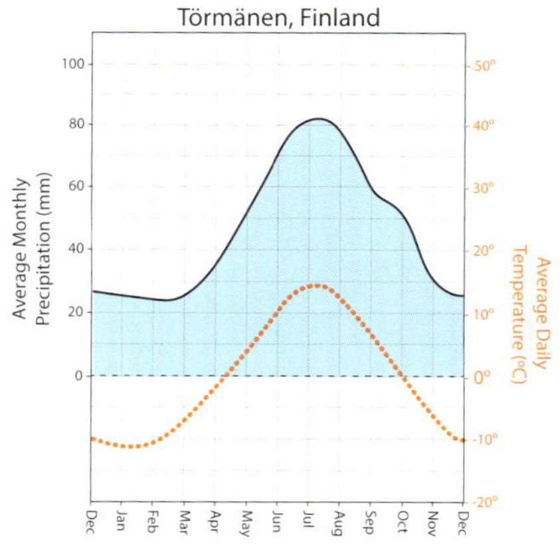

DESCRIPTION: There is a massive taiga belt from Scandinavia to the Urals. This is a mosaic of three kinds of coniferous forests: on the elevated areas, the Pine Taiga (Light Taiga) co-exists with SPRUCE-FIR TAIGA (Dark Taiga), while the very poorly drained areas have CONIFEROUS PEAT WOODLAND. The pine forests of the Pine Taiga are heavily managed, and in the south, few natural forests remain.

The Pine Taiga can handle extremes that Norway Spruce (*Picea abies*) cannot, so it is more common on extensive areas of glacial till (boulder deposits from glaciers); it can occur in waterlogged soils between boulders, such as histosols that are waterlogged for months and then completely dry at other times, and in drier podzols. It also dominates in areas within well-drained and sandy soils, usually podzols with a pronounced humus layer. Consequently, even though it may occur in a similar climate to the Spruce-Fir Taiga, it is locally much more arid. It appears that the more inert the underlying rock type, the greater the likelihood of pines (*Pinus* spp.) growing rather than spruces (*Picea* spp.) or firs (*Abies* spp.). These pine forests also show much more fire resilience than the nearby Spruce-Fir Taiga. Pine forests have many mature trees of varying ages (up to 700 years), in contrast to Spruce-Fir Taiga canopies, with trees of generally similar ages.

Pine Taiga can have a heavy canopy cover but is usually much more open than Spruce-Fir Taiga and can even occur as an open woodland habitat. The canopy is between 20 and 50 m (65–165 ft.) tall, though usually under 30 m (100 ft.). The dominant tree of this habitat is invariably Scots Pine (*Pinus sylvestris*) because of its overall hardiness and great shade tolerance. The other dominant European conifer, the Norway Spruce, is also scattered through the canopy, along with Silver

The Pine Taiga is extremely widespread in Europe's taiga belt. © IAIN CAMPBELL, TROPICAL BIRDING

Pine Taiga will often be open with very little vegetation between the low ground cover and the canopy. © IAIN CAMPBELL, TROPICAL BIRDING

It is always fun to explore the myriad microhabitats to be found in a rockier Pine Taiga.
© IAIN CAMPBELL, TROPICAL BIRDING

Birch (*Betula pendula*), European Aspen (*Populus tremula*), and Downy Birch (*Betula pubescens*) in locally humid areas. European Mountain Ash (*Sorbus aucuparia*) and Grey Alder (*Alnus incana*) are less common but still regular species in the mix.

The forest floor is blanketed in needles, decomposing wood, mosses, and lichens. The lack of thick undergrowth means that you can easily wander through the drier parts of this forest without a trail. Larger shrubs include Common Juniper (*Juniperus communis*), Goat Willow (*Salix caprea*), Grey Willow (*S. cinerea*), and Tea-leaved Willow (*S. phylicifolia*). Small shrubs and dwarf shrubs include Black Crowberry (*Empetrum nigrum*), Common Bilberry (*Vaccinium myrtillus*), and Lingonberry (*V. vitis-idaea*).

Ground cover is nearly complete. In the south, grasses like Sheep's Fescue (*Festuca ovina*) and herbs like Fireweed (*Chamaenerion angustifolium*), May Lily (*Maianthemum bifolium*), and European Lily of the Valley (*Convallaria majalis*) are common. By contrast, the ground cover in northern regions is mostly lichens and mosses, such as Waxyleaf Moss (*Dicranum polysetum*), Red-stemmed Feather Moss (*Pleurozium schreberi*), and Stairstep Moss (*Hylocomium splendens*).

There are very similar taiga forests in e. Asia, but those tend to have a much higher species diversity than taiga forests in Europe. This is because European coniferous forests were likely greatly reduced and stressed during the last glacial maximum (peaking about 20,000 YA) and Younger Dryas mini glaciation (about 12,000 YA). This would have eliminated many species from the European taiga assemblages, while others expanded (or returned) to Europe from the e. Asian refugia. Nowadays, the European Pine Taiga is separated from sister forests in e. Asia by a vast expanse of SIBERIAN LARCH TAIGA.

WILDLIFE: There are some special birds to find in these Pine Taiga, including Grey-headed Chickadee (Siberian Tit), Siberian Jay, Black Woodpecker, Eurasian Three-toed Woodpecker, and grouse such as the Black Grouse and Western Capercaillie. Northern Hawk Owl is found here but is usually reclusive, even when feeding during the summer daylight hours. Other taiga residents include Pine Grosbeak, Bohemian Waxwing, Parrot Crossbill (a Scots Pine specialist), Redpoll, Great Tit, and Willow Tit. Migratory birds here include Fieldfare and Redwing, which both migrate from temperate and oceanic Europe to Pine Taiga, as well as more long-distance migrants such as Brambling, Willow Warbler, and European Pied Flycatcher. Common Sandpipers nest well into the forest on ground between boulders, whereas Wood Sandpiper and Spotted Redshank use the more open bog areas.

The breeding migrant raptor species, such as Eurasian Kestrel, Merlin, Eurasian Hobby, Hen Harrier, and Eurasian Goshawk, generally occur throughout the taiga region.

Herbivorous mammals of this habitat include European Elk (Moose), Western Roe Deer, Eurasian Red Squirrel, and Mountain Hare. Carnivores include the Wolverine, Red Fox, Grey Wolf, and Brown Bear.

Siberian Jays are restricted to the taiga forests of far n. Europe. © EDUARD SANGSTER, AGAMI

The amazing Western Capercaillie gathers in leks in spring, when the males can become quite fearless. © MARKUS VARESVUO, AGAMI

Parrot Crossbills are Scots Pine specialists, using their immensely powerful bills to tackle the hard cones. © MARKUS VARESVUO, AGAMI

CONSERVATION: With global warming, this habitat is being encroached from the south and should be moving north. Much of these Pine Taiga forests have been unattractive for traditional farming, but with warming temperatures much of the region where this taiga grows will be experiencing climates more similar to those of c. Europe today. Overgrazing by livestock and deer is a problem in some areas, reducing non-conifers and canopy saplings in the understorey. Removal of dead trees and logs puts intense pressure on hole nesters, such as woodpeckers, and decreases food for detritivores and, therefore, species higher in the food chain, such as insectivores. The forests are becoming more uniform in structure, with similarly aged trees and little variety of canopy species. Anthropogenic SPRUCE-FIR TAIGA is also replacing Pine Taiga due to reduced fire regimes and deliberate planting.

DISTRIBUTION: Pine Taiga habitat occurs in a mélange with SPRUCE-FIR TAIGA and BOGGY TUNDRA from e. Norway, Sweden (north of Stockholm), and c. Poland eastwards to the Ural Mountains. It is bordered to the south by TEMPERATE MIXED FOREST through much of continental Europe and by FOREST STEPPE in c. Russia. In the north, it blends into TUNDRA TAIGA or changes directly into ROCKY TUNDRA, SHRUBBY TUNDRA, or BOGGY TUNDRA.

WHERE TO SEE: Oulu and Kuusamo regions of Finland; south of Murmansk, Russia.

Grey Wolves still roam across the region, though under constant human pressure. © JARI PELTOMÄKI, AGAMI

Eu1E EUROPEAN SPRUCE-FIR TAIGA

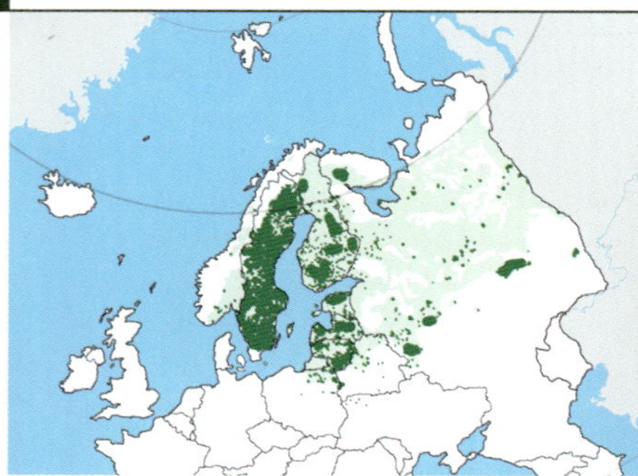

IN A NUTSHELL: These are the endless forests of conifers that people imagine when they think of far n. Europe. **Global Habitat Affinities:** NEARCTIC BOREAL CONIFER FOREST. **Continental Habitat Affinities:** MONTANE SPRUCE-FIR FOREST; PINE TAIGA. **Species Overlap:** PINE TAIGA; CONIFEROUS PEAT WOODLAND.

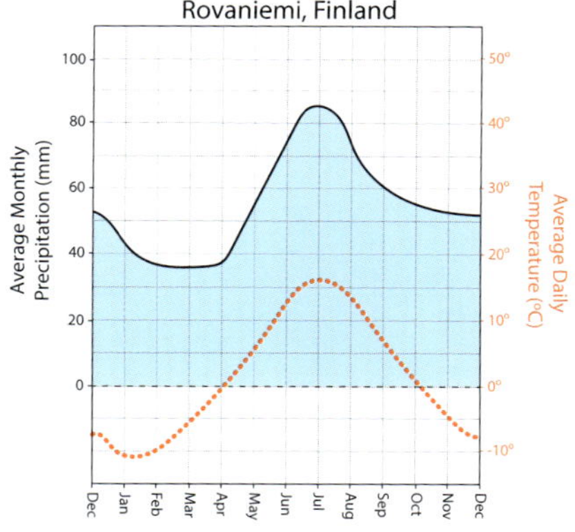

DESCRIPTION: There is a massive belt of coniferous taiga (also called boreal forest) from Norway to the Urals, and indeed all the way to the coast of Kamchatka and n. Japan. When you visit the Spruce-Fir Taiga, it feels very monotonous, certainly much more so than grasslands or deserts, and seems endless. The canopy is thick and 15–20 m (45–60 ft.) high in the north but somewhat taller farther south (30 m/100 ft.), with some trees reaching 50 m (165 ft.) tall.

Most of this forest is rather uniform, with few conifer species in the canopy and few broadleaf tree species. Norway Spruce (*Picea abies*) dominates this habitat in the far north, where it often has an understorey of deciduous species, like European Mountain Ash (*Sorbus aucuparia*), European Aspen (*Populus tremula*), Silver Birch (*Betula pendula*), and Downy Birch (*Betula pubescens*). These species are replaced in the boggiest areas by deciduous broadleaf trees such as Goat Willow (*Salix caprea*), on the lithosols of the rockiest zones by Scots Pine (*Pinus sylvestris*), and close to the tree line by alders such as Grey Alder (*Alnus incana*). Because this forest type covers such a large latitudinal range, from 70°N in Norway to 52°N in Poland, there is a transition in the secondary species that accompany the Norway Spruce, and in the south of its range, the association becomes more biodiverse, with Wych Elm (*Ulmus glabra*), Common Alder (*Alnus glutinosa*), Norway Maple (*Acer platanoides*), Small-leaved Lime (*Tilia cordata*), and English Oak (*Quercus robur*) all occurring as canopy trees.

You can easily walk through the drier parts of this forest without a trail, as there are few shrubs to impede you. The shrubs that dominate the drier areas may form small groves but are rarely extensive and tend to be in thickets at the forest edge. Little light enters the subcanopy of this forest, and only shade-tolerant species thrive here. These include Bird Cherry (*Prunus padus*), Red Raspberry (*Rubus idaeus*), and very widespread species such as Common Juniper (*Juniperus communis*) and Alder Buckthorn (*Frangula alnus*).

The forest floor is covered in a litter of conifer needles, decaying trunks, mosses, and lichens. Generally, mosses dominate the ground cover in the wetter areas (where this habitat transitions into CONIFEROUS PEAT WOODLAND). In the south and in better-drained areas, vascular plants become much more common, and the forest floor can be herb-rich with Common Cow-Wheat (*Melampyrum pratense*), Small Cow-Wheat (*Melampyrum sylvaticum*), many wood sorrels (*Oxalis* spp.), wood ferns (*Dryopteris* spp.), Fireweed (*Chamaenerion angustifolium*), and Arctic Starflower (*Lysimachia europaea*).

Even though precipitation is not high (600 mm/20 in.), the low temperatures in this region mean that precipitation exceeds evaporation. The abundant water causes podzols with a prominent humus layer to form. The climate is subarctic (Köppen **Dfc**) in the north and warm-summer humid continental (**Dfb**) in the south. In regions with similar rainfall but higher temperatures, such precipitation would result in chernozem soils (see appendix), with the likely climax vegetation of TEMPERATE OAK FOREST forming on those soils.

On a regional scale, Spruce-Fir Taiga forests form a mosaic with PINE TAIGA and CONIFEROUS PEAT WOODLAND, where the spruce forests form over the optimal moist but not waterlogged areas with few fires. In areas where the soil becomes more waterlogged, is much drier (such as over glacial

Spruce-Fir Taiga from above. © IAIN CAMPBELL, TROPICAL BIRDING

A gorgeous Spruce-Fir Taiga in autumn, with scattered birches and larches adding lovely rusts and yellows. The hilltop tundras are already brown. © ROB RIEMER, AGAMI

till), or is extremely sandy, the habitat merges into Pine Taiga. The Spruce-Fir Taiga forests tend to have a canopy consisting of uniform, similarly aged trees (up to 400 years) and copious younger trees, because their harmonised circuitry causes trees in close proximity to have a synchronised life cycle. At their elevational limits, these forests can have patches dominated by birch.

This forest exists in both natural and anthropogenic forms. It is a natural climax community formed by conifers replacing pioneer broadleaf trees more typical of the Temperate Oak Forest of the southern part of its range. However, there are also extensive areas where TEMPERATE MIXED FOREST occurs as a climax community in the same broad climatic belt and on similar soils, suggesting that the two habitats can exist in alternate stable states. Over much of the region, these forests are now managed for forestry, and almost none of the regenerated habitat is natural, so people will likely determine any future canopy cover.

The Grey-headed Chickadee (Siberian Tit) is a true northern speciality. © MARKUS VARESVUO, AGAMI

WILDLIFE: The Grey-headed Chickadee (Siberian Tit), Siberian Jay, and Red-flanked Bluetail are the stars of the Spruce-Fir Taiga, but the bird assemblage also contains many woodpeckers, such as the Eurasian Three-toed, Black, and Great Spotted Woodpeckers. Most resident species found in the Spruce-Fir Taiga, such as Western Capercaillie, Pine Grosbeak, Eurasian Treecreeper, Bohemian Waxwing, and Red Crossbill, are found in taiga forests across the top of Eurasia. Passerine migrant breeders that are typical of these forests include Common Chiffchaff, European Robin, Song Thrush, Mistle Thrush, and Eurasian Siskin. Northern Hawk Owl is the most common of the owls here.

A wide range of mammals use these forests, with some of the most remarkable being the Siberian Flying Squirrel, Wolverine, Grey Wolf, European Elk (Moose), and Brown Bear.

CONSERVATION: With rising global temperatures, much of this region will be open to increased agriculture. Clear-felling for grazing land is a serious threat despite the acidic podzol soils severely restricting the land's usefulness to much agriculture. Forestry practices in the remaining stands have a strong influence on the biodiversity of Spruce-Fir Taiga. The removal of dead trees and wood denies breeding habitat for a wide range of invertebrates as well as many hole-nesting birds and mammals. The clearing of undergrowth reduces the structural diversity in the forest and removes food sources for many insectivores and omnivores. The more open forests are then

The smart Red-flanked Bluetail has steadily expanded its range westwards into Europe's Spruce-Fir Taiga in recent decades. © CHRIS VAN RIJSWIJK, AGAMI

more prone to overgrazing, making the forest even more depauperate. The resulting same-aged forests with very uniform forest structures will greatly reduce biodiversity, even though the swaths of forest may look great in satellite images and be considered a conservation success.

DISTRIBUTION: This is the predominant habitat from Sweden north of Stockholm and the Baltic countries east to the Ural Mountains. It is bordered to the south by TEMPERATE MIXED FOREST and TEMPERATE OAK FOREST in n. Poland and c. Europe, and by FOREST STEPPE in Ukraine. In the north, it blends into TUNDRA TAIGA or changes directly into SHRUBBY or BOGGY TUNDRA.

WHERE TO SEE: Oulu and Kuusamo regions of Finland.

The Siberian Flying Squirrel is a habitat specialist of the Spruce-Fir Taiga. Largely nocturnal, it spends its days hidden away in tree cavities. © RALPH MARTIN, AGAMI

Eu1F EUROPEAN MONTANE PINE FOREST

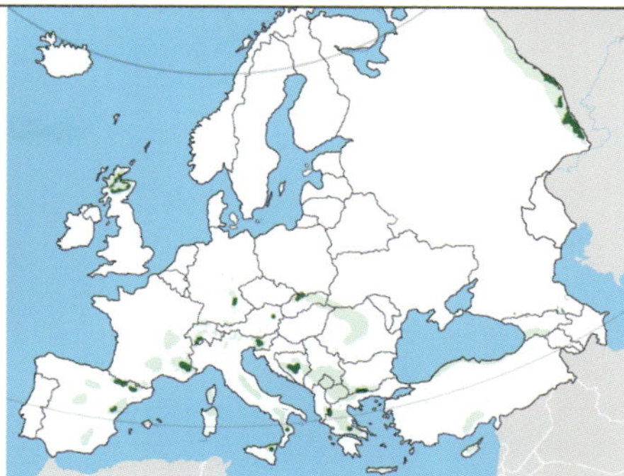

IN A NUTSHELL: Open pine forests in the mountains of most of Europe, often with a strong human influence through clear-cut harvesting and planting. **Global Habitat Affinities:** NEARCTIC HIGH-ELEVATION PINE WOODLAND; HIMALAYAN PINE FOREST. **Continental Habitat Affinities:** MEDITERRANEAN PINE FOREST; MONTANE SPRUCE-FIR FOREST. **Species Overlap:** MONTANE SPRUCE-FIR FOREST; MEDITERRANEAN PINE FOREST.

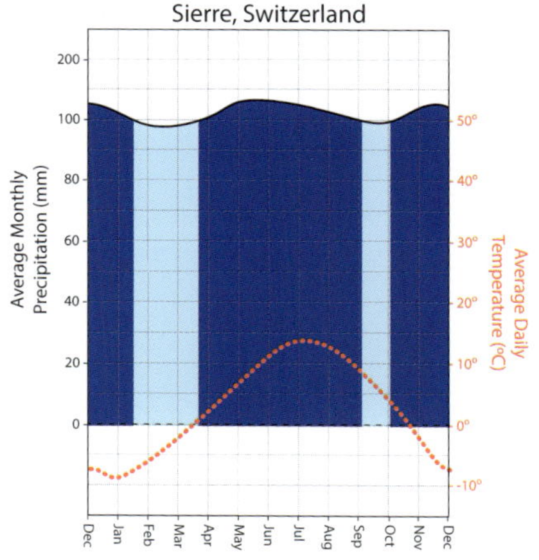

DESCRIPTION: Natural pine forests can be found in most of Europe's mountainous regions (Köppen **Dfb**, **Dfc**), where Scots Pine (*Pinus sylvestris*) or Black Pine (*P. nigra*) dominate an evenly aged canopy. These pines are extremely adaptable and tolerant but grow best with a lot of sun, tending not to regenerate in forest environments. In natural systems, they need fire or treefall to open light gaps for new individuals to move up to the canopy. Nevertheless, both of these pines are valuable timber species, and their forests are often heavily managed with regular clear-cut harvesting and replanting.

Montane Pine Forests tend to be found interwoven between other forest types, particularly MONTANE SPRUCE-FIR FOREST and MONTANE MIXED FOREST. Typically, Norway Spruce (*Picea abies*), European Beech (*Fagus sylvatica*), firs (*Abies* spp.), and European Larch (*Larix decidua*) outcompete Scots and Black Pines, except in extreme and edge conditions. Steep, stony slopes with temperature extremes, the soggy edges of peatlands, as well as underdeveloped, sandy, low-fertility, or dry calcareous soils can all provide conditions harsh enough to allow the adaptable pines to dominate. Deep taproots—even surpassing 6 m (20 ft.) long—help the pines maintain stability on steep, unstable slopes and can also help them access alternative water sources where relatively high heat keeps the surface desiccated. Montane Pine Forests are somewhat azonal, occurring over wide elevational ranges in a variety of climates, though they tend to form best in warm-summer humid continental climates (Köppen **Dfb**) with no dry season and cool winters.

Left: **A typical Montane Pine Forest on a dry south-facing slope. The rocks in the background hold Rock Bunting.** © DALE FORBES

Below left: **Many stunning flowers, such as this Lady's-Slipper (*Cypripedium calceolus*), bring colour to the forests in spring.** © DALE FORBES

Tall, bare trunks ending in a flat or ball-shaped crown mean the forests can often appear quite open. The canopy will typically be formed of a single species of pine along with scattered European Larch, Norway Spruce, European Beech, Sycamore Maple (*Acer pseudoplatanus*), Whitebeam (*Aria edulis*), or other larger trees. These complementary species are typically related to the habitats surrounding the Montane Pine Forest, and intergrades between this and other habitats are common. Grasses (e.g., *Calamagrostis varia*) are abundant, while the shrub layer varies considerably from site to site. Moister, siliceous sites near peatlands and at higher elevations often have a beautiful covering of Common Heather (*Calluna vulgaris*), Common Bilberry (*Vaccinium myrtillus*), Bog Bilberry (*Vaccinium uliginosum*), Bearberry (*Arctostaphylos uva-ursi*), and Common Juniper (*Juniperus communis*). The beautiful mauve flowers of Spring Heath (*Erica carnea*) can carpet Montane Pine Forests on drier, steeper, stonier slopes. Additional ground-cover species in these areas can include Alpine Thrift (*Armeria alpina*), Sheep's Fescue (*Festuca ovina*), various spleenworts (*Asplenium* spp.), and Burnet-Saxifrage (*Pimpinella saxifraga*).

WILDLIFE: The Montane Pine Forests of warm, stony, calcareous, dry, south-facing slopes in the Alps make for a distinct break from the ubiquitous MONTANE SPRUCE-FIR FORESTS that

Warm, sunny Montane Pine Forest can have quite a thick grass layer, perfect for grazing Northern Chamois. © DALE FORBES

surround them—they look, feel, smell, and sound unique. Western Bonelli's Warbler can be truly abundant, whereas it is much thinner on the ground in the spruce-fir forests. Tree Pipit tends to be more common here than in the surrounding habitats. Grey-headed and Eurasian Green Woodpeckers favour these pine forests (whereas Eurasian Three-toed Woodpecker tends to stick to the spruce and larch forests). Eurasian Nightjar is unusual in the Alps, but where it occurs, it favours warm, open Montane Pine Forests. Rock Bunting is

Western Bonelli's Warbler, characterised by the bright lime-green fringes to its wing and tail feathers, is regionally most common in (or restricted to) Montane Pine Forest. © DANIELE OCCHIATO, AGAMI

Above: **Grey-headed Woodpecker can be locally common in this habitat.** © TOMI MUUKKONEN, AGAMI

Left: **Scottish Crossbill is endemic to Scotland's Caledonian pine forests. Constantly under scrutiny by taxonomists, its days as a full species may be numbered!** © DANNY GREEN, AGAMI

best found in steep, open pine woodlands with many small cliffs and rock faces. The classic European forest birds are also common: Great Tit, Eurasian Blue Tit, Crested Tit, Common Chiffchaff, Common Chaffinch, Eurasian Bullfinch, European Greenfinch, Great Spotted Woodpecker, European Robin, Eurasian Wren, Eurasian Nuthatch, Eurasian Blackbird, Song Thrush, Common Buzzard, and Tawny Owl.

The Scottish Crossbill is endemic to Scotland's **Caledonian Forest**, a subtype of Montane Pine Forest. In addition, Britain's only populations of Parrot Crossbill, Western Capercaillie, and Crested Tit are also restricted to this Montane Pine Forest subtype.

Old stands of Corsican Pine (*Pinus nigra* ssp. *laricio*) are the primary habitat of the Corsican Nuthatch on the namesake island. The Corsican

Rock Bunting can be found in open Montane Pine Forests with rocky slopes. © DANIELE OCCHIATO, AGAMI

Corsican Nuthatch occurs only in montane forest dominated by Corsican Pine and is restricted to Corsica. © TOMÁŠ GRIM, AGAMI

Finch is strongly associated with these forests, especially when the forests are a little sparser and more open.

Northern Chamois can be common in Montane Pine Forests, most notably in winter, when they retreat to these warmer, grassy, steep slopes. Western Roe Deer, Eurasian Red Squirrel, Red Fox, and Pine Marten can be harder to find but are invariably present. The Calabrian Black Squirrel is a highly localised species of the Montane Pine Forests in Italy's s. Apennines, where it is heavily dependent on the Black Pine.

A whole host of moths use the pines, including the Pine Processionary Moth (*Thaumetopoea pityocampa*), Pine Arches Moth (*Panthea coenobita*), Pine-tree Lappet (*Dendrolimus pini*), Bordered White (*Bupalus piniaria*), Pine Hawkmoth (*Sphinx pinastri*), and Pine Beauty (*Panolis flammea*).

CONSERVATION: This habitat can be found along a complete spectrum from wild and untouched to heavily managed plantations, with myriad variants between these extremes. Human management of the ecosystem naturally has an enormous effect on the structure of the forests and the wildlife that lives there. Typically, the more heavily managed and neat the forest is, the less space there is for wildlife.

DISTRIBUTION: Montane Pine Forest is found throughout the Alps but is most extensive in France and Italy. Smaller areas can also be found in Austria, France's Massif Central, Italy's s. Apennines, and the w. and far s. Carpathians. Large regions of Montane Pine Forest can also be found in the Balkans, particularly in the Rhodope and Pindus Mountains, but also in the Dinaric Alps and Balkan Mountains. Almost all of Scotland's majestic Caledonian Forest has been lost, and browsing pressure from sheep and deer severely restricts regrowth and replacement.

WHERE TO SEE: Abernethy National Nature Reserve, Scotland, UK; Pfyn-Finges Nature Park, Valais, Switzerland; Pindus National Park, Greece.

Northern Chamois graze in open areas within the pine forests, particularly in heavy winters, when the relative warmth of these slopes means there are more snow-free patches and food is easier to access. © DALE FORBES

Eu1G MEDITERRANEAN PINE FOREST

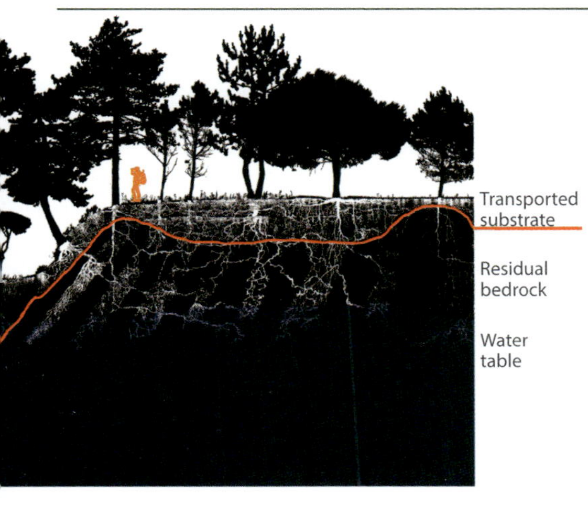

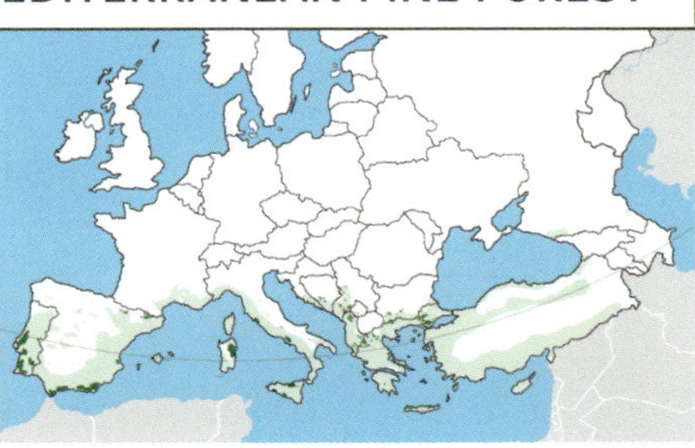

IN A NUTSHELL: Open, generally low conifer woodlands dominated by distinctive umbrella-shaped pine trees with a grassy understorey. **Global Habitat Affinities:** MAGHREB PINE FOREST; NEARCTIC EASTERN PINE SAVANNA; NEARCTIC PONDEROSA PINE FOREST; HIMALAYAN PINE FOREST. **Continental Habitat Affinities:** MEDITERRANEAN JUNIPER AND CYPRESS FOREST; MAQUIS; MEDITERRANEAN OAK FOREST. **Species Overlap:** MEDITERRANEAN JUNIPER AND CYPRESS FOREST; MEDITERRANEAN OAK FOREST.

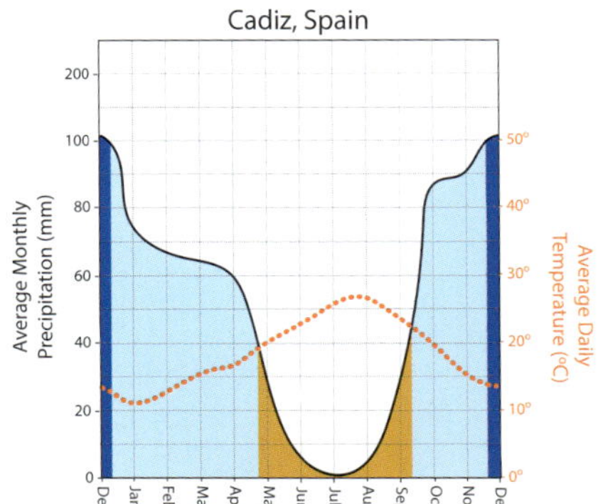

DESCRIPTION: This forest features the most intense soundscape in Europe, with the incessant, ear-splitting churr of Ash Cicadas (*Cicada orni*) during the day. Common Wood-Pigeons try to compete with them at dawn, while Eurasian Scops-Owls and Eurasian Nightjars take over at night.

Mediterranean Pine Forest is the dominant drought-tolerant (xerophytic) forest type found throughout the Mediterranean climate region (Köppen **Csa**, **Csb**) from the Iberian Peninsula to the Middle East. Winters are mild and moist,

These forests are invariably filled with the high-pitched squeal of Ash Cicadas in summer—this is likely Europe's loudest habitat. © DALE FORBES

Patches of Mastic Tree and other small trees have developed a dense understorey in this Mediterranean Pine Forest. © DALE FORBES

Opposite above: **An open canopy and shrubby understorey are characteristic of this habitat. In the background, you can see Maquis on the hotter slopes and Mediterranean Oak Forest developing in the moister, relatively more protected areas.** © DALE FORBES

Opposite below: **A Mediterranean Pine Forest in midsummer, with the grass burnt brown from lack of water and the intense sun.** © DALE FORBES

snow is rare, and frosts are limited. To survive the brutally hot, dry summers, plants need to be highly resistant to drought, desiccating winds, and fire.

Mediterranean Pine Forests have been extensively planted along many Mediterranean coasts, where they may be either stable climax communities or human-maintained forests (plagioclimax communities). The dominant Aleppo (*Pinus halepensis*), Maritime (*P. pinaster*), and Turkish Pines (*P. brutia*) are all of medium height, at about 15–25 m (50–80 ft.), and have an open growth form, red-stained trunk, and long needles. At first glance, Maritime Pine has a similar shape (but not bark) to North America's Ponderosa Pine (*Pinus ponderosa*). The Maritime Pine has a messy, irregular shape, often very lopsided, with some large branches growing low on the trunk, and is much less distinctive than the Aleppo Pine and Turkish Pine. The somewhat shorter Stone Pine (*Pinus pinea*) reaches only about 12 m (40 ft.) tall and has a distinctive umbrella-shaped growth form when young. It is famous for its delicious pignoli (pine nuts), enjoyed in Mediterranean cuisine for millennia. Stone Pine dominates on the sandiest of soils.

In the w. Mediterranean, Maritime and Aleppo Pines will often have an understorey of broadleaf species including oaks, such as Kermes Oak (*Quercus coccifera*) and Holm Oak (*Q. ilex*), as well as Mastic Tree (*Pistacia lentiscus*) and Green Olive Tree (*Phillyrea latifolia*). In the e. Mediterranean,

Turkish Pine forests become more common, although Aleppo Pines are still in the mix and can be dominant in successional stages of forest development. The Turkish Pine forests form one of the dominant forest types from Türkiye to the Caucasus Mountains. These have a less oak-dominated co-canopy, though Golden Oak (*Quercus alnifolia*) does occur alongside Greek Strawberry Tree (*Arbutus andrachne*), Wild Olive (*Olea europaea*), and Syrian Maple (*Acer obtusifolium*) with shrubs such as Jerusalem Thorn (*Paliurus spina-christi*), Tree Heath (*Erica arborea*), and Hairy Thorny Broom (*Calicotome villosa*). In coastal dune systems in most of the area, Maritime and Stone Pines form monospecific groves about 8 m (25 ft.) tall on the first swales behind the beach, with an understorey dominated by junipers that vary with the region, such as Mediterranean Juniper (*Juniperus turbinata*), Portuguese Prickly Juniper (*J. navicularis*), Large-fruited Juniper (*J. macrocarpa*), and Phoenician Juniper (*J. phoenicea*). Mauritanian Grass (*Ampelodesmos mauritanicus*), Rosemary (*Salvia rosmarinus*), Rough Bindweed (*Smilax aspera*), and Mastic Tree can also be common.

Regardless of the region, most Mediterranean Pine Forests have been so extensively modified by grazing, logging, and firewood gathering that few, if any, pristine examples remain. Although these forests can have an understorey, ungrazed examples are so rare that almost all the existing forests have an open understorey and are easy to walk through. During the moist winter, the ground is covered with grasses, forbs, and ferns. In summer, most plants die off, and there are extensive areas of bare, sandy ground. With the exception of the junipers mentioned earlier, most of the shrub-layer plants are shared with MEDITERRANEAN OAK FOREST and the degraded heathlands of the MAQUIS.

Although there is leaf litter, the soil has much less humus than that in wetter environments, and it is not uncommon to see open sandy areas on the forest floor. The forests even sound drier than many other forests, as each step results in the sound of pine needles crackling underfoot, and the drying and cracking of pinecones can sound like corn popping. Mediterranean Pine Forests develop on a wide range of soils in drier and hotter areas but are particularly prevalent on very poorly developed calcareous or siliceous sandy soils such as leptosols (see appendix). These soils are very well drained and create a harsh growing environment, exacerbating the intensity of the summer dry period so that temperate deciduous trees such as beeches (*Fagus* spp.), ashes (*Fraxinus* spp.), and elms (*Ulmus* spp.) struggle. On more nutrient-rich soils in higher-rainfall and higher-elevation areas, pines are restricted to less productive calcareous soils and are outcompeted by firs (*Abies* spp.) and spruces (*Picea* spp.). Where the underlying geology changes rapidly between nutrient-deficient limestones or sandstones and nutrient-rich volcanic rocks, the resulting change in soil type can be seen clearly as an abrupt switch from pine forest to Mediterranean Oak Forest.

Mediterranean Pine Forests are much more fire resilient than the Mediterranean Oak Forests in the region, meaning they have an additional advantage in areas where fires have become more intense or frequent. When fires become too frequent, Stone Pine replaces Aleppo Pine, due to its ability to regenerate faster than other species.

WILDLIFE: Overall, there are few obligate species in this habitat, and most birds are generalists and weak indicators, but Krüper's Nuthatch is found only in these forests and can be regarded as a true obligate. Several resident birds are common throughout Mediterranean Pine Forests, such as Great Spotted Woodpecker, Short-toed Treecreeper, Eurasian Jay, European Robin, Eurasian Blackbird, Mistle Thrush, Coal and Great Tits, Eurasian Nuthatch, European Greenfinch, and the ubiquitous Common Chaffinch. Many species in this habitat are summer-breeding migrants, such as Common Nightingale, Spotted Flycatcher, and both Western and Eastern Bonelli's Warblers. Blue and Common Rock-Thrushes breed in rocky areas. Short-toed Snake-Eagle and Golden, Booted, and Bonelli's Eagles, as well as Eurasian Sparrowhawk and Eurasian Goshawk, all use this habitat.

Right: **The majestic Booted Eagle comes in a pale morph (as depicted) and a less common dark morph. They can frequently be seen soaring over Mediterranean Pine Forests, especially on sunny mornings.** © MARC GUYT, AGAMI

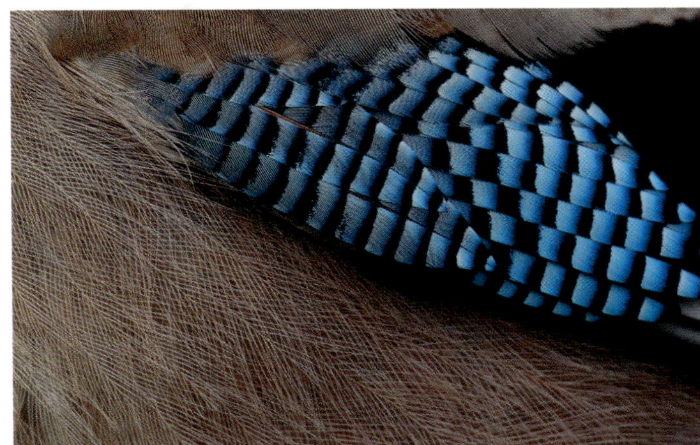

Below right: **The charismatic Eurasian Jay is a widespread species that occurs in a number of habitats but can be particularly abundant in Mediterranean Pine Forests. The incredible vivid blue area on the bend of the wing is a truly spectacular plumage feature when seen up close!** © MARKUS VARESVUO, AGAMI

Below: **The stunning Krüper's Nuthatch is the top prize for birders in the pine forests of the e. Mediterranean, particularly in Türkiye.** © DANIELE OCCHIATO, AGAMI

The cute little Cyprus Scops-Owl (pictured) is restricted to Cyprus, where it is frequently found in coniferous forests, calling monotonously through the night. Eurasian Scops-Owl is common in Mediterranean Pine Forests in other regions. © PETE MORRIS

Eurasian Scops-Owl is typically omnipresent, while the similar Cyprus Scops-Owl is found in this habitat on its namesake island. Red-necked and Eurasian Nightjars can be abundant in more open pine woodlands with few shrubs and abundant grasses. Common aerial feeders over Mediterranean Pine Forests include Common, Alpine, and Pallid Swifts as well as Western House-Martin, Barn Swallow, and Red-rumped Swallow. Both Hawfinch and Red Crossbill prefer Aleppo Pine.

Mammals can be sparse and tend to be small. Northern Small-spotted (Common) Genet, Red Fox, Stone Marten, European Badger, Eurasian Wild Boar, Eurasian Red Squirrel, and Granada Hare or Brown Hare are all generalists and widespread in Mediterranean Pine Forests. Four hedgehog species use these forests, depending on the region (Common, North African, Northern White-breasted, and Southern White-breasted Hedgehogs).

The butterflies can be interesting, particularly in more open Mediterranean Pine Forests. Esper's Marbled White (*Melanargia russiae*) and Tree Grayling (*Hipparchia statilinus*) are more widespread geographically, while Eastern Rock, Delattin's, Freyer's, and White-banded Graylings (*Hipparchia syriaca*, *H. volgensis*, *H. fatua*, and *Pseudochazara anthelea*) are restricted to e. Europe. Corsican Grayling (*Hipparchia neomiris*) is restricted to Corsica, Sardinia, and the Tuscan Archipelago.

CONSERVATION: Most of the original pine forests have been destroyed, and most remaining Mediterranean Pine Forests are managed to some degree for cones or timber. Overgrazing results in similarly aged uniform canopy stands with little undergrowth. While Mediterranean Pine Forests are somewhat resistant to fire, uncontrolled and increasingly frequent fires are a threat.

DISTRIBUTION: Mediterranean Pine Forest ranges from the Iberian Peninsula, where there are extensive forests in the east of Spain, around the northern shores of the Mediterranean Sea, where extensive forests occur from se. Greece to Türkiye. The habitat is found throughout the Mediterranean islands, including in large tracts in s. Cyprus, and in the Caucasus Mountains at lower elevations than MONTANE SPRUCE-FIR FOREST.

WHERE TO SEE: Tarifa, Andalusia, Spain; Maremma Regional Park, Tuscany, Italy; Achladeri Forest, Lesvos, Greece; Marmaris National Park, Muğla, Türkiye.

The cryptic Red-necked Nightjar is a summer migrant to North Africa and the Iberian Peninsula, where it can be found in a variety of habitats, including open coniferous woodland. © EDUARD SANGSTER, AGAMI

The Northern Small-spotted (Common) Genet was brought to Iberia almost 1500 YA, and although its nocturnal ways mean that it is rarely seen, it is found through much of Iberia and s. France. © OSCAR-DÍEZ, AGAMI

Eu1H MEDITERRANEAN JUNIPER AND CYPRESS FOREST

IN A NUTSHELL: The cypress and juniper forests of the Mediterranean and Caucasus. **Global Habitat Affinities:** NEARCTIC PINYON-JUNIPER WOODLAND; NEARCTIC HIGH-ELEVATION PINE WOODLAND; MIDDLE EASTERN JUNIPER WOODLAND. **Continental Habitat Affinities:** MONTANE SPRUCE-FIR FOREST; MEDITERRANEAN PINE FOREST. **Species Overlap:** MONTANE SPRUCE-FIR FOREST.

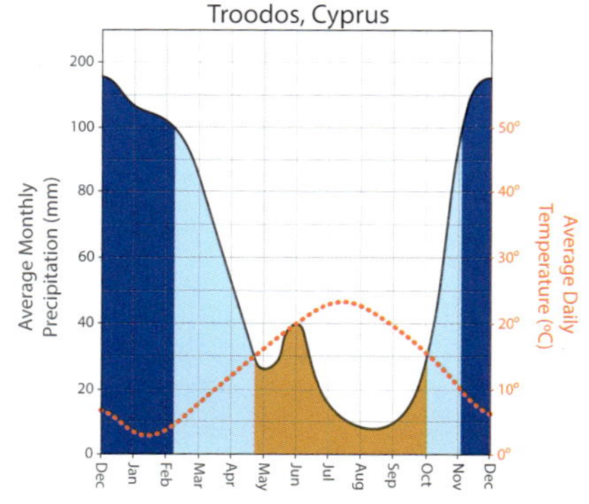

DESCRIPTION: The Mediterranean Juniper and Cypress Forest lies between the MONTANE SPRUCE-FIR FOREST and the MEDITERRANEAN PINE FOREST in that it shares a mix of species with both these other conifer forests, yet it experiences a harsher environment: in addition to the cold winters Montane Spruce-Fir Forest contends with, this forest must also tolerate very dry conditions for much of the year. The forests usually grow where there is a Mediterranean climate (Köppen **Csa**), with hot, dry summers and cool, wet winters. The average high temperatures in the summer months are typically around 28–32°C (82–90°F), while the winter highs range from 8 to 12°C (46–54°F). Nighttime temperatures often drop to near or below freezing. The average annual precipitation is around 600–800 mm (24–31 in.), mostly falling from late autumn to early spring.

Mediterranean Pine Forest dominates the coastal landscape, but farther inland and on hills, Mediterranean Cypress (*Cupressus sempervirens*) and a variety of junipers are the dominant conifers in the landscape. In the Iberian Peninsula, the dominant junipers are Thuriferous (Spanish) Juniper (*Juniper thurifera*) and Common Juniper (*Juniperus communis*), which are typically found at elevations from 800 to 2000 m (2500–6500 ft.) over a wide variety of soils from leptosols to cambisols (see appendix). Thuriferous Juniper can grow very large, up to 25 m (80 ft.) tall with a 2 m (6.5 ft.) diameter trunk. However, it is usually around 10–12 m (32–40 ft.) tall with a characteristic domed shape, although some individuals take on a Christmas tree–like appearance. In Türkiye, juniper forests are dominated by Greek Juniper (*Juniperus excelsa*) and Foetid Juniper (*Juniperus foetidissima*) and are commonly found at elevations from 1000 to 2400 m (3300–7900 ft.). The forests of Georgia and Azerbaijan are dominated by Savin Juniper (*Juniperus sabina*) as well as Common, Greek, and Foetid

A breathtaking Mediterranean Juniper and Cypress Forest landscape near Mt. Olympus, Cyprus. © RALPH MARTIN, AGAMI

Junipers. For visitors to the e. Mediterranean where the Foetid Juniper grows, the habitat can look remarkably similar to the HIGH-ELEVATION PINE WOODLAND of North America's Rocky Mountains, where the junipers resemble the Great Basin Bristlecone Pine (*Pinus longaeva*). The Foetid Juniper can grow to 10–20 m (30–65 ft.) tall, and its trunk is usually gnarled and twisted, reaching up to 1 m (3.3 ft.) in diameter. Consequently, the tree has a pachycaulesque (stubby, stumpy, and bulging) appearance and sometimes a krummholz-type look (see SUBALPINE KRUMMHOLZ), even when it is not affected by strong winds. The bark is thick and fibrous and peels in long strips.

In most Mediterranean Juniper and Cypress Forests, the canopy is shared with a minor broadleaf component, which varies across the region but has some typical species, such as Turkey Oak (*Quercus cerris*), Downy Oak (*Quercus pubescens*), Cretan Maple (*Acer sempervirens*), Mount Atlas Mastic Tree (*Pistacia atlantica*), and Oriental Beech (*Fagus orientalis*). Kermes Oak (*Quercus coccifera*) can grow as a shrub in this woodland but in some instances can grow to become a canopy species. A well-developed shrub layer typically includes Western Prickly Juniper (*Juniperus oxycedrus*), Mediterranean Buckthorn (*Rhamnus lycioides*), Green Olive Tree (*Phillyrea latifolia*), various barberries (*Berberis* spp.), Mediterranean Asparagus (*Asparagus aphyllus*), Tanner's Sumac (*Rhus coriaria*), and Jerusalem Thorn (*Paliurus spina-christi*).

The forests, comprising a wide range of tree sizes within a very small area, are characteristically very messy looking compared with the more uniform stands of Montane Spruce-Fir Forest or Mediterranean Pine Forest. This gives the impression that the forests may have been selectively logged or that many trees have been blown down. This is because their canopy tends to contain more broadleaf trees than the other conifer forests of the Mediterranean region, which breaks the monotony of a monotypic canopy. Plenty of light reaches the understorey and ground, because the forests are open with little canopy overlap. Herbs and forbs become much more prominent in

The Cyprus Warbler is restricted to Cyprus as a breeding species. Its near relative the Sardinian Warbler is rapidly spreading on the island, and in many areas seems to be outcompeting the Cyprus Warbler. One to watch ... © DANIELE OCCHIATO, AGAMI

open areas where the canopy tree cover is less than half the area. Dominant species include the Hoary Rock-Rose (*Cistus creticus*), Little-Robin (*Geranium purpureum*), Mediterranean False-Brome (*Brachypodium retusum*), Wall Germander (*Teucrium chamaedrys*), and the more localised Cretan Pignut (*Scaligeria napiformis*). Grasses include the omnipresent Orchard Grass (*Dactylis glomerata*).

WILDLIFE: These forests are typically not teeming with birdlife, and the species present tend to be generalists from the forests of the region or MAQUIS. Sardinian Warbler, Eurasian Blackbird, Coal Tit, Great Tit, Eurasian Jay, Eurasian Siskin, European Serin, and Common Chaffinch are typically some of the most common birds. Nevertheless, some regional and habitat specialties of somewhat more open Maquis-like Mediterranean Juniper and Cypress Forest include the Cyprus Warbler, Rüppell's Warbler, Cyprus Wheatear, and Masked Shrike. Cyprus Scops-Owl can be fairly common where present. Common and Pallid Swifts, Bonelli's Eagle, and Eurasian Griffon cruise overhead.

Wild mammals are relatively uncommon in these forests, but Mouflon and Red Fox use these forests on Cyprus. On the mainland, mammals common in other forest areas will also use the Mediterranean Juniper and Cypress Forest, like Eurasian Wild Boar, Western Roe Deer, Red Deer, various (regional) hedgehogs, and Brown Bear. Reptile diversity varies by region, but species include Levantine Viper (*Macrovipera lebetinus*), Cyprus Whip Snake (*Hierophis cypriensis*), Large Whip Snake (*Dolichophis jugularis*), Snake-eyed Lizard (*Ophisops elegans*), and Common Chameleon (*Chamaeleo chamaeleon*).

The dapper Rüppell's Warbler can be relatively common in Mediterranean Juniper and Cypress Forest. It is largely monochrome, so it is truly stunning to glimpse those fiery-red eyes and bright orange legs as it skulks through the vegetation. © AURÉLIEN AUDEVARD, AGAMI

The attractive Masked Shrike occurs around the e. Mediterranean, where it preys on large insects and small vertebrates. As with other members of the family, it sometimes impales its prey on thorns. © RALPH MARTIN, AGAMI

CONSERVATION: Centuries (millennia?) of exploitation of Mediterranean Juniper and Cypress Forest has undoubtedly had a profound influence on the extent and health of this habitat. Both wood extraction for timber, firewood, and charcoal production and forest clearance for urban sprawl and agriculture continue to be major threats in places. In addition, effective habitat-level conservation will need to address the threats of habitat fragmentation and develop a balanced understanding of the need for and dangers of fire.

DISTRIBUTION: These conifer forests range from the Iberian Peninsula to the northern shores of the Mediterranean Sea to the mountain ranges of Türkiye and the Caucasus Mountains. They are most prevalent in Türkiye, Crete, and Cyprus. They are generally found above the MEDITERRANEAN PINE FOREST and in drier areas than the MONTANE SPRUCE-FIR FOREST.

WHERE TO SEE: Mt. Olympus, Cyprus; Vashlovani National Park, Georgia.

SIDEBAR 1 DO YOU WANT TO SEE A BIT OF THE MANTLE?

As birders, artists, and historians have their must-see European spots, for tectonics-loving rock-watchers, the Troodos Ophiolite of Cyprus is the ultimate pilgrimage. This is one of the most significant geologic features in the world. Oceans open and close all the time, with the oceanic material (think basalt) being subducted under the continental rocks (think granite or sandstone) and forming ranges such as the Andes or island archipelagoes such as Sumatra or Japan. However, in events much rarer than those that create diamonds or gold, or large meteors crashing into earth, bits of the ocean do not subduct but instead get smeared onto the side of the continent. In the rare event that one of these is located, we get to see a small segment of these rocks. When this happened at Troodos around 90 MYA, some of the Tethys Sea was subducted, but a whole sequence of rocks from below the ocean floor was accreted in a 15 km (9 mi.) series, from the deep-sea sediments that deposited on the ocean to the pillow basalts that formed the seafloor to the dikes of diorite and sheets of gabbro, and down into the peridotite and serpentinite of the earth's upper mantle. This is important because it allows people to see what the upper mantle is made of and to study the petrology of the ocean floor. But as concerns the local ecology, many of these rocks are ultramafic, containing very high levels of iron and magnesium but lower levels of other elements that are useful to plants, such as calcium and potassium. The resulting soils over these rocks are very nutrient deficient, and the vegetation is stunted relative to that rooted in surrounding soils.

Eu1l EUROPEAN MONTANE SPRUCE-FIR FOREST

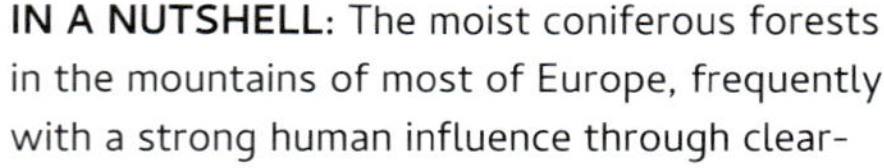

IN A NUTSHELL: The moist coniferous forests in the mountains of most of Europe, frequently with a strong human influence through clear-cut harvesting and planting. **Global Habitat Affinities:** NEARCTIC MONTANE SPRUCE-FIR FOREST; ASIAN MONTANE SPRUCE-FIR FOREST; MAGHREB FIR AND CEDAR FOREST. **Continental Habitat Affinities:** SPRUCE-FIR TAIGA. **Species Overlap:** SPRUCE-FIR TAIGA.

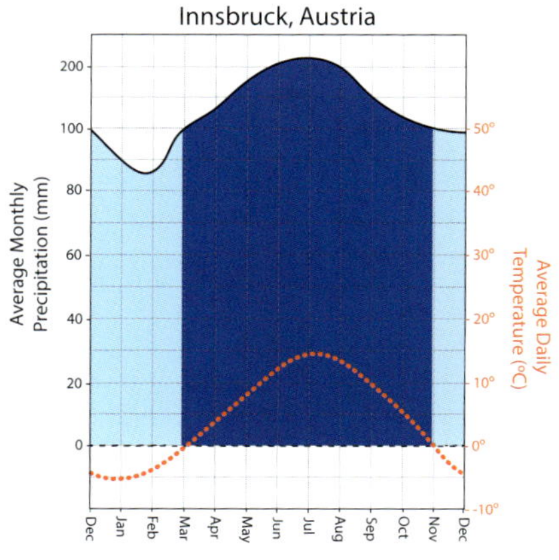

DESCRIPTION: A flock of Red Crossbills chatters high overhead on the sunlit tips of the tallest trees, but down at ground level, deep spring snows mean everything will take longer to wake up. The ground cover is buried deep in the dark forest, and a fox has left a meandering trail. Crested Tits and Goldcrests twitter softly to themselves.

Montane Spruce-Fir Forests are the stereotypical coniferous forests cloaking the montane zone in much of Europe's mountains. The climate of the montane zone at mid-latitudes is similar to that found much farther north in the boreal zone, where a similar SPRUCE-FIR TAIGA develops (both Köppen **Dfb** and **Dfc**), though the growing season in the temperate montane forests is much longer. However, daily temperature fluctuations can be quite extreme, dropping quickly at night and often dipping below freezing even on warmer days in the middle of the growing season. Many months of freeze-thaw cycles increase mechanical rock weathering and create unstable soils. Both the Spruce-Fir Taiga and the Montane Spruce-Fir Forests tend to be dominated by a single tree species. But the complex terrain of the montane forests—and the resulting effects on drainage, sunlight, and soils—means that many more microclimates and complex niches develop, resulting in

Montane Spruce-Fir Forest blankets this Alpine valley. Subalpine Krummholz can be seen on the higher, drier slopes in the upper left. © DALE FORBES

a much more complex forest than the taiga. Montane Spruce-Fir Forest vies with MONTANE PINE FOREST in the montane zone, the spruce or fir dominating on the better, moister soils and the pine relegated to the sandier and poorer soils.

The European Alps are dominated by Norway Spruce (*Picea abies*) forests, with a sprinkling of Silver Fir (*Abies alba*) and European Larch (*Larix decidua*). Most of these forests in the Alps have been heavily managed, clear-cut harvested, and replanted over generations and now are usually experienced as monotonous stands of the same age and size. The tree composition and structural heterogeneity within these forests depend highly on the landowner. Still, given the sheer number of small landowners in the Alps, there is a wide spectrum from the most boring of plantations to wonderfully diverse forests filled with fascinating woodpeckers, tits, and salamanders. Mature stands are typically very open with a low herbaceous layer of variable composition, from a dense layer of Common Bilberry (*Vaccinium myrtillus*) or mosses to looser collections of grasses, ferns, various small shrubs, and European Wood Sorrel (*Oxalis acetosella*). The soils are mostly wetter, nutrient-rich, and acidic, with a strong humus layer (e.g., podzols). Fingers of MONTANE MIXED FOREST and BEECH FOREST run through Montane Spruce-Fir Forests where the climate is milder, while Montane Pine Forests wholly replace them on warm, stony, dry, south-facing slopes. The deeper valley bottoms of the foothills and submontane zones below the Montane Spruce-Fir Forests have mostly been cleared for settlements, pastures, hay meadows, or other agriculture. Nevertheless, some TEMPERATE RIPARIAN FOREST persists along watercourses. At the upper limit of Montane Spruce-Fir Forest, the trees typically thin out, and larch has a greater presence as the forest slowly transitions to open ALPINE TUNDRA, with mats of scrambling Dwarf Mountain Pine (*Pinus mugo*) or open stands of Swiss Pine (*Pinus cembra*) and European Larch (see SUBALPINE TIMBERLINE WOODLAND).

Above: **The scarce Eurasian Three-toed Woodpecker is a specialist of this habitat, with a particular love for bark beetles.** © RALPH MARTIN, AGAMI

Left: **The Eurasian Three-toed Woodpecker carves characteristic dotted rows in spruces and larches to milk the phloem sap in spring.** © DALE FORBES

Below: **The tiny Goldcrest, Europe's smallest bird, is a common breeder in this habitat.** © MARKUS VARESVUO, AGAMI

In cooler regions of the Pyrenees, firs form large, blanketing forests with deep, dark, acidic soils. Spruce is insignificant. In slightly warmer areas, firs are complemented by European Beech (*Fagus sylvatica*) and maples (*Acer* spp.). The mountain ranges generally become drier towards the east, and the Carpathian Mountains have spruce forests in the montane zone and SUBALPINE KRUMMHOLZ at higher elevations.

The Montane Spruce-Fir Forests of the Caucasus and n. Türkiye have Lebanese Cedar (*Cedrus libani*) as a co-canopy species, and in some areas, the cedar can form monotypic stands that feel remarkably similar to the nearly identical stands of Atlas Cedar (*Cedrus atlantica*) in the MAGHREB FIR AND CEDAR FOREST of the Atlas Mountains of North Africa. Lebanese Cedars can be towering giants reaching 60 m (200 ft.) tall, although most are in the 40–50 m (130–160 ft.) range. The very conical shape and lower height (20–25 m/65–80 ft.) of the spruce and fir contrast with the high-domed crown of the cedar. Despite structural differences, this habitat variation cannot be parsed out as a separate habitat, because it occurs as a mélange within the greater Montane Spruce-Fir Forests and has the same wildlife assemblage.

WILDLIFE: Bird densities are low in these montane forests, especially in mature monocultures of spruce or fir, but tend to be higher in matrix, developing, and edge habitats. The avifauna is dominated by the resident tits (especially Coal, Crested, and Great Tits), Eurasian Nuthatch, Eurasian Siskin, Red Crossbill, and Goldcrest, as well as various woodpeckers, with Black Woodpecker and Eurasian Three-toed Woodpecker being easiest to find in this habitat. Keep a look out for the characteristic dotted rows, at waist height, that the Eurasian Three-toed Woodpecker carves in spruces and larches to milk the phloem sap in spring (Great Spotted Woodpecker may also use them). Boreal (Tengmalm's) Owl, Eurasian Pygmy-Owl, Eurasian Goshawk, European Honey-Buzzard, Western Capercaillie, and Eurasian Woodcock are all widespread but invariably hard to find. If you find grouse droppings on the ground, look carefully in the branches above, as a grouse might be roosting right above you. Hazel Grouse prefers Montane Spruce-Fir Forest but is most associated

The diminutive Eurasian Pygmy-Owl, Europe's smallest owl, is the most common owl in many Montane Spruce-Fir Forests.
© MARKUS VARESVUO, AGAMI

The smart Boreal (Tengmalm's) Owl nests in cavities in the conifers, especially in old Black Woodpecker holes. In the Alps, these owls are often found using the margins between older Montane Spruce-Fir Forest and recently clear-cut open areas. © MARKUS VARESVUO, AGAMI

with areas of Green Alder (*Alnus alnobetula*) growth—especially along steeper snow or stream channels through the conifers where the alders can form dense thickets. Spring brings the return of some species from warmer regions in the south, notably Song Thrush, Mistle Thrush, Common Chiffchaff, and much larger numbers of Common Chaffinch. If you can see a Coal Tit, Eurasian Three-toed Woodpecker, and Red Crossbill, you are likely in a Montane Spruce-Fir Forest.

Europe's vast Montane Spruce-Fir Forests provide refuge for some of the continent's greatest wildlife. Healthy populations of Red Deer are found throughout most of the habitat's range. Northern Chamois use these forests all year round, particularly in winter, when large numbers descend from higher elevations. Predators are rare, but this habitat is important for Brown Bear, Grey Wolf, and Eurasian Lynx.

Coal Tit is common in coniferous forests. © RALPH MARTIN, AGAMI

The Alpine Salamander (*Salamandra atra*) is arguably the most remarkable creature of Montane Spruce-Fir Forest. It is almost completely restricted to this habitat, and, unlike most other amphibians, it is wholly terrestrial. The young develop for about three years within the female before being born live (not as eggs). They are about 5 cm (2 in.) long at birth—this is incredible, considering the adult female is only about 12 cm (5 in.) long.

CONSERVATION: Montane Spruce-Fir Forests are of enormous importance to the people of Europe's mountainous regions. Timber is harvested from almost all forests, and many locals enjoy foraging for mushrooms and bilberries. The forests are also important to hunters, who are invariably actively involved in their management. Parts of these forests are still managed for cattle in an ancient tradition of semi-open larch-spruce wooded pastures, in which trees are spaced farther apart, and the understorey is kept open to encourage grass growth. Besides being productive pastures, these are also aesthetically beautiful and great places to look for Grey-headed and Eurasian Green Woodpeckers.

Climate change has an increasingly dramatic and visible effect on Europe's Montane Spruce-Fir Forests. Frequent droughts tax trees, while milder winters allow the European Spruce Bark Beetle (*Ips typographus*) to increase and overwhelm the already weakened trees. The consequent death of infected trees can leave entire hillsides barren, with enormous economic and environmental consequences. The Eurasian Three-toed Woodpecker feeds heavily on bark beetles, so it will likely benefit from these developments (provided foresters allow some nesting trees to remain).

DISTRIBUTION: Montane Spruce-Fir Forests are found throughout Europe's humid and semi-humid mountain ranges, most notably in the Pyrenees, Alps, Carpathians, and Caucasus.

WHERE TO SEE: Karwendel Nature Park, Tyrol, Austria; Martalúzka Nature Reserve, Slovakia; Ordesa y Monte Perdido National Park, Pyrenees, Spain.

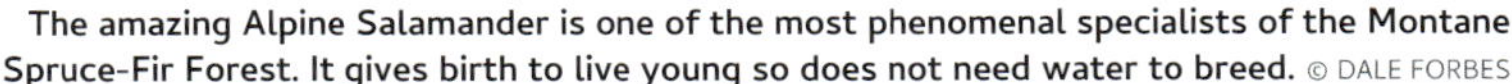

The amazing Alpine Salamander is one of the most phenomenal specialists of the Montane Spruce-Fir Forest. It gives birth to live young so does not need water to breed. © DALE FORBES

Eu1J SUBALPINE KRUMMHOLZ

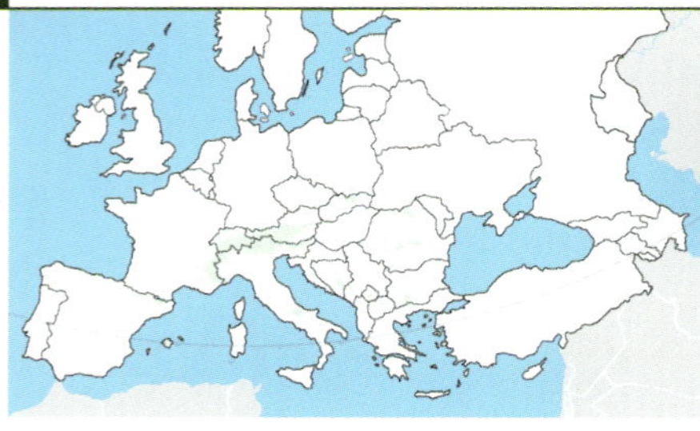

IN A NUTSHELL: Tangled krummholz mats of creeping pines found above Europe's montane forests in the transition to the treeless ALPINE TUNDRA. **Global Habitat Affinities:** NEARCTIC HIGH-ELEVATION PINE WOODLAND; AFROTROPICAL MONTANE DRY MIXED WOODLAND; SUBALPINE EUCALYPT WOODLAND; HIMALAYAN SUBALPINE WOODLAND. **Continental Habitat Affinities:** SUBALPINE TIMBERLINE WOODLAND; SUBARCTIC RIPARIAN WOODLAND. **Species Overlap:** ALPINE TUNDRA.

DESCRIPTION: Trees eking out an existence at the timberline will often be deformed, with an asymmetrical canopy resembling a comb-over, and stunted by frost, heavy snows, and frequent high winds. Dwarf Mountain Pine (*Pinus mugo*) naturally grows in this twisted, stunted form—known as krummholz (German for 'twisted wood')—and cloaks avalanche-prone slopes with looser soils and little to no humus-rich soil buildup.

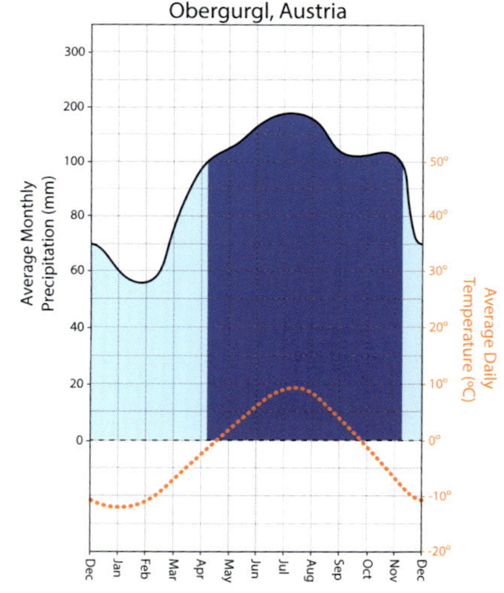

Subalpine Krummholz occurs in the narrow subalpine band (Köppen **Dfc**), which typically covers a band only about 50–200 m (150–650 ft.) wide between the montane forests below and the ALPINE TUNDRA above. The elevation of the timberline (and subalpine habitats) varies by region, from as low as 1200 m (3900 ft.) to as high as 2500 m (8200 ft.), but is most typically at about 1800 m (6000 ft.). It will often grow in a matrix with the more open, savanna-like SUBALPINE TIMBERLINE WOODLAND, with Subalpine Krummholz tending to be found on the poorer soils—it is particularly extensive on steep, calcareous slopes. In contrast, Subalpine Timberline Woodland tends to dominate on slightly better, more stable soils.

The mats of almost impenetrable Dwarf Mountain Pine are often interspersed with grasslands or heathlands, much like the Alpine Tundra. In these more open areas in the Alps, Hairy Alpenrose (*Rhododendron hirsutum*), Bog Bilberry (*V. uliginosum*), Lingonberry (*V. vitis-idaea*), and Common Bilberry (*V. myrtillus*) can be common. Where animal husbandry is more intensive—as in Austria's Alms and Switzerland's Alps—the pine mats are managed, and the spaces between tend to have a short-cropped grass sward. In addition to the pines, the pioneering Green Alder (*Alnus alnobetula*) often forms shrubby masses in avalanche chutes.

Subalpine Krummholz tends to dominate the timberline in the Carpathians, but some Subalpine Timberline Woodlands can also be found here. These are interspersed with grasses, Mountain Juniper (*Juniperus communis* var. *saxatilis*), and Myrtle-leaf Rhododendron (*Rhododendron myrtifolium*).

Dwarf Mountain Pine blankets this slope and can also be seen at a slightly lower elevation at the back of the valley. Montane Spruce-Fir Forest can be seen on the lower slopes in the left of the image. © DALE FORBES

Scattered patches of Dwarf Mountain Pine and open grass are perfect for Mountain Hare, Lesser Whitethroat, and Ring Ouzel. © DALE FORBES

The rather unassuming Dunnock, an accentor, is surprisingly uncommon in Europe's mountainous regions and is typically found only at the timberline. Its delightful song is a classic part of the Subalpine Krummholz habitat in spring. © MARKUS VARESVUO, AGAMI

WILDLIFE: In the spring, these blanketing, entangled masses of scrambling pine resound with the song of Lesser Whitethroat, Dunnock, Citril Finch, and (Lesser) Redpoll. Ring Ouzels can often be seen feeding in the areas between Dwarf Mountain Pine stands where livestock crop the grass short. Black Grouse gathers in leks in open areas before retreating to montane forest during the day. In the Alps, tongues of Green Alder, especially in boggier and somewhat more open areas, provide great habitat for the beautiful and highly localised (Red-spotted) Bluethroat.

Northern Chamois is typically common in Subalpine Krummholz, particularly in the warmer seasons. Red Deer will gladly use this habitat in quieter areas to rest and feed in summer. Red Fox is common, while Brown Bear and Grey Wolf are sporadic. The Mountain Hare is a habitat specialist and highly dependent on Dwarf Mountain Pine, favouring a matrix of this pine and grasses.

Redpolls can be common in the Subalpine Krummholz; they sing from the tops of shrubs, feed on the ground, and dart about in little groups. The Redpolls found in the Alps, like this male, were previously known as Lesser Redpolls. © RALPH MARTIN, AGAMI

Ring Ouzel, an Alpine relative of the Eurasian Blackbird, is commonly found singing from Dwarf Mountain Pines or feeding in the grassy areas between them. © RALPH MARTIN, AGAMI

CONSERVATION: The Dwarf Mountain Pine is important in stabilising loose scree and avalanche-prone slopes above human settlements, so it tends to be well protected and is expanding in many areas, particularly as alpine animal husbandry is abandoned. Developers of ski areas have cut back the pines in some areas to make way for new pistes, but such alteration is rather localised and unlikely to be of great significance to the habitat as a whole.

DISTRIBUTION: Very significant and widespread in the Alps and Carpathians. Rare or sporadic in other subalpine mountainous regions.

WHERE TO SEE: Hohe Tauern National Park, Austria.

Mountain Hare is a habitat specialist in Europe's mountains, doing best in a matrix of Dwarf Mountain Pine and pasture. It assumes a white winter coat, giving it perfect camouflage in the snow. In the summer, its cryptic coat blends perfectly with its lichen-encrusted surroundings. © HUGH HARROP, AGAMI

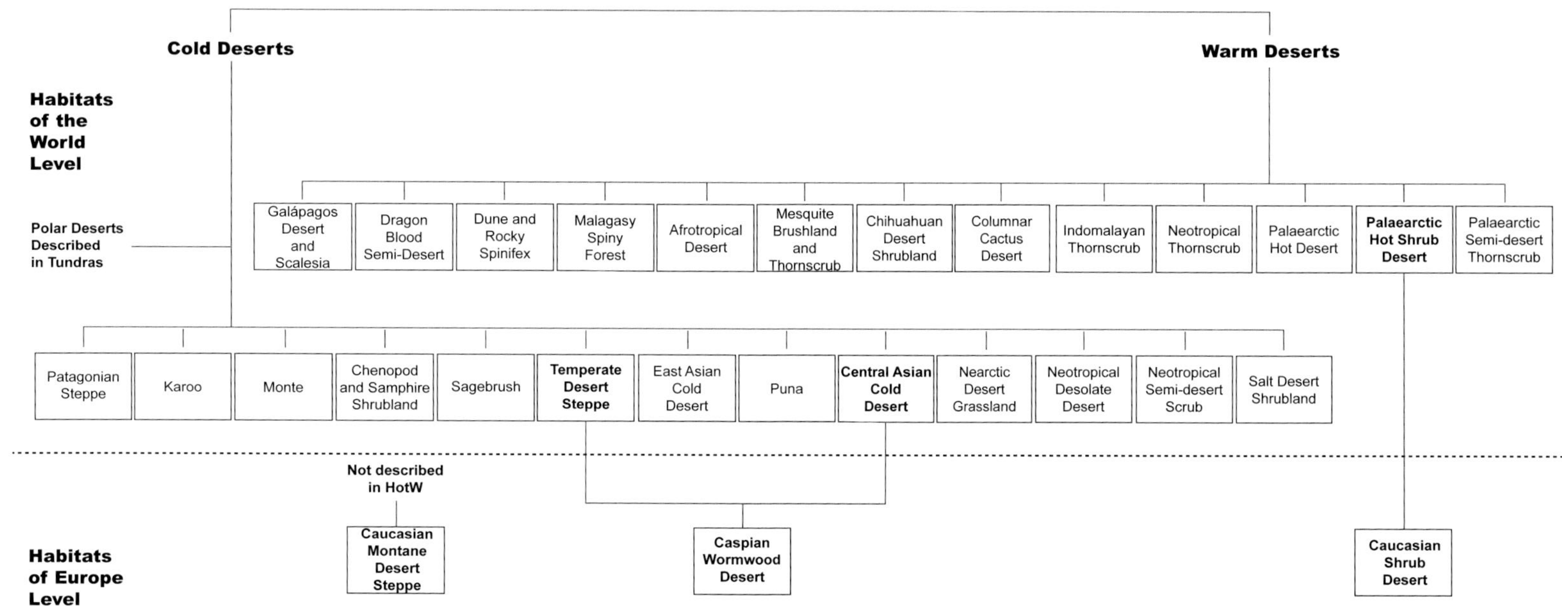
DESERTS
Cold Deserts
Warm Deserts
Habitats of the World Level
Polar Deserts Described in Tundras
Galápagos Desert and Scalesia
Dragon Blood Semi-Desert
Dune and Rocky Spinifex
Malagasy Spiny Forest
Afrotropical Desert
Mesquite Brushland and Thornscrub
Chihuahuan Desert Shrubland
Columnar Cactus Desert
Indomalayan Thornscrub
Neotropical Thornscrub
Palaearctic Hot Desert
Palaearctic Hot Shrub Desert
Palaearctic Semi-desert Thornscrub
Patagonian Steppe
Karoo
Monte
Chenopod and Samphire Shrubland
Sagebrush
Temperate Desert Steppe
East Asian Cold Desert
Puna
Central Asian Cold Desert
Nearctic Desert Grassland
Neotropical Desolate Desert
Neotropical Semi-desert Scrub
Salt Desert Shrubland
Not described in HotW
Habitats of Europe Level
Caucasian Montane Desert Steppe
Caspian Wormwood Desert
Caucasian Shrub Desert

DESERTS

Eu2A CASPIAN WORMWOOD DESERT

IN A NUTSHELL: Cold deserts fringing the Caspian Sea and dominated by small wormwood shrubs. **Global Habitat Affinities:** TURANIAN DUNE DESERT; MONGOLIAN SHRUB DESERT; CHENOPOD SHRUBLAND; CHIHUAHUAN DESERT; SUCCULENT PUNA; NEARCTIC SAGEBRUSH SHRUBLAND. **Continental Habitat Affinities:** CAUCASIAN SHRUB DESERT. **Species Overlap:** CAUCASIAN SHRUB DESERT.

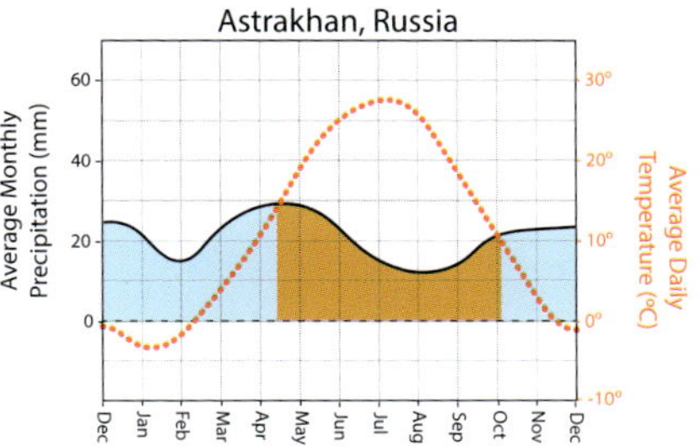

DESCRIPTION: The wildlife of Caspian Wormwood Desert—Saiga, Corsac Fox, Steppe Eagle, Demoiselle Crane, and White-winged Lark—may make you feel like you are standing in c. Asia (despite being in Europe). These shrub deserts are extensive in c. Asia and wrap around the north of the Caspian Sea, just sneaking into Europe. In spring, Caspian Wormwood Desert is flush with ephemeral plants, but in late summer and winter, it dries out, and much of the ground cover disappears. Even then, it does not seem desolate enough to be a *real* desert when compared with the classic sand dune (erg) and pavement (reg) deserts of the Middle East. Nevertheless, Caspian Wormwood Desert still has an evaporation level of over 3 m (10 ft.) annually, which exceeds the level of precipitation by an order of magnitude. The Caspian Wormwood Desert has a cold semi-arid climate (Köppen **Bsk**), with extraordinary temperature extremes. Summers are hot (av. max. 34°C/93°F), and winters are bitterly cold (av. min. −6°C/21°F). This habitat receives between 150 and 250 mm (6–10 in.) of precipitation per year, with the driest period being late summer. This brutal climate is exacerbated by strong desiccating winds throughout the year. In contrast to the CAUCASIAN SHRUB DESERT to the south, which usually develops on bedrock, the Caspian Wormwood Desert is concentrated on regosol soils (see appendix) formed on aeolian wind deposits such as palaeo sand dunes and loess deposits. It also occurs on the palaeo shores of the Caspian Sea where the soils are aridisols (desert soils), developed on coastal sands, and solonchaks (see appendix), those with extreme salinity concentrated around the edge of saline depressions.

The unrelenting summer sun parches the landscape and withers most plants away, leaving ground coverage of as little as 10% and never more than 50%. These wide-open landscapes of short shrubs, generally less than 1 m (3 ft.) tall, are dominated by various wormwoods, such as Field Wormwood (*Artemisia lercheana*), Levant Wormseed (*Artemisia pauciflora*), Fragrant Wormwood

The wide, open plains of the Caspian Wormwood Desert can be quite structurally diverse, offering myriad microhabitats for wildlife. © VINCENT LEGRAND, AGAMI

(*Artemisia fragrans*), and Sand Sagebrush (*Artemisia arenaria*). This plantscape makes the Caspian Wormwood Desert feel much like the CHENOPOD SHRUBLAND of inland Australia.

Early spring rains bring ephemeral forbs and grasses to life and can create almost complete ground cover. A number of beautiful flowering plants are found in the Caspian Wormwood Desert, and many are range-restricted endemics (hence the lack of English common names), with speciation having happened between the barriers of the Caucasus Mountains to the south and the Black and Caspian Seas to the west and east. These include a buttercup (*Ranunculus oxyspermus*), Camelthorn (*Alhagi pseudalhagi*), a tansy (*Tanacetum achilleifolium*), a milk vetch (*Astragalus testiculatus*), Syrian Bean-Caper (*Zygophyllum fabago*), a knotweed (*Calligonum aphyllum*), a poppy (*Papaver arenarium*), Two-flowered Tulip (*Tulipa biflora*), and a thistle (*Carduus uncinatus*). The enormous tumbleweed Prickly Russian Thistle (*Salsola tragus*) is widespread, as are the Leafless Anabasis (*Anabasis aphylla*) and Desert Madwort (*Alyssum desertorum*). The grass sward is dominated by Bulbous Bluegrass (*Poa bulbosa*), Cheatgrass (*Bromus tectorum*), Siberian Lyme Grass (*Leymus racemosus*), Clustered Wheatgrass (*Agropyron desertorum*), and Oriental False Wheatgrass (*Eremopyrum orientale*). Tamarisks are a common feature of more saline soils (solonchak), where Saltcedar (*Tamarix ramosissima*) and Turanian Tamarisk (*Tamarix laxa*) grow about 1.5 m (5 ft.) tall and form thick groves. They spend autumn through winter leafless but in early spring burst with pink and lavender flowers. Black Saxaul (*Haloxylon ammodendron*), a small, slow-growing tree, is rare in Europe but becomes more common farther east where this habitat merges into the Asian TURANIAN DUNE DESERT. Taller vegetation is concentrated in the ribbons of CASPIAN RIPARIAN SCRUB that snake through the Caspian Wormwood Desert.

WILDLIFE: Large mammals are rare in the Caspian Wormwood Desert, but there are several very special ones. The desert around the northern edge of the Caspian Sea holds Saiga, a bizarre-looking antelope with a pair of closely spaced, downward-directed bloated nostrils that give the impression of a character out of *Star Wars*. The Brown Hare is ubiquitous throughout Europe and has also taken to this desert setting, alongside the Great Jerboa, Little Ground Squirrel, Northern Molevole, and Social Vole. These smaller mammals are hunted by African Wildcat, Grey Wolf, Golden Jackal, and foxes. The Corsac Fox scours the desert, although it avoids areas with

Right: **The Corsac Fox scours the desert, although it avoids areas with extensive sandy dunes.** © DANI LÓPEZ-VELASCO, AGAMI

Below: **Europe's only Saigas are found in small numbers in this habitat.** © JAMES EATON, AGAMI

Above left: **Caspian Wormwood Desert is the most important habitat in Europe for the Steppe Eagle.** © SYLVAIN REYT, AGAMI

Above right: **The Black-winged Pratincole is mostly restricted to Caspian Wormwood Desert in Europe. It is an aerial feeder, taking insects on the wing like a giant swallow.** © DANIELE OCCHIATO, AGAMI

Opposite: **The Demoiselle Crane has its European stronghold in the Caspian Wormwood Desert. It can form large flocks when not breeding.** © JAMES EATON, AGAMI

extensive sandy dunes (where the Secret Toadhead Agama, *Phrynocephalus mystaceus*, is to be found). The Red Fox is also found in the Caspian Wormwood Desert but tends to stick to the somewhat more temperate edges nearer waterways, steppes, and savannas. This is also where the Long-eared Hedgehog is found.

The Demoiselle Crane has its European stronghold in the Caspian Wormwood Desert and is one of the region's most magnificent and beautiful birds (Montagu's Harrier is also relatively common and has a similar colour palette). The Black-winged Pratincole is restricted to this habitat and the easternmost PUSZTA AND PONTIC STEPPE. The Caspian Wormwood Desert is the most important habitat in Europe for the Steppe Eagle and is essentially the only habitat it regularly occupies. In addition, Long-legged Buzzard, Black Kite, Common Buzzard, Montagu's Harrier, Pallid Harrier, (Eastern) Imperial Eagle, and Cinereous Vulture scan the landscape from above. Blue-cheeked Bee-eater is almost confined to this habitat (and CAUCASIAN SHRUB DESERT) in Europe, while the European Bee-eater, European Roller, Rosy (Rose-coloured) Starling, Eurasian Hoopoe, and skulking Menetries's Warbler can all be abundant in this habitat. Booted Warbler favours the

Booted Warbler (pictured) favours the Caspian Wormwood Deserts, often feeding near the ground, while the similar Sykes's Warbler is confined to the somewhat taller vegetation of the Caspian Riparian Scrub in the same region. © RALPH MARTIN, AGAMI

The impressive Black Lark is the classic emblem of this habitat. It really is like no other lark.
© EDUARD SANGSTER, AGAMI

Caspian Wormwood Desert, while the similar Sykes's Warbler is confined to the somewhat taller vegetation of the CASPIAN RIPARIAN SCRUB in the same region. Siberian Stonechat, Whinchat, and Lesser Grey Shrike hawk insects from tops of wormwoods and other bushes, while Little Bustard, Tawny Pipit, Eurasian Skylark, and Calandra, Crested, Turkestan Short-toed, and Greater Short-toed Larks run along the open ground. These Caspian Wormwood Deserts are the best places to find White-winged and Black Larks in Europe (the latter mostly in winter). Open areas are additionally important for Isabelline, Pied, and Northern Wheatears, as well as White-tailed Lapwing and Black-bellied Sandgrouse. Black-headed Bunting will use this habitat, although it is more abundant in the MIDDLE EASTERN SAVANNA of the region.

The Caspian Wormwood Deserts have some wonderful reptiles on offer to the avid wildlife enthusiast. The Steppe Runner (*Eremias arguta*), Rapid Racerunner (*Eremias velox*), Central Asian Toadhead Agama (*Phrynocephalus guttatus*), and Secret Toadhead Agama are especially exciting lizards to find, all specialists in this or closely related habitats. The most expected snakes in this habitat include the Caspian Whip Snake (*Dolichophis caspius*), Desert Sand Boa (*Eryx miliaris*), Eastern Montpellier Snake (*Malpolon insignitus*), East Four-lined Rat Snake (*Elaphe sauromates*), and Steppe Rat Snake (*Elaphe dione*). The Afghan Tortoise (*Testudo horsfieldii*) is uncommon but largely restricted to this habitat.

CONSERVATION: A small part of this habitat has been preserved in reserves like the large Chornye Zemli Nature Reserve, Russia (created for the reintroduction of the Saiga). Most deserts found outside reserves are severely degraded from extensive overgrazing by cattle and sheep. This results in less palatable shrubs dominating and significant wind erosion of topsoil. Much of the land has been irrigated and converted to cropland near water sources such as the Volga River. The Aral Sea to the east of this habitat has been converted to an anthropogenic barren desert, and the same fate may await this habitat along the edges of the Ural River and Caspian coast.

DISTRIBUTION: The Caspian Wormwood Desert is concentrated on the western edge of the Caspian Sea, around the northern edge of the Caucasus in southernmost Russia, to the Ural River. There is an outlier in and around Crimea with closely related plant and animal communities.

WHERE TO SEE: Chornye Zemli Nature Reserve, Russia; Mekletinsky State Nature Reserve, Russia; s. Crimea.

Eu2B CAUCASIAN SHRUB DESERT

IN A NUTSHELL: Low, arid shrublands around the Caucasus Mountains and Caspian Sea, extending along s. Türkiye. **Global Habitat Affinities:** CHENOPOD SHRUBLAND; CHIHUAHUAN DESERT; SUCCULENT PUNA; MONTE; NEARCTIC SAGEBRUSH SHRUBLAND; MONGOLIAN SHRUB DESERT; NAMA KAROO. **Continental Habitat Affinities:** CASPIAN WORMWOOD DESERT. **Species Overlap:** CASPIAN WORMWOOD DESERT.

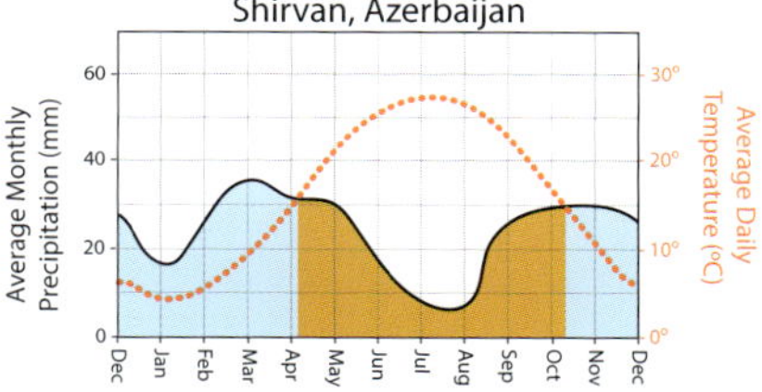

DESCRIPTION: The lowlands between and around the Caucasus Mountains have wondrous steppe deserts filled with endemic reptiles, desert birds rare elsewhere in Europe, and the occasional rare mammal. These shrub deserts are wide, open habitats with scattered shrubs, flushing with ephemeral grasses and forbs after early spring rains. They are extensive through much of c. Asia, just barely making it into Europe as they wrap around the Caspian Sea towards the Black Sea (also see CASPIAN WORMWOOD DESERT).

Hardy wormwoods provide cover for some of the habitat's most interesting wildlife.
© IAIN CAMPBELL, TROPICAL BIRDING

Caucasian Shrub Desert has a cold, semi-arid climate (Köppen **Bsk**), with hot, humid summers and cool, occasionally wet winters. This habitat receives between 150 and 250 mm (6–10 in.) of rain annually, but summers are dry. The aridity is exacerbated by strong winds that parch the landscape. Strong winds are common throughout the year but particularly brutal in summer. Evaporation is extreme and easily exceeds precipitation for most of the year, so plants are subjected to significant water stress in summer, when none of the ephemeral plants are visible aboveground.

This is a cold desert, and, like the chenopod-dominated MONGOLIAN SHRUB DESERT of c. Asia and the NAMA KAROO of s. Africa, it does not seem desolate enough to be regarded as desert, seeming to have too many trees and shrubs. The Caucasian Shrub Desert's vegetation is short, and perennial ground cover is often formed by the widespread Fragrant Wormwood (*Artemisia fragrans*), the endemic Shovista Wormwood (*Artemisia szowitziana*), a whole host of other wormwoods (*Artemisia* spp.), and various saltworts (*Salsola* spp.), making the landscape look much like Australia's CHENOPOD SHRUBLAND. These are generally small shrubs, under 2 m (6 ft.) tall, that whittle down in dry years and then regrow rapidly when conditions are favourable. Between these ground shrubs are perennial grasses such as Bulbous Bluegrass (*Poa bulbosa*), which remain low, generally to around 38 cm (15 in.).

The Caucasian Shrub Desert is much more precipitation-ephemeral in nature than the Caspian Wormwood Desert, in that the growth is less dominated by temperature, because winters are warmer here, and more dominated by rainfall. After seasonal rains, perennial grasses and saltworts (equivalent to the succulents of Australia) are augmented by a burst of ephemeral grasses and shrubs such as Small Medic (*Medicago medicaginoides*), Hoefft's Storksbill (*Erodium hoefftianum*), Two-flowered Tulip (*Tulipa biflora*), Branched Petrosimonia (*Petrosimonia brachiata*), Margined Stickseed (*Lappula marginata*), and the very widespread Clasping Pepperweed (*Lepidium perfoliatum*) and Jagged Chickweed (*Holosteum umbellatum*). The flush of vegetation can increase plant cover to more than 50%.

Dry, desolate Caucasian Shrub Desert in Azerbaijan. © IAIN CAMPBELL, TROPICAL BIRDING

Much of the Caucasian Shrub Desert of Azerbaijan has formed with a peppering of mud volcanoes created by the eruption of fine-grained sediments mixed with gases and water. They range in size from 3 m (10 ft.) wide and 1.5 m (5 ft.) high up to 700 m (2300 ft.) high. They differ from regular volcanoes in that they do not produce lava and are not as hot. In other areas, this habitat occurs mainly on plains or low rises and over a wide variety of substrates, resulting in changes in vegetation composition. These substrates include regosols, durisols, and solonchaks (see appendix). Durisols (aridisols in the USDA soil taxonomy) are thin soils dominated by coarse rock fragments on nutrient-deficient crystalline metamorphic and igneous bedrocks like granites, rhyolites, and quartzites that have been infused with silica, calcium or iron. Regosols developed on sedimentary rocks and unconsolidated Palaeogene sediments, while solonchaks (saline soils) are characterised by extreme salinity and are found around the edge of saline depressions.

WILDLIFE: The deserts in protected areas hold some very rare species and are almost the only areas in Europe where you can find Goitred Gazelle. Other mammals still occurring in this environment include Red Fox, Brown Hare, Golden Jackal, Grey Wolf, Small Five-toed Jerboa, and Jungle Cat. The Southwest Asian Badger and Marbled Polecat are both shy and uncommon but readily use this habitat. Southern White-breasted Hedgehog and Eurasian Wild Boar stick to the somewhat moister and denser vegetation near watercourses, which is also where Northern Lion and Caspian Tiger were concentrated in the recent past (but both are now regionally extinct).

The very dry nature of the habitat becomes obvious when looking at the bird assemblages, with dryland species dominating, such as Chukar, Calandra Lark, Turkestan Short-toed Lark, Crested Lark, Isabelline Wheatear, Lesser Grey Shrike, and Rufous-tailed Scrub-Robin. Cinereous Vulture, Eurasian Griffon, and large numbers of Little Bustards overwinter in this desert. Caucasian Shrub Desert is important for Lesser Kestrel. Saker Falcon is uncommon but a truly phenomenal sight—never more dramatic than when hunting while strong winds are whipping across the plains. Blue-cheeked Bee-eater is almost confined to this habitat (and CASPIAN WORMWOOD DESERT)

The stunning Blue-cheeked Bee-eater breeds in colonies in sandbanks and forages over the surrounding shrub desert. © JOSH JONES, AGAMI

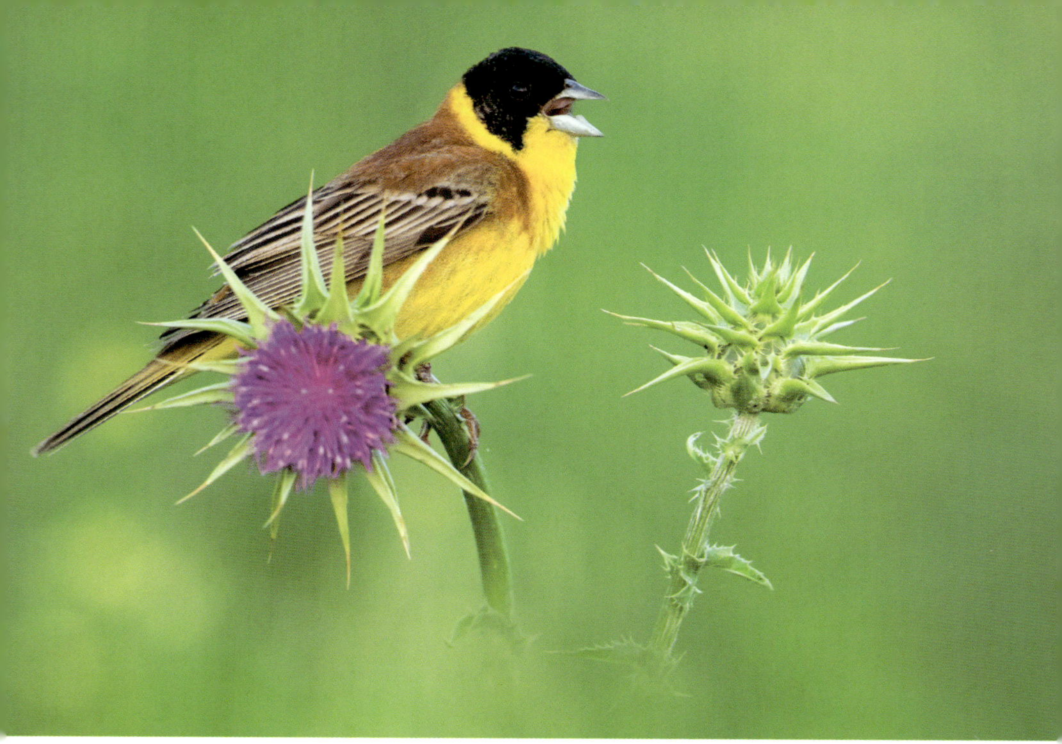

The colourful Black-headed Bunting migrates to the Caucasian Shrub Desert in summer, where it is widespread, especially in areas with enough song perches and thicket for breeding. © DANIELE OCCHIATO, AGAMI

The attractive Black Francolin is almost completely restricted to Caucasian Shrub Desert in Europe. It is far easier to hear than to see, thanks to its far-carrying mechanical song. © DANIELE OCCHIATO, AGAMI

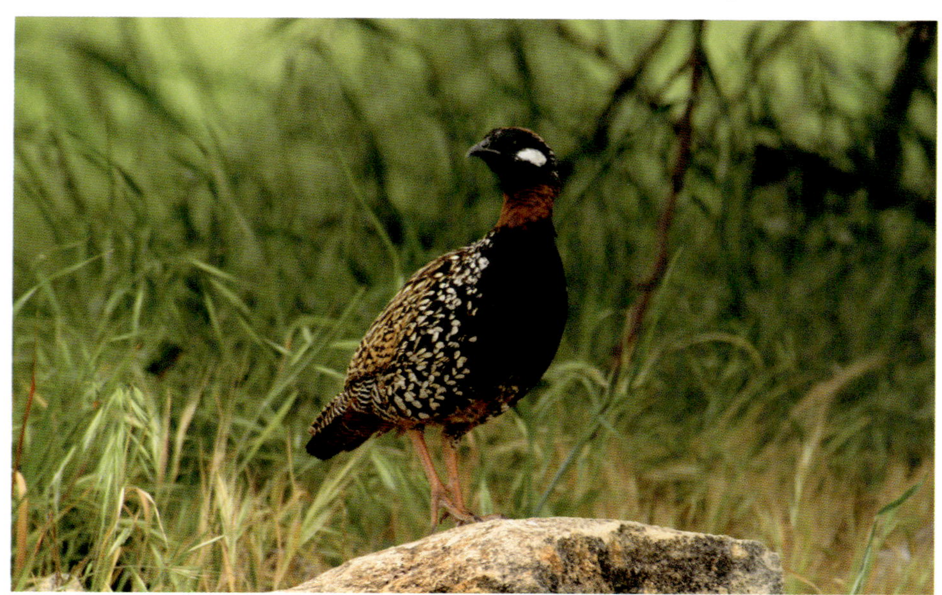

The pocket of Caucasian Shrub Desert on the Turkish border with Syria is particularly interesting, offering the only opportunities in Europe to find See-see Partridge, Cream-coloured Courser, and Pallid Scops-Owl (pictured). © PETE MORRIS

and joins other summer migrants like the European Bee-eater and European Roller. Black-headed Bunting is widespread in this habitat, especially where enough song perches and thickets for breeding are present. White-tailed Lapwing uses this habitat in summer, and Sociable Lapwing on passage. Menetries's Warbler is a good indicator of shrub and wormwood deserts (although it will also use MIDDLE EASTERN SAVANNA in Türkiye). Black Francolin is almost completely restricted to this habitat in Europe.

The pocket of Caucasian Shrub Desert on the Turkish border with Syria is particularly interesting, offering the only opportunities in Europe to see See-see Partridge, Cream-coloured Courser, and Pallid Scops-Owl. The fabulous See-see Partridge can be secretive but likes to sing from exposed rocks. A few other species closely associated with this habitat and region (although occurring sporadically elsewhere) include the Pale Rockfinch, Dead Sea Sparrow, Yellow-throated Sparrow, Eastern Rock Nuthatch, and Iraq Babbler (along watercourses). Little Swift and Pin-tailed Sandgrouse both occur here and in s. Iberia.

The Caucasian Shrub Desert is an exciting habitat for reptile fans, home to many range-restricted and special species. Red-bellied Racer (*Dolichophis schmidti*), Spotted Whip Snake (*Hemorrhois ravergieri*), Levantine Viper (*Macrovipera lebetinus*), Caucasian Agama (*Paralaudakia caucasia*), Snake-eyed Lizard (*Ophisops elegans*), Caspian Bent-toed Gecko (*Tenuidactylus caspius*), European Glass Lizard (*Pseudopus apodus*), Caspian Green Lizard (*Lacerta strigata*), and Rapid Racerunner (*Eremias velox*) are all regional and habitat specialties. However, it is the Urartian Rat Snake (*Elaphe urartica*) that really stands out—it is a local endemic, almost completely restricted to the Caucasian Shrub Desert. The Greek Tortoise (*Testudo graeca*) slowly meanders about among the other reptiles.

CONSERVATION: Much of the region is under intense pressure from overgrazing by sheep and goats. This leads to the suppression of more palatable plants and a considerable loss of biodiversity. Development along the Caspian coast of Azerbaijan is encroaching on the coastal flat areas of this habitat. Reserves such as Shirvan National Park, which was mainly created to protect the Goitred Gazelle, and parks to protect the mud volcanoes serve as a refuge for most of the desert species in Azerbaijan.

DISTRIBUTION: In Europe, this habitat exists on the western edge of the Caspian Sea in Georgia and Azerbaijan between the Greater and Lesser Caucasus. It is also found in the border area between Armenia, Türkiye, Azerbaijan (Nakhchivan), and Iran. The habitat is extensive in Syria (not treated in this book), and a small pocket extends into s. Türkiye. It also extends through Asia in a band from Syria through Iraq and Iran to Afghanistan.

WHERE TO SEE: Shirvan National Park, Azerbaijan; Gobustan National Park, Azerbaijan; Goravan Sands State Sanctuary, Armenia; Birecik, Şanlıurfa, Türkiye.

This is the only habitat in Europe in which the rare Goitred Gazelle is found, albeit rarely.
© VINCENT LEGRAND, AGAMI

Eu2C CAUCASIAN MONTANE DESERT STEPPE

IN A NUTSHELL: Cold desert grasslands found in the Caucasus Mountains. **Global Habitat Affinities:** CHENOPOD SHRUBLAND; SUCCULENT PUNA; CASPIAN WORMWOOD DESERT; SAGEBRUSH SHRUBLAND. **Continental Habitat Affinities:** CAUCASIAN SHRUB DESERT; GARRIGUE. **Species Overlap:** CAUCASIAN SHRUB DESERT.

DESCRIPTION: The Caucasian Montane Desert Steppes are the highland desert grasslands and shrublands of se. Europe. They are a mélange of grassland patches, thornscrubs, and spiny heaths on the sides of dry mountains between about 650 and 2500 m (2000–8200 ft.) elevation. The climate is cold semi-arid, to arid with 300–700 mm (12–28 in.) of rainfall per year (Köppen **Bsk**). Most of the precipitation occurs in the (snowy) winters,

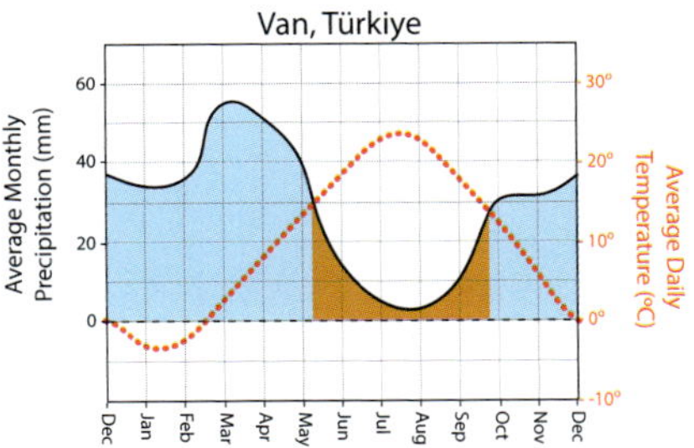

Steeper slopes and mountainsides create a diversity of microhabitats within the Caucasian Montane Desert Steppe. © IAIN CAMPBELL, TROPICAL BIRDING

The Caucasian Montane Desert Steppe can have surprisingly dense vegetation (like a classic steppe) but is dry and desolate at other times (more like a desert).
© IAIN CAMPBELL, TROPICAL BIRDING

when temperatures average around −7 to −3°C (19–27°F). Summers are warm (21–26°C/70–79°F) and dry.

The dry summer months result in extreme plant stress lasting up to five months and mean that the plant communities are dominated by xerophytic (drought-tolerant) shrubs and herbs. Somewhat thicker groves even feel similar to Phrygana, the eastern subhabitat of GARRIGUE. Plant cover is typically 30–100 cm (12–40 in.) high and dominated by species such as the Yellow-flowered Skullcap (*Scutellaria orientalis*), Eastern Catmint (*Nepeta racemosa*), Hydrangea Sage (*Salvia hydrangea*), Sickle Alfalfa (*Medicago falcata*), various spurges (*Euphorbia* spp.), and Volga Pheasant's Eye (*Adonis wolgensis*). Horned Sainfoins (*Onobrychis cornuta*) and others form patches of thorny shrubs. The ground cover between these patches is a mix of the aforementioned herbs and grasses that are also widespread in the lowland steppe, including Valais Fescue (*Festuca valesiaca*), Prairie Junegrass (*Koeleria macrantha*), Horsetail Feathergrass (*Stipa tirsa*), Golden Feathergrass (*Stipa pulcherrima*), and Sheep's Fescue (*Festuca ovina*). Some grasses are, however, more restricted to highlands, such as Hairy Spike Koeleria (*Koeleria eriostachya*) and Wild Barley (*Hordeum brevisubulatum*).

The high percentage of endemic plants is due to the crossover between European and Asian species. Most of these species evolved in the Pleistocene, when multiple glacial events isolated the Caucasus from the European and Asian communities. The Caucasian plant communities have much stronger affinities with the mountain semi-desert environments of c. Asia than they do with the rest of Europe, and this habitat is the European extension of the habitat concentrated in the mountains of Iran and Afghanistan.

Crimson-winged Finch, a Caucasian Montane Desert Steppe habitat specialist, moves high up the mountains when conditions allow but quickly moves back down when snow falls. © DANIELE OCCHIATO, AGAMI

Radde's Accentor is almost completely restricted to Caucasian Montane Desert Steppe, although it will move to lower elevations in winter. © PETE MORRIS

WILDLIFE: The Crimson-winged Finch, Radde's Accentor, and White-throated Robin are almost completely restricted to the Caucasian Montane Desert Steppe within Europe (although they may also use higher MIDDLE EASTERN SAVANNA). A wonderful diversity of ground-feeding wheatears can be found in the summer months, including Northern, Isabelline, Eastern Black-eared, Pied,

The uncommon Mongolian Finch is easiest to find around drinking pools in this dry habitat.

and Finsch's Wheatears. Europe's only Persian Wheatears are found in the dry desert hills of Armenia and Azerbaijan (specifically the Nakhchivan Autonomous Republic). They are joined by other sought-after birds, such as Mongolian Finch, Grey-necked Bunting, Black-headed Bunting, Bimaculated Lark, Pale Rockfinch, Eastern Rock Nuthatch, and Rosy (Rose-coloured) Starling. Chukar is the main partridge of the habitat and remains here throughout the year. Short-toed Snake-Eagle, Golden Eagle, and (Eastern) Imperial Eagle scour Caucasian Montane Desert Steppes from the air. Upcher's Warbler and Rock Sparrow are both strongly associated with this habitat.

The Montane Desert Steppe holds many exciting and localised reptiles, including the Caucasian Agama (*Paralaudakia caucasia*), Medium Lizard (*Lacerta media*), Caspian Green Lizard (*Lacerta strigata*), Dagestan Lizard (*Darevskia daghestanica*), Dahl's Whip Snake (*Platyceps najadum*), and Spotted Whip Snake (*Hemorrhois ravergieri*). The vipers are particularly diverse in this habitat, with some really special species including the Transcaucasian Long-nosed Viper (*Vipera transcaucasiana*), Alburzi Viper (*Vipera eriwanensi*), Wagner's Viper (*Montivipera wagneri*), Caucasus Blunt-nosed Viper (*Macrovipera lebetinus* ssp. *obtusa*), Lotiev's Viper (*Vipera lotievi*), and Steppe Viper (*Vipera renardi*).

CONSERVATION: This habitat is natural in most mountainous areas but anthropogenic in some locations, where extensive clearing of previous JUNIPER AND CYPRESS FOREST, MAQUIS, or MEDITERRANEAN OAK FOREST has resulted in the degradation of xeric scrubs and dryland grasses. Extensive overgrazing by sheep and goats is now a conservation issue, with more palatable plants being consumed and less palatable thorn-cushion plants thriving and dominating. Climate change will likely have a severely detrimental effect, especially on the higher-elevation areas that rely on more fog for moisture, if there are increases in both temperature and aridity.

DISTRIBUTION: The Caucasian Montane Desert Steppe is found in semi-arid areas in both the Greater and the Lesser Caucasus Mountains of Georgia, Russia, Armenia, Azerbaijan, and Türkiye. There are small outliers in Mediterranean regions such as the Italian Peninsula and the Peloponnese of s. Greece. The habitat extends into Syria, Iran, and Afghanistan.

WHERE TO SEE: Nehram Mountains, Nakhchivan, Azerbaijan; Khosrov Forest State Reserve, Armenia; Mt. Tendürek, Ağrı and Van Provinces, Türkiye.

Grey-necked Bunting is a highly sought-after speciality of this habitat. © RALPH MARTIN, AGAMI

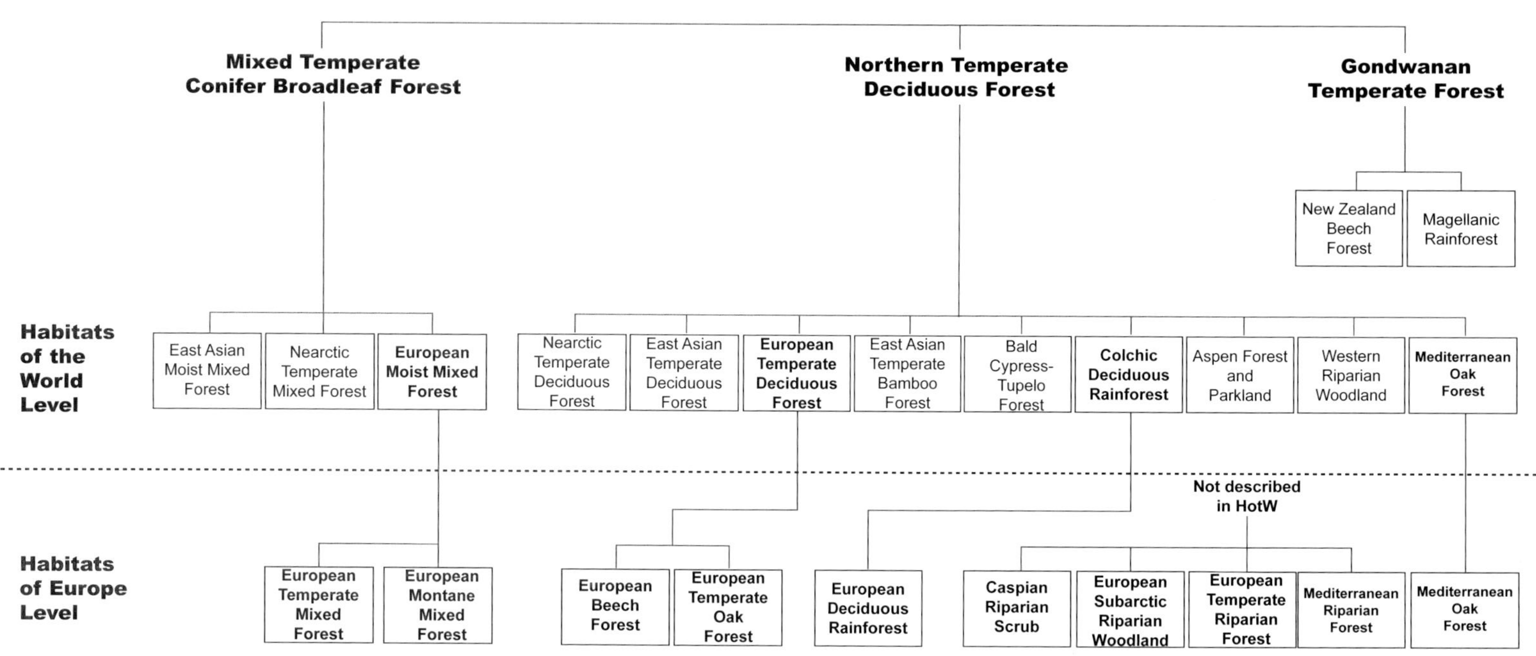
TEMPERATE BROADLEAF WOODLANDS
Mixed Temperate Conifer Broadleaf Forest
Northern Temperate Deciduous Forest
Gondwanan Temperate Forest
New Zealand Beech Forest
Magellanic Rainforest
Habitats of the World Level
East Asian Moist Mixed Forest
Nearctic Temperate Mixed Forest
European Moist Mixed Forest
Nearctic Temperate Deciduous Forest
East Asian Temperate Deciduous Forest
European Temperate Deciduous Forest
East Asian Temperate Bamboo Forest
Bald Cypress-Tupelo Forest
Colchic Deciduous Rainforest
Aspen Forest and Parkland
Western Riparian Woodland
Mediterranean Oak Forest
Not described in HotW
Habitats of Europe Level
European Temperate Mixed Forest
European Montane Mixed Forest
European Beech Forest
European Temperate Oak Forest
European Deciduous Rainforest
Caspian Riparian Scrub
European Subarctic Riparian Woodland
European Temperate Riparian Forest
Mediterranean Riparian Forest
Mediterranean Oak Forest

TEMPERATE BROADLEAF WOODLANDS

Eu3A EUROPEAN TEMPERATE OAK FOREST

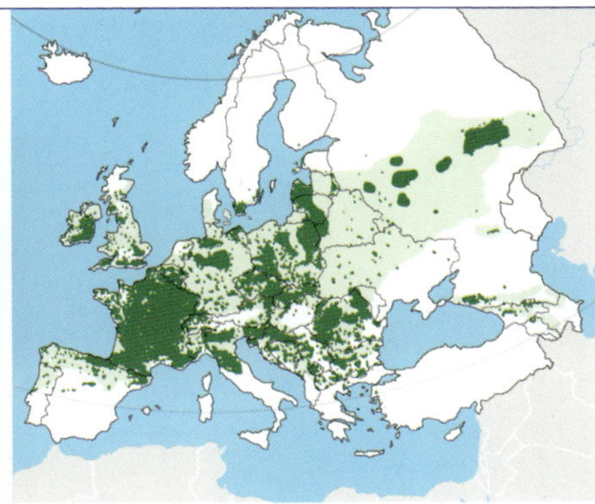

IN A NUTSHELL: The oak-hornbeam forests found throughout much of temperate Europe, particularly in the lowlands where beech is not able to dominate. **Global Habitat Affinities:** NEARCTIC TEMPERATE DECIDUOUS FOREST; EAST ASIAN TEMPERATE DECIDUOUS FOREST. **Continental Habitat Affinities:** MEDITERRANEAN OAK FOREST; FOREST STEPPE. **Species Overlap:** MEDITERRANEAN OAK FOREST; BEECH FOREST.

DESCRIPTION: Temperate Oak Forests are beautiful, enchanting places. Towering oaks, a lush understorey of hornbeams, and diverse undergrowth make for forests filled with lively bird song, and it is easy to imagine Guinevere and Sir Lancelot suddenly appearing around the corner on horseback. Though we would argue that finding a nesting Middle Spotted Woodpecker or hearing the cascading song of a Red-breasted Flycatcher is even better.

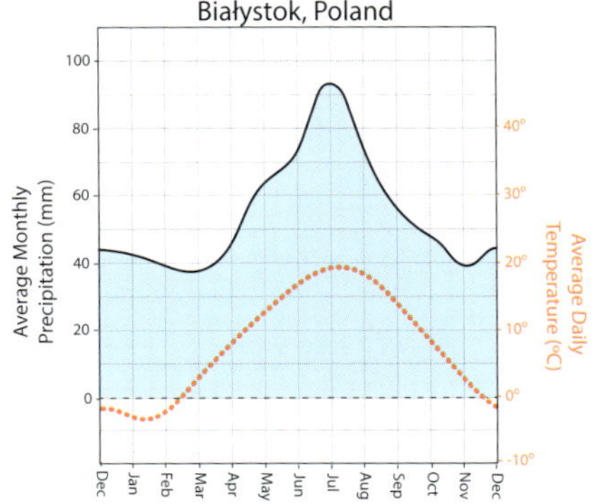

Temperate Oak Forests (also known as Oak-Hornbeam Forests) are widespread throughout Europe and, by some estimates, could potentially cover up to 10% of the region. They are most extensive in France, with significant pockets in the UK, Poland, the Baltic states, and Romania. The forest prefers milder temperatures (av. 9°C/48°F; Köppen **Cfb/Dfb**), so it is mostly found at lower elevations in the north, retreating to higher elevations in the Mediterranean.

The canopy is structurally complex and species-diverse with a large component of oaks. English Oak (*Quercus robur*) and Sessile Oak (*Q. petraea*) are key species, but other oaks may

A sea of Temperate Oak Forest in ne. Poland. © IAIN CAMPBELL, TROPICAL BIRDING

Temperate Oak Forests are a lush dream in springtime, filled with life and interesting creatures to discover. © IAIN CAMPBELL, TROPICAL BIRDING

The oak forest's understorey can be surprisingly open, especially where the canopy is dense and browsing pressure is high. © IAIN CAMPBELL, TROPICAL BIRDING

be regionally important. Other abundant canopy and subcanopy species include the European Hornbeam (*Carpinus betulus*); Small-leaved and Silver Limes (*Tilia cordata, T. tomentosa*); European and Narrow-leaved Ashes (*Fraxinus excelsior, F. angustifolia*); Sweet Chestnut (*Castanea sativa*); Sycamore, Field, and Norway Maples (*Acer pseudoplatanus, A. campestre, A. platanoides*); Service-Tree (*Cormus domestica*); and Wych Elm (*Ulmus glabra*). European Beech (*Fagus sylvatica*) is present in the climatic and geographic zones of transition to BEECH FOREST. The shrub and herb layers are dominated by widely distributed deciduous species, including Common Hazel (*Corylus avellana*), Asarabacca (*Asarum europaeum*), May Lily (*Maianthemum bifolium*), Bastard Balm (*Melittis melissophyllum*), and Sweet Woodruff (*Galium odoratum*). Common Hawthorn (*Crataegus monogyna*) and Midland Hawthorn (*Crataegus laevigata*) are also abundant, and their fruits provide welcome food for Bohemian Waxwings and various thrushes in winter. In spring, their abundant nectar and pollen attract a variety of insects, while their spikiness offers refuge for breeding birds.

Regional specialties, such as Narrow-leaved Lungwort (*Pulmonaria longifolia*), Cuckoo-pint (*Arum maculatum*), Barren Strawberry (*Potentilla sterilis*), Dwarf Masterwort (*Sanicula epipactis*), Butcher's-Broom (*Ruscus aculeatus*), and Blue Anemone (*Anemonoides apennina*), may be important components in local assemblages. This is especially the case with species that are restricted in range but regionally relatively abundant, in southern areas closer to ice-age oak forest refugia.

This habitat transitions to MEDITERRANEAN OAK FOREST at lower elevations and warmer sites with more pronounced winter precipitation. Temperate Oak Forest is unusual in the Alps, found only in warmer, drier locations, particularly deep in the valleys on the first slopes off the valley floor. In addition, these forests are widespread and dominant along the southern rim of the Alps, particularly below about 550 m (1800 ft.). Areas with well-drained, moist soils and a

The scarce Middle Spotted Woodpecker shows a strong preference for oaks. © RALPH MARTIN, AGAMI

The smart Collared Flycatcher is found in deciduous woodland in n. and e. Europe. © RALPH MARTIN, AGAMI

mild climate favour the development of BEECH FOREST. European Beech is an aggressive, dominant tree and will quickly become the most abundant tree in its Goldilocks climatic zone. The balance shifts in favour of Temperate Oak Forest when precipitation is somewhat lower (500–700 mm/20–28 in.) or more unpredictable, with intermittent droughts.

WILDLIFE: The Eurasian Jay is the regent and architect of oak forests, ubiquitous and critical to acorn dispersal. If you see a Middle Spotted Woodpecker or Collared Flycatcher, you are probably in or very close to Temperate Oak Forest (although in some areas, they use mixed-beech forests). White-backed Woodpeckers and Red-breasted Flycatchers in e. Europe are strongly associated with these forests. Hawfinch, Wood Warbler, European Pied Flycatcher, and Common Redstart will all use other habitats but are typically

White-backed Woodpecker and Red-breasted Flycatcher (pictured) in e. Europe are strongly associated with Temperate Oak Forest. © WALTER SOESTBERGEN, AGAMI

The stunning Hawfinch is a surprisingly shy and elusive species that uses its huge bill to crack open hard seeds. © DANIELE OCCHIATO, AGAMI

The tiny Common Firecrest inhabits a variety of mixed and deciduous woodlands and can be abundant in Temperate Oak Forest, particularly around patches of European Holly or Common Yew. © MARKUS VARESVUO, AGAMI

most abundant in Temperate Oak Forest. Europe's classic, generalist woodland birds are naturally plentiful in these forests, including Great, Blue, Marsh, and Long-tailed Tits, as well as Common Chiffchaff, European Robin, Eurasian Nuthatch, Eurasian Blackbird, and Song Thrush. Common Firecrest can be abundant, particularly around patches of European Holly (*Ilex aquifolium*) or Common Yew (*Taxus baccata*). Greater Spotted Eagle readily uses this habitat for breeding in e. Europe, provided enough open areas and wetlands are available nearby for feeding.

European Bison like mosaics of broadleaf and mixed forests, as well as open areas. They are loosely associated with Temperate Oak Forests in ne. Europe. Merck's Rhinoceros would likely have done well in this habitat had it not been driven to extinction during the last ice age. Grey Wolf, European Wildcat, Western Roe Deer, and Eurasian Wild Boar can be widespread, while Crested Porcupine can be found in Italy. Hazel and European Fat Dormice prefer habitats

A Hazel Dormouse eyes up a crop of ripening acorns. Hazel and European Fat Dormice prefer habitats dominated by oak and beech. © VINCENT LEGRAND, AGAMI

dominated by oak and beech. Important bat species include the Brown Big-eared Bat and Western Barbastelle.

The Fire Salamander (*Salamandra salamandra*) is associated with this forest type, although its density in drier versions of this forest is significantly lower than in BEECH FOREST. The Great Capricorn Beetle (*Cerambyx cerdo*) requires large, living oak trees, while the European Stag Beetle (*Lucanus cervus*) prefers decaying trees. The beautiful Purple and Ilex Hairstreaks (*Favonius quercus* and *Satyrium ilicis*) are both oak specialists, while the Eurasian White Admiral (*Limenitis camilla*) and Purple Emperor (*Apatura iris*) are regularly found in Temperate Oak Forest. The White-letter Hairstreak (*Satyrium w-album*) favours Temperate Oak Forest with abundant Wych Elm.

The impressive Great Capricorn Beetle (pictured) is easily recognisable. It requires large, living oak trees, while the European Stag Beetle prefers decaying trees.
© RALPH MARTIN, AGAMI

CONSERVATION: The most biodiverse Temperate Oak Forests are the ancient and primeval forests with complex and diverse age structures. In some forests, up to 30% of the trees can be dead wood, providing wildlife with myriad niches and opportunities. Unfortunately, these forests are found mostly in the lowlands and near human settlements. This proximity has been felt for millennia, and the forests have been heavily managed for timber and livestock, dramatically affecting forest structure and species composition. In addition, they are typically found on relatively well-drained basic soils with moderate to high nutrient levels—perfect for agriculture. As a result, few ancient forests remain, making those like the marvellous Białowieża Forest on the border between Poland and Belarus even more special.

DISTRIBUTION: Temperate Oak Forest is found throughout temperate Europe, with core areas in c. and ne. France as well as the region through s. Poland, Czechia, Slovakia, e. Austria, Slovenia, and n. Croatia. It replaces BEECH FOREST in much of Poland and to the east. Other notable areas include the north coast of Spain, Ireland, se. England, n. Germany, the southern tip of Sweden, and mid-elevations in Italy (especially the southern rim of the Alps up to about 600 m/2000 ft. elevation).

WHERE TO SEE: Boky National Nature Reserve, Zvolen, Slovakia; Zemplen Forest Reserve, Hungary; Maurer Wald, Vienna, Austria; Białowieża Forest, Poland and Belarus; Breite Oak Reserve, Romania.

Eu3B EUROPEAN BEECH FOREST

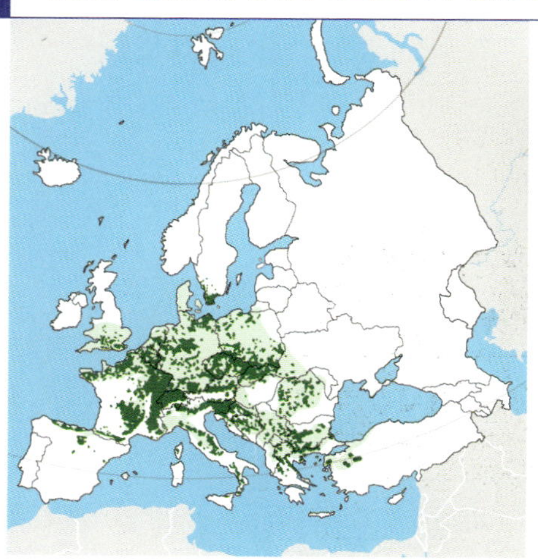

IN A NUTSHELL: Beech forests are rather uniform deciduous forests dominated by beech trees, mostly with a closed canopy, open understorey, and thick leaf litter. **Global Habitat Affinities:** NEARCTIC TEMPERATE DECIDUOUS FOREST; EAST ASIAN TEMPERATE DECIDUOUS FOREST. **Continental Habitat Affinities:** TEMPERATE OAK FOREST. **Species Overlap:** TEMPERATE MIXED FOREST; MONTANE MIXED FOREST.

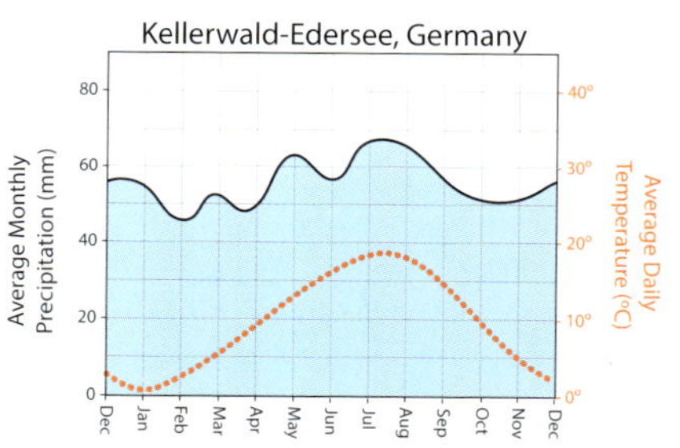

DESCRIPTION: There is something magical about strolling through the deep leaf litter of a Beech Forest on a warm spring morning, dawn sunlight streaming through the canopy, its beams like small, intense spotlights on the ghostly grey beech trunks. The first Wood Crickets (*Nemobius sylvestris*) of the season are chirping, and it is easy to imagine a colourful Fire Salamander (*Salamandra salamandra*) prowling nearby. With luck, you might even come across an inconspicuous White-backed Woodpecker working a fallen log.

The towering, dense canopy is overwhelmingly dominated by the deciduous European Beech (*Fagus sylvatica*) or Oriental Beech (*Fagus orientalis*), and their acidic, growth-inhibiting leaf litter accumulates to form a thick carpet. Decomposition is, however, significantly faster where beech is complemented by other deciduous species such as maples (*Acer* spp.), European Hornbeam (*Carpinus betulus*), European Ash (*Fraxinus excelsior*), or limes (*Tilia* spp.). There is remarkably little undergrowth, and few herbs make it through the leaf litter. Nevertheless, the sprinklings of flowering plants can be an absolute delight, including the Wood Anemone (*Anemonoides nemorosa*), Coralroot (*Cardamine bulbifera*), Sweet Woodruff (*Galium odoratum*), Yellow Archangel (*Lamium galeobdolon*), and Early Dog-Violet (*Viola reichenbachiana*).

The canopy is usually at about 20–30 m (66–100 ft.), but some older emergent trees can reach over 40 m (130 ft.). Gaps in the canopy are quickly filled by existing canopy trees, limiting the ability of other species and individuals to establish. Nonetheless, young beech trees are relatively shade

European Beech (*Fagus sylvatica*) is an aggressive, dominant tree and will quickly become the most abundant tree in its 'Goldilocks' climatic zone.

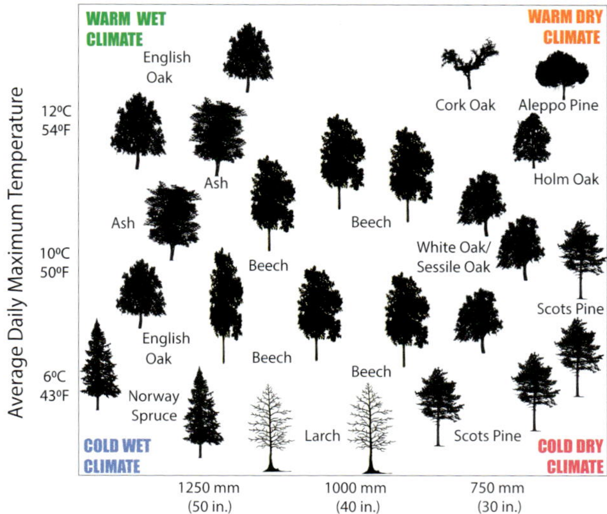

tolerant, thus allowing them to establish and quickly occupy a new gap in the canopy. As a result, 90% of the canopy can be occupied by beech, and it is only when climatic conditions are somewhat harsher that other tree species can compete successfully. Beech Forests find their Goldilocks zone and dominate in moderate climates (Köppen **Cfb**), with an average annual temperature of about 9°C (48°F) and rainfall of about 550–850 mm (21–33 in.) per year.

Beech was one of the last tree species to recolonise large swaths of Europe after the last ice age, spreading up from Mediterranean refugia and gradually becoming likely the most pervasive tree species in European forests. Where the English Oak (*Quercus robur*) was once dominant, beech successively became the most successful tree through its assertive occupation of space, no doubt helped by the human thinning of oaks (*Quercus* spp.), Common Hazel (*Corylus avellana*), and ashes (*Fraxinus* spp.). In areas where beeches have arrived, they invariably

This young Beech Forest has a few scattered Norway Spruce trees, but the canopy is otherwise almost completely dominated by beech. © DALE FORBES

outcompete all other species, relegating them to areas that are too dry, too wet, too hot, or too cold for the beech. Surprisingly, 67% of Germany would likely be covered in Beech Forest were it to be left undisturbed. The post-ice age expansion of beech through Europe continues with the forests slowly creeping deeper into Scandinavia and Poland.

WILDLIFE: The extensive Beech Forests we know through much of Europe have only developed in the past 6000 years or so. Thus, much of the wildlife associated with these forests has only recently started to use the habitat. There are very few habitat specialists,

Left: **Beech Forests can develop on mountain slopes, as pictured here, with Montane Mixed Forest at slightly higher elevation in the background.** © DALE FORBES

Below: **The beautiful autumnal hues of a Beech Forest.** © MENNO VAN DUIJN, AGAMI

Beech Forests are invariably the best places in c. Europe to find White-backed Woodpecker. It prefers old-growth forests, as it needs lots of dead wood, especially logs and trunks, on the ground. © RALPH MARTIN, AGAMI

but myriad species have found it particularly suited to their needs. However, many of these forests have been extensively managed, resulting in neat, clean forests of evenly aged trees. By contrast, old-growth forests with trees of diverse ages, very old trees, and a high density of dead wood offer myriad niches and are much more interesting for wildlife-watchers.

Woodpeckers are the highlight family, and Beech Forest is invariably the best place in c. Europe to find White-backed Woodpecker. However, the woodpecker prefers old-growth forests and need lots of dead wood, especially logs and trunks, on the ground. This is also the breeding habitat of the Red-breasted Flycatcher in c. Europe, especially if European Hornbeam is also present. Old-growth Beech Forests are also the preferred habitat for the remarkable Ural Owl.

Woodpeckers' relatively high density (and diversity) means that a wide range of cavities are made available to a wonderful assortment of birds and other creatures. These cavities are ideal

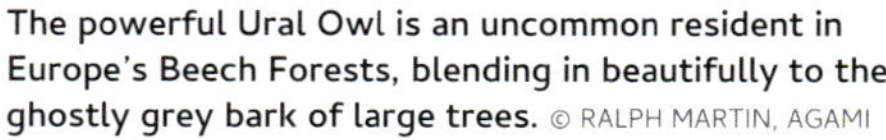

The powerful Ural Owl is an uncommon resident in Europe's Beech Forests, blending in beautifully to the ghostly grey bark of large trees. © RALPH MARTIN, AGAMI

Pine Martens are secretive inhabitants of many of Europe's woodlands but are particularly widespread in Beech Forests. © HAN BOUWMEESTER, AGAMI

for Collared and European Pied Flycatchers. Larger holes—especially those made by the Black Woodpecker—are particularly important to Boreal (Tengmalm's) Owl, Stock Dove, Eurasian Red Squirrel, Pine Marten, and Bechstein's Bat. Other notable mammals in Beech Forests include the Eurasian Wild Boar, Western Roe Deer, various rodents, and the Red Fox, European Wildcat, and Eurasian Lynx that feed on them. Keep a look out for the scratching signs of active European Badgers and Brown Bears, especially in the Carpathians.

Europe's generalist forest birds are naturally also common in these forests: European Robin, Song Thrush, Common Chiffchaff, Wood Warbler, Eurasian Blackcap, Common Chaffinch, and the Eurasian Sparrowhawk. Beech seeds are particularly important to Bramblings in the winter, and regional seeding and weather patterns can cause flocks of millions of birds to gather.

Fire Salamanders are invariably rare and will use a variety of broadleaf forests, but they are most abundant in the thick, moist leaf litter of Beech Forests. They seem to be easiest to find on warm, wet spring days, when they are more likely to explore the forest floor. Fascinatingly, there is a striking overlap in the distribution of Fire Salamander subspecies with the proposed locations of European Beech refugia during the last ice age. This may well have been the mechanism that drove divergence within Europe's Fire Salamanders, and overlaying the patterns of genetic diversity of Fire Salamanders and European Beech may well provide new insights into ice-age forest refugia. By way of example, the location of the Asturian Fire Salamander (*Salamandra salamandra alfredschmidti*) might indicate an as-yet-undescribed Beech Forest refuge.

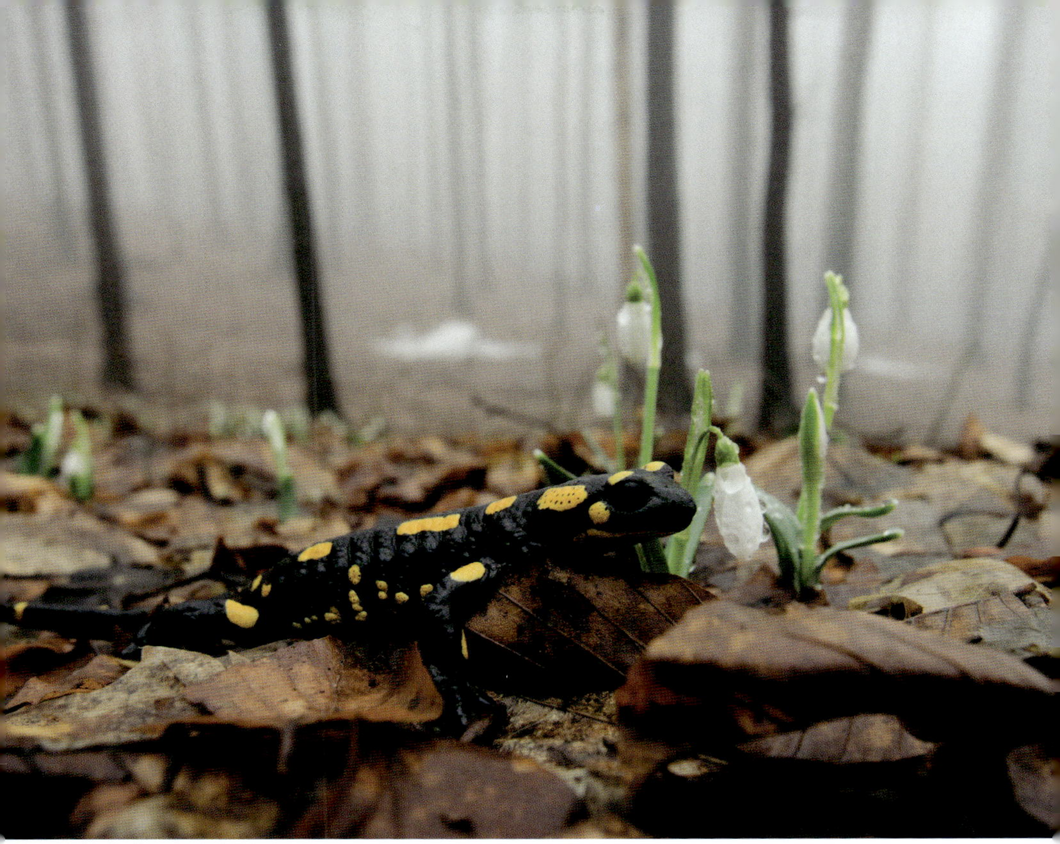

The spectacular Fire Salamander, remaining well concealed most of the time, is easiest to find on warm, wet spring days, when it is more likely to explore the forest floor. Fascinatingly, there is a striking overlap in the distribution of Fire Salamander subspecies with the proposed locations of European Beech refugia during the last ice age.
© ROB DE JONG, AGAMI

Wood Crickets sing on warm days as they clamber through the leaf litter, adding to a wonderful soundscape. A variety of lepidopterans use these forests, including the Tau Emperor Moth (*Aglia tau*). The Violet Click Beetle (*Limoniscus violaceus*) is both beautiful and rare. It is completely dependent on decaying beech and ash and is confined mostly to ancient

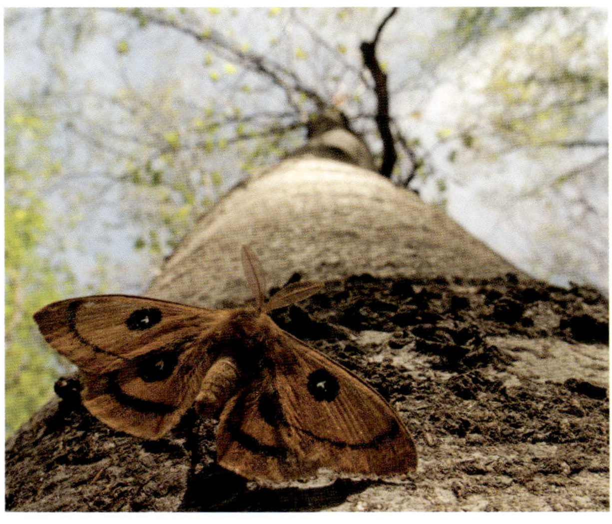

The Tau Emperor Moth, a huge silk moth, is an impressive inhabitant of Beech Forests.
© ROB DE JONG, AGAMI

forests. These forests are also important for the impressive European Stag Beetle (*Lucanus cervus*) and Alpine Longhorn Rosalia (*Rosalia alpina*).

CONSERVATION: Beech trees can be older than 250 years in natural forests, and some individuals in s. Italy are older than 500 years. Nevertheless, in managed forests the trees are typically harvested at 80–120 years. Clear-cutting and harvesting at this age dramatically reduce the biodiversity value of these forests. By contrast, selectively harvested forests with scattered individuals over 180 years old and more than 20 m^3/ha (285 cu. ft./ac.) of dead wood can approach the rich biodiversity of ancient forests. This is especially important for cavity-nesting birds, insects, epiphytes, fungi, and bryophytes.

Much of Europe's Beech Forest has been lost to agriculture and forestry. Scots Pine (*Pinus sylvestris*) became the dominant forestry tree in many areas of w. and c. Europe. However, foresters are increasingly establishing shelterwood practices in mixed-species forests in the hope that they will be more resilient to climate change. This could result in significantly more Beech Forests, but their biodiversity value will depend on their management.

DISTRIBUTION: European Beech Forest runs from Britain and Europe's Atlantic coast in the west to w. Poland, merging into TEMPERATE MIXED FOREST and TEMPERATE OAK FOREST. In Scandinavia, Beech Forest begins south of the TEMPERATE MIXED FOREST and SPRUCE-FIR TAIGA. In the north of its range, it can grow near the coast and in lowlands, but farther south, it retreats to the cooler montane zone. This is the main forest in w. Europe, but it is also found very locally in the Carpathians, Balkans, and even rarely into far w. Türkiye.

WHERE TO SEE: The Chilterns, England, UK; Val Cervara National Park of Abruzzo, Lazio and Molise, Italy; Uholka-Shyrokyi Luh, Zakarpattia Oblast, Ukraine; Kellerwald-Edersee National Park, Hessen, Germany; Kalkalpen National Park, Upper Austria, Austria; Ceahlău National Park, Neamț County, Romania; Sonian Forest, Belgium.

Right: **Beech Forests are important habitat for the amazing Alpine Longhorn Rosalia, one of Europe's most distinctive beetles.** © ROB DE JONG, AGAMI

Opposite: **European Stag Beetles require mature woodland with plenty of dead wood.** © ROB DE JONG, AGAMI

Eu3C EUROPEAN DECIDUOUS RAINFOREST

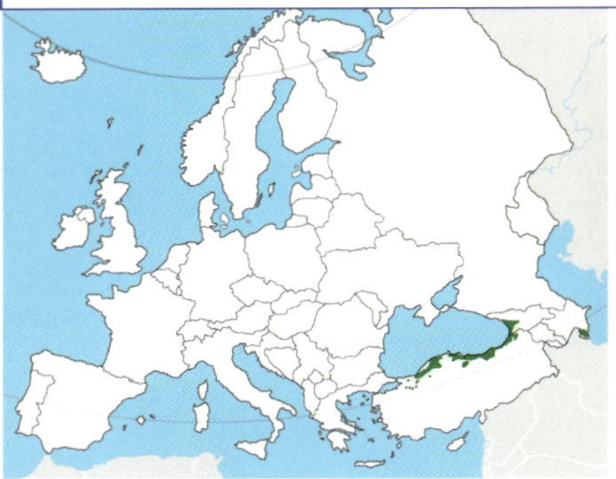

IN A NUTSHELL: Europe's rainforests are a bizarre mixture of deciduous canopy and evergreen undergrowth comprising three subhabitats: Euxine, Colchic, and Hyrcanian Forests. **Global Habitat Affinities:** HYRCANIAN DECIDUOUS FOREST; NEOTROPICAL MAGELLANIC RAINFOREST; NOTHOFAGUS RAINFOREST. **Continental Habitat Affinities:** TEMPERATE OAK FOREST; TEMPERATE MIXED FOREST; BEECH FOREST. **Species Overlap:** TEMPERATE OAK FOREST; TEMPERATE MIXED FOREST; BEECH FOREST.

DESCRIPTION: Lush Deciduous Rainforests hug the southern shores of the Black and Caspian Seas, with towering oaks, hornbeams, and beeches growing alongside firs and spruces. These temperate mixed forests are wet all year round, but, somewhat surprisingly for a rainforest, many of the canopy trees are deciduous. This is in stark contrast with other types of temperate rainforests, including the evergreen conifer NEARCTIC TEMPERATE RAINFOREST (North America) and the mainly non-deciduous MAGELLANIC and NOTHOFAGUS RAINFORESTS (in South America and Australia, respectively).

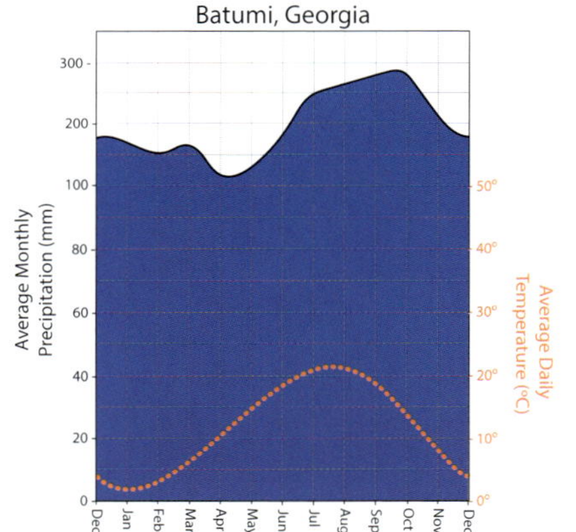

Europe's Deciduous Rainforests can be roughly divided into three subhabitats: the **Euxine Forest** of w. and c. Türkiye, the **Colchic Forest** of the se. Black Sea (in Georgia and e. Türkiye), and the **Hyrcanian Forest** skirting the s. Caspian Sea (mainly in Iran but also just making it into se. Azerbaijan). The diverse climatic conditions, varied mountain landscape forms, and location at the junction of temperate Europe with subtropical Asia combine to create a fascinating and unique habitat. Combined, these three Deciduous Rainforests encompass one of the most interesting forest blocks in the world.

Euxine Forest, though relatively drier than the other two subtypes, still gets 900–1500 mm (35–59 in.) of precipitation per year, and even the driest (spring) months get some rain (>50 mm/2 in.). The moist, temperate climate (Köppen **Cfa**, **Cfb**) is quite similar to the TEMPERATE OAK FOREST and TEMPERATE MIXED FOREST of c. Europe and shares many corresponding species. Sessile Oak (*Quercus petraea*), Turkey Oak (*Quercus cerris*), Oriental Beech (*Fagus*

Colchic Forest, Georgia. © IAIN CAMPBELL, TROPICAL BIRDING

orientalis), Common Hazel (*Corylus avellana*), Trojan Fir (*Abies nordmanniana* ssp. *equi-trojani*), and Scots Pine (*Pinus sylvestris*) are among the most important tree species.

Farther east, the **Colchic Forest** is fed by a steady stream of moisture-laden air, making it even wetter and thicker. The winds in this region are predominantly westerlies, and as they cross the Black Sea, they pick up a lot of evaporation. These moisture-laden air masses are funnelled between mountain ranges on the southern and northeastern shores of the Black Sea. When they hit the steep mountains of the southeastern coast, they drop their moisture as orographic rainfall.

Walking through the Colchic Forest of sw. Georgia in summer, with a rhododendron understorey, mosses, and water dripping from the trees, feels very similar to being in the HIMALAYAN TEMPERATE DECIDUOUS FOREST of the e. Himalayas. In winter, the feeling is starkly different, the canopy trees are leafless save the occasional evergreen conifer, but a seemingly impenetrable mass of evergreen shrubs covers the forest floor. It is this difference that makes this forest a truly special habitat in Europe.

The Colchic Forest region has a wet, almost subtropical, warm-temperate climate (Köppen **Cfa**) unlike any other in Europe. Summers are warm for Europe, averaging 21°C (70°F), and winters are cool, averaging 7°C (45°F). These temperatures are much like those in Barcelona, yet the Colchic region receives much more rain: 2400–4500 mm (95–177 in.) annually, compared to just 600 mm (24 in.) for Barcelona. Precipitation is much higher than in most other parts of Europe and distributed relatively evenly throughout the year. Even the driest months (in spring) see almost

100 mm (4 in.) of rain falling. There can be substantial snow cover in the Colchic Forest in winter, especially at higher elevations.

The makeup of the Colchic Forest changes from sea level to the tree line, but the extreme humidity remains. Throughout the elevational range, the Colchic Forest feels much more like Asian forests than other European ones, and anyone familiar with the Himalayan forests of Nepal or Bhutan will notice the similarities. Plant diversity is high in the lower elevations of the forest's range, below 500 m (1500 ft.). A suite of localised trees dominates the canopy and subcanopy, including Caucasian Fir (*Abies nordmanniana* ssp. *nordmanniana*), Caucasian Birch (*Betula pubescens* var. *litwinowii*), a subspecies of Common Alder (*Alnus glutinosa* ssp. *barbata*), Oriental Spruce (*Picea orientalis*), Oriental Beech (*Fagus orientalis*), Cappadocian Maple (*Acer cappadocicum*), Sweet Chestnut (*Castanea sativa*), and various oaks (including *Quercus hartwissiana*). The understorey is dominated by evergreen plants adapted to spending time under snow cover, where they are protected from severe frosts. Rhododendrons, such as Pontic Rhododendron (*Rhododendron ponticum*) and Ungern's Rhododendron (*Rhododendron ungernii*), are found throughout the elevational range of the forests. Other evergreen shrubs such as Pontic Daphne (*Daphne pontica*), Cherry Laurel (*Prunus laurocerasus*), and Alexandrian Laurel (*Danae racemosa*) are a major component of the understorey of the lower elevations and continue as a significant shrub layer species to the tree line. The ground between the shrubs is laden with a thick fern layer.

Between 500 and 1000 m (1500–3300 ft.) elevation, the canopy loses biodiversity and becomes dominated by Oriental Beech and Sweet Chestnut, while other canopy species from below

Deciduous Rainforests, not surprisingly, can be thick with vegetation, especially when relatively young. © IAIN CAMPBELL, TROPICAL BIRDING

Hyrcanian Forest, Azerbaijan. © IAIN CAMPBELL, TROPICAL BIRDING

become minor components. In contrast, the 3–4 m (9–12 ft.) tall understorey becomes very diverse, with many species of evergreen bushes that are more typical of a Himalayan moist forest than a European one, such as many rhododendron species, hollies, and Cherry Laurel. Above 1000 m (3000 ft.), Oriental Beech forests with rhododendron understoreys dominate, transitioning into MONTANE SPRUCE-FIR FOREST.

Hyrcanian Forest on the southern shores of the Caspian Sea is fascinating in its stark contrast to the surrounding deserts and steppes. Unlike Colchic Forest, Hyrcanian Forest is dominated by trees that are sensitive to frost and snow. Many of the most important plant species are localised, and the resulting community is quite distinct from those of other European forests. Trees of note include Chestnut-leaved Oak (*Quercus castaneifolia*), Caucasian Alder (*Alnus subcordata*), Velvet Maple (*Acer velutinum*), Persian Ironwood (*Parrotia persica*), and Caspian Locust (*Gleditsia caspia*). Conifers are rare. Oriental Beech is dominant in the montane zone, alongside European Hornbeam (*Carpinus betulus*) and Persian Oak (*Quercus macranthera*). Russian Ivy (*Hedera pastuchowii*) will often grow up into the canopy 30 m (100 ft.) overhead.

The difference between the Colchic and Hyrcanian Forests is more obvious in the undergrowth, because the Hyrcanian Forest floor does not accumulate as much snow as the Colchic Forest, so the understorey plants are not protected from desiccating winds. The forest floor is much more dominated by ferns, along with graminoids such as Spiked Sedge (*Carex spicata*), Slender False-Brome (*Brachypodium sylvaticum*), Wavyleaf Basketgrass (*Oplismenus undulatifilius*), Tor-Grass (*Brachypodium pinnatum*), and Southern Woodrush (*Luzula forsteri*).

This area remained forested during the Pleistocene ice ages, when the cold, dry conditions converted much of Europe to tundra or steppe. Consequently, this habitat was a refugium for many of the species found in Beech, Temperate Oak, and Temperate Mixed Forests. It was from here that much of the region's deciduous forest species recolonised a warming Europe.

These are the best forests in Europe for Green Warblers. © DANIELE OCCHIATO, AGAMI

Right: The Caucasian form of Mountain Chiffchaff (sometimes treated as a full species) is restricted to this region. © DANIELE OCCHIATO, AGAMI

Below: The stunning Common Firecrest occurs in mixed and deciduous forests across the region. © WALTER SOESTBERGEN, AGAMI

WILDLIFE: Botanical similarities and the general feel between these forests and those of e. Asia are not mirrored in their wildlife, with these forests being extremely depauperate relative to similar-looking forests of the Himalayas. It also seems incongruous that a forest that is botanically so distinct from any other in the European region does not have an equally distinctive animal assemblage. The European Deciduous Rainforest is stark in its lack of resident bird species, but it is likely the best habitat in Europe to see the Green Warbler. The endemic Caucasian Chiffchaff (a subspecies of Mountain Chiffchaff) occurs here, along with widespread species such as Common Firecrest, Short-toed Treecreeper, Middle Spotted and Grey-headed Woodpeckers, Red-breasted Flycatcher (especially in the Hyrcanian Forest), Eurasian Blackcap, Semicollared Flycatcher, Common Redstart, and European Robin. Europe's only Shikras are found in and around the Hyrcanian Forest, and the Caspian Tit is wholly restricted to this forest. The Deciduous Rainforest zone is an important funnel for raptor migration,

Caspian Tit is restricted to the Hyrcanian Forests of Azerbaijan and Iran. © PETE MORRIS

Shikra is predominantly an inhabitant of drier habitats in Africa and Asia but sneaks into Europe in Azerbaijan's Hyrcanian Forests. © ARIE OUWERKERK, AGAMI

and more than 1 million birds of 35 species use it, including over half the world's populations of European Honey-Buzzard, Levant Sparrowhawk, and Booted Eagle.

Caspian Tigers hunted Eurasian Wild Boars in the Deciduous Rainforests and surrounding riparian forests well into the 20th century. Caucasian Squirrel and Southern White-breasted Hedgehog can be locally common. The Iranian Fat Dormouse is restricted to the Hyrcanian Forest.

Amphibians seem much more indicative of the special nature of the Deciduous Rainforests. Keep a look out for Caucasian Toad (*Bufo verrucosissimus*), Caucasian Parsley Frog (*Pelodytes caucasicus*), Caucasian Salamander (*Mertensiella caucasica*), and Caucasian Banded Newt (*Ommatotriton ophryticus*).

CONSERVATION: Illegal logging and expansion of farming threaten the Deciduous Rainforest, with the situation in Azerbaijan and Georgia being worse than that in Türkiye. Azerbaijan has increased efforts to monitor and control illegal logging activities, undertaken extensive reforestation, and created Hirkan National Park to protect these unique forests. International recognition as the Hyrcanian Forests UNESCO World Heritage Site is bringing attention to the area and increasing the tourism potential of se. Azerbaijan. Ecotourism in the Colchic Forest of Georgia has resulted in better conservation in the touristed areas and better control of illegal logging and poaching in the region.

DISTRIBUTION: European Deciduous Rainforest is found in a belt along the southern edges of the Black and Caspian Seas. It ranges from sea level to 2000 m (6500 ft.). The drier Euxine Forest extends from the Türkiye-Bulgaria border (where it merges with BEECH FOREST and TEMPERATE OAK FOREST) to e. Türkiye. Colchic Forest is found around the southeastern corner of the Black Sea and mainly occurs in Georgia and far ne. Türkiye. Hyrcanian Forest occurs in the southwest of the Caspian Sea lowlands and Talish Mountains of se. Azerbaijan, continuing into the Elburz Mountains of Iran.

WHERE TO SEE: Colchic Forest—Mtirala National Park, Georgia; **Hyrcanian Forest**—Hirkan National Park, Azerbaijan; **Euxine Forest**—Yedigöller National Park, Türkiye.

The localised Caucasian Squirrel lives in a variety of deciduous and mixed forests but is likely easiest to find in Euxine and Colchic Forests. © VINCENT LEGRAND, AGAMI

Eu3D EUROPEAN TEMPERATE MIXED FOREST

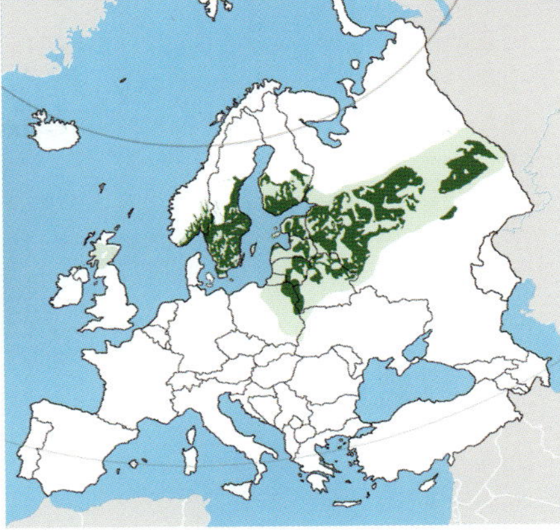

IN A NUTSHELL: Mixed deciduous and coniferous forest, typically with beech or oak combined with pine or spruce. **Global Habitat Affinities:** NEARCTIC TEMPERATE MIXED FOREST; MANCHURIAN DECIDUOUS FOREST. **Continental Habitat Affinities:** MONTANE MIXED FOREST. **Species Overlap:** TEMPERATE OAK FOREST; BEECH FOREST; MONTANE MIXED FOREST.

DESCRIPTION: Europe has pure broadleaf forests, pure coniferous forests, and everything in between. When the balance is roughly even (30–70% of each type), the wildlife community resembles a mixture of broadleaf and coniferous assemblages. These are some of the continent's richest and most interesting forests. European Badgers snuffle around for worms, Eurasian Woodcocks rode (perform display flights) overhead, and any of Europe's tits could be hopping about. The main canopy species are Scots Pine (*Pinus sylvestris*), Norway Spruce (*Picea abies*), various oaks (especially English Oak, *Quercus robur*), Silver Birch (*Betula pendula*), Common Alder (*Alnus glutinosa*), European Hornbeam (*Carpinus betulus*), and European Beech (*Fagus sylvatica*). All are usually found in mosaics of different monotypic clusters, but complex mélange-like mixtures are also common. Spruce and pine dominate the extremes of nutrient-poor, boggy, or dry, sandy soils. Pedunculate Oak (*Quercus robur*), European Hornbeam, and Small-leaved Lime (*Tilia cordata*) are more common on heavier clay-rich and relatively fertile soils where conditions are not so extreme. These can develop into TEMPERATE OAK FOREST, often with admixtures of spruce.

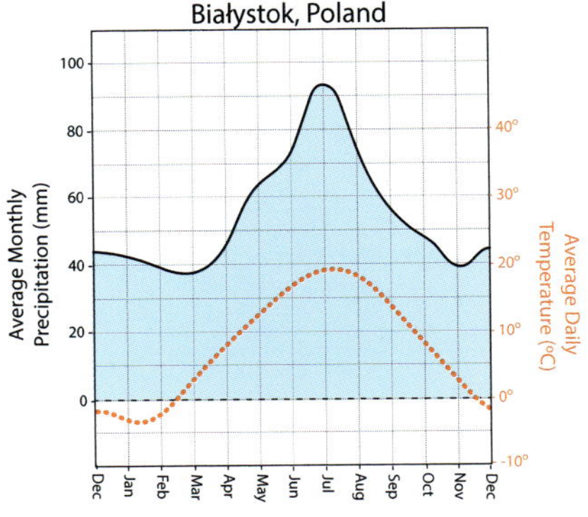

The climate of these c. European forests tends to be much milder (Köppen **Dfb**) than that of the MONTANE MIXED FOREST to the south or the conifer forests to the east and north. Average temperatures range from −5 to 18°C (23–65°F), and precipitation is fairly consistent throughout the year. There is often a weak understorey of mature trees, and much light reaches the forest floor. The shrub layer is surprisingly thin and dominated by shrubs and forbs rather than grasses, including Alder Buckthorn (*Frangula alnus*), Common Heather (*Calluna vulgaris*), Common Juniper (*Juniperus communis*), Common Bilberry (*Vaccinium myrtillus*), Lingonberry (*Vaccinium vitis-idaea*), and Lesser Rattlesnake Plantain (*Goodyera repens*). Mosses can be diverse and extensive, and the assemblage may include haircap mosses (*Polytrichum* spp.), Pincushion Moss (*Leucobryum glaucum*), plaitmosses (*Hypnum* spp.), and Stag's-horn Clubmoss (*Lycopodium clavatum*). Large bare patches without undergrowth can develop where pine needles or beech leaves accumulate.

In e. Europe, the climate becomes much more severe, with hotter summers and colder winters. Here, beech becomes much less common, reaching its limits in Poland and w. Ukraine. From Estonia to the Urals, the forests lack beech and become much more diverse as a mélange rather than a mosaic (a subhabitat called **Sarmatic Mixed Forest**). The Pedunculate Oak and European Hornbeam dominate (see TEMPERATE OAK FOREST) but may be joined by codominant conifers (especially Norway Spruce, often as a canopy emergent, and Scots Pine). Other canopy species include Sycamore Maple (*Acer pseudoplatanus*), Norway Maple (*Acer platanoides*), European Ash (*Fraxinus excelsior*), European Aspen (*Populus tremula*), Common Alder, and Silver Birch. They are magnificent in their messiness: there can be groves of low alder and birch 15 m (45 ft.) tall and towering emergent Norway Spruce at 40 m (120 ft.), making the birch appear as a mere understorey; turn another way, and there can be old, yet stunted Scots Pine forming a dense, tall grove of equal height. This biodiversity and myriad growth forms and canopy structure in such a small area make walking through this forest interesting at every turn.

Temperate Mixed Forest, Poland. © IAIN CAMPBELL, TROPICAL BIRDING

Temperate Mixed Forest, Lithuania. © IAIN CAMPBELL, TROPICAL BIRDING

Sarmatic Mixed Forest, Latvia. © IAIN CAMPBELL, TROPICAL BIRDING

WILDLIFE: These forests can teem with life and hold a wonderful diversity of species. They really can feel like the best of both coniferous and broadleaf worlds. Coal Tit, Red Crossbill, Eurasian Three-toed Woodpecker, Eurasian Pygmy-Owl, and Boreal (Tengmalm's) Owl are all associated with coniferous forests but readily use mixed forests too. By comparison, predominantly broadleaf-favouring species that also use mixed forest include Red-breasted Flycatcher, White-backed Woodpecker, and Short-toed Treecreeper (which especially likes a mix of oaks and pines). Additional birds to look out for include Lesser Spotted Eagle, Eurasian Woodcock, Redwing (provided there is also a mosaic of open areas), European Pied Flycatcher, and Greenish Warbler. The Middle Spotted Woodpecker is strongly associated with oaks, so if you are watching one and can hear a Coal Tit or Red Crossbill, you are likely standing in a Temperate Mixed Forest.

Eurasian Pygmy-Owl is a fierce predator despite its tiny size, sometimes taking prey almost as big as itself! © MARKUS VARESVUO, AGAMI

Eurasian Woodcock is a shy denizen of the forest floor. © ARTO JUVONEN, AGAMI

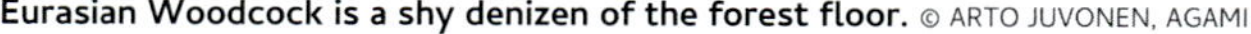

The migratory European Pied Flycatcher can be relatively common in this forest type. © SERGIO PITAMITZ, AGAMI

Greenish Warbler is uncommon and localised in Europe, found almost only in Temperate Mixed Forest, especially Sarmatic Mixed Forest. © RALPH MARTIN, AGAMI

This habitat is home to Europe's most charismatic mammals, including European Bison, European Wildcat, Grey Wolf, and Brown Bear. Other more common and widespread mammals include Red Deer, Western Roe Deer, Brown Hare, rodents, Pine Marten, Eurasian Wild Boar, and European Badger.

Some characteristic butterflies to keep a look out for include Poplar Admiral (*Limenitis populi*), Eurasian White Admiral (*Limenitis camilla*), and Dryad (*Minois dryas*).

CONSERVATION: Much of this forest has been cleared for agriculture over the millennia. In addition, the popularity of pine and spruce for timber has resulted in the conversion of vast areas to coniferous monocultures. Monocultures are invariably sad, dreary places for wildlife enthusiasts. However, climate change and recent research into tree growth rates have led to a rethinking in European forestry, with a major move towards mixed forests. Oaks, hornbeams, maples, lindens, and other trees are increasingly being planted or allowed to develop under and among older conifers. In the coming decades, we will see more and more mixed forests in Europe, and even if they are plantations, they will inevitably be better for biodiversity.

DISTRIBUTION: Temperate Mixed Forest is found from about 60°N in far s. Finland, s. Sweden, and n. Estonia south into Germany and across to the Ural Mountains. Smaller areas of this forest are also found in the Scottish Highlands, as well as n. Spain, and other mountainous areas of Europe (not all mapped).

WHERE TO SEE: Białowieża Forest, Poland and Belarus; Düben Heath Nature Park, Saxony-Anhalt, Germany; Brienz, Bern, Switzerland.

Small populations of Grey Wolf cling on in Europe, though as the human population increases, this macro-predator is forced into more and more remote areas. It would naturally thrive in Temperate Mixed Forest.
© SERGIO PITAMITZ, AGAMI

Below: European Bison went extinct in the wild in the 1920s, but captive breeding, reintroductions, and protection have meant that Europe's largest extant mammal can be seen in the wild again.
© MENNO VAN DUIJN, AGAMI

Eu3E EUROPEAN MONTANE MIXED FOREST

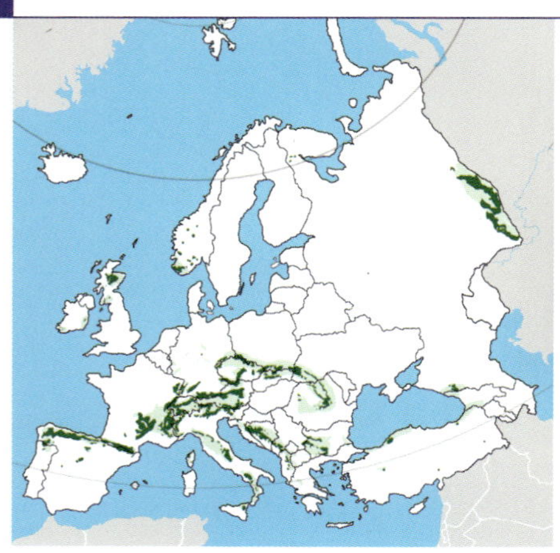

IN A NUTSHELL: The vast mixed forests of Europe's mountains, dominated primarily by European Beech, Norway Spruce, and Silver Fir. **Global Habitat Affinities:** NEARCTIC MONTANE MIXED-CONIFER FOREST; HIMALAYAN MONTANE MIXED FOREST. **Continental Habitat Affinities:** MONTANE SPRUCE-FIR FOREST. **Species Overlap:** MONTANE SPRUCE-FIR FOREST; MONTANE PINE FOREST; BEECH FOREST.

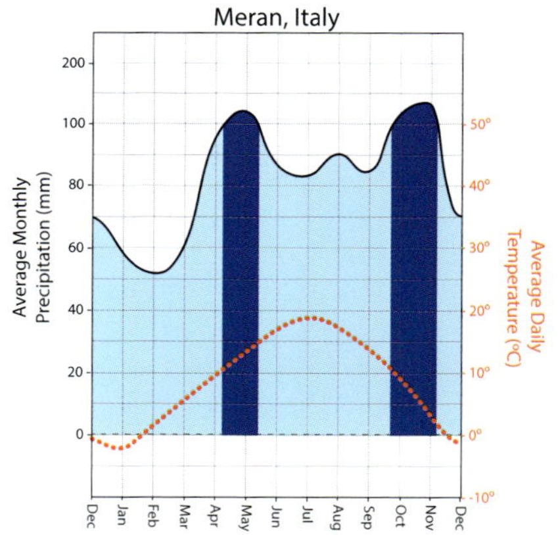

DESCRIPTION: Just the thought of bears, wolves, lynx, and bison lurking around the next corner is absolutely thrilling. Even without the 'big and hairies', Montane Mixed Forest is an absolute delight for the wildlife enthusiast. The somewhat higher diversity in tree species creates diverse niches for a wonderful array of other plants, as well as invertebrates, birds, and mammals.

Europe's montane and submontane forests include extensive mixed intergrades between the predominant areas of MONTANE SPRUCE-FIR FOREST, MONTANE PINE FOREST, BEECH FOREST, and TEMPERATE OAK FOREST. This typically results in greater biodiversity within these mixed forests, with assemblages from both the conifer-dominated and the angiosperm-dominated forest types. Moreover, there are large regional differences in canopy species in these mixed forests.

Coniferous species gain a competitive advantage over broadleaf species in harsher climates, while deciduous species can dominate in more temperate locations. Nebulous intergrades and mélanges form in climatically intermediate areas (see Introduction: Types of Habitat Boundaries and Ecotones). Large areas can appear in some regions as a blend of broadleaf and coniferous tree species (with a nebulous boundary). The situation is more complex in areas with diverse and varied microclimates. Here, homogeneous mixtures are found alongside patches of purer BEECH FOREST in more humid and sheltered areas. Equally, drier areas transition to more MONTANE PINE FOREST or TEMPERATE OAK FOREST.

In the Alps, Montane Mixed Forests are most common on soils formed over calcareous or granitic substrates (especially leptosols and cambisols). They prefer the milder outer regions of the

Montane Mixed Forest, Austria. © DALE FORBES

Alps, where they can even reach the overlying SUBALPINE TIMBERLINE WOODLAND. Norway Spruce (*Picea abies*), Silver Fir (*Abies alba*), and European Beech (*Fagus sylvatica*) are the keystone species of Montane Mixed Forest in the Alps. Other tree species of regional or complementary importance include Scots Pine (*Pinus sylvestris*), European Larch (*Larix decidua*), Norway Maple (*Acer platanoides*), Sycamore Maple (*Acer pseudoplatanus*), Silver Birch (*Betula pendula*), Downy Birch (*Betula pubescens*), European Ash (*Fraxinus excelsior*), European Mountain Ash (*Sorbus aucuparia*), and English Oak (*Quercus robur*). Notable plants in the herbaceous layer include a variety of orchids—for example, White Helleborine (*Cephalanthera damasonium*), Narrow-leaved Helleborine (*C. longifolia*), Red Helleborine (*C. rubra*), Broad-leaved Helleborine (*Epipactis helleborine*), and the saprophytic Bird's-nest Orchid (*Neottia nidus-avis*)—as well as Snowy Mespilus (*Amelanchier ovalis*), Bastard Balm (*Melittis melissophyllum*), the beautiful Dark Columbine (*Aquilegia atrata*), and a variety of sedges, including White Sedge (*Carex alba*) and Soft-leaved Sedge (*Carex montana*). Montane Mixed Forests are much more restricted on siliceous soils and are typically found only in particularly mild sites with nutrient-rich neutral soils. The plant diversity of mixed forests provides myriad microhabitats and a mix of wildlife assemblages. White-backed Woodpeckers will happily use this habitat (if there is more than 30% beech) alongside the spruce-favouring Eurasian Three-toed Woodpecker. Similarly, the Fire Salamander (*Salamandra salamandra*) can be found alongside the Alpine Salamander (*Salamandra atra*; see MONTANE SPRUCE-FIR FOREST).

In the Pyrenees, Silver Fir (*Abies alba*) and European Beech (*Fagus sylvatica*) form mixed forests on wetter slopes in the montane zone (~1200–1800 m/3900–6000 ft.), especially those with calcareous bedrock. The mixed forests intertwine and transition to TEMPERATE OAK FOREST at lower elevations, particularly in drier areas. Pyrenean Mountain Pine (*Pinus uncinata*) SUBALPINE TIMBERLINE WOODLAND replaces the Montane Mixed Forest at higher elevations. As in many European forests, the effects of logging and forestry are very evident, and it takes at least 200 years for the structure of these forests to return to a semi-natural state. Walking through an ancient Montane Mixed Forest in the Pyrenees, you will notice that beech is somewhat dominant over Silver Fir, and leaf litter can be thick. There may be the occasional Scots Pine, Common Yew (*Taxus baccata*), maple (*Acer* spp.), or Sessile Oak (*Quercus petraea*) in sunnier locations. If you are extremely lucky, you might even encounter the critically endangered European Mink hunting Pyrenean Frogs (*Rana pyrenaica*) or Pyrenean Brook Salamanders (*Calotriton asper*) along a mountain stream.

Mixed beech-fir forests are also important in Italy's Apennine Mountains—the last refuge of the Italian Wolf. The high rainfall (1000–2400 mm/40–95 in.) and milder temperatures made these forests important ancient refugia of plant biodiversity during the ice ages. The forests were greatly

Montane Mixed Forest, Austria. © DALE FORBES

reduced with human population growth in the 5th–8th centuries. Thereafter, political instability and waves of plague in the Middle Ages led to the abandonment of vast areas of the Apennines, resulting in the widespread expansion of Silver Fir in the region. More recent human pressures have again reduced Silver Fir in the region. Importantly, Silver Fir is highly shade tolerant and can even establish and slowly invade BEECH FOREST. This is a slow process, but many protected areas of the Apennines are starting to see the slow shift from pure BEECH FOREST to Montane Mixed Forest. Additional tree species in the Apennine Montane Mixed Forests include European Mountain Ash, Lobel's Maple (*Acer cappadocicum* ssp. *lobelii*), and Field Maple (*Acer campestre*). As is often the case in beech-rich forests, the shrub layer is impoverished, but various blackberries (*Rubus* spp.) may be prominent. Herbs include the Round-leaved Bedstraw (*Galium rotundifolium*), Early Dog-Violet (*Viola reichenbachiana*), Sweet Woodruff (*Galium odoratum*), Bastard Agrimony (*Aremonia agrimonoides*), Wood Sanicle (*Sanicula europaea*), and Wall Lettuce (*Mycelis muralis*). Mixed forests can also be found in the submontane belt, with Silver Fir and various pines (*Pinus* spp.) intermixed with TEMPERATE OAK FOREST.

The Montane Mixed Forests in the Dinaric Alps, Balkans are similar to those in the Apennines. Here, beech is complemented by Norway Spruce, Silver Fir, Scots Pine, Black Pine (*Pinus nigra*), Macedonian Pine (*P. peuce*), and Bosnian Pine (*P. heldreichii*). In places, they mix with TEMPERATE OAK FOREST, with the Hungarian Oak (*Quercus frainetto*) being particularly important. While the wolf reigns supreme in the Apennines, it is the Eurasian Lynx that is the symbol of the Dinaric forests.

The widespread Coal Tit prefers woodland with at least some conifers. © RALPH MARTIN, AGAMI

The forest matrix of the Carpathians, however, is likely the most important bastion for Europe's three great predators: Brown Bear, Grey Wolf, and Eurasian Lynx. Here, you will find a wondrous mélange of mixed forests between the MONTANE SPRUCE-FIR and BEECH FORESTS. Various combinations of Silver Fir, Norway Spruce, European Larch, and Scots Pine mix with European Beech, Silver Birch, Downy Birch, European Aspen (*Populus tremula*), Sycamore Maple, and Norway Maple.

The tree species in the Pontic and Caucasus Montane Mixed Forests may differ from those farther west, but the structure is largely the same. In the submontane zone, Oriental Beech (*Fagus orientalis*) mixes with various conifers, including Oriental Spruce (*Picea orientalis*), Caucasian Fir (*Abies nordmanniana*), Caucasian Pine (*Pinus sylvestris hamata*), and Black Pine. On drier sites, Persian Oak (*Quercus macranthera*) and other species of submontane TEMPERATE OAK FORESTS replace Oriental Beech in a mixture with the montane conifers.

WILDLIFE: Montane Mixed Forests can have a wonderful mix of assemblages. European Robins and Eurasian Wrens sing incessantly in the spring, the sound punctuated by the explosive song of the Common Chaffinch. The classic coniferous forest birds (Coal Tit, Crested Tit,

Eurasian Wren has an amazingly loud voice for such a tiny bird. It is catholic in its habitat choice and is found throughout most of temperate Europe. © RALPH MARTIN, AGAMI

The Black Woodpecker is Europe's largest woodpecker by far, and its holes are incredibly important for a whole suite of other wildlife. This is the red-capped male. © MARKUS VARESVUO, AGAMI

Goldcrest, Red Crossbill, and Eurasian Siskin) are joined by Hawfinch, Eurasian Jay, and a greater abundance of Common Firecrest. Eurasian Three-toed Woodpecker and Black Woodpecker are both more associated with coniferous forests, while the White-backed Woodpecker is more associated with deciduous forests. However, a good Montane Mixed Forest forms a fascinating realm where you can potentially see Black, Eurasian Three-toed, White-backed, Great Spotted, Eurasian Green, and Grey-headed Woodpeckers all in the same small area. The enormous Western Capercaillie and the diminutive Boreal (Tengmalm's) Owl can both do well in Montane Mixed Forest. European Honey-Buzzard is secretive, tending to stay within forests as it follows wasps and hornets back to their nests.

The secretive European Honey-Buzzard is a summer migrant to Europe and is unusual in that it specialises in feeding on the larvae of bees, wasps, and hornets, though it will take other prey. It is typically hard to see during the breeding season, spending most of its time hidden deep in the forest. © DANIELE OCCHIATO, AGAMI

Stone Marten is a secretive denizen of woodlands through much of Europe. © HANS GERMERAAD, AGAMI

Europe's Montane Mixed Forests are extremely important for our large predators: Brown Bear, Eurasian Lynx, and Grey Wolf. Other notable mammals include Red Fox, Eurasian Red Squirrel, Pine Marten, Stone Marten, European Badger or Southwest Asian Badger, Western Roe Deer, and Red Deer. The European Bison has been reintroduced in the Romanian and Slovakian Carpathians (see Sidebar 2: Rewilding Europe). The rare European Mink uses streams in the Montane Mixed Forests of the Pyrenees, where it is found alongside the range-restricted Pyrenean Frog and Pyrenean Brook Salamander. The Fire Salamander is regularly found in this habitat (although not as abundantly as in BEECH FOREST). At the same time, the Alpine Salamander will also occasionally use Montane Mixed Forests in the Alps (where it is found mainly in MONTANE SPRUCE-FIR FOREST).

CONSERVATION: Forestry and planting regimes continue to significantly impact the tree-species composition of much of Europe's forests. Many natural mixed forests have been converted into Scots Pine or Norway Spruce monocultures. However, forestry thinking is changing, and there is a strong push towards reestablishing mixed forests. A flood of research over the past decade has shown the myriad benefits of mixed forests, including increased timber production, greater resilience to climate change and pests, and higher overall biodiversity. Monocultures have never been much fun for wildlife-watchers.

European Badger uses a wide range of habitats but does well in mixed forests. © HANS GERMERAAD, AGAMI

DISTRIBUTION: Montane Mixed Forests grow in all humid and semi-humid mountain ranges, including the Alps, Pyrenees, Apennines, Didaric Alps, Balkan Mountains, Carpathians, Pontic Mountains, and Caucasus Mountains. They are estimated to cover 10 million ha (25 million ac.).

WHERE TO SEE: Aztaparreta Forest Reserve, Navarre, Spain; Pollino National Park, Italy; National Nature Reserve Dobročský prales, Banská Bystrica, Slovakia; Făgăraș Mountains, Romania.

SIDEBAR 2 REWILDING EUROPE

European Bison tear the bark off and kill large trees, smash their way through thickets, and dig up earth with their hooves, leaving a trail of destruction everywhere they go. So many of us have grown up with a romanticised version of nature and conservation, assuming that this 'damage' must naturally be bad for the forests and plants because they would grow better without it. We are slowly learning that landscape engineers—like bison—are incredibly important for natural systems in Europe. This is because our native plant and animal assemblages actually evolved with the disturbance of large mammals (see Sidebar 4: Prehistoric Europe, p.208).

It feels strange to see cattle chewing and bashing their way through nature reserves, but this is becoming an increasingly common sight across Europe as conservationists realise the critical importance of large animals in the system. Cattle are the niche replacements for the extinct Aurochs, while horses, donkeys, water buffalo, and others are the domestic counterparts of wild forms that would naturally have been found here. Crunching hooves open up space for seedlings to establish, compacted paths provide niches for disturbance-adapted plants, chewed saplings keep glades open, bark-stripped trees open up new spaces, and muddy wallows are great for a wide suite of insects and herps. Introducing keystone species like vultures, lynx, and bison or the pragmatic use of domestic counterparts is one of the tenets of rewilding.

The initiative Rewilding Europe states, 'Rewilding is a progressive approach to conservation. It's about letting nature take care of itself, enabling natural processes to shape land and sea, repair damaged ecosystems, and restore degraded landscapes'.

This may seem straightforward, but rewilding is beautifully multifaceted in its approach to conservation, including dedicating space and time for nature to recover, working together with communities, embedding local customs, creating sustainable livelihoods with nature, and introducing keystone species. The philosophy reflects a sense of solidarity with the people and nature in a landscape, potentially even showing a new way forwards for humanity and how we interact with nature.

The Rewild Podcast is a beautifully produced dive into some of Europe's most inspirational rewilding projects—well worth a listen.

Eu3F MEDITERRANEAN OAK FOREST

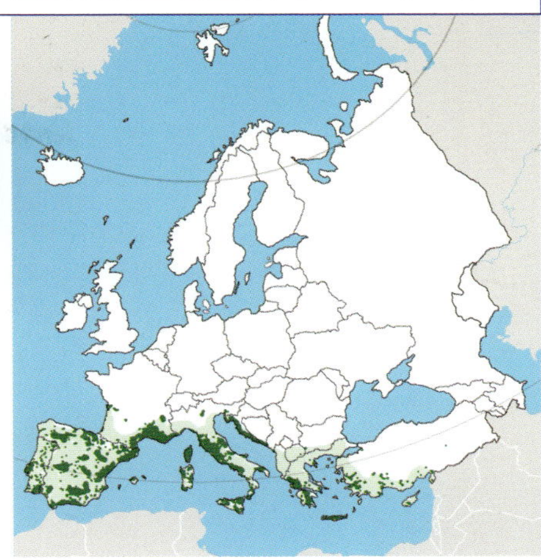

IN A NUTSHELL: The typical low-canopy broadleaf forests of the warmer Mediterranean realm. **Global Habitat Affinities:** MADREAN ENCINAL; MAGHREB BROADLEAF WOODLAND; NEARCTIC FOOTHILL OAK SHRUBLAND. **Continental Habitat Affinities:** TEMPERATE OAK FOREST. **Species Overlap:** OAK DEHESA; TEMPERATE OAK FOREST.

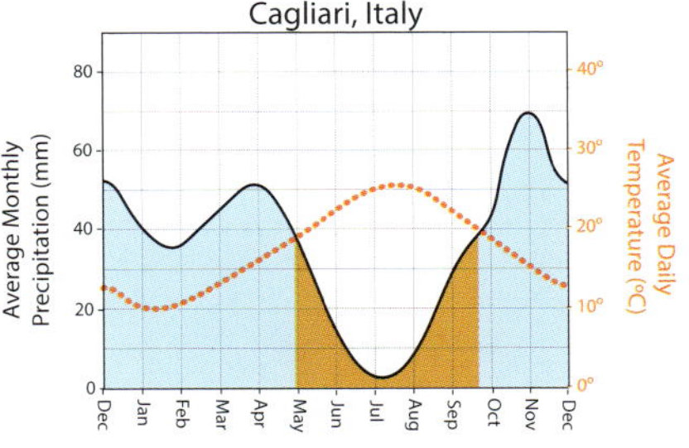

DESCRIPTION: You leave the blistering heat of the steppes and MAQUIS and step into a Mediterranean Oak Forest. The forest's low canopy and dense vegetation create a cool, shaded haven. The air is filled with the melodious songs of robins, while Short-toed Treecreepers clandestinely navigate the tree trunks. A majestic Black Kite glides by overhead, and somewhere in the thick undergrowth, a family of Eurasian Wild Boars finds relief from the day's heat.

The Mediterranean has not always had the hot, dry climate we experience today (Köppen **Csa**, **Csb**, **Bsk**). The past 2.6 million years have seen repeated glaciations in Europe with unfathomable quantities of ice and snow. Europe was significantly colder, but the Mediterranean region would have had glaciers only in the mountains. The greatest impact of the Pleistocene ice ages was arguably the lack of water. So much was frozen in c. and n. Europe that the entire continent was dramatically drier. Trees in the Mediterranean realm survived these cold, dry periods only in the warmest and wettest locations, and even then, mostly in savannas and open woodlands. This explains why most of the birds in Mediterranean Oak Forests are generalist species equally happy in savannas. Tall, closed-canopy forests were likely very scarce and confined to small, protected pockets. River valleys fed by glacial meltwater were undoubtedly important as refugia. During this time, the woodlands would have had a greater proportion of trees adapted to somewhat cooler climates, such as various deciduous oaks (*Quercus* spp.), European Hornbeam (*Carpinus betulus*), Field Maple (*Acer campestre*), and even European Beech (*Fagus sylvatica*). Despite the warm, dry climate of the Mediterranean realm in modern times, these trees persist, albeit mostly at cooler, moister sites.

The oak forests on northern slopes can be particularly dense, lush, and enchanting, growing as tall as 15 m (50 ft.). These slopes are cooler, retain more moisture, and can develop deep, rich soils. By contrast, oak forests on southern slopes tend to be more open, with drought-tolerant

The bark of the amazing Cork Oak is typically harvested every nine years. © DALE FORBES

This tall Mediterranean Oak Forest in Italy is growing in a somewhat sheltered and protected location in a mosaic with coastal Maquis. © DALE FORBES

Maquis-like sclerophyllous vegetation filling the gaps. The soils of ancient oak forests do not have the intense red staining from iron oxyhydroxides of the soils in the surrounding MAQUIS. This suggests that these forests kept the soils moister despite the intense summer droughts typical of the Mediterranean realm.

The most important oak species in modern Mediterranean Oak Forests vary widely across the region. Mirbeck's Oak (*Quercus canariensis*) and Cork Oak (*Q. suber*) dominate the forests of Andalusia, while Sweet Acorn Oak (*Q. rotundifolia*) joins Cork Oak in the drier parts of the Iberian Peninsula. Farther east, Downy Oak (*Q. pubescens*) and Holm Oak (*Q. ilex*) become more common. In the forests of Sardinia, Italy, agriculturalists have favoured Cork Oak because of its valuable bark, and entire forest swaths—established in the last century or so—are dominated by Cork Oaks. However, Cork Oaks need a lot of light to regenerate, so they are slowly replaced with Holm and Downy Oaks as well as a suite of other tree species. A similar pattern is seen throughout Europe, where oak regeneration within forests is extremely low.

Acorns that birds disperse are more likely to survive and germinate than those that fall below the parent tree. Eurasian Jays are particularly important in this role, flying up to 4 km (2.5 mi.) to cache the seeds. Their hiding sites are invariably in open areas, not in forests, and it turns out that being buried in a non-forested location is optimal for oak establishment. It may well be that many of the oak forests we experience today are not climax communities but rather long-persisting, evenly aged transitional states, having established after the original forest was cleared or when pastures were abandoned (compare OAK DEHESA).

Ancient oak forests have a complex canopy, with trees of vastly different ages where the natural death of old trees opens gaps for the regeneration of young oaks. Most of Europe's oak forests, however, are heavily managed and populated with trees of a similar age. As a result, canopies tend

This Mediterranean Oak Forest in Croatia is in a mosaic with orchards and other croplands on deeper, inland soils. © DALE FORBES

to be uniform in size and height. While oaks overwhelmingly dominate the canopy, the forests will invariably include species like hornbeams (*Carpinus betulus* and *C. orientalis*), Manna Ash (*Fraxinus ornus*), Aleppo Pine (*Pinus halepensis*), Sweet Chestnut (*Castanea sativa*), Mastic Tree (*Pistacia lentiscus*), Terebinth (*Pistacia terebinthus*), Strawberry Tree (*Arbutus unedo*), Narrow-leaved Mock Privet (*Phillyrea angustifolia*), and Green Olive Tree (*Phillyrea latifolia*). Significant amounts of light penetrate the semi-open canopy in large, older Mediterranean Oak Forests, allowing for strong growth below the canopy. Western and Eastern Prickly Junipers (*Juniperus oxycedrus* and *J. deltoides*), Butcher's-Broom (*Ruscus aculeatus*), Mediterranean Buckthorn (*Rhamnus alaternus*), Common Hawthorn (*Crataegus monogyna*), Tree Heath (*Erica arborea*), Common Ivy (*Hedera helix*), and Common Box (*Buxus sempervirens*) can all be abundant.

The high-pitched trilling and twittering of European Serin are common sounds in these forests. © MARKUS VARESVUO, AGAMI

Eurasian Jay and Eurasian Sparrowhawk are both typical of this habitat. © MARKUS VARESVUO, AGAMI

WILDLIFE: The Eurasian Jay is the lord of oak forests; it is not only ubiquitous but also plays a critical role in seed dispersal and determining where oaks will germinate. The classic birds of Mediterranean Oak Forest are generalist, broadleaf woodland species, including the Lesser Spotted Woodpecker, European Robin, Great Tit, Eurasian Blue Tit, Long-tailed Tit, Common Firecrest, Common Chiffchaff, Short-toed Treecreeper, Eurasian Nuthatch, Common Chaffinch, and Hawfinch. All these species are present throughout the year, but additional individuals from more northerly breeding areas join Mediterranean communities in the winter. Birds of prey include the Eurasian Sparrowhawk; Eurasian Goshawk; Bonelli's, Booted, and Spanish (Imperial) Eagles; and Tawny Owl. Summer communities are complemented by migrants such as Black Stork, Spotted Flycatcher, European Pied Flycatcher, European Serin, Common Nightingale, Eastern and Western Orphean Warblers, and Iberian Chiffchaff. Western Bonelli's Warbler is most common in Mediterranean Oak Forests in Spain, France, and Italy, while Eastern Bonelli's Warbler uses these forests in se. Europe.

Most of Europe's charismatic mammals are found in the Mediterranean Oak Forest, including the Iberian Lynx, Brown Bear, Red Deer, European Wildcat, and European Badger. Eurasian Wild Boar can be particularly abundant.

Several insects specialise in oaks, including the beautiful Purple and Spanish Purple Hairstreaks (*Favonius quercus* and *Laeosopis roboris*) and the incredibly camouflaged Great Oak Beauty (*Hypomecis roboraria*), but the beautiful Oak Hawkmoth (*Marumba quercus*) is arguably the most characteristic. The Oak Hawkmoth requires good structural heterogeneity, so measures to clear undergrowth, open forests, and homogenise the canopy are all real threats to the species.

Above: **Common Nightingale prefers areas of oak forest with a well-developed understorey, from which it delivers its superb song, often right through the night.**

© DANIELE OCCHIATO, AGAMI

Eurasian Wild Boar is typically shy but can be incredibly abundant in Mediterranean Oak Forests.

© DANNY GREEN, AGAMI

The huge European Rhinoceros Beetle, surely one of Europe's most spectacular invertebrates, and its predator, the Mammoth Scoliid Wasp, are both associated with this habitat. © MENNO VAN DUIJN, AGAMI

The Southern White Admiral (*Limenitis reducta*) is characteristic of Mediterranean Oak Forest, especially around forest clearings with abundant honeysuckles (*Lonicera* spp.).

The Great Capricorn Beetle (*Cerambyx cerdo*) is one of the largest beetles in Europe and requires very large living oak trees for its larvae. The European Stag Beetle (*Lucanus cervus*) also prefers oaks but, by contrast, needs decaying snags and other dead wood. Both the Mammoth Scoliid Wasp (*Megascolia maculata*) and its prey, the European Rhinoceros Beetle (*Oryctes nasicornis*), are associated with this habitat.

CONSERVATION: Mediterranean Oak Forests face challenges similar to those faced by many other habitats. Overzealous management of the forests for wood production, including a desire to make the forests 'neat' by removing dead wood and clearing brush, has disastrous effects on biodiversity. Nature does not like neatness.

DISTRIBUTION: The Mediterranean Oak Forest extends throughout the Mediterranean realm. The Cork and Holm Oak forests in Portugal and Spain occur in relatively wetter and cooler locations than the surrounding MAQUIS and MEDITERRANEAN PINE FOREST. This habitat is widespread on the Mediterranean islands, in Italy, and in s. France. The forest skirts the Alps to the south, where it occurs in drier and lower elevations than the nearby TEMPERATE OAK FOREST, BEECH FOREST, and MONTANE SPRUCE-FIR FOREST. It occurs in coastal areas of the Balkans, Türkiye, and around the Black Sea.

WHERE TO SEE: Douro International Natural Park, Bragança and Guarda Districts, Portugal; Monfragüe National Park, Extremadura, Spain; Sierra de Andújar Natural Park, Andalusia, Spain; WWF Oasis Monte Arcosu, Sardinia, Italy.

Eu3G EUROPEAN SUBARCTIC RIPARIAN WOODLAND

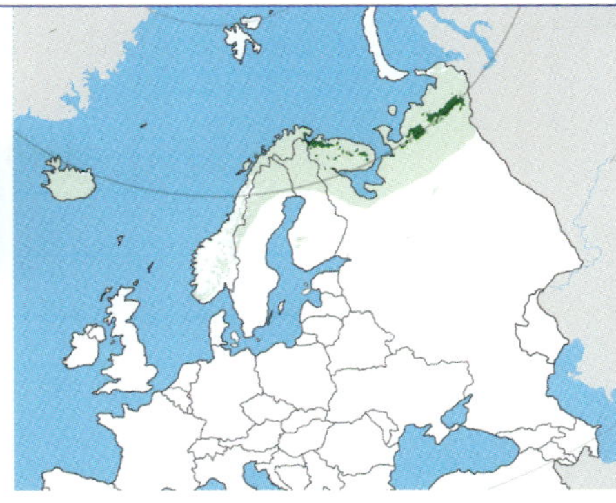

IN A NUTSHELL: Deciduous shrubs and trees that grow along rivers and protected areas within the tundras and taigas. **Global Habitat Affinities:** NEARCTIC SUBARCTIC RIPARIAN WOODLAND AND BOREAL SHRUBLAND MOSAIC; ASIAN SUBARCTIC RIPARIAN WOODLAND. **Continental Habitat Affinities:** CONIFEROUS PEAT WOODLAND; TEMPERATE RIPARIAN FOREST; TUNDRA TAIGA. **Species Overlap:** TEMPERATE RIPARIAN FOREST.

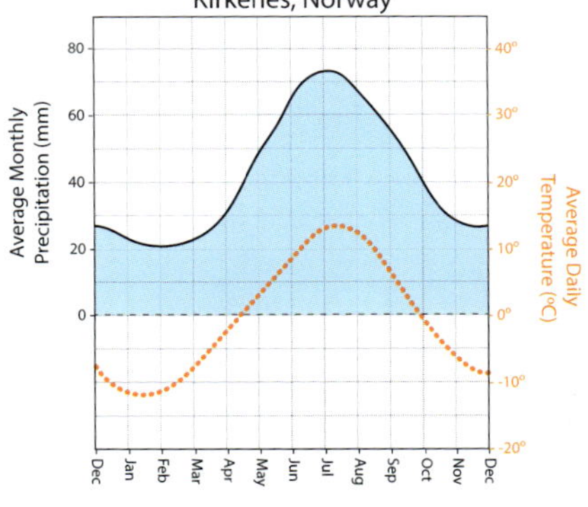

DESCRIPTION: A common misconception is that conifers are the northernmost trees of Europe. However, there is an Arctic scrub of birch, willow, and aspen in protected wet environments on the southern edge of the tundra and in low mountains in extreme subarctic conditions. The climate is harsh (Köppen **Dfc**), with an extremely short growing season, abundant snows, high winds, and permafrost below.

Where these groves exist between the conifers and tundra, they expand in favourable years and contract in more severe years. In the toughest conditions of the subarctic, conifers such as spruce and fir are unable to survive through the winter, because they are evergreen; any tree that carries leaves at all, and that thus needs to eke out water from the permafrost during the winter months, finds it difficult to survive. When these evergreens succumb, they are replaced by colonist deciduous angiosperms, birches (*Betula* spp.), and deciduous conifers like Siberian Larch (*Larix sibirica*). This deciduous trade-off does mean that for most of the year, these habitats appear as a series of bare branches, bursting into life only in mid-spring. If you visit from October through April, expect things to be very dreary. These groves are generally very open, with a krummholz canopy (windblown in one direction), usually around 1.2 m (4 ft.) tall in exposed areas and 6 m (20 ft.) tall in more protected areas, especially where there are snowbanks. On drier slopes, these shrublands and forest groves are dominated by Dwarf Birch (*Betula nana*), Downy Birch (*Betula pubescens*), European Aspen (*Populus tremula*), Tea-leaved Willow (*Salix phylicifolia*), and Least Willow (*Salix herbacea*). Underneath, the groves are dominated by taller versions of the same plant species that grow in the SHRUBBY TUNDRA and more exposed areas, such as Black Crowberry (*Empetrum nigrum*), Lingonberry (*Vaccinium vitis-idaea*), Common Bilberry (*V. myrtillus*), Bog Bilberry (*V. uliginosum*), and Marsh Labrador Tea (*Rhododendron tomentosum*). The ground cover is dominated by sedges, such as Globular Sedge

Subarctic Riparian Woodland can be open and scrubby in nature (above) but can also form closed-canopy forests (below). © IAIN CAMPBELL, TROPICAL BIRDING

(*Carex globularis*), and grasses, like Wavy Hair-Grass (*Avenella flexuosa*). In contrast to the soils of the tundra, these shrublands cause the development of a strong podzol soil that is heavily leached at the surface.

Where this habitat grows in riparian or boggy areas—such as palsa mounds or aapa mires (see Sidebar 6: A Brief Overview of Europe's Diverse Peatlands, p.332)—the main trees remain the same. Although they grow taller than in the drier areas, they often have a scraggly appearance, as though they are barely holding on in horrible conditions. This is exactly what is happening; they are eking out an existence in unfavourable conditions. Downy Birch is the dominant tree, with a minor canopy component of Grey Alder (*Alnus incana*), Common Alder (*Alnus glutinosa*), and European Mountain Ash (*Sorbus aucuparia*). There is the occasional Scots Pine (*Pinus sylvestris*) and rarely a Norway Spruce (*Picea abies*) in the canopy mix. Because this can also be a pioneer habitat, over time the mass of spruces or pines may replace the canopy as the forest slowly develops into a CONIFEROUS PEAT WOODLAND. Some of the understorey plants are the same as in the drier areas, such as the Common Bilberry and Bog Bilberry, but willows are much more common here. Eared Willow (*Salix aurita*) and Grey Willow (*Salix cinerea*) dominate the shrub assemblage along with small shrubs such as Alder Buckthorn (*Frangula alnus*), Cross-leaved Heath (*Erica tetralix*), and Wild Rosemary (*Andromeda polifolia*). As would be expected, graminoids are very common, including Purple Moor Grass (*Molinia caerulea*), Smooth-stalked Sedge (*Carex laevigata*), Tussock Cottongrass (*Eriophorum vaginatum*), Soft Rush (*Juncus effusus*), and Wavy Hair-Grass, as are ferns, such as Spreading Wood Fern (*Dryopteris expansa*). It is the density of bryophytes (mosses and similar plants) that distinguishes this boggy form of Subarctic Riparian Woodland from the drier forms, with many of the same species that occur in the Coniferous Peat Woodland, such as the sphagnums Papillose Peatmoss (*Sphagnum papillosum*), Russow's Sphagnum (*Sphagnum russowii*), and Fringed Bogmoss (*Sphagnum fimbriatum*), along with Common Haircap Moss (*Polytrichum commune*), Ribbed Bogmoss (*Aulacomnium palustre*), and the plant with arguably the most delightful name in Europe, Golden Fuzzy Fen Moss (*Tomentypnum nitens*).

WILDLIFE: As with other Arctic and subarctic habitats, this forest is very quiet for most of the year. Among the very few bird species found here through the year, some of the most obvious are Eurasian Magpie, Lesser Spotted Woodpecker, and Common (Northern) Raven. In contrast with the similar CONIFEROUS PEAT WOODLAND, most of the canopy cover is lost in winter, so life is very difficult for the resident species, and even woodpeckers from nearby conifers avoid this habitat in winter. A variety of passerines more typical of c. Europe do make the journey north to feed on the massive burst of insect

The tiny Lesser Spotted Woodpecker is Europe's smallest woodpecker, the size of a sparrow. This male is just about able to eke out an existence in the harsh winter environment of Subarctic Riparian Woodland.

The abundance of singing Willow Warblers in spring in the Subarctic Riparian Woodland makes for a truly delightful soundscape. © SAVERIO GATTO, AGAMI

The attractive Redwing is a common sight in the summer. © TOMI MUUKKONEN, AGAMI

life in spring, and the sheer abundance of Willow Warblers, Bluethroats, and Ring Ouzels shows these woodlands to be very different from CONIFEROUS PEAT WOODLANDS. Bramblings breed in very high densities in these birch forests. In addition, small breeding migrants to this forest include Bohemian Waxwing, Twite, Eurasian Bullfinch, European Pied Flycatcher, and Redpolls. Dunnock and Spotted Flycatcher also breed here but do not make it to the extreme north in big numbers. Redwing and Fieldfare are two thrushes that nest here in large numbers and call incessantly through the summer. Ring Ouzel and Mistle Thrush are more common on the edges of these groves than deep in the woodlands. Merlin migrates into the region in spring to hunt the abundant passerines.

The smart Ring Ouzel chooses harsh, open habitats in which to breed and is most common on the edges of Subarctic Riparian Woodland. Its simple, repetitive, far-carrying song can be heard on spring mornings. © MARKUS VARESVUO, AGAMI

In contrast with birds, the mammal assemblage in these shrublands is the same as that in the surrounding conifer forests, though the mammals use the two habitats at different times. Brown Bear is rare in the Subarctic Riparian Woodland, and this habitat is about as far north as the species reaches in Europe. European Elk (Moose) can be very common in this habitat, and wild and semi-domesticated Reindeer (Caribou) roam the forests.

CONSERVATION: This habitat is fascinating in that, as a coloniser and sometimes successional habitat, it is quick to take advantage of changing conditions. It is becoming common in northernmost Fennoscandia, with small groves replacing the ROCKY TUNDRA and SHRUBBY TUNDRA. As global warming continues, vast regions of northernmost Europe will change to a climate much more conducive to the growth of conifer forest and these Subarctic Riparian Woodlands than to tundra (see SHRUBBY TUNDRA). Because conifers are much slower at advancing than poplar, birch, and willow, the potentially massive void will be first exploited by this habitat. Things are not looking so conducive to habitat expansion at the other end of the distribution. There has been a lot of peat extraction in Finland, Russia, and Norway, and although extraction seems to have halted in w. Europe, extensive drainage of the peatlands and peat extraction continue in Russia. The other major threat to the habitat is extreme overgrazing of the understorey by livestock and deer, leading to diminished biodiversity of the understorey and evenly aged canopies.

DISTRIBUTION: This habitat is found in the transition zone between the tundra and the taiga forests in n. Fennoscandia and Russia. Farther south, this habitat transitions to TEMPERATE RIPARIAN FOREST.

WHERE TO SEE: Kirkenes, Norway.

European Elk (Moose) can be very common in Subarctic Riparian Woodland. © ALAIN GHIGNONE, AGAMI

Eu3H EUROPEAN TEMPERATE RIPARIAN FOREST

IN A NUTSHELL: The diverse forests lining watercourses, often in a state of active disturbance and succession. Species composition is quite variable but can include willows, poplars, ashes, or alders. **Global Habitat Affinities:** AUSTRALIAN SHEOAK RIPARIAN WOODLAND; EAST ASIAN RIPARIAN FOREST. **Continental Habitat Affinities:** SUBARCTIC RIPARIAN WOODLAND; MEDITERRANEAN RIPARIAN FOREST; CASPIAN RIPARIAN SCRUB. **Species Overlap:** TEMPERATE OAK FOREST; BEECH FOREST.

DESCRIPTION: With a dramatic splash, a spooked Eurasian Beaver heads home for the day. It has been working on a large poplar, which will likely fall tonight. In the canopy, a Eurasian Golden Oriole belts out its delightful bubbly, fluty song. Eurasian Penduline-Tits flit back and forth, building a nest, and a flash of Common Kingfisher zips past, just above the water's surface. A Banded Demoiselle (*Calopteryx splendens*) ignores the commotion in the regal belief that it is, in fact, the most beautiful creature of Temperate Riparian Forests.

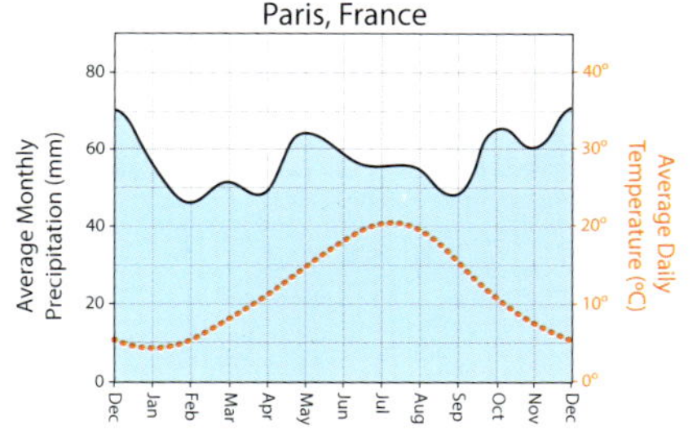

These ecosystems are critical agents of regional environmental health and serve as important breeding, stepping-stone, and dispersal habitat for wildlife. The forests that develop along watercourses—from small, fast-flowing creeks to large, winding rivers that break their banks annually—are typically quite distinct from the habitats through which they snake. High or fluctuating water tables and periodic flooding greatly affect the plant species that establish and thrive in these ecosystems.

In the temperate lowlands (Köppen **Cfb**, **Dfb**), this habitat is the riverine representation of the temperate deciduous forests such as TEMPERATE OAK FOREST and BEECH FOREST. In s. Europe, this habitat is replaced by MEDITERRANEAN RIPARIAN FOREST where the regional habitats are the warmer and drier MAQUIS and OAK DEHESA (Köppen **Csa**, **Csb**, **Bsk**). This habitat merges into SUBARCTIC RIPARIAN WOODLAND in n. Europe, where the riverine areas are surrounded by habitats such as SPRUCE-FIR TAIGA (Köppen **Dfc**).

In their natural hydrological state, large, gently flowing rivers would tend to flood occasionally, inundating the immediate surroundings. These flooding events can deposit large amounts of nutrient-rich alluvial soils (creating luvisol; see appendix) and diverse debris. Still, they also tend to be quite mechanically destructive to the vegetation in this habitat. Softwood forests of willows (including White Willow, *Salix alba*; Goat Willow, *S. caprea*; and hybrid Crack Willow, *S.* × *fragilis*) and poplars (including White Poplar, *Populus alba*; European Aspen, *P. tremula*; and Black Poplar, *P. nigra*) thrive under these conditions and develop wonderful tall, closed-canopy forests. Willows will tend to dominate where flooding is roughly annual, whereas poplars become relatively more important in areas that are flooded every few years. Both willows and poplars are typically fast to grow and quick to coppice after flood damage. In this habitat, they are variably complemented by Common Alder (*Alnus glutinosa*), European Ash (*Fraxinus excelsior*),

Temperate Riparian Forest, Austria. © DALE FORBES

Temperate Riparian Forest, Poland. © IAIN CAMPBELL, TROPICAL BIRDING

Downy Birch (*Betula pubescens*), maples (*Acer* spp.), and elms (*Ulmus* spp.), among others. The understorey is typically thick in the summertime, making it very hard to scramble through, with species including Common Hazel (*Corylus avellana*), European Dewberry (*Rubus caesius*), Guelder-Rose (*Viburnum opulus*), Wayfaring Tree (*Viburnum lantana*), and Great Stinging Nettle (*Urtica dioica*). Scrambling lianas and vines like Catchweed Bedstraw (*Galium aparine*), Hedge Bindweed (*Calystegia sepium*), Common Hops (*Humulus lupulus*), and Bittersweet Nightshade (*Solanum dulcamara*) are also typical components of this ecosystem. The abundance of European Mistletoe (*Viscum album*) is most obvious in winter, when the willow and poplar hosts lose their leaves, and the parasitic mistletoe stands out as tight green balls of vegetation in the otherwise open canopies.

In areas where larger rivers rarely flood the surrounding land, impressive, complex galleries of oaks, elms, and ashes can develop. A complex multistorey layering of other trees, shrubs, climbers, and forbs makes for a wonderfully biodiverse habitat that is a thrill to visit.

Smaller rivers and streams of various speeds favour the development of alder and alder-ash forests. Periodic flooding or a consistently high water table creates these swampy environments and maintains the species balance. At the ecotonal outer edges of the habitat—where the ground tends to be drier—alders (*Alnus glutinosa* and *A. incana*) and ashes (*Fraxinus excelsior* and *F. angustifolia*) start to be complemented with elms and other upland species. The shrub and herb layer can vary according to the soil, light, and flooding conditions. The thick shrub layer could include Bird Cherry (*Prunus padus*), Guelder-Rose, Common Dogwood (*Cornus sanguinea*), Common Privet (*Ligustrum vulgare*), and Alder Buckthorn (*Frangula alnus*). On wetter, marshy soils, species may include Common Reed (*Phragmites australis*), Greater Tussock-Sedge (*Carex paniculata*), Meadowsweet (*Filipendula ulmaria*), Marsh Marigold (*Caltha palustris*), or Great Stinging Nettle. As with the willow-poplar riparian forests, these alder-ash forests will also typically have good numbers of climbing plants, adding interesting structural heterogeneity to the forest and creating greater microhabitats for invertebrates and larger wildlife.

WILDLIFE: The Eurasian Beaver is the quintessential animal of riparian forests, actively forcing change and the development of microhabitats within the riparian belt. The soft wood of willows and poplars allows beavers to quickly open a closed-canopy forest and allow natural WET GRASSLAND to develop. In the past, Aurochs, Common Hippopotamus, Merck's Rhinoceros, and European Elk (Moose) would also have kept some of these riparian areas open. In addition, when considering the destruction of periodic flooding, it is easy to understand how Temperate Riparian Forests have evolved as ecosystems in continual transition. Eurasian Wild Boar, Red Fox, Western Roe Deer, and European Fallow Deer readily use the diversity in riparian belts both as living spaces and as conduits between larger habitats.

The 'destruction' by Eurasian Beavers is incredibly important to riparian forest ecosystems. These forests would have evolved with beavers, Aurochs, water buffalos, hippos, and the like in a continuous tension between opening up wet meadows and forming closed forests. © HARVEY VAN DIEK, AGAMI

Above: **Icterine Warbler is a great songster and an excellent mimic commonly found in Temperate Riparian Forests.** © MARKUS VARESVUO, AGAMI

Right: **Eurasian Penduline-Tit is easy to find in Temperate Riparian Forests, where its large globular nest is often the first giveaway of its presence.** © SAVERIO GATTO, AGAMI

Below: **In May, the fluting song of the Eurasian Golden Oriole can often be heard in stands of riparian poplars.** © JACQUES VAN DER NEUT, AGAMI

Goldfinches and tits buzz about while robins sing and Fieldfares chatter (unmelodiously). With some luck, a Hawfinch pair will be feeding overhead as a Short-toed Treecreeper skulks by. Large rivers are important conduits and orientation markets for migrating birds and other wildlife, making the protection of this habitat of particular importance to Europe's biodiversity. The bird assemblage varies by region, but in much of Europe, you will want to be in this habitat to find Lesser Spotted Woodpecker, Icterine Warbler, Marsh Tit, Eurasian Penduline-Tit, or Eurasian Golden Oriole. Thrush Nightingale,

The secretive River Warbler spends most of its life skulking around on the ground like an avian rodent, but in the spring the male sits up and belts out its monotonous song, often in plain view. © RALPH MARTIN, AGAMI

River Warbler, and Azure Tit are associated with this habitat in e. Europe. In winter, riverside alders host large numbers of hungry Redpolls and Eurasian Siskins.

One of Europe's largest butterflies—the rare Poplar Admiral (*Limenitis populi*)—is found mainly in this habitat, as is the beautiful Lesser Purple Emperor (*Apatura ilia*). Other butterflies of Temperate Riparian Forests include the Camberwell Beauty (Mourning Cloak; *Nymphalis antiopa*), European Peacock Butterfly (*Aglais io*), Map (*Araschnia levana*), and European Comma (*Polygonia c-album*), as well as Small, Large, Scarce, and Compton Tortoiseshells (*Aglais urticae*, *Nymphalis polychloros*, *N. xanthomelas*, and *N. l-album*).

The Poplar Admiral is one of Europe's finest butterflies. It is found mostly in riparian poplar forests. © DICK FORSMAN, AGAMI

Beautiful and Banded Demoiselles (*Calopteryx virgo* and *C. splendens*) are relatively common along streams and rivers in addition to clubtails (family Gomphidae) and myriad other possible dragonflies and damselflies. The (mostly) aquatic Grass Snake (*Natrix natrix*) or Barred Grass Snake (*Natrix helvetica*) are commonly found in this habitat throughout the region. The Agile Frog (*Rana dalmatina*) and European Common Frog (*Rana temporaria*), among others, can be found in streams and oxbows.

CONSERVATION: Riparian ecosystems have developed with cycles of flooding and high water tables. However, as with so many other European habitats, major changes to how water systems work have enormously impacted modern Temperate Riparian Forests. Drainage ditches dry agricultural land while dams and dikes are built to minimise flooding, all while asphalt, concrete, and stormwater systems exacerbate runoff and catalyse flash floods. Invasive plants from other continents, like Himalayan Balsam (*Impatiens glandulifera*) and Virginia Creeper (*Parthenocissus quinquefolia*), establish quickly in the pioneering nature of riverside forests, forcing out native species. Temperate Riparian Forests are cleared for timber and to make space for farmland and housing, thus cauterising some of Europe's most important biodiversity highways.

DISTRIBUTION: Across w. and c. Europe along watercourses from the lowlands into the montane belt.

WHERE TO SEE: The Broads of East Anglia, England, UK; Hortobágy, Hungary; Donau-Auen National Park, Lower Austria, Austria; Kühkopf-Knoblochsaue Nature Reserve, Hesse, Germany.

The gorgeous Banded Demoiselle can often be found flapping lazily over slow-flowing rivers.
© WIL LEURS, AGAMI

The monochrome plumage of the migratory Black Stork is broken up by its vivid red legs and bill. It readily nests in Temperate Riparian Forests.
© MARC GUYT, AGAMI

Eu3l MEDITERRANEAN RIPARIAN FOREST

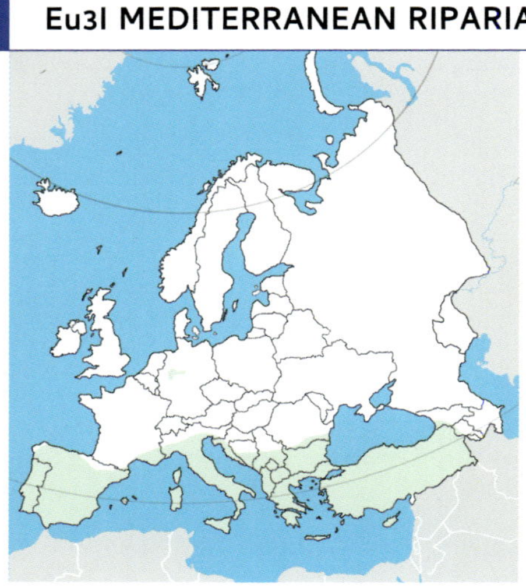

IN A NUTSHELL: The deciduous willow, poplar, or plane tree woodlands and tamarisk thickets associated with permanent and periodic watercourses in s. Europe. **Global Habitat Affinities:** NEARCTIC WESTERN RIPARIAN WOODLAND. **Continental Habitat Affinities:** CASPIAN RIPARIAN SCRUB; TEMPERATE RIPARIAN FOREST. **Species Overlap:** TEMPERATE RIPARIAN FOREST.

DESCRIPTION: Narrow ribbons of Mediterranean Riparian Forest snake through the Mediterranean realm, their relatively cooler climate, greater water availability, and higher productivity creating an oasis effect. This makes them vital refuges in a landscape changed by people. They are particularly important in urban and agricultural areas, where they can represent the only remaining (semi-)natural habitat. The enchanting song of Common Nightingales is complemented by burbling Eurasian Golden Orioles and enthusiastic Melodious Warblers. Chirping crickets are omnipresent.

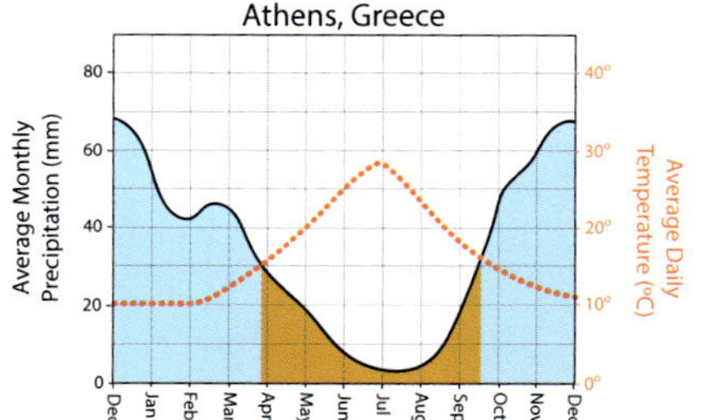

Mediterranean Riparian Forests extend deep into Iberia and farther north into c. Europe in warmer and drier river valleys (Köppen **Csa**, **Csb**, **Bsk**). In somewhat more temperate climates, this habitat is replaced with the rich willow, poplar, and ash galleries of the TEMPERATE RIPARIAN FOREST to the north. In the core regions of the Mediterranean and Macaronesia (Cape Verde,

Scattered trees and reeds lining a small river in Spanish cropland.

Tamarisks along a watercourse in a mosaic with Coastal Salt Marsh in Italy. © DALE FORBES

In protected sites, Mediterranean Riparian Forest can form tall, closed-canopy forests reminiscent of those in Temperate Riparian Forests, but it is most commonly encountered as a narrow riparian belt snaking through the landscape, as pictured here. © MARTIN KELSEY

Canary Islands, Madeira, and Azores), these Mediterranean Riparian Forests are typically narrow, resource-rich, diverse slivers through a dry, scrubby landscape, representing incredibly important areas for regional biodiversity. Geographic location, soil type, aridity, frequency of flooding, salinity, and human disturbance all contribute to determining the exact structure and species composition of this habitat in any one location.

Some areas develop deep alluvial soils, allowing for richer galleries reminiscent of TEMPERATE RIPARIAN FORESTS. These poplar, plane, and willow forests can also be found on more nutrient-rich, salt-poor soils in humid environments. Nowadays, the best examples are mostly found in steeper, hard-to-access gorges with ideal microclimates and some measure of protection from the destructive influences of people and their livestock.

In more arid areas, the coarse soils are often relatively little developed, poorly stabilised, and well drained. This favours the development, commonly in lower thickets, of hardier plants such as various tamarisks (*Tamarix* spp.), Oleander (*Nerium oleander*), and Lilac Chaste Tree (*Vitex agnus-castus*). Watercourses are typically periodic or intermittent and fed by winter or spring rains. Similar tamarisk communities also develop in much wetter conditions—for example, near coastal marshes—where the salinity limits the growth of other woody species, and tamarisk's ability to cope with salt helps it become the dominant shrub or tree.

Climax forests develop in somewhat more moderate climates and on sheltered, protected sites. They tend to be dominated by poplar species (especially *Populus alba*), which are often complemented by willows (like *Salix alba*), alders (*Alnus* spp.), and ashes (especially *Fraxinus angustifolia*). In the Balkans, Greece, and some e. Mediterranean islands, these forests are regularly dominated by fast-growing, large Oriental Plane Trees (*Platanus orientalis*), with complementary

The beautiful European Turtle-Dove is still relatively common in s. Europe, particularly on the edges of Mediterranean Riparian Forest. © DANIELE OCCHIATO, AGAMI

species as in other regions. The lush forests—especially in well-protected gorges—can have fascinatingly diverse shrub and forbs layers, including myriad ferns, mosses, and lichens. Foragers delight in the fruits of Holy Bramble (*Rubus creticus*), Elmleaf Blackberry (*Rubus ulmifolius*), Common Fig (*Ficus carica*), and European Wild Grape (*Vitis vinifera* ssp. *sylvestris*), but toxic fruits like those of Italian Arum (*Arum italicum*) and Black Bryony (*Dioscorea communis*) also abound.

WILDLIFE: There is something magical about walking through a Mediterranean Riparian Forest with the smell of blossoms in the air and the vibrant songs of Melodious Warblers, Common Nightingales, and Eurasian Golden Orioles filling the air. Eurasian Penduline-Tits are a riparian forest specialist, but many other forest and woodland birds can also be found in these forests. Eurasian Blue Tit, Great Tit, Eurasian Nuthatch, European Robin, and Eurasian Blackcap are invariably present. Eurasian Hobby, Red-footed Falcon, Levant Sparrowhawk (in e. Europe), and Eurasian Sparrowhawk nest and exploit the abundance of prey in these very productive forests. Black-crowned Night Herons and various other heron species regularly nest in Mediterranean Riparian Forest. European Turtle-Doves are frequently seen resting or cooing in the trees before flying off to feed in the more open habitats of the surrounding farmland.

Above right: **Melodious Warbler is a summer migrant to the Mediterranean region often found in riparian thickets, from where its characteristic song can often be heard on a fine spring morning.** © DANIELE OCCHIATO, AGAMI

Right: **The Black-crowned Night Heron favours riparian forest for breeding and is largely crepuscular and nocturnal. It is extremely widely distributed, with an almost global distribution.** © TOMÁŠ GRIM, AGAMI

The Iberian Grass Snake is one of a number of *Natrix* species found across Europe that are primarily associated with wetland habitats. © SYLVAIN REYT, AGAMI

The tiny Pygmy White-toothed Shrew favours Mediterranean Riparian Forest. At just 1.8 g (1/16 oz.), it is the smallest living mammal. You would need more than two of these shrews to add up to the weight of a Euro 10-cent coin! Riparian habitats are also ideal for most bat species of the Mediterranean zone but are particularly important to Bechstein's Bat, Pygmy Pipistrelle, and Western Barbastelle, which use them year-round. Woodpeckers work the soft wood of poplars and willows, creating cavities that are great for roosting bats, and the flying insects at a high density are an important food source. Bats also frequently use riparian forests as linear channels to navigate and move through the landscape.

The five *Natrix* grass snake species are closely associated with water and commonly found in this habitat throughout the region, with the exact species composition changing from west to east, from the Iberian Grass Snake and Viperine Snake (*N. astreptophora* and *N. maura*) in greater Iberia, the Barred Grass Snake (*N. helvetica*) in central longitudes, and the Tessellated Water Snake (*N. tessellata*) and Grass Snake (*N. natrix*) being found from about Italy eastwards into Asia. Similarly, the nine marbled and crested newt species (*Triturus* spp.) have mostly separated distributions across Europe's southern latitudes, from the cute Pygmy Marbled Newt (*T. pygmaeus*) in sw. Iberia to the Southern Crested Newt (*T. karelinii*) in the Caucasus. The Agile Frog (*Rana dalmatina*) and European Common Frog (*R. temporaria*), among others, can be found in streams and oxbows.

Rivers and riparian zones offer fantastic habitats for a great diversity of odonates. Local species diversity varies widely, but Banded Demoiselles (*Calopteryx splendens*) and various clubtails (family Gomphidae) are often about. Butterfly life can also be wonderful; the gorgeous Freyer's Purple Emperor (*Apatura metis*) is found in se. Europe, while the Lesser Purple Emperor (*Apatura ilia*) is widespread in this habitat throughout the region.

CONSERVATION: Clearing for agriculture and plantations, gravel and sand extraction, wood harvesting, livestock pressure, disturbance of the natural hydrology, and the spread of non-native plant species have all drastically reduced the extent of intact, climax-community Mediterranean Riparian Forest. Cycles of disturbance, flooding, drought, and the addition of nutrients open new niches and areas for colonisation and make riparian ecosystems particularly prone to invasion by non-native plants. Pioneer invasive plants establish quickly and become major, dominating forces in the habitat. Species from other Mediterranean-climate zones worldwide are particularly problematic, as they are well adapted to s. Europe but have fewer natural enemies controlling their growth than the native flora.

Mature riparian forests are significantly more useful and important for wildlife than young thickets and forests. The greater habitat heterogeneity offers more available niches, but the dead wood is particularly important for a wide range of (saproxylophagous) insects and the animals that

feed on them. Nonetheless, even moderately intact riparian forests can be invaluable conduits for animal movement.

DISTRIBUTION: The Mediterranean realm and warmer parts of Iberia and c. Europe.

WHERE TO SEE: Vikos Gorge, Greece; Byala Reka, Bulgaria; Katinata Protected Area, Zagrazhden, Bulgaria; Sotos y Bosque de la Ribera de Cañaverosa Nature Reserve, Murcia, Spain; Río Sella, Valencia, Spain.

Newts, like this Marbled Newt, become aquatic in the spring, when they mate and lay eggs. Nevertheless, they spend most of their time foraging in moist areas away from water. © NICOLAS BASTIDE, AGAMI

Eu3J CASPIAN RIPARIAN SCRUB

IN A NUTSHELL: Woodlands and scrublands along rivers that drain e. Europe's cold deserts and dry steppes. **Global Habitat Affinities:** AUSTRALIAN SHEOAK RIPARIAN WOODLAND. **Continental Habitat Affinities:** MEDITERRANEAN RIPARIAN FOREST. **Species Overlap:** CASPIAN WORMWOOD DESERT; CAUCASIAN SHRUB DESERT.

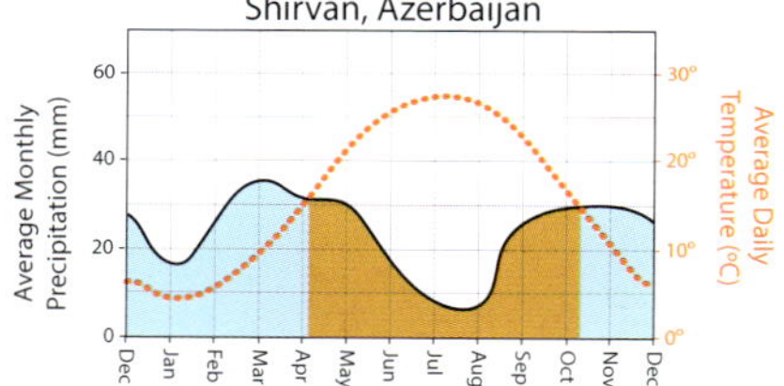

DESCRIPTION: Riparian scrublands form in a variety of environments within the arid regions of e. Europe, including temporary pans, rivers, and drainage channels. They are essentially oases in cold deserts, most of which have been heavily modified or destroyed by farming. As with the surrounding cold deserts, the scrubland climate is of warm, dry summers and bitterly cold winters. The rainfall is around 300 mm (12 in.) per year, which places it at the boundary between semi-arid and desert (Köppen **Bsk**). Average temperatures range from −15°C (5°F) in January to 25°C (77°F) in July. Summer has blistering highs up to 46°C (115°F).

This habitat ranges from shrublands to forests and extends far to the east into the cold deserts of Asia. In Europe, it occurs mainly in the low valleys or swales in the deserts where shrublands of very closely spaced bushes follow streams and other watercourses. The groves can form an impenetrable scrub about

3–4 m (9–12 ft.) high, dominated by tamarisk shrubs, such as Saltcedar (*Tamarix ramosissima*), Turanian Tamarisk (*Tamarix laxa*), and Graceful Tamarisk (*Tamarix gracilis*). Taller emergents are especially significant in somewhat more temperate environments, where Black Poplar (*Populus nigra*), Russian Olive (*Elaeagnus angustifolia*), White Willow (*Salix alba*), Goat Willow (*Salix caprea*), and sometimes even Grey Willow (*Salix cinerea*) develop as larger trees. In the moister areas, Branched Petrosimonia (*Petrosimonia brachiata*), Tuberous Bulrush (*Bolboschoenus glaucus*), Meyer's Sea-Lavender (*Limonium meyeri*), Blue Lettuce (*Lactuca tatarica*), and Marsh Mallow (*Althaea officinalis*) occur as ground cover. Common Reed (*Phragmites australis*) and REEDBED develop in the wettest of areas.

Poorly drained soils away from the water tend to be solonchaks. These are typical of moister areas within deserts and are characterised by high concentrations of soluble salts, often appearing as white crusts on the surface. In these highly saline outer edges of the groves, the Saltcedars become shorter, and the willows are replaced by Replicate Atraphaxis (*Atraphaxis replicata*) and European Ephreda (*Ephedra distachya*). In addition, halophytic plants like Saline Wormwood (*Artemisia santonicum*) are more widely spaced, growing amid a ground cover of succulent

Caspian Riparian Scrub can be more open in places (like this example in Azerbaijan), making it perfect for shrikes, bee-eaters, and other perch-and-pounce/sally hunters. © IAIN CAMPBELL, TROPICAL BIRDING

A thick tamarisk tangle in Azerbaijan, perfect habitat for Menetries's and Sykes's Warblers.
© IAIN CAMPBELL, TROPICAL BIRDING

chenopods, such as Fivehorn Smotherweed (*Bassia hyssopifolia*), Sedum-like Smotherweed (*Grubovia sedoides*), Tatarian Saltbush (*Atriplex tatarica*), Aucher's Saltbush (*Atriplex aucheri*), and Russian Atriplex (*Atriplex micrantha*). The European Ephreda is part of an ancient group of gymnosperms that evolved over 100 MYA and occur on the edge of these scrublands before they merge into habitats such as CASPIAN WORMWOOD DESERT and CAUCASIAN SHRUB DESERT.

WILDLIFE: While these areas are very important for bird migration routes, they are rather depauperate compared to more humid deciduous forests and desert scrublands. These riparian scrubs provide an oasis in arid lands, and many waterbirds associated with the wetlands need these scrubs to nest and shelter. This habitat is regularly used by species such as Great Egret, Grey Heron, Glossy Ibis, and Common Sandpiper. Some of the other birds expected in these scrublands include European and Blue-cheeked Bee-eaters, European Roller, Eurasian Golden Oriole, Red-backed Shrike, Great Grey Shrike, Lesser Grey Shrike, and Common Redstart. There is invariably a host of warblers, especially during migration, including the highly range-restricted Menetries's Warbler (which breeds in the tamarisk) and Upcher's, Eastern Olivaceous, Paddyfield, and

Above right: **The beautiful Menetries's Warbler breeds in tamarisks and is almost completely restricted to this habitat in Europe.**
© TOMI MUUKKONEN, AGAMI

Fabulously colourful Blue-cheeked Bee-eaters are common along watercourses, where they breed in sandbanks.
© VINCENT LEGRAND, AGAMI

Sykes's Warbler (pictured), best identified by its song, is confined to Caspian Riparian Scrub in Europe, while the similar Booted Warbler sticks to the shorter vegetation of the Caspian Wormwood Desert in the same region. © VINCENT LEGRAND, AGAMI

Marsh Warblers, as well as Common Chiffchaff and Lesser Whitethroat. Sykes's Warbler is confined to Caspian Riparian Scrub in Europe, while the similar Booted Warbler, found in the same region, sticks to the shorter vegetation of the CASPIAN WORMWOOD DESERT. Hunting these migrants are Levant and Eurasian Sparrowhawks. The somewhat taller vegetation of these riparian belts can allow for the establishment of Rook colonies; these in turn attract Red-footed Falcons, which use the Rook nests for breeding.

Veins of Caspian Riparian Scrub run through more arid and open desert landscapes and provide many animals with refuge and passage. They are important for Eurasian Wild Boars and the Caspian Tigers that, up until a few decades ago, hunted them. Long-eared Hedgehog and Northern White-breasted Hedgehog are both more common here than in the surrounding deserts.

Levant Sparrowhawk is a secretive breeding species but is regularly seen hunting smaller birds in and around Caspian Riparian Scrub. © VINCENT LEGRAND, AGAMI

The impressive Tessellated Water Snake is usually found close to water. © ROB OLIVIER, AGAMI

The Tessellated Water Snake and Grass Snake (*Natrix tessellata* and *N. natrix*) can both be relatively common here. They hunt smaller fish and amphibians, such as the Marsh Frog (*Pelophylax ridibundus*), Green Toad (*Bufotes viridis*), Taurus Frog (*Rana macrocnemis*), and Pallas's Spadefoot (*Pelobates vespertinus*).

The Southern Darter (*Sympetrum meridionale*), Blue-tailed Damselfly (Common Bluetail, *Ischnura elegans*), Southern Migrant Hawker (Blue-eyed Hawker, *Aeshna affinis*), Common Winter Damselfly (*Sympecma fusca*), Keeled Skimmer (*Orthetrum coerulescens*), and Black-tailed Skimmer (*O. cancellatum*) can all be relatively common. Some cool mantids use the Caspian Riparian Scrub, including the Transcaucasian Giant Mantis (*Hierodula transcaucasica*), European Mantis (*Mantis religiosa*), Dot-winged Mantis (*Iris polystictica*), and Eastern Conehead Mantis (*Empusa pennicornis*). Butterflies include many widespread species, including the Painted Lady (*Vanessa cardui*), Silver-studded Blue (*Plebejus argus*), Oriental Meadow Brown (*Hyponephele lupinus*), Old World Swallowtail (*Papilio machaon*), and Eastern Bath White (*Pontia edusa*).

CONSERVATION: Most areas where forest occurred in this habitat have been cleared for agriculture. The tamarisk scrubs are in a slightly better condition, as, in the absence of irrigation, they are not readily used for agriculture other than grazing. However, modern irrigated farming will increase clearing pressure and increase salination of the soil profile. Just east of Europe, in Asia, extensive Caspian Riparian Scrub existed around the former Aral Sea. The clearing and irrigation there have turned the former seafloor into the world's first anthropogenic desert, surrounded by remnants of a dying woodland. Unfortunately, we are seeing similar developments in the Caspian Sea, where global warming and land-use changes in the Ural River catchment mean that its water level is likely to drop by a staggering 9–18 m (30–60 ft.) in the 21st century.

DISTRIBUTION: Caspian Riparian Scrub occurs through the arid lands and deserts of Europe, around the Crimean Peninsula, to the coast of the Caspian Sea, and through Asia to China. Very small patches occur on islands in the Mediterranean, with a mix of this habitat and MEDITERRANEAN RIPARIAN FOREST. They are not big enough to contain the typical wildlife assemblage of this habitat and are included in the surrounding habitat.

WHERE TO SEE: Shirvan National Park, Azerbaijan; Gobustan National Park, Azerbaijan; Goravan Sands State Sanctuary, Azerbaijan.

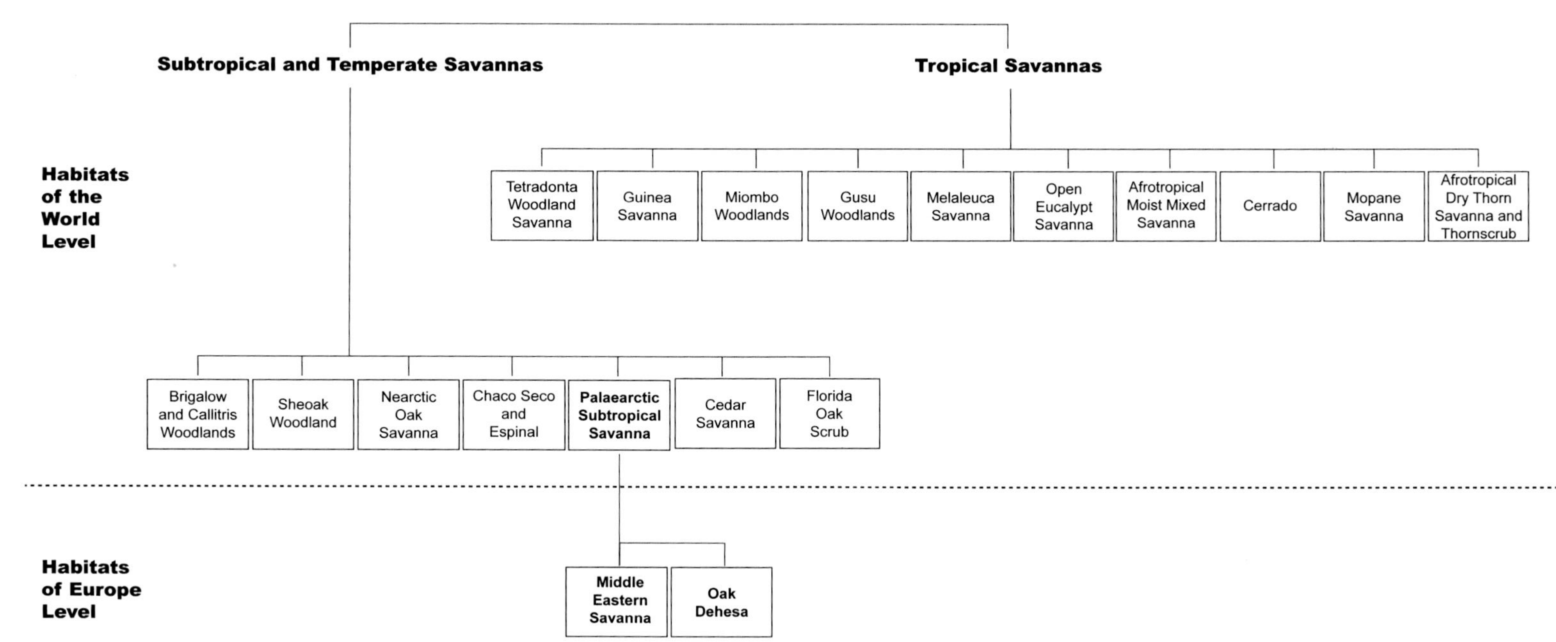
SAVANNAS
Subtropical and Temperate Savannas
Tropical Savannas
Habitats of the World Level
Tetradonta Woodland Savanna
Guinea Savanna
Miombo Woodlands
Gusu Woodlands
Melaleuca Savanna
Open Eucalypt Savanna
Afrotropical Moist Mixed Savanna
Cerrado
Mopane Savanna
Afrotropical Dry Thorn Savanna and Thornscrub
Brigalow and Callitris Woodlands
Sheoak Woodland
Nearctic Oak Savanna
Chaco Seco and Espinal
Palaearctic Subtropical Savanna
Cedar Savanna
Florida Oak Scrub
Habitats of Europe Level
Middle Eastern Savanna
Oak Dehesa

SAVANNAS

Eu6A MIDDLE EASTERN SAVANNA

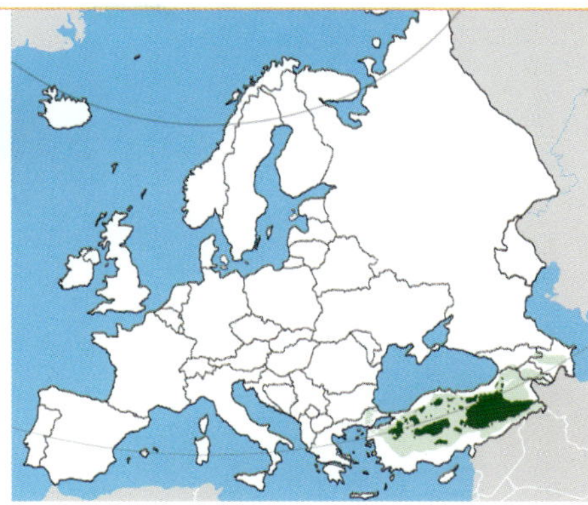

IN A NUTSHELL: Temperate and subtropical savanna of extensive grasslands peppered with oaks and other trees. **Global Habitat Affinities:** DECCAN SAVANNA; AFROTROPICAL GUSU; CALIFORNIA OAK SAVANNA. **Continental Habitat Affinities:** OAK DEHESA. **Species Overlap:** CAUCASIAN SHRUB DESERT; MEDITERRANEAN OAK FOREST.

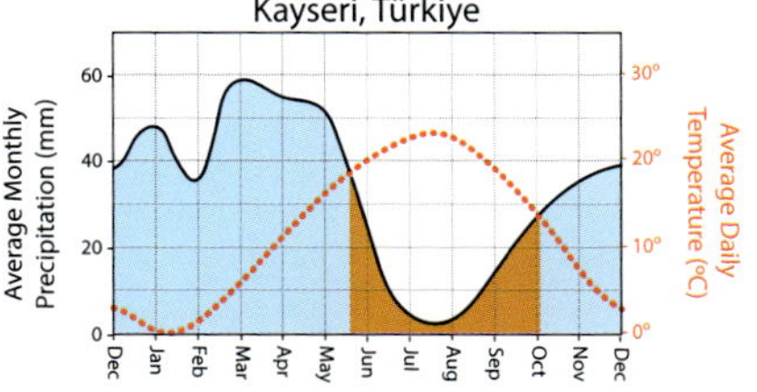

DESCRIPTION: Most people imagine Africa when thinking about savannas, but the Middle East also has some wonderful savannas. They are baking hot in midsummer, when the annual grasses and herbs are burnt to a crisp, and flocks of domestic goats shimmer in the mirage-filled shade of scattered oak and juniper trees. Nighttime provides some respite and is the most rewarding time to look for specialties like Striped Hyaena, Indian Crested Porcupine, Southwest Asian Badger, or even a Leopard!

The Middle Eastern Savanna is a predominantly Asian habitat extending into e. Türkiye, Georgia, Armenia, and Azerbaijan, occurring at the intersection of MEDITERRANEAN PINE FOREST, MEDITERRANEAN OAK FOREST, and MAQUIS with CAUCASIAN SHRUB DESERT or CAUCASIAN MONTANE DESERT STEPPE. Between these other habitats, open woodlands and grassy savannas are peppered with 10 m (30 ft.) tall junipers and oaks. They can sometimes resemble open woodlands, with trees only 8 m (25 ft.) apart, but can equally be more open savannas with 20 m (65 ft.) or more between trees. They look very similar to the OAK DEHESA of w. Europe and feel much like CALIFORNIA OAK SAVANNA or Africa's GUSU woodlands. These Middle Eastern Savannas have been around for millennia but are still poorly understood. At least some of the habitat is in a natural state, but humans undoubtedly have influenced large swaths in much the same way as they have OAK DEHESA.

In Armenia and the Anatolia region of e. Türkiye, the landscape is predominantly shaped by extremes in temperature and rainfall. The climate (**Dsa** or **Dsb**) is much like an extreme semi-arid Mediterranean climate with large temperature fluctuations; most of the 400 mm (7 in.) of precipitation falls in the spring and during snowy winters, when temperatures can get down to −32°C (−26°F). With prolonged droughts from May through October, summers can hit a scorching 50°C (122°F). Spring rains flush the landscape green, but the summer's low rainfall and high temperatures mean high evapotranspiration—up to 1800 mm (70 in.) annually—subjecting plants

A relatively open Middle Eastern Savanna in Türkiye with small, young, coppiced trees. © DOMINIC MITCHELL

This well-developed Middle Eastern Savanna in Türkiye has high structural diversity, with young and old trees as well as denser and more open areas. © DOMINIC MITCHELL

SIDEBAR 3 THE ILLUSION OF EUROPE

To even attempt to understand the habitats of Türkiye, we need to take a step back and examine the geology and geomorphology of the diverse region. We understand Türkiye and the Caucasus to be the crossroads of Europe and Asia, but this is an artificial construct. Eurasia has existed since Baltica (think Europe) joined Asia in the early Devonian around 420 MYA. This all happened when the region was in the Southern Hemisphere, and since then, it has joined and separated from North America (Laurentia) not once but twice. Arabia joined, India collided with Asia, and Japan formed.

If we look at palaeontology and biogeography as indicators, we see that Eurasia formed when terrestrial flora was limited mainly to such early plants as early bryophytes, prototype mosses, liverworts, and hornworts. There were early vascular plants, called hyniophytes, though they lacked true leaves or roots. Animals were limited to arthropods such as millipedes, proto-arachnids, and very primitive insects. The parts of Eurasia have had a shared history for the past 400 million years through the development of terrestrial evolution, including the vast majority of all animal and plant orders and all terrestrial plant and animal families.

to extreme water stress. The plants and animals of these dry savannas are arguably some of the hardiest in the world, able to tolerate drought, extreme temperature ranges, and fire.

Downy and Aleppo Oaks (*Quercus pubescens* and *Q. infectoria*) mix with some Turkish Pines (*Pinus brutia*) and smaller trees such as Persian Oak (*Quercus brantii*) and Oleaster-leaved Pear (*Pyrus elaeagrifolia*) in the drier and/or well-drained western parts of these savannas. In other areas, such as in e. Georgia, the woodlands are dominated by the widespread Pedunculate Oak (*Quercus robur* ssp. *pedunculiflora*) along with Georgian Oak (*Quercus petraea* ssp. *polycarpa*), Foetid Juniper (*Juniperus foetidissima*), and Wild Pistachio Tree (*Pistacia atlantica* ssp. *mutica*). Wild Pistachio is a much more important component of this habitat in w. Asia, where it occurs with occasional White Saxaul (*Haloxylon persicum*) trees and desert sedges that extend into the TURANIAN DUNE DESERT. The grasses and forbs are more ephemeral and annual in this habitat's eastern and southern parts, while they are perennial in the western regions.

WILDLIFE: Some exciting predators roam the Middle Eastern Savannas, from the Golden Jackal and Striped Hyaena to the (rare) Leopard and African Wildcat. Even the Northern Lion survived in this habitat well into the 19th century, and the Caspian Tiger likely went extinct in Türkiye only in the 1990s. The savanna also boasts a rich array of other mammals, including Indian Crested Porcupine, Southwest Asian Badger, Wild Goat, Williams's Jerboa,

Some exciting predators roam the Middle Eastern Savannas, from Golden Jackal (pictured) and Striped Hyaena to (rare) Leopard and African Wildcat. © HAN BOUWMEESTER, AGAMI

The endearing Long-eared Hedgehog is more likely to be encountered at night. © VINCENT LEGRAND, AGAMI

Persian Jird, Grey Dwarf Hamster, and Long-eared Hedgehog.

The skies are filled with thrilling raptors such as Long-legged Buzzard, Common Buzzard, Short-toed Snake-Eagle, (Eastern) Imperial Eagle, Saker Falcon, Egyptian Vulture, and Cinereous Vulture. Interesting ground birds include Chukar, Eurasian Thick-knee (Eurasian Stone-Curlew), Sociable Lapwing (on migration), Pin-tailed Sandgrouse, Calandra and Crested Larks, Black Redstart, Eastern Black-eared Wheatear, Finsch's Wheatear, and Rufous-tailed Scrub-Robin. White-throated Robin is quite a special bird of this habitat (and CAUCASIAN MONTANE DESERT STEPPE). Middle Eastern Savanna is an absolute stronghold of the European Roller. Black-headed Buntings sing from the scattered trees and shrubs, while Long-tailed, Lesser Grey, and (localised) Masked Shrikes use them as hunting posts, dropping down on invertebrates below or sallying out to grab something flying by. Upcher's Warbler and Greater Whitethroat tend to remain more hidden in the vegetation. Great Spotted Cuckoo is mostly restricted to this habitat (and OAK DEHESA). Laughing Dove can be common in this habitat and nearby human settlements.

Spotted Whip Snake (*Hemorrhois ravergieri*) is strongly associated with the Middle Eastern Savanna, while Red-bellied Racer (*Dolichophis schmidti*) is found both here and in neighbouring, related habitats (especially CAUCASIAN SHRUB DESERT). Caucasus Blunt-nosed Viper (*Macrovipera*

Black-headed Bunting is one of the last spring migrants to arrive on Middle Eastern Savanna, but once it does, the air is filled with its melodious song. © DANIELE OCCHIATO, AGAMI

Finsch's Wheatear prefers rockier areas within the Middle Eastern Savanna. © DANIELE OCCHIATO, AGAMI

The pallid Long-legged Buzzard patrols the savanna looking for unsuspecting rodents. It can be common in places within this habitat. © MARKKU RANTALA, AGAMI

lebetinus ssp. *obtusa*) and Caucasian Agama (*Paralaudakia caucasia*) both use rocky areas of this habitat. Greek Tortoise (*Testudo graeca*) is widespread.

CONSERVATION: Savannas are typically ecosystems that, for biodiversity to thrive, require some disturbance, be it browsing, fire, or tree management. But the habitat's richness quickly disappears when the disturbance factors get too great, and large areas of Middle Eastern Savanna suffer from overgrazing, deforestation, conversion to intensive agriculture, irrigation, or clearance for human settlements. At the other end of the spectrum, the abandonment of animal husbandry (and consequent removal of grazers from the system) and the arguably misguided planting of forests in their place are also threatening these systems. The effect of humans might be omnipresent, but Middle Eastern Savannas are actually ancient, old-growth ecosystems, and effective conservation strategies will need to strike the right level of disturbance to maintain them.

DISTRIBUTION: This habitat is more widespread in Asia than in Europe. In Europe it extends from w. Türkiye through c. Türkiye into Georgia, Armenia, and Azerbaijan.

WHERE TO SEE: Vashlovani National Park, Georgia; Kozanlı Sazlığı National Park, Türkiye.

Eu6B OAK DEHESA

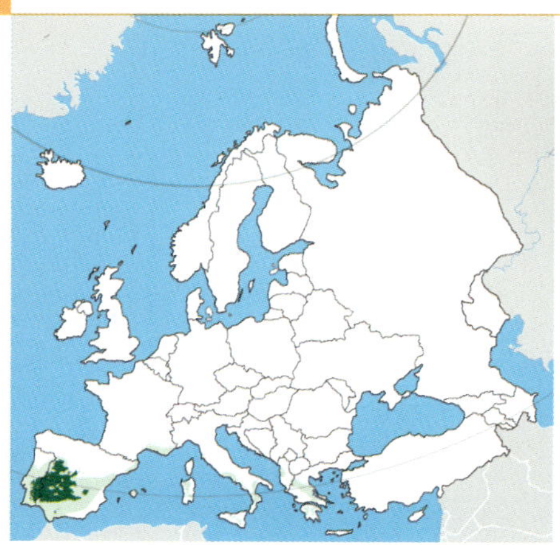

IN A NUTSHELL: The dry oak savannas of the Mediterranean realm. **Global Habitat Affinities:** CALIFORNIA OAK SAVANNA; MAGHREB BROADLEAF WOODLAND; DECCAN SAVANNA. **Continental Habitat Affinities:** MIDDLE EASTERN SAVANNA. **Species Overlap:** MEDITERRANEAN OAK FOREST; GARRIGUE; MAQUIS.

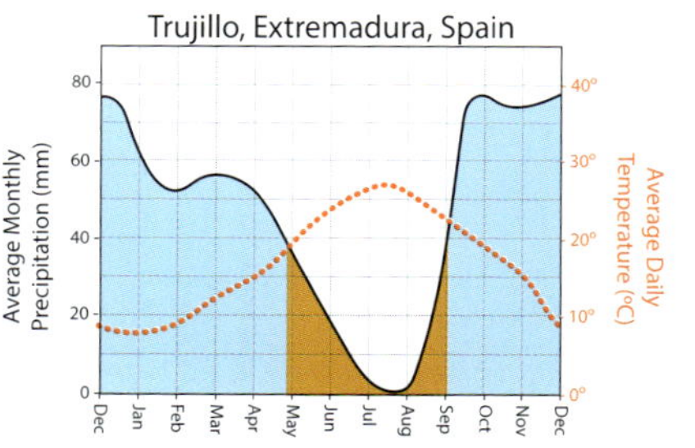

DESCRIPTION: Oak Dehesa is a managed savanna ecosystem of open pastures with scattered evergreen oak trees. Pastoralists have maintained dehesas for at least 6000 years. Still, the range of wildlife adapted to and thriving in Oak Dehesa suggests that similar habitats have existed in the region for considerably longer. Oak and pine savannas have been widespread in s. Europe over the past 2.6 million years (see Sidebar 4: Prehistoric Europe, p.208). Repeated ice ages locked up vast amounts of water in the glaciers of the mountains and n. Europe, meaning that s. Europe was considerably drier. This water scarcity meant steppes and savannas dominated the landscape, while cooler temperatures pushed more temperate fauna and flora farther south. Relatively warmer and moister periods between ice ages (interglacials) shifted the balance to more savannas, while drier, colder periods saw the expansion of steppes. Throughout the Pleistocene, the interplay of climate, geology, hydrology, browsing pressure, and fire would have created an ever-changing matrix of habitats from open steppes and savannas to denser MEDITERRANEAN OAK FOREST.

Oak Dehesa is found in Mediterranean and meso-Mediterranean climates (Köppen **Csa, Bsk**) with hot, dry summers and wet winters. It is most extensive in Portugal (known as *Montado*) and Spain but also occurs to a lesser extent in s. France and Italy, as well as in parts of the Balkans and Greece. Tree diversity at any one site is normally rather low, with one or two species dominating. Sweet Acorn Oak (*Quercus rotundifolia*) and Cork Oak (*Q. suber*) are the most characteristic tree species in the Iberian Oak Dehesa. Drier and alkaline locations tend to favour the growth of Sweet Acorn Oak, while Cork Oak prefers slightly moister sites, often in valleys or on granite tors. Downy Oak (*Q. pubescens*), Holm Oak (*Q. ilex*), and Cork Oak dominate French and Italian dehesas. A suite of other oak species (including *Q. coccifera*, *Q. cerris*, *Q. frainetto*, *Q. ithaburensis*, *Q. pyrenaica*, and *Q. petraea*) and other trees such as Sweet Chestnut (*Castanea sativa*), Eastern Hornbeam (*Carpinus orientalis*), Manna Ash (*Fraxinus ornus*), Strawberry Tree (*Arbutus unedo*), and Wild Olive (*Olea europaea*) can be regionally important.

Early in spring, carpets of flowers transform the landscape of Europe's Oak Dehesas, High Nature Value farmlands in which low intensity farming and diverse use support high biodiversity. © ROB RIEMER, AGAMI

Oak Dehesas are designated High Nature Value farmlands in which low intensity farming and diverse use support high biodiversity. Modern Oak Dehesas are managed pastoral and agricultural habitats, with farmers influencing the density of trees, tree shapes, the thickness of the shrub layer, grazing pressure, and the growing of any crops. Poor soils have, however, typically moderated agricultural ambitions and led to less intensive land use and management. This has allowed the dehesas to remain critical ecosystems throughout much of their range, with myriad fauna and flora taking advantage of the diverse and dynamically changing niches available.

The oak trees are typically pollarded at about 3 m (10 ft.). In this process, the crown is thinned to a handful of major branches and encouraged to grow outwards. The consequence is that the oak trees spread out wider (not unlike the thorn trees of an African savanna), significantly increasing the yield of acorns and providing more shade from the torturous heat of the sun. Periodic cutting also appears to slow the aging process, with oaks in dehesas typically living longer than in forests. Pruned branches are used to produce hard, aromatic charcoal for cooking and curing meats, and the harvested leaves are used to help feed livestock during the dry summer months.

Many agriculturalists of the Iberian dehesas favour Sweet Acorn Oak because of the copious quantities of sweet, edible acorns it produces. Black Iberian pigs raised in the dehesas in autumn and winter yield *jamón ibérico de bellota* (acorn-fed Iberian ham). A diet rich in acorns makes the ham distinctively flavoursome and rich in nuttiness. The farming, pigs, and hams are of great cultural importance for the dehesa regions.

Acorns are also an incredibly important food source for the Common Crane, and a considerable proportion of Europe's cranes overwinter in c. Iberia. These numbers are buoyed by irrigated maize and rice agriculture outside the dehesas. During drought periods, however, farmers are forced to switch to more drought-resistant crops, like winter cereals or beans. This forces the cranes to disperse over a much greater area in the dehesas, plains, and fields.

The poor nature of the soils in the dehesas means that crops can be effectively grown only every 5–10 years. Grains such as barley, wheat, and oats and nitrogen-fixing legumes like Common Vetch (*Vicia sativa*) are favoured and grown as fodder for livestock. Interestingly, crop production is greatest beneath trees, as soil fertility and microclimate are significantly more favourable here than away from trees (in unfertilised fields). After the harvest, the land lies fallow to recover, with some farmers planting legumes to help enrich the soil. As the vegetation develops and animals' droppings are added, the vegetation slowly changes, thus creating a dynamic suite of microhabitats for a diversity of wildlife.

Above: **Black-winged Kite can frequently be seen hovering over open areas or perched at the top of an oak.** © RALPH MARTIN, AGAMI

Below: **Oak Dehesa dries out quickly in summer and by May can already be rather brown.** © DALE FORBES

Hunting is a significant facet in the diverse use of Oak Dehesas, and many dehesas have strong populations of Red Deer, Eurasian Wild Boar, Mouflon, European Rabbit, and Red-legged Partridge. Hunting is common alongside livestock production, but some estates are managed solely for wildlife. If grazing and browsing pressure is too low, the habitat thickens and can significantly decrease biodiversity. In addition, the brushy vegetation is more likely to be considered a fire hazard. Consequently, some farmers will clear-cut the brush vegetation to reduce the fire risk. While this keeps the habitat open, it does not, unfortunately, mimic the function of the wildlife and livestock, resulting in a lower overall plant-species diversity and loss of dehesa-specialist species.

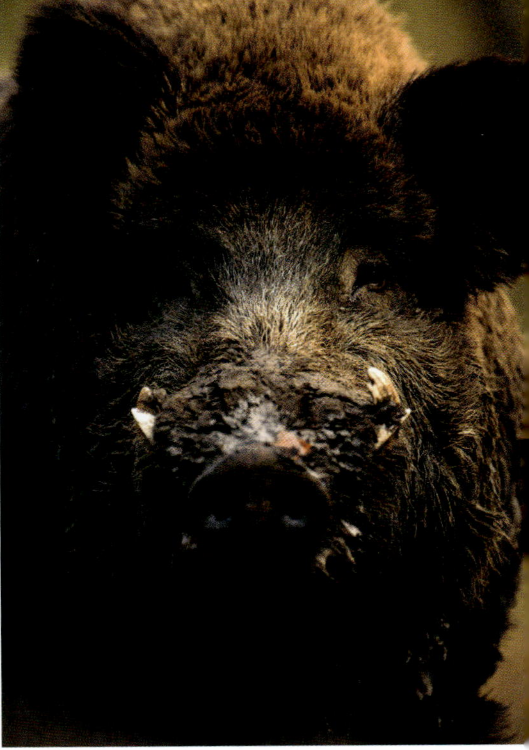

Eurasian Wild Boar forages noisily for acorns and is popular with Spanish hunters. © DANNY GREEN, AGAMI

Goat and sheep husbandry has a long tradition in the dehesas. Both are kept for their milk to produce a splendid array of cheeses, and the merino wools produced in the dehesas were a mainstay of Iberian agriculture until about the 1950s, when alternative fabrics rose in popularity, and cheap wools (especially from Australia) flooded the market. However, consumer interest and demand for merino wool have shown robust growth in recent years, making sheep farming somewhat more attractive again. Nevertheless, cows have come to dominate the livestock scene in many regions. This shift to cattle has evidently been driven by lower caretaking needs, greater demand for beef, and the European Union's Common Agricultural Policy incentives. Abundant grass growth during the (winter) rainy season is great for livestock, but as the land dries going into summer, livestock needs to be moved to other regions or provided with supplemental feed. Some dehesas now have three times the number of animals per hectare (per 2.5 ac.) than in the 1950s, with profound consequences to the landscape and cycles of change within the habitat.

The pastures can be cropped down extremely low where grazing and browsing pressure is high. Iberian Grey Shrike and European Bee-eater like the resulting open pastures with scattered, large oak trees, and Thekla's and Crested Larks are particularly common. Nonetheless, the beautiful and unusual Eurasian Hoopoe is the true icon of short-cropped dehesas: the open ground is perfect for foraging, and the old, gnarled oaks make fantastic breeding sites with abundant natural cavities. Wood-boring beetles—especially longhorn beetles like Great Capricorn Beetle (*Cerambyx cerdo*), as well as *C. welensii*, and *Prinobius myardi*—open cavities where rot can take hold in the wood. This is great for cavity-nesting birds and a natural part of the ecosystem. Still, when combined with other environmental stressors, especially drought, it can cause major damage and tree death.

New oak recruitment is of concern to pastoralists, especially where livestock pressure is high, as livestock, when at higher densities, tends to crop the dehesas shorter and limit the development of shrubs that provide a protective environment in which young oaks can establish. Spanish Heath (*Erica australis*), Pincushion Gorse (*Genista hirsuta*), and Rosemary (*Salvia rosmarinus*) are particularly important in facilitating oak recruitment.

Iberian Lynx is the iconic apex predator of Oak Dehesa. © OSCAR DÍEZ, AGAMI

Oak Dehesas with more structure—scattered rocky outcrops and vegetation—become more interesting for the reclusive Eurasian Thick-knee (Eurasian Stone-Curlew). Woodchat Shrike is much more obvious, as it intermittently drops to the floor to pick up insects. The abundant beetles, hairy caterpillars, diverse insect larvae, millipedes, and other insect life are also the focus of the habitat's archetypal species: the Iberian Magpie.

If allowed, the understorey of Oak Dehesa can also develop a bushier, denser, lower vegetation reminiscent of GARRIGUE or MAQUIS, attracting species from those habitats. Dartford, Western Subalpine, Western Orphean, and Sardinian Warblers chatter from the scrub, while European Serins and European Greenfinches display overhead and Ladder Snakes (*Zamenis scalaris*) slither by quietly. European Rabbits take advantage of the protective cover of the vegetation, creating vast warrens where softer soils allow. Rabbits are ecosystem engineers, and their burrows, feeding, and latrines create diverse niches for plants and wildlife, significantly increasing the local biodiversity.

Rabbits are also the principal prey items of another two of the dehesas' most iconic species: Spanish (Imperial) Eagle and Iberian Lynx. Both species concentrate their hunting and breeding in the dehesas. Spanish Eagles nest in tall trees, particularly in Sweet Acorn and Cork Oaks in the dehesas, while using various pines (especially *Pinus pinaster*) in fringe habitats. The Spanish Eagle's habitat specialisation suggests that, while the modern dehesas are agricultural landscapes, something akin to them must have existed for millennia in the Iberian Peninsula. The dehesas represent a sweet spot of high productivity and protective shelter for many wildlife species.

Cork Oaks often stand out in the dehesas, as they grow much larger than the Sweet Acorn Oak and other oaks. Large Cork Oaks are also particularly interesting as nesting trees for a wide range of raptors. In addition, their strongly fissured bark creates innumerable nooks and crannies for invertebrates. This is also reflected in the birdlife, with Lesser Spotted Woodpecker, Crested

The powerful and rare Spanish (Imperial) Eagle is the avian showpiece of the dehesa. © OSCAR DÍEZ, AGAMI

Tit, Short-toed Treecreeper, and Eurasian Wryneck being particularly abundant where Cork Oaks are common. Their acorns are not as good for feeding pigs as those from Sweet Acorn Oaks, but the cork itself is a valuable crop. Farmers carefully remove the cork bark from the trees in the summer months, endeavouring to do this in the biggest planks possible. The first two harvests produce a lighter cork, used for insulation or floats. Thereafter, the cork develops a more suitable structure for wine bottle stoppers and is harvested every nine years for about 150 years.

Desert truffles (*Terfezia* spp.) grow well in many dehesas and have become an important part of the regional cuisine and a valuable complementary income source.

WILDLIFE: Iberian Lynx, Iberian Magpie, and Spanish Eagle embody the great wildlife found in Oak Dehesa. Raptors can be diverse and abundant, including Black-winged, Red, and Black Kites; Bonelli's and Booted Eagles; Short-toed Snake-Eagle; and Eurasian (Common) Kestrel. Iberian Oak Dehesas are the best places in Europe to see vultures, with fairly large numbers of Eurasian

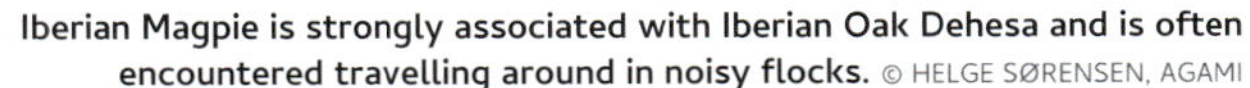

Iberian Magpie is strongly associated with Iberian Oak Dehesa and is often encountered travelling around in noisy flocks. © HELGE SØRENSEN, AGAMI

Cinereous Vulture, one of Europe's scarcer breeding raptors, is easily found in extensive areas of dehesa.
© DALE FORBES

Griffon, Cinereous Vulture, and Egyptian Vulture in some areas. Woodchat Shrike and Iberian Grey Shrike hawk from exposed perches, while Sardinian, Dartford, Western Orphean, and Western Subalpine Warblers skulk in the bushes. Open areas attract Thekla's, Greater Short-toed, Crested, and Calandra Larks, as well as Eurasian Hoopoe, Red-legged Partridge, Little Bustards, and Cirl Bunting. European Bee-eaters are common near breeding sandbanks and are joined in the air by Pallid, Common, and Alpine Swifts in addition to the almost ubiquitous European Red-rumped Swallow. Red-necked Nightjar, Eurasian Nightjar, Eurasian Scops-Owl, Little Owl, and Eurasian Thick-knee (Eurasian Stone-Curlew) work the night shift.

Wild mammals can be abundant in Oak Dehesa, which supports good populations of Eurasian Wild Boar, Red Deer, European Fallow Deer, European Rabbit, Granada Hare, Common Hedgehog, and European Badger. Predators include Red Fox, European Wildcat, Egyptian Mongoose, and Stone Marten. Northern Small-spotted (Common) Genet is scarce and reclusive but in Europe does seem to favour Oak Dehesas, especially those with access to shrub cover and rocky ground or cliffs. Modern Oak Dehesas are human-maintained ecosystems, but Europe's great megafauna would have been the ecosystem engineers in the past (see Sidebar 4: Prehistoric Europe, p.208). Straight-tusked Elephants would have broken and pushed over trees, keeping vegetation relatively open. Both the elephant and the Narrow-nosed Rhinoceros were mixed browsers and grazers, while stronger grazing pressure came from the enormous Aurochs, Common Hippopotamus, Wild Horse, and European Wild Ass. The temperate megafauna would have had a substantial role in maintaining the ecosystem matrix, resulting in the evolution of many interesting species in Europe's savannas. Unfortunately, humans seem to have dealt a death blow to this phenomenal collection of species as the last ice age pushed it into smaller refuge areas in s. Europe.

Abundant insect life in the dehesas makes the habitat ideal for bats. Some species here include Nathusius's Pipistrelle, Pygmy Pipistrelle, Kuhl's Pipistrelle, and Lesser Noctule.

The warm, thriving ecosystems of the Oak Dehesas mean that reptiles are widespread and relatively abundant. Keep a look out for the Iberian False Smooth Snake (*Macroprotodon brevis*), Western Montpellier Snake (*Malpolon monspessulanus*), Horseshoe Whip Snake (*Hemorrhois hippocrepis*), Ladder Snake, Ocellated Lizard (*Timon lepidus*), and Large Psammodromus (*Psammodromus algirus*). Spiny-footed Lizard (*Acanthodactylus erythrurus*) prefers drier, more open dehesas, using cork bark or rocky areas for shelter. Two worm snakes occur in the Iberian dehesas: Southwest Iberian Worm Lizard (*Blanus cinereus*) and Central Iberian Worm Lizard (*B. vandellii*). These bizarre, enigmatic subterranean reptiles are rarely seen but might be found by searching under rocks.

The dehesas hold some interesting mantids, from the Iberian Mantis (*Apteromantis aptera*), introduced Giant African Mantis (*Sphodromantis viridis*), and delightfully cute European Dwarf

Mantis (*Ameles spallanzania*) to the frankly peculiar Mediterranean Conehead Mantis (*Empusa pennata*) with its fantastic headwear. Sweat bees (*Lasioglossum* spp.), Western Honeybee (*Apis mellifera*), and the Small Shaggy Bee (*Panurgus calcaratus*) are typically the most common bees in Spanish Oak Dehesa. The Common Globetail (Long Hoverfly, *Sphaerophoria scripta*) is an important pollinator in some areas, with its black and yellow striping resembling that of a wasp (a Batesian mimicry defence). Specialist and interesting butterfly species include the False Ilex Hairstreak (*Satyrium esculi*), Purple Hairstreak (*Favonius quercus*), and Spanish Purple Hairstreak (*Laeosopis roboris*).

Giant African Mantis, truly impressive when seen close up, is one of a multitude of similar mantids in European Oak Dehesa. It is, however, an introduced species. © RALPH MARTIN, AGAMI

CONSERVATION: Despite their great biodiversity and cultural value, Oak Dehesas are facing great pressures from the intensification of land use (especially overgrazing) and abandonment. Both extremes in land-use management result in profound changes to the ecosystem. This is exacerbated when the management is homogenised over large areas such that the dehesas lose the biodiversity benefits of a matrix ecosystem comprising a variety of micro-niches. Low to non-existent tree regeneration and climate change–aggravated desiccation are additional challenges for the habitat.

DISTRIBUTION: Found within the Mediterranean region, Oak Dehesas are most extensive in Spain (~1.55 million ha/3.8 million ac.) and Portugal (~1.05 million ha/2.6 million ac.). They are also found in France, Italy, Croatia, Bosnia and Herzegovina, and Greece. See MIDDLE EASTERN SAVANNA for a similar habitat in Türkiye and the Caucasus region.

WHERE TO SEE: Trujillo, Extremadura, Spain; Mértola, Alentejo, Portugal; Monte Pisanu, Sardinia, Italy.

SIDEBAR 4 PREHISTORIC EUROPE: WHY WE HAVE THE SPECIES WE DO

Picture a wildlife-filled savanna. Grasses sway in a gentle breeze as a herd of bison slowly moves past a solitary grazing rhino. In the background, a herd of elephants pushes over a tree to reach tender leaves. Can you hear the lark singing peacefully overhead? A lion roars somewhere off to the south. This was Europe.

Europe has changed a lot over the millennia since early humans first arrived. The climate has been changing slowly but continually in flux between colder, drier glacial periods and warmer interstadials. Colder periods saw Arctic and cold-adapted communities and habitats moving farther south. During warmer periods, species that preferred more temperate and warmer conditions were able to extend their ranges towards the Arctic. This process had started long before our ancestors reached Europe and has been one of the three most important drivers for today's wildlife communities. The others are the extermination of the extraordinary wildlife described in the opening paragraph of this sidebar and the large-scale transformation of habitats.

The past 2.6 million years have seen repeated glacial periods: colder temperatures resulted in extensive glacial sheets covering much of n. and c. Europe. So much water was locked up in ice and snow that the remaining ice-free regions of s. Europe were rather dry. Trees were forced south of the ice sheets. Moreover, the arid conditions meant that they would likely have been found only in open savannas, with forests persisting only in moist, protected valleys along watercourses. Small forest refuges and widespread savannas would have reduced animals that were forest specialists and created a relatively depauperate assemblage of generalists. We see this most obviously with our forest birds, most of which do as well in open forest ecosystems as in almost any other forest type (e.g., Great Tit, Eurasian Nuthatch, and Eurasian Wren). The somewhat more specialised birds of MONTANE SPRUCE-FIR FOREST are also found in many coniferous and mixed forests, and those of BEECH FOREST are found in most deciduous and mixed forests.

Open savannas, grasslands, and heathlands would have dominated the ice-free regions of Europe for much of the past 2 million years (the Pleistocene). A dizzying array of birds, invertebrates, and plants pay testament to the long periods in which open habitats dominated the European landscape. Grazing Woolly Mammoths were found alongside Woolly Rhinoceros, Steppe Bison, Muskox, Reindeer, Saiga, Scimitar-toothed Cat, Grey Wolf, Steppe (Cave) Lion, and Cave Hyaena. These were the architects of the mammoth steppe—a highly productive, dry, cold grassland habitat that was once one of the most extensive habitats on the planet. During the last glacial maximum (peaking about 20,000 YA), these cold-adapted species were pushed farther south and east as rainfall and wind patterns changed. This was as humans were expanding north into more frigid climes. Most of our megafauna did not survive, and humans proliferated.

If we look back to the Eemian (last interglacial period), about 120,000 YA, we find a climate very similar to that of modern Europe and potentially a little warmer. This gives us the clearest idea of what Europe could have looked like without the impact of our species. It makes our imagination run wild, dreaming about what we could have experienced. The Straight-tusked Elephant was a browser and mixed feeder and undoubtedly had a similar effect on the landscape to that of African Elephants. Herds of Wild Horses, European Wild Asses, and Aurochs were very significant grazers and added to the safari feeling of Europe's warmer steppes. Narrow-nosed Rhinoceros fed on grasses, forbs, and other low-growing vegetation (à la Africa's White Rhinoceros), while Merck's Rhinoceros was a browser and likely preferred somewhat denser vegetation (à la Black Rhino). The influence of Europe's megafauna was so great that these animals kept more than half of Europe as grasslands or savanna despite the climate being suitable for extensive forests. The vegetarian Cave Bear was significantly bigger than the other local bear, the mostly carnivorous Brown Bear. The former is now extinct, while the latter has become almost exclusively vegetarian. This is likely because farmers targeted Brown Bears with a predilection for livestock and hence selected for a slow drift to greater vegetarianism. The Dhole, Spotted Hyaena, and Leopard all had widespread European subspecies. After the large, maneless Steppe Lion was driven to extinction, the Northern Lion expanded into Europe before disappearing again in about the 10th century.

Wild rivers and streams are quite different from the controlled channels that they have become in much of Europe. Meandering rivers would have regularly formed oxbow lakes, while beavers supported flooding and opened riparian forests. The resulting glades were likely the favoured habitat for European Water Buffalo, Common Hippopotamus, Aurochs, and European Elk (Moose). WET GRASSLANDS formed, with the large beasts carving out paths, open patches, muddy scrapes, and shallow pools. This created myriad microhabitats for invertebrates, amphibians, reptiles, birds, and plants.

Our influence on European habitats has accelerated since the agricultural revolution, with large swaths of the continent being transformed into CROPLAND, managed pastures, depauperate plantations, and URBAN ENVIRONMENTS. Waves of change through the Pleistocene have favoured generalists and made our continent's species rather adaptable. Nevertheless, the rate of change over the past century is proving tragically challenging for many species, as our climate is changing 30 times faster than at any other time in the planet's history. Agricultural intensification favours vast fertilised and pesticide-sprayed monocultures. Essentially, Europe should be a diverse and ever-changing mixture of habitats likely more akin to Africa's wildlife-filled savannas and woodlands than the endless dark forests of the Brothers Grimm. We may not be able to return to this ideal, but as a society, we could choose to allow biodiversity more space between our fields and consciously use large mammals to help shape ecosystems in a semi-natural way.

A reconstructed image of Narrow-nosed Rhinoceros, Straight-tusked Elephant, and Steppe Bison. Europe's native megafauna were important landscape engineers and would have contributed significantly to keeping parts of the landscape open.

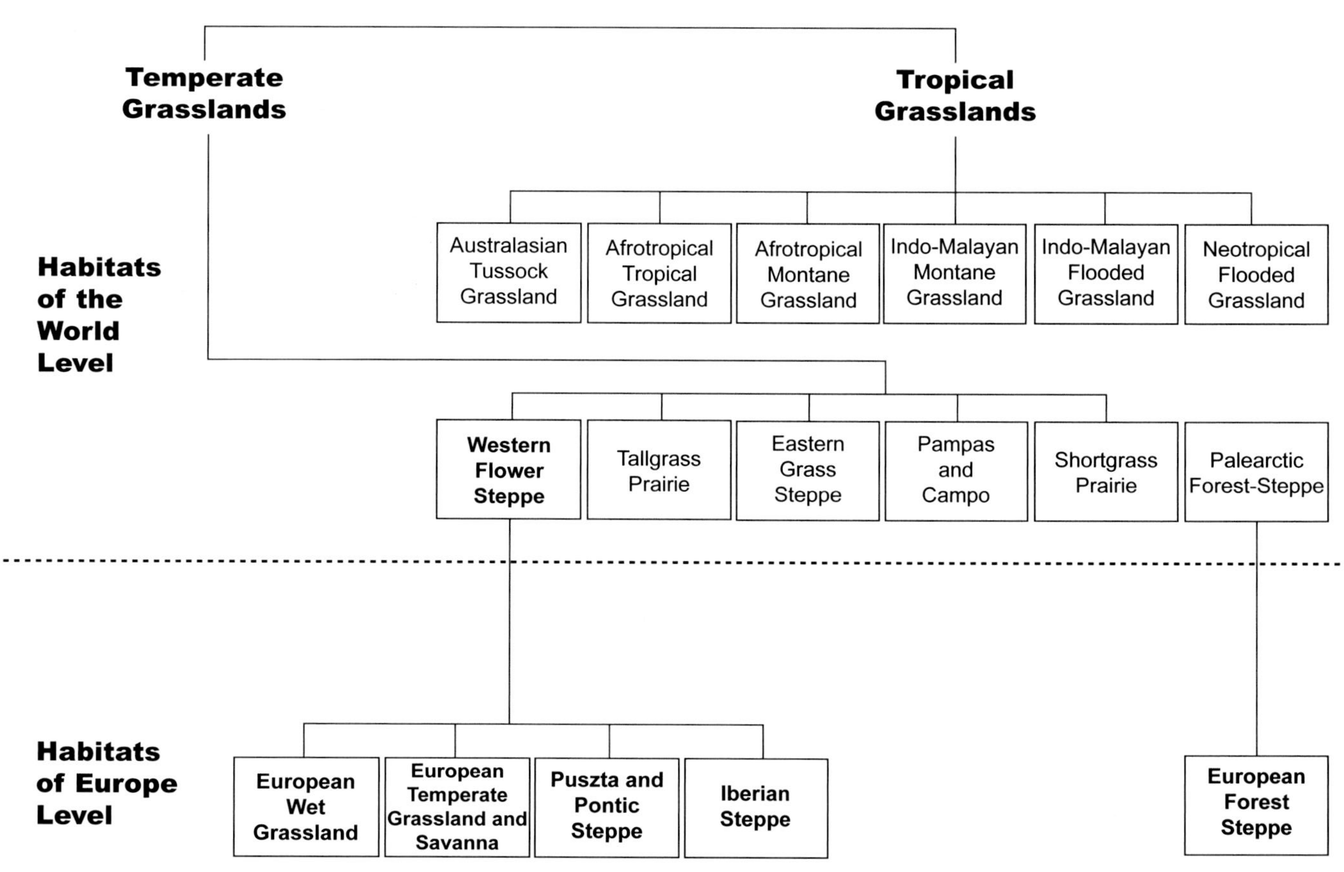
GRASSLANDS AND STEPPES
Temperate Grasslands
Tropical Grasslands
Habitats of the World Level
Australasian Tussock Grassland
Afrotropical Tropical Grassland
Afrotropical Montane Grassland
Indo-Malayan Montane Grassland
Indo-Malayan Flooded Grassland
Neotropical Flooded Grassland
Western Flower Steppe
Tallgrass Prairie
Eastern Grass Steppe
Pampas and Campo
Shortgrass Prairie
Palearctic Forest-Steppe
Habitats of Europe Level
European Wet Grassland
European Temperate Grassland and Savanna
Puszta and Pontic Steppe
Iberian Steppe
European Forest Steppe

GRASSLANDS AND STEPPES

Eu7A EUROPEAN WET GRASSLAND

IN A NUTSHELL: Wet pastures and hay meadows on flat or gently sloping ground, often in a matrix with wetlands, mires, drier grasslands, or other habitats. **Global Habitat Affinities:** NEARCTIC SEDGE AND GRASSLAND MARSHES; ASIAN FLOODED GRASSLAND. **Continental Habitat Affinities:** SHALLOW FRESHWATER MARSH. **Species Overlap:** SHALLOW FRESHWATER MARSH.

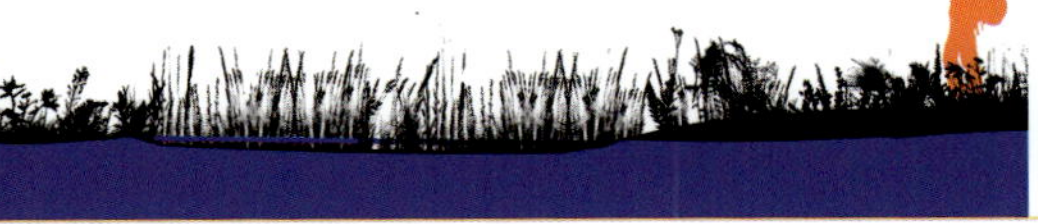

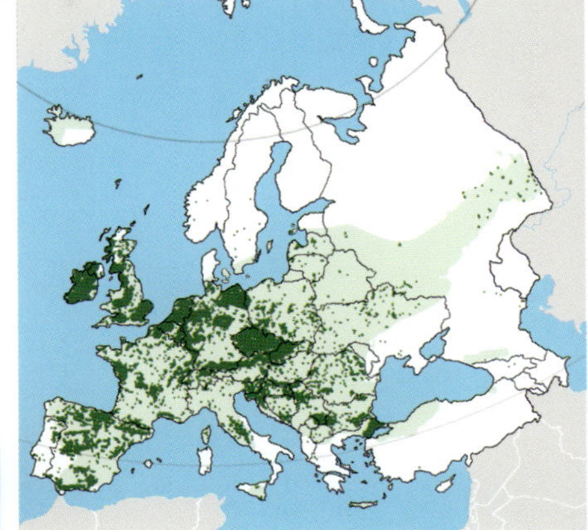

DESCRIPTION: These are muddy, squelchy places best explored with rubber boots—and a sense of adventure, for a hunkered-down Jack Snipe might explode from under your feet at any moment! The unstable footing can make Wet Grassland hard to move through, so sticking to paths and roads is often your best bet, especially when birds are breeding.

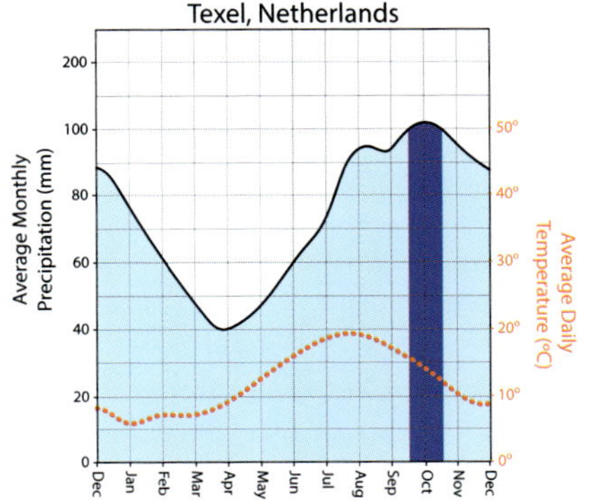

Wet Grasslands form on and near valley floors where water accumulates and the water table is high. They range in elevation from lowlands to the montane zone and in size from small dales and glades to extensive floodplain grasslands around lakes or watercourses. Flooding can be seasonal, and many of these grasslands will be partially inundated in winter and spring and dry by summer.

The plant and animal communities of Wet Grassland are determined by two major factors: whether they are in floodplains or areas that are rarely flooded and whether they are wildflower meadows or heavily grazed pastures. Soils on floodplains and around lakes can be nutrient-rich, making for a wonderfully diverse ecosystem, with myriad wildflowers, dancing damselflies, croaking frogs, and breeding shorebirds. Periodic flooding by a river flushes the habitat with fresh, nutrient-rich soils and organic matter, effectively fertilising and energising the system. In contrast, long periods of inundation, especially deep into the warmer months, create an anoxic environment in the soil and favour marsh plant species and the development of SHALLOW FRESHWATER MARSH.

Wet Grassland, Germany. © DALE FORBES

The plant and animal communities associated with Wet Grassland evolved with Europe's megafauna, and this was the preferred habitat of the European Water Buffalo, Aurochs, and Common Hippopotamus. Together with Straight-tusked Elephant and Merck's Rhinoceros, these landscape architects would have kept the habitat open and allowed the incredible diversity of species to evolve. Sadly, all five of these charismatic large mammals are now extinct in Europe, and the hippopotamus survives only in Africa. Nowadays, active management is required to maintain Wet Grassland systems, without which encroachment by bushes and trees is inevitable. The conscious use of horses, cattle, sheep, and mowing can keep Wet Grassland free of trees and ideal for plant diversity. In addition, managing the structure of the sward allows a complex matrix of microhabitats to be created according to the needs of different species.

Traditionally, floodplain hay meadows were mown once a year and were only briefly, lightly grazed. This allowed plenty of time for grassland wildlife to reproduce and for plants to flower and set seed. Wet Grassland supports a dazzling array of herbs, including Marsh Marigold (*Caltha palustris*), Ragged-Robin (*Silene flos-cuculi*), Marsh Horsetail (*Equisetum palustre*), Creeping Buttercup (*Ranunculus repens*), Meadow Pea (*Lathyrus pratensis*), Meadow Foxtail (*Alopecurus pratensis*), Meadowsweet (*Filipendula ulmaria*), Greater Bird's-foot Trefoil (*Lotus pedunculatus*), Great Burnet (*Sanguisorba officinalis*), Fen Bedstraw (*Galium uliginosum*), Brown Sedge (*Carex disticha*), and Soft Rush (*Juncus effusus*). These rich, knee-high meadows are the best places to listen on warm summer evenings for the rasping *krek-krek* of advertising Corn Crakes.

Grazing—especially by cattle and water buffalo—changes the grassland structure, opening paths, bare ground, miniature pools, and a matrix of short and tall vegetation. This can stimulate biodiversity through the creation of myriad microhabitats and realms for a wide range of plants as well as invertebrates and larger animals. Nevertheless, high levels of grazing tend to reduce plant diversity and encourage a community of species tolerant of trampling, soil compaction, and heavy grazing. There tend to be fewer showy flowers, and invertebrate diversity is correspondingly lower. Creeping Bent (*Agrostis stolonifera*) dominates the sward, but other grasses include Perennial Ryegrass (*Lolium perenne*), Water Manna Grass (*Glyceria fluitans*), Marsh Foxtail (*Alopecurus geniculatus*), and Purple Moor Grass (*Molinia caerulea*). Additional hardy species include various rushes (such as *Juncus inflexus*, *J. acutiflorus*, *J. subnodulosus*, and *J. articulatus*), Creeping Buttercup, White Clover (*Trifolium repens*), Strawberry Clover (*Trifolium fragiferum*), Pennyroyal (*Mentha pulegium*), Meadow Fleabane (*Pentanema britannica*), Greater Plantain (*Plantago major*), Common Silverweed (*Argentina anserina*), Curled Dock (*Rumex crispus*), and Tubular Water-Dropwort (*Oenanthe fistulosa*).

Common Snipe prefers wet pastures during both the breeding and the non-breeding seasons. Ideal snipe habitat comprises about two-thirds taller tussocks (~60 cm/2 ft. high) and one-third shorter grasses (5–15 cm/2–6 in.) with smaller open areas. The ground should be soggy or wet. The snipe does not require open water but will use the edges of pools when suitable habitat is limited. It will avoid harder soils, extensive short grass, grazing pressure, and frequent disturbance.

Similarly, large, open wet pastures with a mixed sward height of about 30 cm (12 in.) and 30% rush cover make an ideal habitat for Eurasian Curlew. Common Redshank and Black-tailed Godwit prefer shorter swards (<15 cm/6 in.), but some taller tussocks are important for nests and protective cover for the chicks. Both species need shallow open water nearby for feeding. Northern Lapwing prefers even shorter swards (70% at <5 cm/2 in. high), with some scattered 30 cm (12 in.) tussocks. The lapwing does well on moist soils but is not as dependent on them as some other Wet Grassland breeding shorebirds. As a result, lapwings are often found on short agricultural fields but invariably choose wide, open areas, presumably so they can spot potential predators early. Eurasian Wigeon, swans, and geese also feed readily on floodplain pastures with short swards, especially in fields where White Clover is abundant in the winter. Western Yellow Wagtail feeds on well-trampled, open pastures while breeding in thicker, higher tussocks.

Wet Grassland can also develop in depressions in the landscape far away from a floodplain. This type is usually found in a matrix with TEMPERATE PEATLAND and TEMPERATE GRASSLAND AND SAVANNA, from the lowlands to the montane zone. It can be regularly inundated with water, especially in winter, but dries out in the warmer months. However, without

Corn Crake is particularly dependent on Wet Grasslands, but the intensification of agriculture has had a severely detrimental effect on this and many other species. © BENCE MÁTÉ, AGAMI

Attractive marsh orchids (*Dactylorhiza* spp.) add colour to Wet Grassland in spring. © DALE FORBES

Below left: **Common Redshanks relentlessly and vocally defend their territories in Wet Grassland.** © JACOB GARVELINK, AGAMI

Below right: **The Slender-billed Curlew is now, sadly, extinct. It tended to be found in Wet Grassland, Coastal Salt Marsh, and other open habitats.** © HANS GEBUIS, AGAMI

regular flooding, the soils tend to be nutrient-poor. Productivity is, therefore, not as high as in the nutrient-rich floodplains, and these grasslands are usually only lightly grazed or mown once a year. Invertebrate and plant diversity can be quite high, with beautiful, colourful highlights, including Siberian Iris (*Iris sibirica*), Marsh Gentian (*Gentiana pneumonanthe*), Heath Spotted Orchid (*Dactylorhiza maculata*), Broad-leaved Marsh Orchid (*Dactylorhiza majalis*), and Devil's-bit Scabious (*Succisa pratensis*). The sward is grassy and dominated by Purple Moor Grass, sometimes with Quaking-Grass (*Briza media*). Peatier soils have more sedges (such as *Carex nigra* and *C. panicea*) and rushes (such as *Juncus acutiflorus* and *J. conglomeratus*). Corn Crake readily uses this habitat when it has a good sward height and is relatively undisturbed.

WILDLIFE: Wet Grasslands are lively places in springtime, with birds and buzzing insects everywhere. Common Redshanks cruise about calling incessantly, but Eurasian Curlews undoubtedly have the more beautiful repertoire. With some luck, you might find the more localised Black-tailed Godwit, the secretive Common Snipe, or maybe even a Great Snipe! However, Corn Crake and Common Quail take secrecy to the next level: they are relatively easy to hear in taller wet meadows but nearly impossible to see. Shorter

A number of forms of Western Yellow Wagtails occur in Wet Grasslands across our region. This is a male of the 'blue-headed' form. © MENNO VAN DUIJN, AGAMI

Wet Grasslands with open areas attract Western Yellow Wagtail and White Wagtail, with the former needing more tussocky habitat nearby to breed. The Citrine Wagtail—arguably the most beautiful of Europe's wagtails—also favours this habitat to breed. A tall sward with even taller tussocks attracts Reed Bunting. Whinchat, European Stonechat, Red-backed Shrike, Meadow Pipit, and Yellowhammer all readily use Wet Grassland, provided there are enough singing and hunting posts. All these breeding birds, invertebrates, and small mammals offer plentiful food for Western Barn Owl, Short-eared Owl, Montagu's Harrier, Eurasian Hobby, Eurasian (Common) Kestrel, Peregrine Falcon, and many other raptors.

Red Fox and Western Roe Deer are probably the two wild mammals most seen in Wet Grassland, although a whole host of species will use the habitat. This is where you are most likely

Citrine Wagtail forages for small invertebrates in short Wet Grassland. This species has spread west in recent decades. © RALPH MARTIN, AGAMI

The Common Spreadwing can often be found in rushes at the margins of shallow pools in Wet Grassland. © ONNO WILDSCHUT, AGAMI

to see a European Elk (Moose) as it carefully picks out soft leaves and flowers from among the rougher grasses (which it will not eat).

Grass Snake (*Natrix natrix*), Iberian Grass Snake (*Natrix astreptophora*), and Barred Grass Snake (*Natrix helvetica*) are commonly found in this habitat (with the species varying by geographic region) as they pursue diverse amphibians, including the European Toad (*Bufo bufo*) and European Common Frog (*Rana temporaria*).

Wet Grasslands, especially those adjacent to water bodies, are often alive with dragonflies and damselflies in the summer. Common Spreadwing (*Lestes sponsa*), Common Blue Damselfly (Common Bluet, *Enallagma cyathigerum*), Azure Damselfly (Azure Bluet, *Coenagrion puella*), and Large Red Damselfly (*Pyrrhosoma nymphula*) are especially widespread. Darters (*Sympetrum* spp.) can be particularly abundant in late summer, providing plentiful food for Eurasian Hobbies.

Butterflies of note include the Marsh, Bog, and Lesser

The lovely Marsh Fritillary can be found sipping nectar on various flowering plants in Wet Grassland. © WIL LEURS, AGAMI

Marbled Fritillaries (*Euphydryas aurinia*, *Boloria eunomia*, and *Brenthis ino*), Violet Copper (*Lycaena helle*), Brown Hairstreak (*Thecla betulae*), and Marbled White (*Melanargia galathea*), as well as the bumblebee-mimicking Narrow-bordered Bee Hawkmoth (*Hemaris tityus*). The Large Copper (*Lycaena dispar*) is largely restricted to Wet Grasslands with docks (*Rumex* spp.). Caterpillars of the Alcon Large Blue (*Phengaris alcon*) feed almost exclusively inside the flowers of Marsh Gentian. When large enough, they drop to the ground and produce a chemical that entices (mainly) *Myrmica* ants to carry the parasitic caterpillar into their nest. Feeder ants then provide for the caterpillar alongside the ant larvae. The story gets even more bizarre when the fascinating *Ichneumon* parasitic wasp enters the picture. It specialises on Alcon Large Blues and enters the ant nests, emitting a pheromone that confuses the attacking ants. It then lays an egg in the caterpillar, and the wasp larva pupates within the butterfly pupa.

CONSERVATION: Changing agricultural practices have put many of Europe's Wet Grasslands at risk. Water management can stop flooding or dry out soils, causing slow shifts in plant (and animal) communities. Abandonment of grazing leads to bush and tree encroachment, while overgrazing creates a uniform low-cropped sward unsuitable for many breeding birds and other wildlife. However, land-use intensification is the most significant pressure in many parts of Europe. Hayfields are regularly sprayed with manure mixes or chemical fertilisers, stimulating plant growth and dramatically reducing plant diversity. Grasses dominate, sometimes accompanied by a single flowering species (e.g., dandelions, *Taraxacum* spp.). These 'improved' grasslands may still look attractive, but their uniformity makes for impoverished invertebrate communities. Removing hedges, shrubs, and other 'disturbing' structures, as well as frequent mowing, make the wildlife communities sadly depauperate. Taken to the extreme, water levels are controlled, and crops are planted, eliminating wildlife habitat altogether.

A great variety of butterflies, such as this Violet Copper, are attracted to flowers in Wet Grassland.
© WIL LEURS, AGAMI

DISTRIBUTION: Wet Grasslands are widespread throughout Europe, from the lowlands to the montane zone. They are primarily associated with watercourses and lakes but also form in valley bottoms. Brackish Wet Grassland can develop alongside COASTAL SALT MARSH and other coastal wetlands, especially in the Baltic region.

WHERE TO SEE: Dartmoor, Devon, England, UK; Nene Washes, Cambridgeshire, England, UK; Rhine delta, Vorarlberg, Austria; Texel, Netherlands.

Eu7B EUROPEAN TEMPERATE GRASSLAND AND SAVANNA

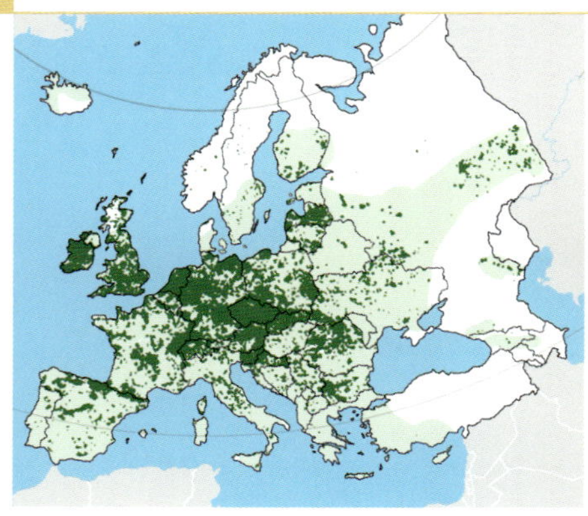

IN A NUTSHELL: Open, grassy habitat found throughout Europe's temperate zone. It is maintained through cutting (meadows) or livestock grazing (pastures), but biodiversity plummets when fertilised. **Global Habitat Affinities:** NORTH AMERICAN PASTURELAND AND RANGELAND; AUSTRALIAN MONTANE GRASSLAND. **Continental Habitat Affinities:** PUSZTA AND PONTIC STEPPE; IBERIAN STEPPE; OAK DEHESA; MIDDLE EASTERN SAVANNA. **Species Overlap:** LOWLAND HEATH.

DESCRIPTION: It is a warm summer morning, and your path snakes through the knee-high grasses. Multicolour blossoms decorate the field. A circling Red Kite searches for rodents while European Field Crickets (*Gryllus campestris*) sing under the hungry eye of a Red-backed Shrike. The tangy smell of cow dung wafts through the air.

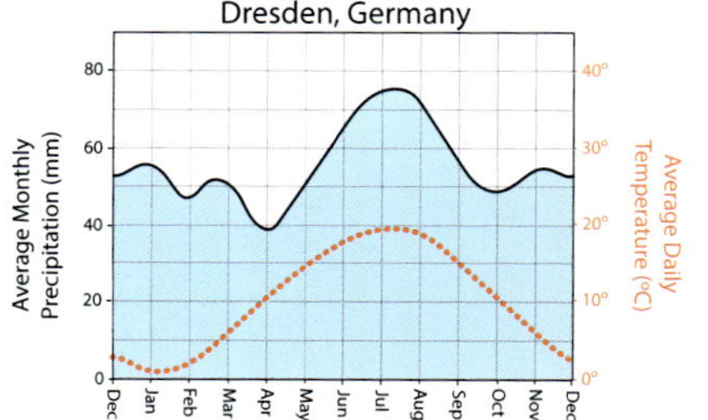

Temperate Grasslands and Savannas are common across Europe's temperate zone (Köppen **Cfb**, **Dfb**). They are invariably closely tied to animal husbandry and used directly as pastures or maintained as meadows for silage or hay production. Considering this, it is easy to think of them only as non-natural farmlands, but grassland ecosystems are very much a natural part of the European landscape. In fact, during the last period with a similar climate to today's (the Eemian interglacial, ~120,000 YA), more than 50% of Europe was covered in open or semi-open vegetation. Elephants, bison, Aurochs, equines, and other Pleistocene megafauna maintained open habitats in a matrix with savannas and forests (see Sidebar 4: Prehistoric Europe, p.208). A wide diversity of plant and animal species evolved over the millennia to produce myriad communities and habitat subtypes. Lacking large numbers of wild herbivores, most present-day grasslands need livestock grazing, mowing, or some other active intervention to keep them open.

The nature of our modern Temperate Grassland and Savanna varies according to climate, the local bedrock, and management practices. Calcareous grasslands are generally more species-rich than those on acidic, siliceous soils. Deeper, drier calcareous soils can produce wonderfully diverse wildflower communities but with species composition largely dependent on the relative importance of Mediterranean, continental, or oceanic influences. Some attractive, diagnostic flowers include the yellow Lady's Bedstraw (*Galium verum*) and the lavender-coloured Large Thyme (*Thymus pulegioides*), Hairy Violet (*Viola hirta*), Meadow Sage (*Salvia pratensis*), and Greater Knapweed (*Centaurea scabiosa*). Nevertheless, it is the diverse orchids that are arguably the highlight, including Bee Orchid (*Ophrys apifera*), Fly Orchid (*Ophrys insectifera*), Early Purple Orchid (*Orchis

Temperate Grassland in the Outer Hebrides, Scotland. © BILL BASTON, AGAMI

Meadow in s. Germany. © DALE FORBES

Temperate Grassland and Savanna in Tuscany, Italy. © DALE FORBES

mascula), Lady Orchid (*Orchis purpurea*), Green-winged Orchid (*Anacamptis morio*), and Military Orchid (*Orchis militaris*). The small Burnt-tip Orchid (*Neotinea ustulata*) is what the Pompadour Cotinga would look like if it were a plant. Tor-Grass (*Brachypodium pinnatum*) and Quaking-Grass (*Briza media*) will often dominate the sward, but even the grass diversity can be wonderfully high. Unfortunately, this delightful diversity quickly disappears with agricultural 'improvement', especially fertilisation. When grazing or mowing is removed, trees establish, and many of these grasslands will develop into forests.

Acid grasslands on siliceous soils are typically less productive and are never as diverse as calcareous grasslands. Grasses like Colonial Bent (*Agrostis capillaris*) and Sheep's Fescue (*Festuca ovina*) dominate, with a light sprinkling of wildflowers, including Tormentil (*Potentilla erecta*) and Heath Bedstraw (*Galium saxatile*). Acid grasslands managed traditionally as hay meadows typically have more wildflowers with greater overall biodiversity, while a lighter general grazing regime allows MONTANE HEATH AND MOORLAND to develop. It is relatively common to find both of these habitats in a matrix together, depending on how individual landowners manage the landscape.

Nevertheless, Europe's most extensive Temperate Grasslands are on deeper mesic soils. When traditionally managed, these hay meadows can be wonderfully biodiverse and harbour species like Common Eyebright (*Euphrasia nemorosa*), Black Knapweed (*Centaurea nigra*), Changing Forget-Me-Not (*Myosotis discolor*), Oxeye Daisy (*Leucanthemum vulgare*), Lady's Bedstraw, and Bird's-foot Trefoil (*Lotus corniculatus*). Grass-species diversity can be great but invariably includes the wonderfully fragrant Sweet Vernal Grass (*Anthoxanthum odoratum*), as well as Yorkshire Fog (*Holcus lanatus*), Red Fescue (*Festuca rubra*), and Downy Oat Grass (*Avenula pubescens*).

Traditional farming methods across Europe often saw the development of pastures and meadows with scattered trees, with the species involved depending on the region and local

Meadow Pipit has an impressive display flight and can frequently be seen 'parachuting' over Temperate Grasslands and Savannas. © MENNO VAN DUIJN, AGAMI

Barn Swallow and other insectivorous species can often be seen flying over insect-rich grasslands. © DANIELE OCCHIATO, AGAMI

traditions. Some of the more distinctive species include various oaks (*Quercus* spp.), fruit trees, Wild Olive (*Olea europaea*), European Beech (*Fagus sylvatica*), maples (*Acer* spp.), birches (*Betula* spp.), Sweet Chestnut (*Castanea sativa*), pines (*Pinus* spp.), and European Larch (*Larix decidua*). Besides their visual beauty, wooded pastures also emulate the savannas of Europe during the ice ages (Pleistocene), and wildlife can thrive in this environment.

WILDLIFE: The delightful song of the Eurasian Skylark often forms the soundtrack to Temperate Grassland and Savanna. Barn Swallows strongly favour pastures for hunting. Tree Pipit and Wood Lark readily add their melodies where scattered trees are present in a savanna-like setting. Meadow Pipit, Red-backed Shrike, Yellowhammer, Ortolan Bunting, Cirl Bunting, and Eurasian Green Woodpecker also favour these settings, but their songs are somewhat less musical. In

Yellowhammer is one of several bunting species adapted to Temperate Grassland and Savanna. © DANIELE OCCHIATO, AGAMI

The attractive Ortolan Bunting is one of many species that have declined rapidly in recent decades. Dwindling insect populations and the intensification and standardisation of agriculture are having profound effects on Europe's ecosystems. © DANIELE OCCHIATO, AGAMI

somewhat warmer climates, Eurasian Hoopoe, European Roller, Eurasian Scops-Owl, Cirl Bunting, Eurasian Thick-knee (Eurasian Stone-Curlew), and Woodchat Shrike depend heavily on this habitat and its even warmer, Mediterranean equivalent, OAK DEHESA. Citril Finch is almost completely dependent on this habitat in the montane zone. Twite needs biodiverse upland hay meadows for feeding near its MONTANE HEATH AND MOORLAND breeding sites.

European Fallow and Western Roe Deer, Brown Hare, and European Rabbit readily use Temperate Grassland and Savanna. Eurasian Wild Boar and Red Fox leave the protective cover of forests at night to feed in grasslands and agricultural fields. The Eurasian Hamster is uncommon but largely confined to this habitat.

European Rabbit is common in many of Europe's grasslands, especially where soils are soft or sandy. © DANNY GREEN, AGAMI

Common Blue and a number of other attractive butterflies can be found sipping nectar from the abundant flowers on summer days. © ROB DE JONG, AGAMI

Wildflower meadows teem with a dizzying array of insects. Some characteristic butterflies include Dark Green, High Brown, Niobe, and Lesser Marbled Fritillaries (*Argynnis aglaja, A. adippe, A. niobe,* and *Brenthis ino*), Marbled White (*Melanargia galathea*); Meadow Brown (*Maniola jurtina*); a variety of diminutive blues (subfamily Polyommatinae), including Common Blue (*Polyommatus icarus*); and skippers (family Hesperiidae). There are also various black and scarlet burnet moths (*Zygaena* spp.). Strolling through calcareous wildflower grasslands on a warm summer evening is the best way to find the charming European Glow-Worm (*Lampyris noctiluca*). With some luck, your search will be accompanied by the song of the European Field Cricket. Two other 'singers' of Temperate Grassland and Savanna are the Meadow and Common Green Grasshoppers (*Pseudochorthippus parallelus* and *Omocestus viridulus*).

European Field Cricket makes a loud chirping sound from the entrance to its burrow. © WIL LEURS, AGAMI

As with other open habitats, Temperate Grassland and Savanna can be good for finding reptiles, including Adder (*Vipera berus*), Common Slowworm (*Anguis fragilis*), Sand Lizard (*Lacerta agilis*), and Common Lizard (*Zootoca vivipara*).

CONSERVATION: The intensification of European agriculture has meant that trees and hedges have been removed through ploughing and reseeding; chemical fertilisers and manure slurry are frequently used to 'improve' grasslands and increase production, but species diversity plummets. White Clover (*Trifolium repens*), Creeping Buttercup (*Ranunculus repens*), and ryegrasses (*Lolium* spp.) take over. Invertebrates become rarer, and their predators—such as Whinchat and Red-backed Shrike—disappear. Whinchat, European Stonechat, Meadow Pipit, Corn Bunting, Ortolan Bunting, Grey Partridge, Eurasian Linnet, and many more species have been hard hit. Of all the threatened wildlife in Europe, this group of farmland birds is most under pressure.

Temperate Grassland and Savanna can be restored to species-diverse wildflower habitats, with 40–90% of the cover being (desired) herbaceous plants. An annual cutting (usually in July) and/or active livestock grazing can rehabilitate semi-improved grasslands in 1–9 years by effectively suppressing dominant grasses and herbs. Restoration of fertilised land can take considerably longer—anywhere from 4 to 30 years, depending on how enriched the soil has been. In such cases, land managers may even resort to inversion ploughing to pull nutrient-poor subsoil to the surface or completely remove the topsoil (stripping) to provide wildflowers with the impoverished soil they need. The most fascinating approach to driving restoration is the active use of Yellow Rattle (*Rhinanthus minor*). This semi-parasitic herb gets some of its energy from the roots of nearby grasses and legumes (such as clovers), consequently reducing their vigour and allowing other species to be more competitive. Combined with livestock and/or mowing, Yellow Rattle can effectively restore biodiverse grasslands.

DISTRIBUTION: This habitat is found widely across temperate Europe, from n. Spain through c. Europe, the UK, and parts of the Nordic and Baltic states. It is extensive in e. Europe and is found in somewhat temperate, upland areas in Italy and the Balkans. Temperate Grasslands and Savannas are invariably encountered in a matrix of forests, heaths, and ares of more intensive agricultural use.

IBERIAN STEPPE and OAK DEHESA are the ecological equivalents in the warmer, drier Mediterranean realm, particularly on the Iberian Peninsula. Drier PUSZTA AND PONTIC STEPPE is also found in the Pannonian Basin and around the Black and Caspian Seas.

WHERE TO SEE: Kingcombe Meadows, Dorset, England, UK; Yorkshire Dales National Park, England, UK; Hesselberg Natura 2000, Bavaria, Germany; Bucovina region, Romania and Ukraine.

Lesser Marbled Fritillary favours damp meadows and is widely distributed across Europe, though absent from the UK.
© WIL LEURS, AGAMI

Eu7C PUSZTA AND PONTIC STEPPE

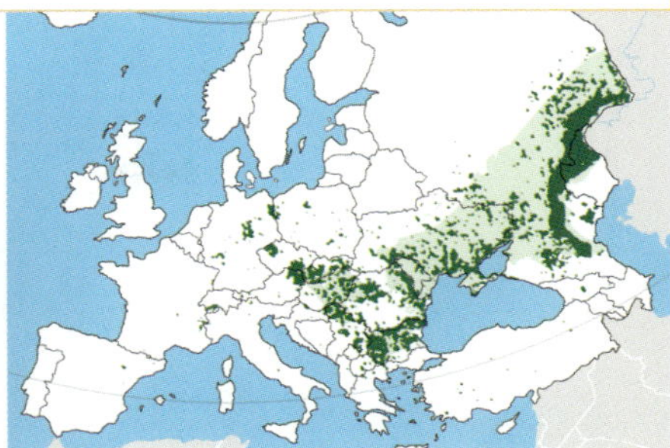

IN A NUTSHELL: The open steppes of e. Europe, where dry summers, harsh winters, and high salt concentrations in the soil restrict the vegetation to grasses, forbs, and small shrubs. **Global Habitat Affinities:** ASIAN FLOWER STEPPE; NEARCTIC TALLGRASS PRAIRIE. **Continental Habitat Affinities:** IBERIAN STEPPE. **Species Overlap:** SODA PAN AND INLAND SALT MARSH.

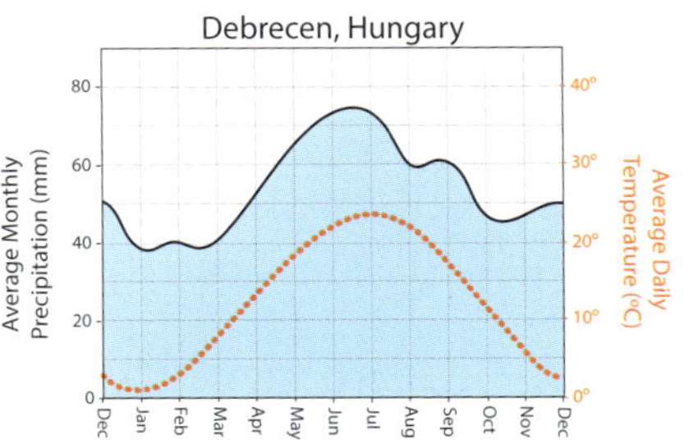

DESCRIPTION: Puszta and Pontic Steppe represents the westernmost parts of the great Eurasian steppes, extending from the Puszta Steppe of Austria and Hungary through the Pontic Steppe around the Black Sea all the way out to e. Russia. At first glance, the steppe—natural grassland largely devoid of trees and larger shrubs—appears uniform and rather boring, but with time and attention, it slowly gives up its secrets and reveals its incredible diversity and splendour. Subtle differences in topsoil depth, salinity, geology, and hydrology create a matrix of diverse plant communities, from salt-determined shortgrass steppes through fertile loess steppes and wonderful floral steppes to vast springtime marshlands. Harsh winters and dry summers limit the growing season (Köppen **Dfa**, **Dfb**). Salts in the sandy soils, strong solar radiation, and desiccating winds make for challenging growing conditions.

The topsoil layer is thin and lies over an alkaline subsoil that has accumulated salts over the millennia (mainly since the last ice age, which peaked ~20,000 YA). Groundwater moving through the carbonate-rich loess leaches out salts, and evaporation on the surface draws these mineral-rich waters upwards (termed a 'capillary pump'). As the water evaporates, the minerals are deposited in the soil and build up over time. Rainwater and snowmelt in late winter and spring flood much of the steppe and essentially wash some of these minerals out of the topsoil, making it somewhat more habitable to salt-tolerant, shallow-rooted plants. This system driving the buildup of salts reaches its extreme in the SODA PAN AND INLAND SALT MARSH habitat that peppers the landscape.

Thin topsoils tend to support shortgrass steppes, with fescues (*Festuca* spp.), feathergrasses (*Stipa* spp.), and the wonderfully scented Saline Wormwood (*Artemisia santonicum*). These are complemented by Sea Aster (*Tripolium pannonicum*), Sea Plantain (*Plantago maritima*), Siberian Statice (*Limonium gmelinii*), Low Baby's-Breath (*Psammophiliella muralis*), and Steppe Buttercup (*Ranunculus pedatus*), among other herbs. Large, costly blossoms tend to be unusual in the shortgrass steppes, and simple, wind-pollinated flowers are most common in this windswept

The relatively flat Puszta Steppe is a harsh, windblown, and bitterly cold environment in winter. © DALE FORBES

Rolling hills characteristic of the Pontic Steppe, s. Russia. © DAVID MONTICELLI, AGAMI

Spring on the steppes can be wonderfully floral. © IAIN CAMPBELL, TROPICAL BIRDING

environment. The shortgrass steppes have been the home of pastoral peoples for millennia. Old breeds of livestock—like the Hungarian Grey cattle and Hortobágy Racka sheep—are closely associated with this habitat and have replaced the ecological role of Saiga, Aurochs, and European Wild Ass. Even our modern horse is said to have been first domesticated in the Pontic Steppes of modern-day Ukraine and Russia. The extremes of overgrazing and abandoning grazing both negatively affect the ecology of the shortgrass steppes.

Thicker, more fertile loess topsoils allow taller grasses and forbs to grow. The lower salt levels in these soils allow for a much more diverse and colourful plant community, including Purple Mullein (*Verbascum phoeniceum*), Prostrate Speedwell (*Veronica prostrata*), Pannonian Dianthus (*Dianthus pontederae*), Bieberstein's Toadflax (*Linaria biebersteinii*), Purple Wood Sage (*Salvia nemorosa*), Common Chicory (*Cichorium intybus*), and Tuberous Jerusalem Sage (*Phlomoides tuberosa*). Even woodier species, like Dog Rose (*Rosa canina*), can grow in places. Their (relatively) fertile soils and lower salt content make these steppes particularly vulnerable to exploitation for agriculture. Extensive areas of this habitat have been ploughed to plant wheat and other grains.

Sandy steppes do not necessarily have high salt concentrations and can even be acidic. As the soil holds little water, the vegetation must cope with very dry conditions for much of the year, particularly in summer. Only scattered, hardy trees can grow in these conditions, and natural grasslands form.

Spring rains and snowmelt flood large expanses of steppe, forming vast wetland systems that can change rapidly. The intense summer sun slowly dries out the steppe, and the plants face extreme water stress by late summer. Consequently, the vegetation of these areas needs to cope with winter snows, flooded springs, and dry summer heat compounded by soil salts and desiccating winds. But when they do flood, they are a dream for migrating waterfowl and shorebirds, which spread out over the vast flooded marshes in breathtaking numbers.

The spectacular European Bee-eater swoops over the steppe in search of insects. © MARKUS VARESVUO, AGAMI

Eurasian Hoopoes favour areas of shorter vegetation in which to forage. © BENCE MÁTÉ, AGAMI

WILDLIFE: The songs of Eurasian Skylark and Crested Lark set the soundscape for the Puszta and Pontic Steppe—a beautiful, melodic cacophony of flowing trills and warbles. The seasonally flooded steppes are filled with breeding European Fire-bellied Toads (*Bombina bombina*), and their distinctive whooping calls add to the unique sounds of the steppe. Snipe, egrets, herons, marsh terns, and a dazzling array of waterfowl and shorebirds take advantage of the seasonal marshy steppes for breeding or while on migration. Spectacular dancing Ruffs can gather in numbers in the marshy steppe in spring, and the Aquatic Warbler can still be found breeding sporadically in sedge fens (see TEMPERATE PEATLAND and Sidebar 7: Saving the Aquatic Warbler, p.336) despite dramatic population declines in the past century.

Great Bustard, Tawny Pipit, European Stonechat, Eurasian Hoopoe, European Bee-eater, and the nomadic Rosy (Rose-coloured) Starling are also closely associated with steppe habitats. The European populations of Black-winged Pratincole are largely restricted to the easternmost portions of the Pontic Steppe and the CASPIAN WORMWOOD DESERT. Lesser Grey Shrike, European Roller,

Colourful European Rollers often sit prominently on any available high perch. © MARKUS VARESVUO, AGAMI

Right: **Red-footed Falcon is largely insectivorous, taking much of its prey on the wing.**
© MARKUS VARESVUO, AGAMI

Below: **The powerful Saker Falcon can occasionally be found hunting over the steppe. Seeing it fly on windy days is a mind-blowing experience, and it is obvious that it evolved to take advantage of the winds that tear across the landscape.**
© ARIE OUWERKERK, AGAMI

and Red-footed Falcon are largely insectivorous steppe birds, but the falcon needs old corvid nests to breed. It is consequently most often found within flying distance of a forest patch with a Rook colony. Somewhat larger predators include (Eastern) Imperial Eagle, Steppe Eagle, Saker Falcon, Long-legged Buzzard, and various harrier species. These compete with Steppe Polecat and Red Fox for the abundant steppe rodents. Large flocks of geese—including Greylag, Greater White-fronted, and Red-breasted Geese—use steppes and CROPLAND during winter.

European Ground Squirrel and Bobak Marmot are likely the most important grazers of the drier steppes, and their burrowing brings important dynamism to the ecosystem. Eurasian Hamster is also found in these dry steppes but has become rather uncommon and localised. The strange Saiga used to be widespread in the Eurasian steppes. Small populations can still be found in the Pontic-Caspian Steppes around the Black and Caspian Seas.

Grass Snake (*Natrix natrix*) takes advantage of the seasonally flooded steppes as Sand Lizard (*Lacerta agilis*) retreats to slightly higher areas. The Steppe Viper (*Vipera renardi*) is a habitat

Large flocks of Red-breasted Geese gather in the Puszta and Pontic Steppe and surrounding croplands in winter. © BAS VAN DEN BOOGAARD, AGAMI

European Ground Squirrel is never too far from a hole to dive down at the first sign of danger. © HAN BOUWMEESTER, AGAMI

specialist in the Pontic-Caspian Steppes. Wonderfully diverse clouded yellows (*Colias* spp.), coppers (*Lycaena* spp.), and fritillaries (tribe Argynnini)—such as the beautiful Cardinal Butterfly (*Argynnis pandora*)—float through the steppes in summer. The Dark Spreadwing damselfly (*Lestes macrostigma*) and Broad Scarlet (*Crocothemis erythraea*) stand out in the marshy steppe, as they can withstand somewhat salty water.

CONSERVATION: Draining and lowering the water table in the steppes slowly decreases the salinity, causing long-term changes to the ecosystem and allowing more generalist and woody species to be established. The subsequent ploughing and use for agriculture are omnipresent and direct threats.

DISTRIBUTION: The Puszta Steppe can be found across much of Hungary and the neighbouring countries of the Pannonian Basin, but large areas have been converted to agriculture or disturbed in other ways. Some lovely examples remain in Hungary's Hortobágy National Park and Austria's Neusiedler See-Seewinkel National Park. These steppes are considered an exclave of the great Eurasian steppes, with the Carpathians separating the Puszta Steppe of the Pannonian Basin from the Pontic-Caspian Steppes found around the Black Sea. Vast stretches of Pontic Steppe can still be found in Romania, Ukraine, and Russia, with additional, relatively smaller areas in the Balkans and Türkiye (the Central Anatolian Steppe).

WHERE TO SEE: Yelanets Steppe Nature Reserve, Ukraine; Măcin Mountains National Park, Romania; Hortobágy National Park, Hungary; Neusiedler See-Seewinkel National Park, Austria.

The amazing Cardinal Butterfly, a stunning species of fritillary. © ROB DE JONG, AGAMI

Eu7D IBERIAN STEPPE

IN A NUTSHELL: The steppes of the Iberian Peninsula, where low rainfall, almost constant wind, and hot, dry summers keep the landscape open. Dwarf Shrub Steppe is found mostly inland, behind the rain shadows of mountains or in the upland *parameras*, while Grassy Steppe is found in a mosaic with OAK DEHESA. **Global Habitat Affinities:** NEARCTIC MIXED-GRASS PRAIRIE; MONGOLIAN GRASS STEPPE. **Continental Habitat Affinities:** PUSZTA AND PONTIC STEPPE. **Species Overlap:** OAK DEHESA.

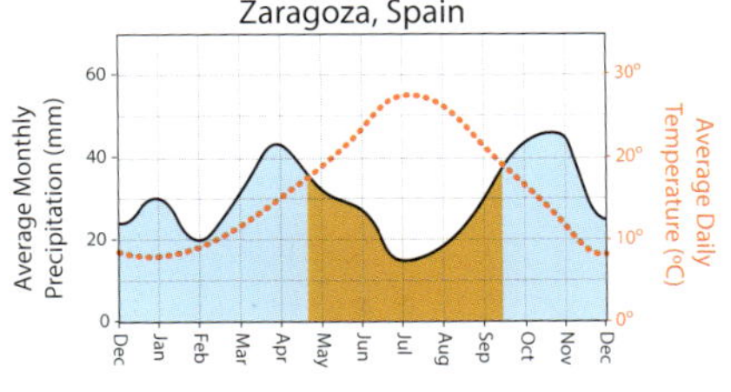

DESCRIPTION: Dawn on the Iberian Steppe in spring is wonderfully charming. As a displaying bustard does his best to be an enormous ball of candyfloss, larks generate their melodic songs. The first rays of sunlight catch a pair of sandgrouse flying by as a Great Spotted Cuckoo lands on a fence wire and belches out a squawk. A true highlight for birders, Iberian Steppe is relatively extensive in Spain and Portugal. It occurs in two subtypes: **Grassy Steppe**, found in a complex with sparsely treed savannas (see OAK DEHESA); and **Dwarf Shrub Steppe**, which occurs in even more arid zones where harsh environmental conditions inhibit tree growth.

Iberian Steppe is an ancient treeless ecosystem that was one of the key habitats of the region through the long, dry ice ages (see Sidebar 4: Prehistoric Europe, p.208). As the region warmed and rainfall increased, trees became a more prominent part of the landscape, and oak savannas became relatively more widespread through the dry interior of Iberia (see OAK DEHESA). Heavy timber extraction and agriculture by the Romans and subsequent peoples have opened and maintained more extensive **Grassy Steppe**. This effect is particularly noticeable around ancient cities.

The heavy hand of humans in shaping the landscape has led some to call Iberia's grasslands 'pseudo-steppes' to distinguish them from the great natural steppes across Eurasia (see PUSZTA AND PONTIC STEPPE). This view considers only the relatively recent agricultural influences of the past two millennia. Nevertheless, it is safe to assume that much of Iberia would naturally have been covered in a matrix of savannas and steppes, a landscape kept open by the Pleistocene megafauna. Straight-tusked Elephant, Narrow-nosed Rhinoceros, Wild Horse, European Wild Ass, and the Aurochs—the incredible ancestor to our cattle—would all have played a role in shaping these landscapes. Fluctuating densities of large herbivores, regional weather patterns, fire, and local soil conditions would have created an ever-changing landscape between open Grassy Steppes and savannas akin to the modern-day OAK DEHESA.

Scanning for some of the many special birds on the wide-open Iberian Steppe, Extremadura, Spain. © DALE FORBES

Grassy Steppe is typically found in a hot-summer Mediterranean climate (Köppen **Csa**) on soils that are nutrient-poor and littered with slate outcrops, making agriculture a real challenge. Cattle and sheep are grazed, particularly in the winter rainy season, while somewhat more productive areas are ploughed and sowed with drought-resistant winter cereal crops. Provided insecticide use is limited, these crop fields can be interesting places to look for Great and Little Bustards, as they resemble the birds' preferred natural habitat of tall Grassy Steppe. After harvest, fields are left as stubble, while those that will be planted with winter cereals are often ploughed in late spring to reduce water loss over the hot, dry summer months. These open fields are typically the best places to look for feeding Black-bellied Sandgrouse. Calandra Larks, Greater Short-toed Larks, and Corn Buntings often join them as they move between the ploughed fields and newly seeded grasslands or CROPLAND. Crop fields will typically be left fallow for several years to allow the soil to recover. Grazing on these fallow grasslands helps create myriad microhabitats for a great diversity of insects and birds. With low herbivore pressure, abandoned steppes slowly change their structure, as bushes like Spanish Heath (*Erica australis*), Pincushion Gorse (*Genista hirsuta*), Rosemary (*Salvia rosmarinus*), Yellow Bridal Broom (*Retama sphaerocarpa*), and Gum Rock-Rose (*Cistus ladanifer*) establish. Thekla's Lark and European Stonechat favour bushy steppes, and as bush encroachment increases, so too does the presence of reclusive birds such as Dartford, Spectacled, Western Subalpine, and Sardinian Warblers. The protected environments in and around bushes also create nestled nurseries for oaks to establish as part of a natural progression towards OAK DEHESA.

In contrast, the cold semi-arid climate (Köppen **Bsk**) of the **Dwarf Shrub Steppe** is too harsh for treed savannas to establish. This subhabitat is generally found at somewhat higher elevations (above ~1000 m/3500 ft.) with cooler temperatures, on windswept plains known as *parameras*. Dwarf Shrub Steppe also develops in dry interior depressions in the rain shadows of significant ridgelines (e.g., in the Tagus/Tejo and Ebro river valleys). Water stress is integral to all Iberian Steppes but is particularly extreme in Dwarf Shrub Steppe. Rainfall is low and occurs mostly in winter, making for a hot, desiccated summer with tough growing conditions. Soils are generally underdeveloped, nutrient-poor regosols, but the remnants of ancient lakes in some areas mean that marl-gypsum and salt deposits are extensive. Temporary SODA PANS AND INLAND SALT MARSHES are peppered through the flat gypsum steppes.

Dwarf Shrub Steppe is similar in structure to other semi-desert areas around the Mediterranean basin. Poor soils, water stress, and millions of years have driven the evolution of endemic species, and an incredible 42% of the steppe plants are endemic to the Iberian Steppe region. Examples include *Vella bourgaeana* and *Teucrium intricatum* of the Almería steppes and *Vella pseudocytisus* of the Duero/Douro and Ebro steppes. These three rain-shadow valley steppes have developed their own largely unique plant communities, isolated from other similar habitats. By contrast, the upland *parameras* are somewhat more alike, as climatic changes during the Pleistocene caused the frequent joining and separating of habitat islands. Nevertheless, diverse distinct shrubland communities have been identified in the *parameras*, with typical species including brooms (*Genista scorpius*, *G. versicolor*, and *Erinacea anthyllis*), thymes (*Thymus mastigophorus* and *T. zygis*), Spanish Common Sage (*Salvia officinalis lavandulifolia*), and Spike Lavender (*Lavandula latifolia*). Thuriferous (Spanish) Juniper (*Juniperus thurifera*) can grow into full, large trees at somewhat protected sites in the *parameras*.

Salt steppes and temporary salt pans can be found in areas with extensive deposits from ancient water bodies. These are very similar systems to those found in the PUSZTA AND PONTIC STEPPES with their associated Soda Pans. Grasses and other shallow-rooted plants can survive in the very top layer of soil from which rainfall has flushed out some of the concentrated salts. Trees have little chance of establishing, but salt-tolerant plants like pickleweeds (*Salicornia* spp.) and sea-lavenders (*Limonium* spp.) thrive.

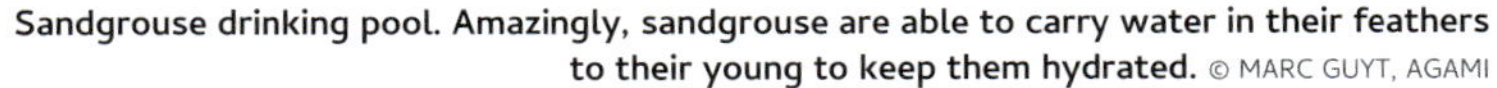

Sandgrouse drinking pool. Amazingly, sandgrouse are able to carry water in their feathers to their young to keep them hydrated. © MARC GUYT, AGAMI

Great Spotted Cuckoo, a brood parasite, patrols the area looking for magpie nests in which to lay its eggs, to be raised by the unsuspecting host. © HELGE SØRENSEN, AGAMI

WILDLIFE: The Iberian Steppes are among the oldest habitats in Europe and were likely even more extensive during the Pleistocene ice ages, when much of the continent's water was locked away in ice and snow. They are not only botanically interesting; unique animal communities have also developed, creating one of Europe's most interesting and exciting regions for bird- and wildlife-watchers.

Most of the world's Great Bustards are found in Iberia, especially in Spain's Castile and León and Castilla–La Mancha. They are best found in undulating, wide-open tallgrass or cereal landscapes. Females choose the cover of taller vegetation to breed, while males need open areas to display, particularly favouring short-cropped grazing land. After breeding, Great Bustards move to more arable land, especially stubble. Little Bustard likes similar habitats to the Great Bustard but tends to select areas with a somewhat more complex matrix of microhabitats, including grasslands, cereals, legume fields, and vineyards. As with the Great Bustard, females tend to choose taller grass or cereal for cover to breed, while males favour areas with open patches or rocks from which to display (but will also do a fun jumping display if the grass grows too high). Little Bustards are most abundant at 300–700 m (1000–2300 ft.) elevation. Males abandon breeding areas early and move to irrigated and better feeding grounds. The females and young are left behind as the increasingly hotter summer months parch and bake the steppe. Lower survival rates on the plains might explain why there are considerably more male than female Little Bustards in Spain and why the population has plummeted in the past few decades.

Seven species of larks are regularly found in the Iberian Steppes. Iberia's dry pastures are incredibly important for Eurasian Skylark in winter, but the bird heads to higher elevations to breed, when it is the most abundant lark in many Dwarf Shrub Steppes on the *parameras*. There it selects somewhat shorter grasslands, fallow fields, and areas of low-intensity agriculture,

A male Great Bustard, Europe's heaviest flying bird, weighs up to 14 kg (31 lb.). © OSCAR DÍEZ, AGAMI

particularly where multiple crops are growing within the range of a breeding territory. It tends to nest in herbaceous cover and avoid areas with too many trees or larger bushes.

Thekla's Lark favours Mediterranean scrub but readily uses shortgrass steppes with scattered bushes or exposed rocks. Crested Lark is found mostly on short cereal fields, along road edges, around settlements, and in other disturbed areas with little vegetation. Calandra Lark favours flat, drier steppes and is especially associated with the *paramera* steppes. However, it will also breed in short-cropped Grassy Steppe, and large post-breeding flocks can be found in ploughed fields. Mediterranean Short-toed Lark is found on arid salt steppes with lots of open ground and dwarf bushes, especially Shrubby Seablite (*Suaeda vera*). Greater Short-toed Lark is somewhat more of a generalist but is usually found scurrying over ploughed fields or bare, cleared firebreaks,

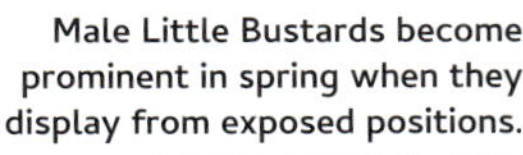

Male Little Bustards become prominent in spring when they display from exposed positions. © MENNO VAN DUIJN, AGAMI

Dupont's Lark is likely the most sought-after of the Iberian larks. It is restricted to Spain's central dry, flat Dwarf Shrub Steppes. © RAN SCHOLS, AGAMI

Corn Bunting prefers wide-open habitats without trees. Its jangling song can be heard throughout the steppes. © MARKUS VARESVUO, AGAMI

although it will also use Dwarf Shrub Steppe with some herb and grass cover. Dupont's Lark is likely the most sought-after of the Iberian larks, with fewer than 2000 pairs in 24 populations. It is restricted to Spain's central, dry, flat Dwarf Shrub Steppes and is heavily threatened by anthropogenic habitat change (wind farms, intensive agriculture) and the abandonment of traditional low-intensity sheep farming. Tawny Pipit and Western Black-eared Wheatear both select nest sites similar to those of Dupont's Lark, needing lots of open ground with dwarf shrubs for cover. Short grass, dwarf shrubs, and lots of bare ground are also good for Eurasian Thick-knee (Eurasian Stone-Curlew).

Corn Bunting can be abundant in wide, open Grassy Steppe but also regularly uses ploughed fields. Black-bellied Sandgrouse is best found in ploughed fields or heard flying over the steppes at dawn. Listening at dawn is also the best way to find Pin-tailed Sandgrouse, as they will cover great distances between their regular drinking holes and the close-grazed sheep pastures where they tend to feed. Both sandgrouse species also use stubble fields, especially in autumn and winter, and can sometimes be found in mixed flocks. Interestingly, Pin-tailed Sandgrouse often feed around Little Bustards and are thought to use the taller birds as look outs for danger.

Lesser Kestrels depend highly on the Iberian Steppe, especially during the breeding season. The plains are abuzz with activity in spring as adult Lesser Kestrels dart between White Storks and Black Kites to collect grasshoppers and crickets for their insatiable chicks. Egyptian Vulture, European Bee-eater, Spanish Sparrow, Rock Sparrow, and many other species make the Iberian Steppe a great birding environment. Vertical cliffs attract Black Wheatears.

The stunning Pin-tailed Sandgrouse is an iconic species of the steppe. It will cover great distances between its regular drinking holes and the close-grazed sheep pastures where it tends to feed. © MARC GUYT, AGAMI

Mammals of the Iberian Steppe include Granada Hare, European Rabbit, European Badger, Eurasian Wild Boar, Western Roe Deer, and Red Fox. Larger mammals are somewhat more likely to be found in nearby OAK DEHESA and MEDITERRANEAN OAK FOREST. Western Montpellier Snake and its prey—lizards such as Large Psammodromus (*Psammodromus algirus*)—can be abundant in the steppes. It is also worth keeping an eye out for the enormous Ocellated Lizard (*Timon lepidus*), which can get up to 90 cm (3 ft.) in length!

The butterfly diversity of the Iberian Steppes is a true delight. Keep a look out

Egyptian Vulture can frequently be seen patrolling the plains. © WIL LEURS, AGAMI

A Provence Hairstreak shows off its stunning colours. © NICOLAS BASTIDE, AGAMI

for Provence Hairstreak (*Tomares ballus*) where medicks (*Medicago* spp.) are present, Panoptes Blue (*Pseudophilotes panoptes*) on flowery steppes, Spanish Fritillary (*Euphydryas desfontainii*), Striped Grayling (*Hipparchia fidia*), Hermit (*Chazara briseis*), and Great Banded Grayling (*Brintesia circe*), as well as Iberian, Western, and Spanish Marbled Whites (*Melanargia lachesis*, *M. occitanica*, and *M. ines*).

CONSERVATION: The intensification of livestock farming in the Grassy Steppes has created larger tracts of uniformly short-cropped pasture. This is disastrous for many classic steppe birds, like European Roller, Great Bustard, Little Bustard, Montagu's Harrier, and Iberian Grey Shrike, which all do best with high habitat heterogeneity. But on the flip side, higher livestock densities and lower supervision have greatly increased the availability of carcasses for vultures. This has supported a tremendous recovery of Cinereous Vulture and Eurasian Griffon in the past few decades. However, crops are increasingly being grown for livestock and harvested earlier than those grown for human consumption. This is catastrophic for ground-nesting birds.

DISTRIBUTION: Dwarf Shrub Steppes are found in many semi-arid river systems, including those of the Ebro, Tagus (Tejo), Douro (Duero), and Segura Rivers. Similar, related systems are found near Spain's southwestern coast. The upland *parameras* of c. Spain—found especially in Castile and León—hold biologically important dry steppe communities. Grassy Steppes are most extensive within the OAK DEHESA savannas of Extremadura and Castilla-La Mancha, Spain, and Alentejo, Portugal.

WHERE TO SEE: Altos de Barahona and Paramos de Layna, both in Castile and León, Spain; Saladas de Sástago-Bujaraloz, Aragón, Spain; Trujillo, Extremadura, Spain.

Eu7E EUROPEAN FOREST STEPPE

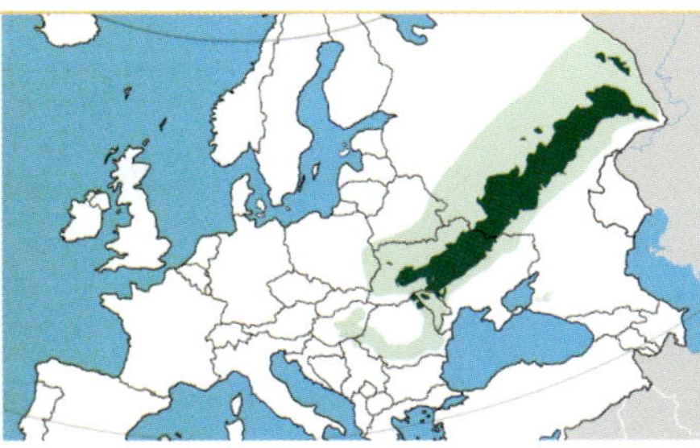

IN A NUTSHELL: A mélange of forest patches and grasslands wedged between the temperate forests to the north and the dry steppes to the south. **Global Habitat Affinities:** CALIFORNIA OAK SAVANNA; ASIAN FOREST STEPPE. **Continental Habitat Affinities:** MIDDLE EASTERN SAVANNA; PUSZTA AND PONTIC STEPPE; TEMPERATE MIXED FOREST. **Species Overlap:** SPRUCE-FIR TAIGA; PUSZTA AND PONTIC STEPPE.

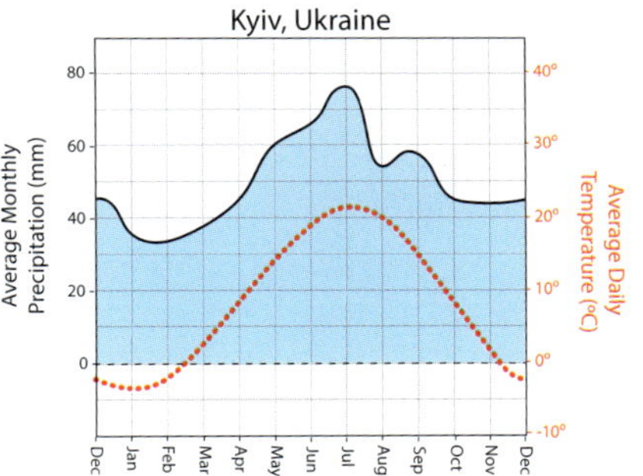

DESCRIPTION: A cultivated landscape of gently rolling hills with intertwined meadows, pastures, and woodlots is intimately familiar to most Europeans. But there is a wild version of this landscape in the east, in a narrow band stretching from Romania to the Urals (and well beyond). Wide-open meadow steppes are scoured by (Eastern) Imperial Eagles and Montagu's Harriers. At the same time, scattered forest patches hide Eastern Roe Deer patiently waiting for the cover of darkness before moving out onto the steppes to feed.

This fascinating landscape has developed in a Goldilocks zone (Köppen **Dfb**) wedged between the dry steppes to the south and wetter forests to the north. In this transition zone, a mosaic of forest patches in a sea of grass and flowers makes for incredible biodiversity and wildlife-watching possibilities. Forest steppes occur over a variety of landscapes, from flatlands to rolling hills, and range in elevation from 300 to 1500 m (900–4500 ft.). The forest groves are somewhat more prominent on north-facing slopes, in valleys, and on mountain tops. By contrast, flatter south-facing slopes tend to be dominated by grasslands; desiccating winds restrict tree growth and generally keep the sward shorter.

Within this transition zone, the vegetation changes along gradients as precipitation decreases and summer temperatures rise. Snowfall in spring and rainfall in summer bring most of the annual precipitation (400–600 mm/16–24 in., drier to the east and south). Average yearly temperatures range from 6 to 12°C (40–54°F). However, it is the continental extremes that govern this habitat, with average summer temperatures as high as 24°C (75°F) and winter averages as low as −16°C (3°F), making it very difficult for plants, as they must handle both bitter winters and scorching summers.

The compositions of the forests and the grasslands change from west to east and from north to south. In general, the forests in the Forest Steppe are oak dominated and closely related to TEMPERATE OAK FOREST, especially in the western parts of the habitat's range, where coniferous

Forest Steppe showing the classic rolling hills with forest patches and open steppe grasslands.

trees are unusual. English Oak (*Quercus robur*), Downy Oak (*Q. pubescens*), and Sessile Oak (*Q. petraea*) grow alongside other broadleaf trees, including Silver Birch (*Betula pendula*) and European Aspen (*Populus tremula*). It may seem incongruous to find Downy Birch (*Betula pubescens*) as an important component of these woodlands, given that it grows farther north than any other tree. Nevertheless, when we consider the brutal winters, with their very dry, desiccating winds, it becomes clear that the harsh conditions limiting trees 2000 km (1200 mi.) to the north are also at play in the Forest Steppes of Russia.

To the east, oaks diminish in importance, while Small-leaved Lime (*Tilia cordata*) and conifers like Scots Pine (*Pinus sylvestris*), Siberian Larch (*Larix sibirica*), European Larch (*Larix decidua*), and Common Juniper (*Juniperus communis*) become increasingly dominant. The habitat continues into Asia (ASIAN FOREST STEPPE), where the forests are strongly related to the coniferous boreal taiga forests, as opposed to the mixed conifer-oak assemblages we see in European Forest Steppe. Water availability (rather than temperature) is evidently the driving factor behind this shift from oak to mixed and to coniferous forests along the west–east gradient, as conifers can better handle drier conditions than oaks.

The meadows, sometimes called flower steppes, are dominated by some attractive temperate-climate grasses, such as Bushgrass (*Calamagrostis epigejos*), Furrowed Fescue (*Festuca rupicola*), Horsetail Feathergrass (*Stipa tirsa*), European Feathergrass (*Stipa pennata*), and Brown Bent (*Agrostis vinealis*). Valais Fescue (*Festuca valesiaca*) is a grass from this habitat that has been introduced to North America, where it grows in areas that were naturally TALLGRASS PRAIRIE. It makes sense that it would do well there, as it is, in many ways, the American equivalent of its native habitat. As in the Tallgrass Prairie, the grasses grow to over 1.5 m (4 ft.) tall. As the name flower steppe suggests, the grasses are mixed with many species of colourfully blooming forbs—such as the lovely yellow Spring Adonis (*Adonis vernalis*) and Lady's Bedstraw (*Galium verum*) and the lavender-coloured Meadow Sage (*Salvia pratensis*) and Peach-leaved Bellflower (*Campanula persicifolia*)—as well as a range of white flowers, including Mountain Clover (*Trifolium montanum*), Dropwort (*Filipendula vulgaris*), and the near globally introduced Oxeye Daisy (*Leucanthemum vulgare*).

On the southern edge of the habitat, closer to the PUSZTA AND PONTIC STEPPE, the forests thin to scattered individual trees in a temperate savanna. The open areas look much more like the true steppes to the south and begin to appear similar to the SHORTGRASS PRAIRIE of North America, with fewer flowers and more xerophytic (dry-climate) short grasses and forbs, including the Tartar Breadplant (*Crambe tataria*), Nodding Sage (*Salvia nutans*), and beautiful scarlet Fern-leaf Peony (*Paeonia tenuifolia*).

Soils in the meadows and broadleaf forests tend to be very nutrient-rich chernozems, though they vary from black soils supporting broadleaf forests to sandy soils supporting pine forests. Much of the flatlands here has developed on the very widespread loess deposits that extend through much of c. Asia. The forest groves are in more exposed areas in the more northerly, colder, moister regions. Farther south, where it is relatively warmer and drier, the forests tend to be in gullies and areas with more water accumulation. Small patches of conifers tend to occur on poorer soils, and the increased acidity from the pine needles can change the chernozems to podzols, where they encroach onto meadows.

People have been farming the Forest Steppe for thousands of years, and almost half of the land has been transformed into cropland, especially winter wheat and maize. © VLADIMIR YU. ARKHIPOV

The beautiful song of the Thrush Nightingale is a standout in Europe's wildlife. The bird can be common in forest patches of Forest Steppe. © MARKUS VARESVUO, AGAMI

WILDLIFE: The birdlife of the Forest Steppe is a fascinating mixture of forest, savanna, and grassland birds. The forest birds tend to be widespread generalists, like Great Tit, European Robin, Eurasian Bullfinch, Common Chaffinch, Eurasian Siskin, Hawfinch, and the wonderful songster Thrush Nightingale. Syrian, Black, and Grey-headed Woodpeckers are found alongside the ubiquitous Great Spotted Woodpecker in somewhat larger forest patches. These larger forests can also be good spots to see Eurasian Goshawk. The steppe bird assemblages unsurprisingly contain Eurasian Skylark, Meadow Pipit, Whinchat, and European Stonechat with a sprinkling of Siberian Stonechat and Booted Warbler, all keeping a watchful eye on the sky as (Eastern) Imperial Eagle, Booted Eagle, Montagu's Harrier, and Eurasian (Common) Kestrel cruise by. Rough-legged Hawk (Rough-legged Buzzard) visits in winter. The forest-steppe mosaic is great for Fieldfare, Wood Lark, Tree Pipit, Yellowhammer, Ortolan Bunting, Grey Partridge, and Red-backed Shrike. Forest Steppe is the core zone for the Lesser Grey Shrike and the

Lesser Grey Shrike favours savannas and a mixture of forest and open areas—and does well in Forest Steppe. © RALPH MARTIN, AGAMI

Top: **The powerful (Eastern) Imperial Eagle is one of the top avian predators in Forest Steppe.** © DANIELE OCCHIATO, AGAMI

Bottom: **Splendid Montagu's Harriers can be seen patrolling areas of open steppe during the summer months.** © DANIELE OCCHIATO, AGAMI

Greater Spotted Eagle, with the latter needing a matrix of forest and larger marshes or wetland areas.

Unfortunately, the classic megafauna of the region (see Sidebar 4: Prehistoric Europe, p.208) disappeared a long time ago, but you can still find Eastern Roe Deer, Eurasian Wild Boar, Grey Wolf, Eurasian Lynx, Red Fox, and European Badger in some areas. Eurasian Red Squirrels can still be relatively common in some forest patches. The Greater Blind Mole-Rat is almost completely restricted to Forest Steppe, as is the rare Speckled Ground Squirrel. Bobak Marmot can be present in more open southerly sites, while the Eurasian Hamster is uncommon but widespread.

The stunning, black (or dark) Nikolsky's Viper (*Vipera nikolskii*) is strongly tied to the Forest Steppe but sticks to the wooded areas, especially along watercourses. By contrast, the Steppe Viper (*Vipera renardi*) uses the open steppes of Forest Steppe and Pontic Steppe. Adder (*Vipera berus*) typically finds its niche between Nikolsky's and Steppe Vipers in forest edge and somewhat more complex habitats. Common Lizard (*Zootoca vivipara*), Sand Lizard (*Lacerta agilis*), Eastern Slowworm (*Anguis colchica*), and Smooth Snake (*Coronella austriaca*) are all widespread, while the Steppe Runner (*Eremias arguta*) is limited to the drier, more open areas of the southern Forest Steppes.

The Forest Steppe holds a wealth of interesting butterfly species, including Large, Scarce, and Compton Tortoiseshells (*Nymphalis polychloros*, *N. xanthomelas*, and *N. l-album*); Hungarian Glider (*Neptis rivularis*); Pallas's Sailer (*Neptis sappho*); and Dryad (*Minois dryas*).

CONSERVATION: People have been farming the Forest Steppe for thousands of years. This is unsurprising, given that the chernozem soils of this habitat are so fertile, and the open-and-closed

Adder (pictured) is best found in edge habitats of Forest Steppe, while Nikolsky's Viper tends to be found in the forest patches, and Steppe Viper in the open steppe grasslands. © NICOLAS BASTIDE, AGAMI

mosaic landscape of the Forest Steppe allows for both farming and protection from the elements. These savannas and forest-grassland mosaics are undoubtedly ancient, natural ecosystems, but human intervention in shaping these landscapes is everywhere to be seen. Almost half of the land has been transformed into CROPLAND, especially winter wheat and maize. Uncontrolled fires and overgrazing have also greatly affected the remaining land. It is unclear to what extent the 'open' areas have been increased. Nevertheless, the cutting of the forest groves and ploughing of the land for crop production have been so extensive that it is difficult to distinguish the purely natural and anthropogenic versions of this habitat. What is clear is that when fire and grazing are limited, trees and shrubs are quick to establish. European Aspen is typically among the first woody colonisers, slowly changing much of the fallow land to forest blocks over time.

Very little Forest Steppe remains intact, due to relatively high population densities and enormous pressure from farming, oil drilling, and infrastructure.

DISTRIBUTION: The Forest Steppe occurs as a band from the northern edge of the Carpathians through to Inner Mongolia of China, as a broad zone ranging from 50 to 650 km (30–400 mi.) wide. In Europe, the Forest Steppe occurs from e. Romania and n. Ukraine to s. Russia, across the north of the Caucasus, skirting around the n. Caspian Sea to the Volga River and the Urals.

WHERE TO SEE: Macin Mountains National Park, Romania; Hetmanskyi National Nature Park, Ukraine; Kaluzhskiye Zaseki Nature Reserve, Russia.

The cryptic underwing of the Large Tortoiseshell helps to hide it during its winter hibernation. © WIL LEURS, AGAMI

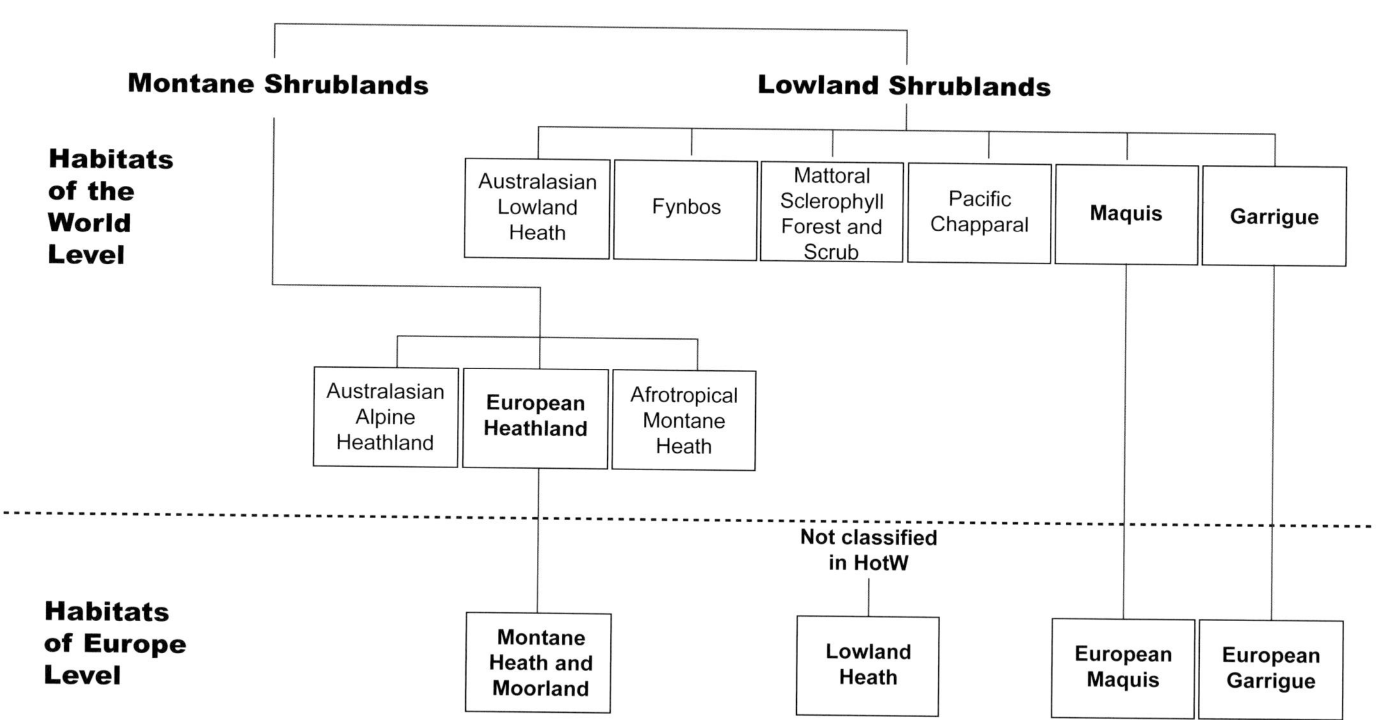
MEDITERRANEAN SHRUBLANDS
Montane Shrublands
Lowland Shrublands
Habitats of the World Level
Australasian Lowland Heath
Fynbos
Mattoral Sclerophyll Forest and Scrub
Pacific Chapparal
Maquis
Garrigue
Australasian Alpine Heathland
European Heathland
Afrotropical Montane Heath
Not classified in HotW
Habitats of Europe Level
Montane Heath and Moorland
Lowland Heath
European Maquis
European Garrigue

MEDITERRANEAN SHRUBLANDS

Eu8A EUROPEAN GARRIGUE

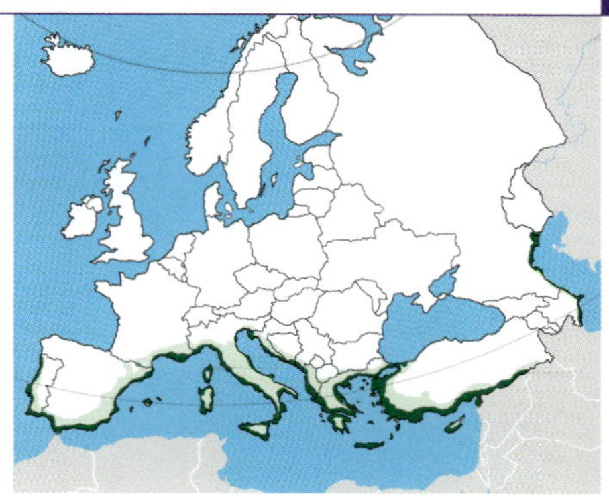

IN A NUTSHELL: A very low, open scrub habitat found around much of the Mediterranean Sea. **Global Habitat Affinities:** MAGHREB GARRIGUE; FYNBOS; WALLUM AND AUSBOS. **Continental Habitat Affinities:** MAQUIS; CAUCASIAN SHRUB DESERT. **Species Overlap:** MAQUIS; CAUCASIAN SHRUB DESERT.

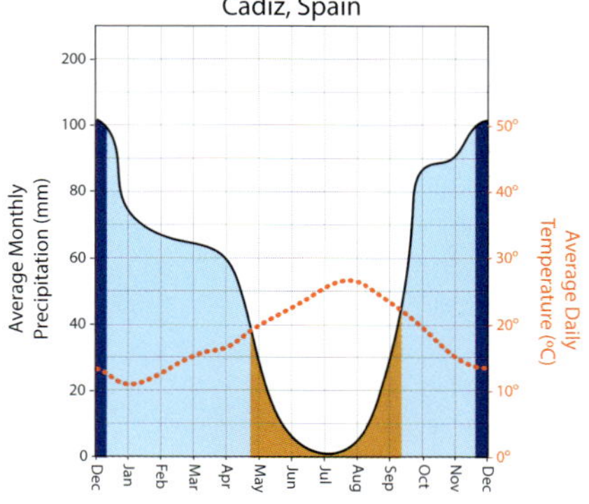

DESCRIPTION: This shrubland is a very depauperate, short, and scrubby counterpart of MAQUIS. Garrigue is typically less than 2 m (6 ft.) high, with a mixture of tree species much like those characteristic of MAQUIS, though these are usually overgrazed or at least much shorter and shrubbier in this habitat. It is generally found in hotter parts of the region and tends to have a drier microclimate than MAQUIS (though still Köppen **Csa**) or is found on nutrient-deficient soils developed over limestone, marble, quartzite, or granite. MAQUIS is more resistant to degradation where soils are deeper, more nutrient-rich, and derived from bedrocks such as mudstone and basalt, so it would seem intuitive to expect that less Garrigue forms on these soils. However, because these rich soils are so good for cultivation, most of the MAQUIS there has been converted to agriculture, and where soils have been overexploited, Garrigue grows in fallow land.

The habitat can be divided between more natural Garrigue forming around the coast on nutrient-deficient, free-draining soils and Garrigue farther away from the coastlines that is thought to be of anthropogenic origin. Garrigue that forms on the coast has more shrub variety and bushes of the same species that grow as trees in MAQUIS, such as Wild Olive (*Olea europaea*), Strawberry Tree (*Arbutus unedo*), Libyan Strawberry Tree (*Arbutus pavarii*), and Mastic Tree (*Pistacia lentiscus*), and many smaller shrubs and forbs, such as Rosemary (*Salvia rosmarinus*), Spiny Burnet (*Poterium spinosum*), Gum Rock-Rose (*Cistus ladanifer*), and Spiny Broom (*Calicotomo villos*). In

Coastal Garrigue in Croatia showing the typical scattered, low, scrubby vegetation. © DALE FORBES

the e. Mediterranean, where Spiny Burnet becomes more dominant, Garrigue habitat is referred to as **Phrygana** (or, in some regions, **Batha**), but the general wildlife assemblage does not change. Phrygana can be regarded as a subhabitat of Garrigue where thorny plants become much more common. No matter where you are in the Garrigue, however, walking off trail is a painful, bloody endeavour.

Garrigue that has formed farther from the coast on better soils is more likely to be the direct result of degradation by humans and replacement of MEDITERRANEAN OAK FOREST or MEDITERRANEAN PINE FOREST. Trees like Sweet Acorn Oak (*Quercus rotundifolia*), Holm Oak (*Quercus ilex*), Portuguese Oak (*Quercus faginea*), and Thuriferous (Spanish) Juniper (*Juniperus thurifera*) tend to remain in the mix as seedlings and stunted remnants.

By European standards, these habitats are regarded as having reasonable biodiversity, but this obscures the striking difference between this and the seemingly analogous habitats of FYNBOS in s. Africa and WALLUM AND AUSBOS in s. Australia. Two of the most florally diverse ecosystems on the planet, they present a stark contrast to the depauperate wildlife assemblages in the Garrigue of Europe. Fynbos is part of the Cape Floristic Region, home to over 9000 plant species, and WALLUM AND AUSBOS contains over 6500 plant species, while Garrigue has just hundreds of species in a very similar climate. The three habitats represent a fascinating example of how plants have adapted to similar climatic conditions in different parts of the world with vastly different outcomes in terms of biodiversity.

Above: **Coastal Garrigue in Italy. Walking through this thorny vegetation quickly results in scratched and bleeding legs.** © DALE FORBES

Right: **Western Rock Nuthatch builds its prominent mud nest directly over crevices on inaccessible rock faces.** © DUBI SHAPIRO, AGAMI

WILDLIFE: Birdlife in this depauperate habitat is similar to that in MAQUIS but is much reduced in both species and numbers. The more open nature of Garrigue means that wildlife species from drier and sparser habitats can also be abundant. Birds that take advantage of Garrigue include Western Rock Nuthatch, Spectacled Warbler, Western Black-eared Wheatear, Black Wheatear, Masked Shrike, Cretzschmar's Bunting, Dupont's Lark, and a variety of other larks and pipits. Northern Bald Ibis has been extirpated but has recently been reintroduced in s. Spain in Garrigue and the surrounding steppe-like farmland.

Mammal diversity is limited, but European Rabbit, Brown Hare, and Granada Hare are all found here. By contrast, a wealth of

Cretzschmar's Bunting is a colourful inhabitant of Garrigue in se. Europe. © RALPH MARTIN, AGAMI

Open Garrigue interspersed with rocky areas is the perfect habitat for Western Black-eared Wheatear. © MARC GUYT, AGAMI

reptiles takes advantage of the warm, open Garrigue. Green Whip Snake (*Hierophis viridiflavus*) can be surprisingly common where present. Some of the other frequently encountered reptiles include Ladder Snake (*Zamenis scalaris*), Western Montpellier Snake (*Malpolon monspessulanus*), Horseshoe Whip Snake (*Hemorrhois hippocrepis*), Large Psammodromus (*Psammodromus algirus*), and various wall lizards (*Podarcis* spp.). Greek, Hermann's, and Marginated Tortoises (*Testudo graeca, T. hermanni* and *T. marginata*) meander about, while the agama-like Bedriaga's Rock Lizard (*Archaeolacerta bedriagae*) is found in rocky areas on Corsica and Sardinia.

The butterfly diversity can be especially great in flowery Garrigue. Keep a look out for Pea Blue (*Lampides boeticus*), Lang's Short-tailed Blue (*Leptotes pirithous*), and Black-eyed Blue (*Glaucopsyche melanops*), as well as Two-tailed Pasha (*Charaxes jasius*), Chapman's Green Hairstreak (*Callophrys avis*), Southern White Admiral (*Limenitis reducta*), Striped Grayling (*Hipparchia fidia*), and Hermit (*Chazara briseis*).

CONSERVATION: Garrigue is regarded as both a natural and, more commonly, an anthropogenic habitat, because if protected from fire and overgrazing, it would likely return to MAQUIS or even to MEDITERRANEAN PINE FOREST or MEDITERRANEAN OAK FOREST. Given that this habitat is the result of human overuse, it is no wonder that it is found in disturbed areas around the Mediterranean.

DISTRIBUTION: This habitat is very widespread on Mediterranean islands and all around the Mediterranean coast. It also exists away from the coast on the Iberian Peninsula, on the Italian Peninsula, and through Türkiye. It extends into Syria, where it merges into CAUCASIAN SHRUB DESERT.

WHERE TO SEE: Tarifa, Andalusia, Spain; Calanques National Park, Bouches-du-Rhône, France; Isola di Capraia, Tuscany, Italy.

Black-eyed Blue is a characteristic species of w. Mediterranean Garrigue. © WIL LEURS, AGAMI

Eu8B EUROPEAN MAQUIS

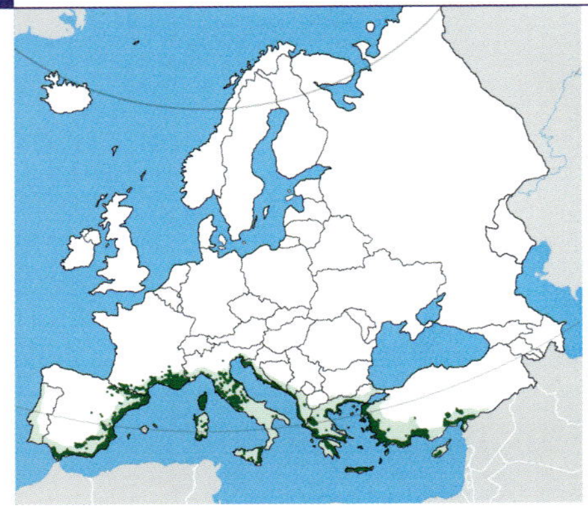

IN A NUTSHELL: Dry, sometimes anthropogenic, thicket heathland around the Mediterranean with trees of similar species to surrounding woodlands. **Global Habitat Affinities:** AUSTRALIAN TEMPERATE HEATH THICKET; FYNBOS; MAGHREB MAQUIS; NEARCTIC PACIFIC CHAPARRAL. **Continental Habitat Affinities:** GARRIGUE; MEDITERRANEAN OAK FOREST; CAUCASIAN SHRUB DESERT. **Species Overlap:** GARRIGUE; MEDITERRANEAN OAK FOREST.

DESCRIPTION: Maquis (also known as Macchia in Italy and Matorral in Spain) is a dense shrub or small tree community with a mainly closed canopy between 1 and 6 m (3–20 ft.) high, most often around 3 m (10 ft.). Much of Europe's Maquis is found in a Mediterranean climate (Köppen **Csa**), with brutally hot, dry summers (av. daily high temperature >31°C/88°F) and cool, wet winters (high 10°C/50°F) during which monthly rainfall can be more than three times higher than in summer months. Nevertheless, the climate can be somewhat milder right on the coast, where the sea has an ameliorating effect, creating a warm-summer Mediterranean climate (Köppen **Csb**).

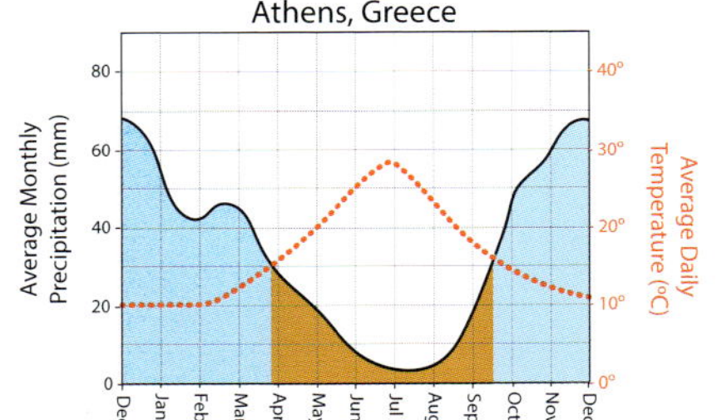

Plants have had to adapt to deal with the harshness of the warm, dry months, so the vegetation consists mainly of evergreen sclerophyllous (hard, waxy-leaved) canopy plants such as Carob (*Ceratonia siliqua*), Strawberry Tree (*Arbutus unedo*), Tree Heath (*Erica arborea*), Mastic Tree (*Pistacia lentiscus*), Wild Olive (*Olea europaea*), Bay Laurel (*Laurus nobilis*), and oaks such as Kermes Oak (*Quercus coccifera*), Portuguese Oak (*Q. faginea*), and Holm Oak (*Q. ilex*). Conifers also feature in the low canopies, with species such as Mediterranean Cypress (*Cupressus sempervirens*), Aleppo Pine (*Pinus halepensis*), and a suite of junipers, including Western Prickly Juniper (*Juniperus oxycedrus*), Phoenician Juniper (*J. phoenicea*), and

Mediterranean Juniper (*J. turbinata*). Smaller shrubs like Oleander (*Nerium oleander*) and Grey-leaved Cistus (*Cistus albidus*) grow between the stunted trees. In more open areas, many annuals grow until sclerophyllous plants shade them out.

Walking through Maquis is a challenging endeavour, as the canopy cover, at eye level, forms a nearly impenetrable barrier. With most of the plants exhibiting shrubby growth forms, the canopy seldom reaches a height that allows for comfortable passage beneath it. Small branches ascend from the trunks, and multiple trunks often sprout from a single base, creating a dense and intricate thicket. This environment receives the bulk of its rainfall during the winter months, while summer droughts are harsh and unforgiving for the vegetation. As a result, many plants are sclerophyllous, bearing leathery leaves with a waxy coating that helps to minimise water loss. The leaves tend to be narrower than those found in broadleaf deciduous forests. Some non-sclerophyllous shrubs have adapted to the dryness by becoming dry-deciduous, shedding their leaves in summer to avoid desiccation.

The original habitat of s. Europe, n. Africa, and the Middle East during the early Holocene to Mesolithic periods remains a subject of ongoing debate. Some suggest that it was predominantly a mixed-evergreen woodland of cypress, juniper, and oak and that there has been an anthropogenic replacement of these forests. Others think it was a fire-adapted wooded savanna or that the Maquis that exists now is a natural community on a xeric (arid and semi-arid) site with a Mediterranean climate (Köppen **Csa**) of mild, wet winters and hot, dry summers. Although Maquis is often regarded as a human-induced, disturbed (plagioclimax) habitat, it is likely that in the early Holocene, a Maquis existed as an alternate stable state (climax as opposed to plagioclimax) in gaps within mixed woodland, oak woodland, conifer woodland, or a savanna-type habitat. There is also ample evidence that the now-extinct megafauna kept the Maquis stable, as it did the OAK DEHESA, and that the 'thickening' of the habitat to MEDITERRANEAN OAK FOREST and JUNIPER AND CYPRESS FOREST is the result of the reduction of browsing pressure (see Sidebar 4: Prehistoric Europe, p.208).

Maquis, Italy. © DALE FORBES

Above and below: **Maquis, Spain.** © IAIN CAMPBELL, TROPICAL BIRDING

Maquis is often imagined to develop only on calcareous soils overlaying limestones, though it can also form in soils overlaying rocks with very high silica, such as sandstones, and acidic soils. The habitat does tend to develop more on sandy, well-drained soils, but this is more a function of grain size and drainage rather than the soil parent material.

In recent post-industrial times, an increase in fire frequency, overgrazing by domestic sheep and goats, clearing for agriculture, and the development of olive groves have all but eliminated the extensive oak and conifer forests around the Mediterranean coastline. Completely natural Maquis is very limited in extent, but native Maquis plants have a massive advantage in this human-altered

The beautiful Iberian Lynx is one of the world's rarest and most threatened cats. It does well in sandy Maquis with strong rabbit populations. Secretive for much of the year, it becomes a little more active in daylight during its winter mating period. © VINCENT LEGRAND, AGAMI

environment. Maquis is consequently one of the most widespread habitats around the Mediterranean Basin and through the western parts of the Middle East.

WILDLIFE: Animal assemblages in the Maquis have been drastically affected by 4000 years of intense human pressure, resulting in the extinction of many mammals. Nevertheless, Iberian Lynx still holds on in Andalusia, Barbary Macaque is found in Gibraltar, and Crested Porcupine is found in Italy. Eurasian Wild Boar, Red Fox, European Badger, and European Rabbit are all widespread and can be common. The hedgehog diversity is fascinating. In the western parts of the habitat's range, you are more likely to find Common and North African Hedgehogs, while Northern White-breasted and Southern White-breasted Hedgehogs are found farther east.

Maquis holds many resident birds, like Red-legged Partridge, Little Owl, European Serin, and Sombre Tit, as well as some restricted-range ones, such as Cyprus Warbler, Cyprus Wheatear,

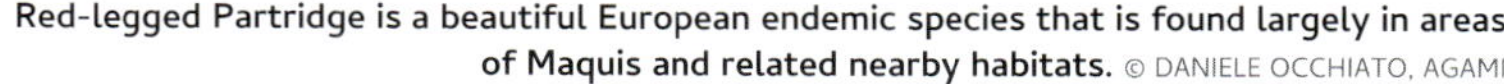

Red-legged Partridge is a beautiful European endemic species that is found largely in areas of Maquis and related nearby habitats. © DANIELE OCCHIATO, AGAMI

Spectacled Warbler is one of several sylviid warblers that frequent this habitat. It is often found in areas of lower vegetation dominated by salt-tolerant species. © DANIELE OCCHIATO, AGAMI

and Corsican Finch on their namesake islands. This habitat supports a stunning array of warblers. Some of these little beauties include Dartford, Western Subalpine, Western Orphean, Spectacled, Tristram's, Marmora's, and Sardinian Warblers. Maquis is important as wintering grounds for

Maquis provides the perfect hunting ground for the feisty Woodchat Shrike, which can often be seen perched prominently, surveying the surroundings for its next meal. © RALPH MARTIN, AGAMI

species that breed farther north, such as Eurasian Blackcap and Song Thrush. In spring and summer, Maquis hosts breeding migrants such as Red-necked Nightjar, Woodchat Shrike, and European Bee-eater. This habitat also becomes vitally important as the first feeding place for spring migrant passerines that have crossed the Sahara on their way to the mixed forests of n. Europe. Following these birds are numerous accipiters and falcons, along with other raptors, such as Short-toed Snake-Eagle and Booted and Bonelli's Eagles. Eleonora's Falcon breeds on Mediterranean sea cliffs and is truly breathtaking when seen hunting or cruising over nearby Maquis. Vultures are relatively common over Maquis in some areas. Birding in spring can be amazing, and April is a great time to be in the Iberian Peninsula, Corsica, Greece, or Türkiye.

Maquis has many more reptiles than most other habitats of Europe, from lizards and snakes to Common Chameleons (*Chamaeleo chamaeleon*) and tortoises. Wall lizards (*Podarcis* spp.) are ubiquitous and incredibly diverse, with each region typically having only one species. These include Catalonian, Common, Italian, Tyrrhenian, Lilford's, Erhard's, Peloponnese, Ionian, Milos, and Skyros Wall Lizards (*P. liolepis*, *P. muralis*, *P. siculus*, *P. tiliguerta*, *P. lilfordi*, *P. erhardii*, *P. peloponnesiacus*, *P. ionicus*, *P. milensis*, and *P. gaigeae*). Hermann's Tortoise (*Testudo hermanni*) is invariably the most abundant tortoise, but Marginated and Greek Tortoises (*T. marginata* and *T. graeca*) can be locally important. Snakes include the beautiful Asp Viper (*Vipera aspis*) as well as Western Montpellier Snake (*Malpolon monspessulanus*), Viperine Snake (*Natrix maura*), Green Whip Snake (*Hierophis viridiflavus*), and Ladder Snake (*Zamenis scalaris*).

Opposite: **The smart Marmora's Warbler is a localised endemic breeder that is largely confined to the Maquis of Corsica and Sardinia.** © DANIELE OCCHIATO, AGAMI

Right: **Hermann's Tortoise (pictured) is invariably the most abundant tortoise in Maquis, but Marginated and Greek Tortoises can be locally prominent.** © NICOLAS BASTIDE, AGAMI

The stunning Two-tailed Pasha—surely Europe's most dazzling butterfly—is largely associated with Maquis. © RALPH MARTIN, AGAMI

The Two-tailed Pasha (*Charaxes jasius*) is one of Europe's largest and most beautiful butterflies. It is strongly tied to Maquis and related habitats because of the presence of its larval host plant, Strawberry Tree, which is also used by Chapman's Green Hairstreak (*Callophrys avis*). It is also worth keeping a look out for Black-eyed Blue (*Glaucopsyche melanops*) and Southern White Admiral (*Limenitis reducta*).

CONSERVATION: Because much of modern Maquis is anthropogenic or fire dependent, a product of the modification of MEDITERRANEAN PINE FOREST and MEDITERRANEAN OAK FOREST, it can revert to these forests in reserves where fires are prevented or grazing reduced. Outside such reserves, a change to GARRIGUE is likely where grazing and fire pressure are high. Much of the coastal Maquis has been turned over to cultivation, and further pressure is added by urban development and tourism infrastructure. In the more arid areas of e. Türkiye, Maquis is being degraded into CAUCASIAN SHRUB DESERT. Higher temperatures are likely due to climate change, but the real unknown is the possible change in precipitation cycles. These overgrown heathlands are often on poorly developed soils with little moisture-holding capacity, so a decrease in rainfall over the already very dry summers will result in some shrubs being unable to survive. The protection of Maquis is vital for the survival of many European migrant birds. It is vitally important as a feeding and resting stop for migrating bird species after they cross the Sahara on their northerly journey or as the last real vegetation they encounter on their southerly return journey.

DISTRIBUTION: This habitat is very widespread and common below 1100 m (3500 ft.) on the Mediterranean islands and around the Mediterranean coast from Portugal to Türkiye.

WHERE TO SEE: Tarifa, Andalusia, Spain; Arrábida Natural Park, Portugal; Calanques National Park, Bouches-du-Rhône, France; Isola di Capraia, Tuscany, Italy.

Eu8C LOWLAND HEATH

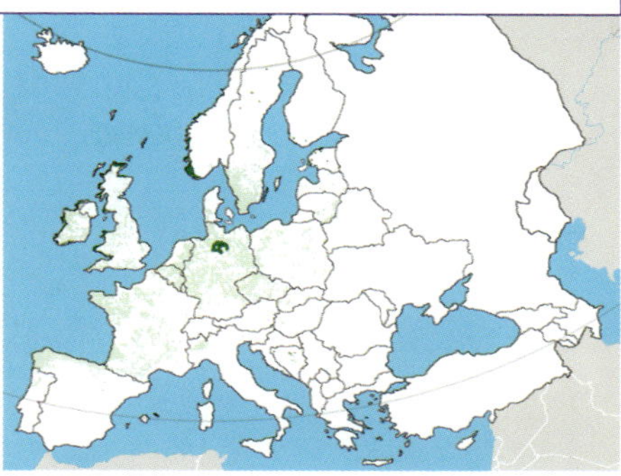

IN A NUTSHELL: An open, low habitat of ericoid dwarf shrubs in exposed areas of the cooler parts of the region. **Global Habitat Affinities:** FYNBOS; WALLUM AND AUSBOS; NEARCTIC PACIFIC CHAPARRAL. **Continental Habitat Affinities:** MAQUIS; GARRIGUE; MONTANE HEATH AND MOORLAND. **Species Overlap:** MONTANE HEATH AND MOORLAND.

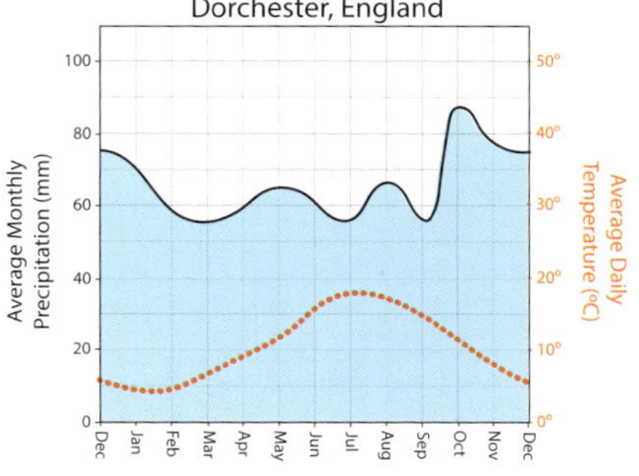

DESCRIPTION: Standing alone in the hauntingly beautiful and stark landscape of a heath conjures up images of a tormented King Lear and his fool stumbling through a storm. It is no wonder that literature has frequently turned to the rawness of the heath as a reflection of human turmoil, anguish, and solitude.

Heathlands are open habitats dominated by abundant small, sclerophyllous, ericoid plants (largely members of Ericaceae, the erica or heath family), their tiny blossoms turning rolling hills a delightful mauve in late summer. Ground cover is near universal, the lower stratum typically about 30 cm (12 in.) high. Common Heather (*Calluna vulgaris*) blankets many acidic heathlands, where it is complemented by other heath species (*Erica* spp.), gorses (*Ulex* spp.), Common Milkwort (*Polygala vulgaris*), various grasses, and Common Bracken (*Pteridium aquilinum*). The open landscapes are often peppered with larger shrubs (reaching 1 m/3 ft.) and trees (6–10 m/20–30 ft.). Depending on the region, these can include isolated Common Yew (*Taxus baccata*), the occasional Scots Pine (*Pinus sylvestris*), and thickets of hawthorn (*Crataegus* spp.) and juniper (*Juniperus* spp.). Ideally, heaths can show a relatively wide diversity of plant species without any group being particularly dominant, but in reality, most heaths are species-poor, with an almost complete dominance of a few heath and grass species.

Heathland types can be sliced and diced in myriad ways, including their elevation, their general climate, the soils on which they form, how wet they are, their geographic location, and their grazing-dependent openness.

Lowland Heath is found in low-elevation areas of Europe's temperate oceanic climate zone (Köppen **Cfb**), while MONTANE HEATH AND MOORLAND develops at higher elevations in the montane life zone (Köppen **Cfc**). GARRIGUE and MAQUIS are heathlands that develop in the hot-summer Mediterranean climatic region (Köppen **Csa**).

Lowland Heath is often found on soils that are relatively unfavourable for most other plant assemblages, especially on very acidic sandy soils (from weathered silicates) but also on extremely alkaline soils (from limestone). Sandy soils produce dry heaths with very little humus. Common Heather, Bell Heather (*Erica cinerea*), and gorses (including Dwarf Gorse, *Ulex minor*) are common

A typical heathland scene with lovely purple blooms of heather. © MARC GUYT, AGAMI

in these environments. Black Crowberry (*Empetrum nigrum*) is more abundant on dry heaths farther north, especially in Scandinavia.

Somewhat moister soils develop heath communities that include Western Gorse (*Ulex gallii*) and Bristle Bent (*Agrostis curtisii*), as well as various mixtures of Common Heather, Bell Heather, Cornish Heath (*Erica vagans*), St. Dabeoc's Heath (*Daboecia cantabrica*), Cross-leaved Heath (*Erica tetralix*), and Common Bilberry (*Vaccinium myrtillus*). These can be particularly stunning along salty, wind-whipped sea cliffs and coasts, where the maritime heaths hold relatively diverse plant communities.

Wet heaths are a transitional habitat between drier heaths and TEMPERATE PEATLAND where drainage is impeded, causing their soils to be waterlogged for extended periods. Cross-leaved Heath and Common Heather do well on these wetter, peaty soils, as do Purple Moor Grass (*Molinia caerulea*), Grass-like Sedge (aka Carnation Sedge, *Carex panicea*), Deergrass (*Trichophorum cespitosum* ssp. *germanicum*), Marsh Gentian (*Gentiana pneumonanthe*), Bog Asphodel (*Narthecium ossifragum*), and even some sphagnum mosses (e.g., Low Peatmoss, *Sphagnum compactum*).

Heathlands can form climax communities in soggy areas, on extremely nutrient-deficient soils, or where strong, desiccating winds make the development of trees impossible. Nevertheless, most of Europe's heathlands were created by tree clearing during the Bronze Age and exist as subclimax communities. Without continual grazing and management of shrubs and trees, many European heaths would slowly change into forests. Heathlands are often seen as human-derived

Dartford Warbler (pictured) regularly uses European Stonechat as a predator lookout when feeding in exposed areas. © BILL BASTON, AGAMI

ecosystems because of their reliance on active management. However, this stands in perplexing contrast to the great biodiversity and biological importance of heathlands and other open habitats. Large grazers and browsers were the norm in Europe until waves of humans arrived and decimated their populations. Up until that point, our native megafauna had had a strong role as landscape architects across the continent. During the Eemian (~120,000 YA), the last warmer interglacial, when temperatures were comparable with current times, more than half of Europe was covered in open savannas or steppes. Lightly wooded Lowland Heaths are undoubtedly an ancient, natural ecosystem, with our cattle, sheep, and ponies now fulfilling the ecological role of Aurochs, Narrow-nosed Rhinoceros, Straight-tusked Elephant, Wild Horse, and European Wild Ass (see Sidebar 4: Prehistoric Europe, p.208).

WILDLIFE: The beautiful Dartford Warbler is the bird most associated with Lowland Heath, where the low, thorny gorse cover provides safe nesting sites. It feeds mainly in bushes but will often follow European Stonechats and feed in open areas on the ground below them. It is quite possible that the warbler is using the stonechat as a predator lookout when it is exposed, but this evidently reduces the stonechat's feeding success rate, so it will often fly off to try to find a new spot without a warbler. Like the Dartford Warbler, both European Stonechat and Whinchat take advantage of gorse for nesting. Eurasian Nightjar and Wood Lark are both strongly associated with Lowland Heaths, especially those with scattered trees for singing posts. Eurasian Skylark provides the soundscape for the habitat, while Eurasian Hobby frequently hunts over heathlands.

European Fallow Deer, Red Deer, and Western Roe Deer, as well as the introduced Sika Deer, all regularly use Lowland Heath for feeding, particularly when it is close to forests for shelter. With some luck, you might see a Eurasian Stoat dash across a path as it searches for European Wood Mouse, Bank Vole, Field Vole, or other small prey.

Lowland Heath is generally great for finding reptiles, and within the UK, Smooth Snake (*Coronella austriaca*) is restricted to Lowland Heath. Sand Lizard (*Lacerta agilis*) is found in open heathland with bare, sandy patches, while Common Lizard (*Zootoca vivipara*) and Barred Grass Snake (*Natrix helvetica*) prefer wetter heaths. Adder (*Vipera berus*) and Common

Eurasian Hobby is an expert aerial predator that frequently hunts over heathlands. © HARVEY VAN DIEK, AGAMI

In the UK, the secretive Smooth Snake is found only on Lowland Heath. © NICOLAS BASTIDE, AGAMI

Heaths with regular disturbance, younger heath plants, and some open areas are good for the Silver-studded Blue. This beautiful little butterfly lives in tight-knit colonies, invariably near an active Black Garden Ant or Cornfield Ant nest, as these ants protect the eggs and caterpillars. © WIL LEURS, AGAMI

Slowworm (*Anguis fragilis*) can be relatively common.

The diversity and abundance of flowering plants on heath make it a great habitat for a wide variety of invertebrates. Heaths with regular disturbance, younger heath plants, and some open areas are good for Silver-studded Blue (*Plebejus argus*), which lives in tight-knit colonies in a very restricted area, typically experienced as a cloud of beautiful little blue butterflies. These are invariably near an active Black Garden Ant (*Lasius niger*) or Cornfield Ant (*Lasius alienus*) nest, as these ants protect the butterfly's eggs and caterpillars. In return, the caterpillars provide the ants with a sweet, amino-acid-filled secretion. Another blue butterfly, the Alcon Large Blue (*Phengaris alcon*), is found only on wetter Lowland Heath in which Marsh Gentian grows.

Horse Chestnut Moth (*Pachycnemia hippocastanaria*), True Lover's Knot (*Lycophotia porphyrea*), Beautiful Yellow Underwing (*Anarta myrtilli*), and Heath Rustic (*Xestia agathina*) are all associated with Lowland Heath. The enormous day-flying Emperor Moth (*Saturnia pavonia*) is never common, but with some luck, you might spot one flying over heathland looking for a mate; it lays its eggs on heather, a favoured food plant of the impressive larvae.

Emperor Moth lays its eggs on heather, a favoured food plant of the impressive larva (pictured). By midsummer, the larva will be getting ready to pupate in the ground. © BAS HAASNOOT, AGAMI

The enormous Hornet Robber Fly, most often found on Lowland Heath, is a powerful predator, catching dung beetles, bees, and caterpillars on the wing. Its life cycle is intricately associated with that of herbivores (and their dung). © RALPH MARTIN, AGAMI

Golden-ringed Dragonfly (Common Goldenring, *Cordulegaster boltonii*) is often seen hunting over Lowland Heath far from water. Additional odonate species indicative of heathlands (or associated mires) include Four-spotted Skimmer (Chaser, *Libellula quadrimaculata*), Keeled Skimmer (*Orthetrum coerulescens*), Black Darter (*Sympetrum danae*), Common Spreadwing (*Lestes sponsa*), Small Red Damselfly (*Ceriagrion tenellum*), and Southern Damselfly (Mercury Bluet, *Coenagrion mercuriale*).

The enormous Hornet Robber Fly (*Asilus crabroniformis*) is most often found on Lowland Heath. It is 2.5 cm (1 in.) long, and its hornet-like appearance is no doubt a protective mechanism against would-be predators. It is itself a powerful predator, catching dung beetles, bees, and caterpillars on the wing. The fly's life is intricately associated with that of herbivores, especially large ones, such as cattle, horses, and European Bison (see Sidebar 2: Rewilding Europe, p.164). The fly lays its eggs in dung piles, where its larvae feed mainly on dung beetle larvae. Nevertheless, this complex system works only when herbivores are not regularly dewormed. For all the benefits that preventative deworming brings for animal husbandry, it is a disaster for creatures that live around and feed off dung.

CONSERVATION: Agriculture, plantations, natural succession, and urban development have meant that an estimated 70% of heathland has been lost in the last couple of centuries.

DISTRIBUTION: Most Lowland Heath can be found in the UK. Dry heath is most extensive in Europe's oceanic climates with high wind and rainfall, especially in Spain, the UK, and Ireland. Larger areas in continental France, Germany, and Poland can be found on siliceous, sandy soils. Wet heaths occur in the Atlantic regions of nw. Europe, with the majority being within the UK and Ireland, but some also in n. Spain, w. France, Belgium, the Netherlands, and Denmark.

WHERE TO SEE: Thursley Common, Surrey, England, UK; New Forest National Park, England, UK; Lüneburg Heath, Lower Saxony, Germany.

Eu8D MONTANE HEATH AND MOORLAND

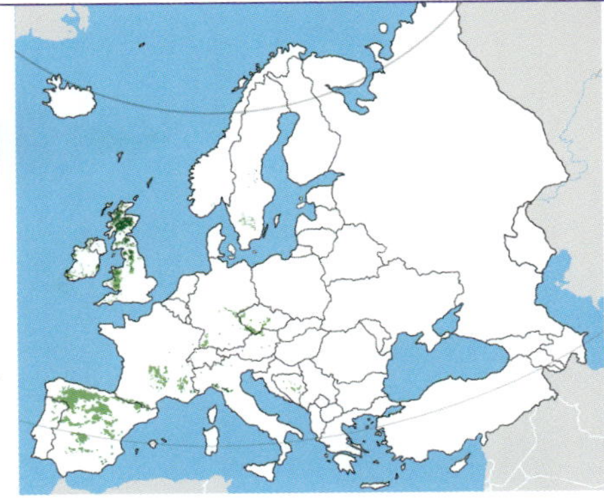

IN A NUTSHELL: A low, open habitat of ericoid dwarf shrubs (especially heather) in the cooler montane zone below the tree line. **Global Habitat Affinities:** AUSTRALIAN MONTANE HEATHLAND; NEOTROPICAL MAGELLANIC BOFEDALES. **Continental Habitat Affinities:** SUBALPINE TIMBERLINE WOODLAND; ALPINE TUNDRA; LOWLAND HEATH. **Species Overlap:** ALPINE TUNDRA.

DESCRIPTION: The wide, rolling hills are blanketed in the lavender hues of heather. There is invariably a light drizzle, and only the bubbling 'go back' call of a Red Grouse and the song of a distant skylark break the eerie silence. A lone Red Deer wades through the mist.

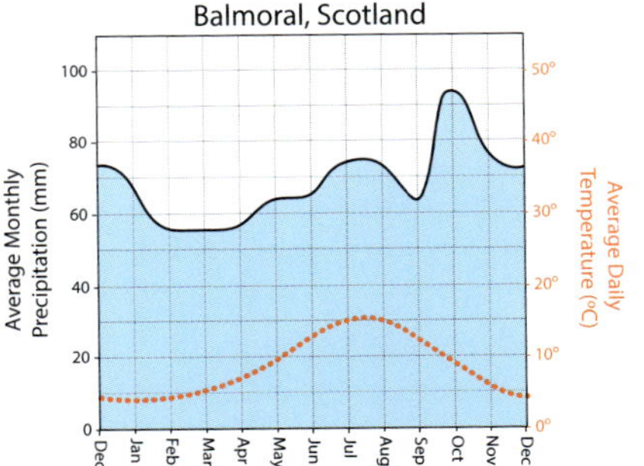

Montane Heath and Moorland is a charming open habitat of ericoid subshrubs (largely members of Ericaceae, the erica or heath family) and grasses with few scattered trees (Köppen **Cfc**). It is higher and cooler than LOWLAND HEATH (**Cfb**) and

Nearly all of Britain's upland moorlands have been extensively modified by the effects of drainage, grazing, and intensive management for the grouse-hunting industry. © PETE MORRIS

Heathland management will often result in a patchwork mélange of various microhabitats. © PETE MORRIS

found up to the tree line, where the harsher growing conditions naturally inhibit tree growth (**Dfc**, **Dfd**). Above this, the habitat transitions to SUBALPINE TIMBERLINE WOODLAND and ALPINE TUNDRA. It is often found in mosaics with blanket bogs (a type of TEMPERATE PEATLAND), various montane forests, or TEMPERATE GRASSLAND AND SAVANNA, and there is considerable species overlap between these habitats. In the UK, heathlands in the montane life zone are called 'upland heaths' or 'moorlands' (while heaths in the ALPINE TUNDRA are often misleadingly called 'montane heaths', despite not being in the montane life zone). The term 'moorland' is often used to refer to this mosaic of upland open habitats or alternatively just for Montane Heath (we use the narrower sense in this book). Confusingly, 'moor' is also a false friend of the German *Moor*, meaning bog, a type of TEMPERATE PEATLAND.

The impoverished, acidic mineral soils of Montane Heath and Moorland can develop a moderate peat layer, so they regularly feel soggy underfoot. A harder layer of deposited minerals leached from the topsoil can exacerbate water retention, and areas that are less steep transition to blanket bogs. Forests of birches (*Betula* spp.), Scots Pine (*Pinus sylvestris*), or Norway Spruce (*Picea abies*) could develop, but browsing, fire, and active tree removal limit tree density and keep the habitat open. Heavy grazing can force a transition to transition to TEMPERATE GRASSLAND AND SAVANNA.

Common Heather (*Calluna vulgaris*), Bell Heather (*Erica cinerea*), and Common Bilberry (*Vaccinium myrtillus*) are invariably the most common species, especially on acidic soils. A host of other Arctic-alpine and boreal species are complementary, including Lingonberry (*Vaccinium vitis-idaea*), Black Crowberry (*Empetrum nigrum*), Tormentil (*Potentilla erecta*), and Wavy Hair-Grass (*Avenella flexuosa*), as well as Reindeer Lichen (*Cladonia portentosa*) and Iceland Lichen (*Cetraria islandica*). Common Juniper (*Juniperus communis*) and Bearberry (*Arctostaphylos uva-ursi*) can be complementary on more

Twite is a subtly attractive finch that is typically found breeding in moorland habitats. © PETE MORRIS

Red Grouse is the iconic species of Britain's moorlands. © THEO DOUMA, AGAMI

northern moorlands, while Western Gorse (*Ulex gallii*) can be significant on those farther south. Wetter moorlands transitional to bogs will see more Cross-leaved Heath (*Erica tetralix*), Common Cottongrass (*Eriophorum angustifolium*), Bog Cranberry (*Vaccinium oxycoccos*), Bog Asphodel (*Narthecium ossifragum*), and sphagnum mosses. Purple Moor Grass (*Molinia caerulea*) is almost ubiquitous and can become dominant where browsing pressure is high (from sheep) but there is little grazing to push back the grasses.

WILDLIFE: No animal represents the moorlands quite like the Red Grouse. Formerly considered a subspecies of Willow Ptarmigan, it is now often treated as a full species, endemic to the UK and Ireland. It is a moorland specialist that does best with regular burning that provides Common Heather of various ages for feeding and cover. Most of the UK's Black Grouse are confined to the edges of moorlands, favouring vast heathlands and semi-open savanna-like ecosystems where some trees are present (even if they are just from conifer plantations).

The song of Eurasian Skylark is a delight on the Montane Heathlands; the skylark is often joined by Ring Ouzel and Northern Wheatear in rockier heaths. Meadow Pipit is ubiquitous. Whinchat favours open heathlands, particularly when gorse or other larger bushes provide good vantage points. Northern Lapwing and Eurasian Curlew nest in short moorlands, as does the European Golden-Plover, which favours recently burnt heaths and short, wet heaths. Common Snipe and Common Redshank will readily use wet moorlands. Twite is strongly tied to heath moorlands for breeding but also needs nearby grasslands. Moorlands are incredibly important for Hen Harrier, Merlin, and Short-eared Owl, with taller and thicker heather providing good cover for nesting. These birds of prey are not to be expected around Red Grouse shooting estates.

Mammals found on moorlands include Western Roe and Red Deer, Mountain and Brown Hares, Red Fox, Eurasian Stoat, and Least Weasel, although predator numbers are heavily restricted on

The tiny Eurasian Pygmy Shrew can be quite common in this habitat, though it spends most of its time well hidden. © THEO DOUMA, AGAMI

hunting estates. Interestingly, Eurasian Pygmy Shrew can be quite abundant in Montane Heath and Moorland, likely using European Mole tunnels during winter to continue to find 125% of its body weight in invertebrate food per day!

The impressively large Emperor Moth (*Saturnia pavonia*) and the beautiful Oak Eggar (*Lasiocampa quercus*) are day-flying moths strongly associated with heather and best found on heaths (although they both have a wide range of food plants). Scotch Argus (*Erebia aethiops*) is a butterfly typically found in grasslands and open pine woodlands. However, it will use moorlands extensively, as Purple Moor Grass and Blue Moor Grass (*Sesleria caerulea*) are both important larval host plants. Cross-leaved Heath is the favoured food plant of the Large Heath (*Coenonympha tullia*); this butterfly can be seen readily on wetter moors, often alongside a selection of dragonflies characteristic of moorlands and associated bogs, such as the Black Darter (*Sympetrum danae*), Azure Hawker (*Aeshna caerulea*), and Four-spotted Skimmer (Chaser, *Libellula quadrimaculata*). Sedge Darner (Moorland Hawker, *Aeshna juncea*) can be common near moorland pools, while Golden-ringed Dragonfly (Common Goldenring, *Cordulegaster boltonii*) will venture far from water to hunt over heathlands.

Cool temperatures in Montane Heath and Moorland mean that reptiles are scarce, but Common Slowworm (*Anguis fragilis*), Adder (*Vipera berus*), and Common Lizard (*Zootoca vivipara*) readily use moorlands with good structural diversity.

CONSERVATION: Ideally, heaths will have a high diversity of plant species without any group being particularly dominant. Nevertheless, large areas of Britain's moorlands are intensively managed for Red Grouse hunting, and burning and cutting are used to create an almost complete dominance of Common Heather of various ages. In addition, removing almost all mammalian and avian predators from British moorlands has knocked many natural systems out of balance. Nature can play her orchestral piece only when all the instruments are in place. Our own fear of death and (understandable) inability to understand nature means that we are in sad denial of the importance of wolves, bears, harriers, and eagles.

Scotch Argus is a classic inhabitant of this habitat.
© WIL LEURS, AGAMI

Human intervention in the form of wetland restoration, fire, and browsing is essential to keeping Montane Heaths and Moorlands open and the density of invading trees low. Open or savanna-like heaths were likely widespread in the Pleistocene, with our native megafauna keeping trees in check. Of greatest importance on Montane Heaths and Moorlands would have been larger, cold-adapted mammals, including Reindeer (Caribou), Red Deer, Irish Elk, Muskox, Woolly Mammoth, Woolly Rhinoceros, Wild Horse, and European Wild Ass (see Sidebar 4: Prehistoric Europe). Nowadays, sadly, browsing on moorlands is limited mostly to sheep, cattle, and Red Deer. The natural diversity of browsing and grazing strategies would undoubtedly have done wonders for creating a complex matrix of microhabitats in the heaths and advancing their biodiversity.

DISTRIBUTION: This habitat is more extensive in the UK than anywhere else in Europe. Almost 30% of Scotland is Montane Heath and Moorland, and extensive moorlands also occur in Wales and England, most notably in the Pennines. Important montane heathlands can also be found in Spain (especially northern, including through the Pyrenees), France, Germany, and Scandinavia.

WHERE TO SEE: Cairngorms National Park, Scotland, UK; Forest of Bowland, Lancashire, England, UK; Glaslyn, Powys, Wales, UK; Rothaar Mountains, North Rhine-Westphalia and Hesse, Germany.

SIDEBAR 5 WHAT ARE KEY BIODIVERSITY AREAS AND WHY DO THEY MATTER?

Key Biodiversity Areas (KBAs) are sites of global significance for preserving biodiversity. They contain a globally significant population of one or more species, a globally significant extent of an ecosystem, or a globally significant area of outstanding ecological integrity. KBAs are identified by 11 quantitative criteria to make them comparable between countries within different regions of the world. As a result, KBAs are used as important indicators for the sustainable development goals and the biodiversity plan established by the Convention on Biological Diversity, a multilateral treaty that tracks the progress by governments in achieving conservation goals. KBAs are also used by the private sector to avoid and minimise impacts on biodiversity. In order to apply the KBA ecosystem criteria, we need a good map of ecosystems that covers their global extent. These maps should be at a relevant scale within a universal ecosystem typology. The Habitats of the World project is facilitating the timely identification, classification, description, and conservation of these KBAs.

TUNDRAS

Polar Tundras
Alpine Tundras
Habitats of the World Level
Arctic Polar Desert
Nearctic Rocky Tundra
Eurasian Rocky Tundra
Antarctic Tundra
Eurasian Boggy Tundra
Nearctic Boggy Tundra
Nearctic Alpine Tundra
Eurasian Alpine Tundra
African Montane Heath
Paramo
Habitats of Europe Level
European Polar Desert
European Cryptic Tundra
European Rocky Tundra
European Shrubby Tundra
European Boggy Tundra
European Alpine Tundra
European Nival Rocky Tundra

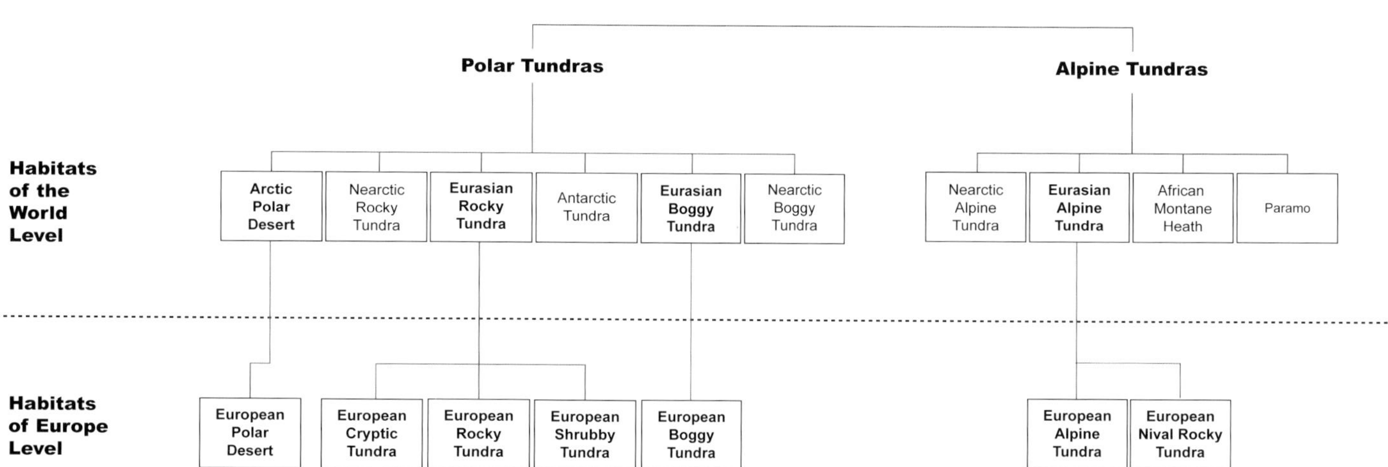

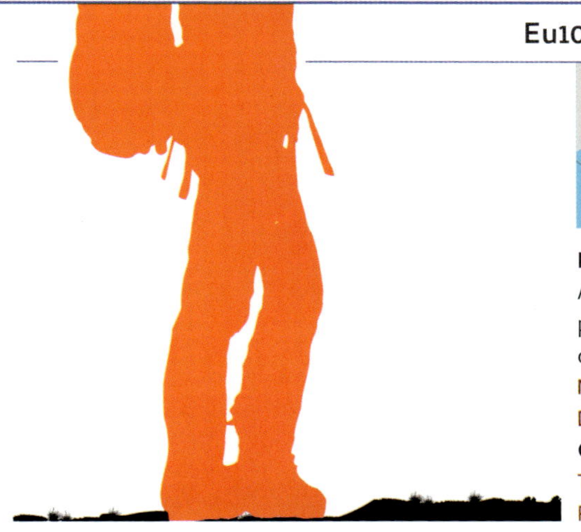

Eu10A EUROPEAN POLAR DESERT

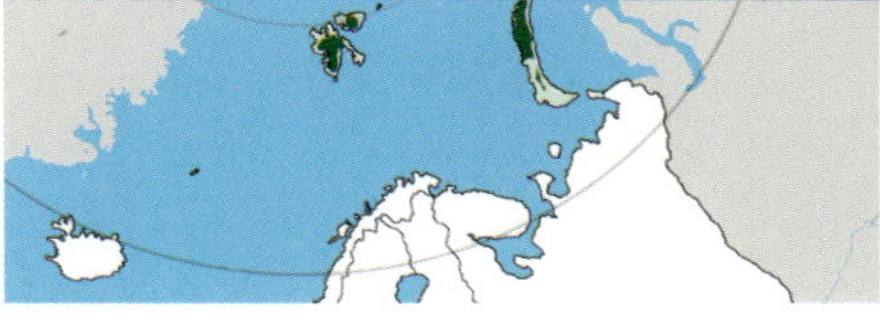

IN A NUTSHELL: The habitat of the High Arctic at the very edge of where life is possible. There is almost no vegetation of any kind. **Global Habitat Affinities:** NEARCTIC POLAR DESERT; ASIAN POLAR DESERT; ANTARCTIC POLAR DESERT. **Continental Habitat Affinities:** CRYPTIC TUNDRA. **Species Overlap:** CRYPTIC TUNDRA; ROCKY TUNDRA.

DESCRIPTION: The northernmost vegetated part of the planet is one of both bitter cold and aridity (Köppen **EF**). The Polar Desert has no month when temperatures average over 0°C (32°F) and receives less than 250 mm (10 in.) of precipitation per year. It is the extreme aridity and year-round bitter cold that separate this climate regime from other habitats. Although photosynthesis is possible below freezing, most plants require water to grow, so photosynthesis becomes more effective over 2°C (36°F) but is halted when temperatures drop back below −5°C (23°F). Consequently, plant life is limited to the hardiest of species.

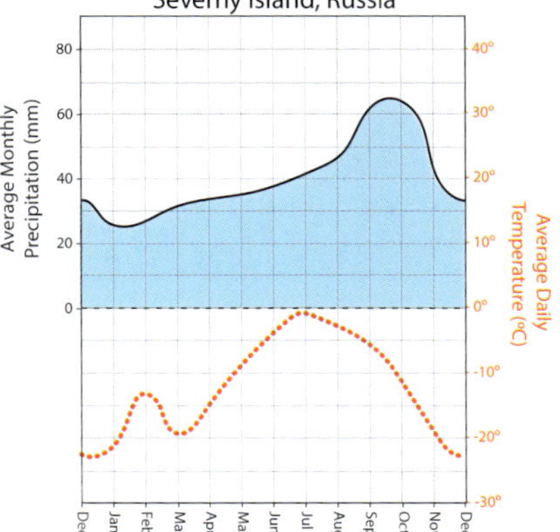

The ground is sparsely covered, with no closed vegetation cover, and over 90% of the ice-free surface is bare rock. Plants, fungi, and algae exist in sheltered areas in cracks and hollows and consist mainly of crustose (flat-lying) lichens, such as Arctic Saucer Lichen (*Ochrolechia frigida*). Some fruticose (free-standing) lichens, such as Snow Foam Lichen (*Stereocaulon rivulorum*), survive in the most protected areas. Mosses occur only where fine soils and moisture have accumulated in the best-protected areas. Forbs, such as Arctic Chickweed (*Cerastium arcticum*), Pygmy Saxifrage (*Saxifraga hyperborea*), and Purple Saxifrage (*Saxifraga oppositifolia*), and grasses and similar plants, such as Ice Grass (*Phippsia algida*), Few-flowered Whitlow-Grass (*Draba pauciflora*), and Arctic Wood-Rush (*Luzula nivalis*), will occasionally be able to establish in sheltered nooks and crannies.

Low temperatures and lack of water mean that there is almost no chemical weathering of the rocks here, and most of the disintegration of rock material is through frost and wind abrasion.

Sea ice at the foot of a bleak yet stunning Polar Desert landscape. The enormity of the scene makes the Polar Bear on the sea ice look tiny. © IAIN CAMPBELL, TROPICAL BIRDING

The nature of mechanical weathering processes (especially ablation and frost heaving) means soil development is limited to regosols. These are essentially minute fragments of the parent material and have very heterogeneous grain sizes from silts to cobbles. The lack of chemical weathering means that very few nutrients are released, and the parent material (source rock or sediment) is not an important factor in the soil's development. Consequently, there is rarely a relationship between flora, algae, and fungi and the underlying rock type. Nutrients are derived either from the rotting of existing flora or the occasional input from defecation or rotting of seabirds and the occasional mammal, such as Walrus or Polar Bear. Permafrost is pervasive within the shallow soils.

WILDLIFE: Non-migratory birds and terrestrial animals cannot survive here. Those birds and other animals that migrate here in summer also occur to the south in other habitats. Birds like Black-legged Kittiwake and Northern Fulmar use cliffs for nesting in summer but feed out in the ocean. No terrestrial mammals reside here, though seals, Walruses, and Polar Bears use the fringes of the land as haul-outs. No insects or reptiles can survive in the true Polar Desert environment. However, a few insects live in transitional areas between Polar Desert and CRYPTIC TUNDRA on Svalbard. Springtails (Collembola) are a group of cryptic terrestrial arthropods related to insects that spend most of their time in soils and under rocks. There are over 70 springtail species on Svalbard, some eking out an existence on the edge of the Polar Desert.

Black-legged Kittiwakes fly before an impossibly blue glacier face. These gulls use cliffs in the Polar Desert for nesting in summer but feed out on the ocean. © SERGIO PITAMITZ, AGAMI

CONSERVATION: Increasing global temperatures will result in CRYPTIC TUNDRA and ROCKY TUNDRA encroaching into this habitat, and because this is the coldest environment in the Northern Hemisphere, there is nowhere for this habitat to move. Increased transportation through the Arctic Ocean is likely to result in development and increased pollution along the coastlines of the Arctic.

DISTRIBUTION: This habitat is limited to the highest latitudes of the Arctic in Russia and Svalbard, Norway. Most people encounter it on the northernmost and higher parts (above 200 m/650 ft.) of Svalbard or Russia's Victoria Island, Novaya Zemlya, or Franz-Josef Land.

WHERE TO SEE: Cruises from Svalbard, Norway, that go to the north of the archipelago pass by this habitat.

The harsh Polar Desert provides some of the most beautiful scenery in Europe. Although over 90% of the ice-free surface is bare rock, some plants, fungi, and algae manage to eke out an existence in sheltered cracks and hollows. © SERGIO PITAMITZ, AGAMI

Eu10B EUROPEAN CRYPTIC TUNDRA

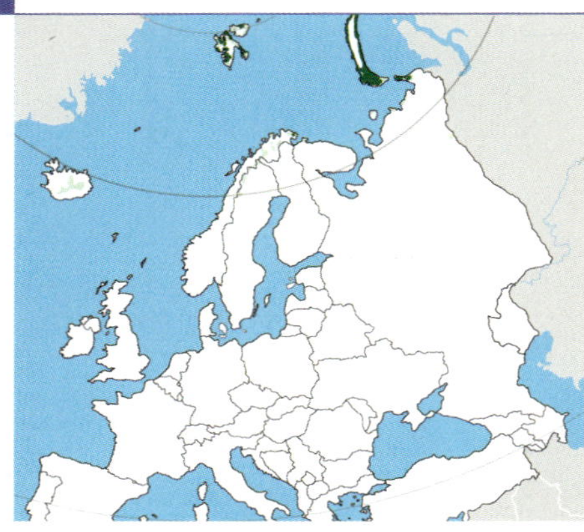

IN A NUTSHELL: Circumpolar at very high latitudes, an almost plantless environment with only very short mosses, lichens, and similar growth. **Global Habitat Affinities:** NEARCTIC CRYPTIC TUNDRA; ASIAN CRYPTIC TUNDRA. **Continental Habitat Affinities:** ROCKY TUNDRA; NIVAL ROCKY TUNDRA. **Species Overlap:** ROCKY TUNDRA; POLAR DESERT.

DESCRIPTION: 'Cryptic Tundra', 'cryptogram barren', and 'High Arctic vegetation' are terms describing this circumpolar habitat in the extreme north of Europe, North America, and Asia, as well as higher-elevation areas, such as ridgelines in areas dominated by ROCKY TUNDRA. Most of the surface area of the regions around the North Pole has no vegetation, so this habitat exists as a mosaic with glaciers and barren rock fields. A very uniform habitat where no trees or woody plants grow,

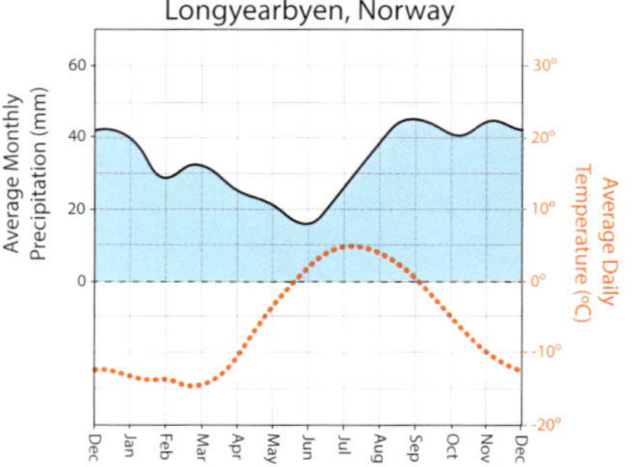

Much of the ground is completely bare in Cryptic Tundra, but where there is ground cover, the so-called cryptogram layer makes up 60% of it. © IAIN CAMPBELL, TROPICAL BIRDING

Vegetation is somewhat more extensive in more sheltered areas and spots where moisture can collect. © IAIN CAMPBELL, TROPICAL BIRDING

Cryptic Tundra differs from POLAR DESERT in that it does have vascular plants, and there is water in the environment. The vascular plants, which include forbs, grasses, cushion plants, and rosette plants, make up less than 10% of the habitat's botanical plant species and only 2% of the biomass, with the remainder dominated by fungi, algae, lichens, mosses, and liverworts. The structure of the tundra can be divided into three layers. The 'canopy' is a prostrate dwarf shrub layer less than 5 cm (2 in.) high. The occasional emergent grasses or forbs grow through this shrub canopy to as high as 10 cm (4 in.). Much of the ground is completely bare, but where there is ground cover, the so-called cryptogram layer, generally about 3 cm (1 in.) high and comprising fungi, algae, lichens, and mosses, makes up 60% of it.

This is among the most inhospitable terrestrial environments in the world (along with the ARCTIC POLAR DESERT and ice cap). The very low polar angles of sunlight mean essentially two to three months of complete darkness, two to three months of daylight, and only four to six months with air temperatures above freezing. Permafrost (frozen soil) is a defining feature, and little snowmelt occurs much below the surface. Consequently, the growing season is extremely short. These tundras experience very low temperatures throughout the year (Köppen **ET–EF**). Winters are particularly cold,

Generally about 3 cm (1 in.) high, the cryptogram layer includes fungi, algae, lichens, and mosses. © IAIN CAMPBELL, TROPICAL BIRDING

with average temperatures well below freezing, averaging −20 to −14°C (−4 to 7°F) and sometimes as low as −40°C (−40°F). Summer temperatures are relatively milder but remain very cold, with the average usually around 3–7°C (37–45°F). The European Arctic is moderated by temperate ocean currents that curve around the top of Norway from the North Atlantic, so it has a much less severe climate than both Siberia and Canada, where the coldest temperatures are affected by extreme continentality.

Regions of Cryptic Tundra are usually very dry, with precipitation around 300 mm (12 in.), mostly from snow. Such low precipitation levels in most locations on the planet would result in a desert. Nevertheless, low evapotranspiration means some surface water is usually present in summer, and the habitat can even give the impression of being humid. In contrast with the ROCKY TUNDRA, even the better-protected snowbanks cannot support shrubs, so this habitat rarely has patches of SHRUBBY TUNDRA nearby.

Extremely little chemical weathering occurs here; almost all weathering is mechanical, with freeze-thaw weathering and abrasion being particularly important. Yet paradoxically, changes in underlying rock chemistry from acidic to alkaline are the main determinants of the plants that grow on these lithosols. Calcareous rocks, such as limestones, are dominated by Greenland Fork-Moss (*Dicranum groenlandicum*). On more acidic soils formed on igneous rocks such as granites or metamorphic rocks such as schist, the globally widespread Broom Fork-Moss (*Dicranum scoparium*) is more common, along with the free-standing

Below: **A few specialised plants, such as this Tufted Saxifrage, have adapted to the harsh conditions in Cryptic Tundra.** © SERGIO PITAMITZ, AGAMI

Reindeer (Caribou) is the only large herbivore in Europe's Cryptic Tundra. Polar Bears feed mainly on seals and other marine mammals, but some individuals seem to be successful at hunting Reindeer. © SERGIO PITAMITZ, AGAMI

Snow-bed Iceland Lichen (*Cetrariella delisei*), Green Reindeer Lichen (*Cladonia arbuscula*), and Crinkled Snow Lichen (*Flavocetraria nivalis*). Tufted Saxifrage (*Saxifraga cespitosa*), Purple Saxifrage (*Saxifraga oppositifolia*), and Moss Campion (*Silene acaulis*) are among the few angiosperms able to eke out an existence in the Cryptic Tundra.

WILDLIFE: The extreme climate of the Cryptic Tundra is such that almost no vertebrates can live here year-round. Amphibians and reptiles are both absent. The only large grazer on Svalbard, Norway is the Svalbard Reindeer, a small subspecies—only about half the size of the Reindeer (Caribou) on continental Europe—that somewhat resembles a barrel on tiny legs. Arctic Fox lives in Cryptic Tundra and feeds predominantly on migrating birds, marine mammal carcasses, and, since the mid-1900s, the introduced East European Vole. Polar Bears are found in coastal Cryptic

The amazing Walrus spends most of its time at sea but hauls out to rest and to breed on coastal Cryptic Tundra. © SERGIO PITAMITZ, AGAMI

Tundra but also wander many kilometres inland. Walrus and various seals haul out and breed on coastal Cryptic Tundra.

The only regular migrant passerines to this harshest of environments are the Snow Bunting and Northern Wheatear, and even the latter rarely makes it to Svalbard or Russia's Novaya Zemlya. The bird assemblage of Cryptic Tundra tends to be an impoverished version of the assemblage of ROCKY TUNDRA. Most other birds that migrate here to breed are shorebirds that arrive in early summer to take advantage of the insect life on the summer tundra. Common Ringed Plover, Dunlin, Purple Sandpiper, and Red Phalarope can be particularly common, especially with pools about. Eurasian Dotterel favours this habitat in continental Europe. Rock Ptarmigan lives close to this environment year-round but heads downslope or slightly south to ROCKY TUNDRA for winter. Many seabirds use the cliffs on the coastline to breed but do not feed on land.

In the spring, as the days start to warm and the snow slowly recedes, rocks are exposed first. Birds are drawn to these patches, and the lichens that grow on these rocks are the focus of Reindeer, both domestic and wild. Reindeer also retreat to these exposed rocks to cool off once the snow melts and enjoy the (relatively) lower insect numbers there during the warmer summer months.

CONSERVATION: The Arctic is the region most affected by climate change, because the temperature is rising there more than twice as fast as in the tropical and subtropical parts of the world, a phenomenon known as Arctic amplification. Because the Arctic Ocean binds the Arctic region in Europe, there is little room for Cryptic Tundra to expand north as the planet warms. As ROCKY TUNDRA and SHRUBBY TUNDRA slowly move up from the south, they wedge the Cryptic Tundra into an ever-decreasing space. Although it is an extremely cold environment, it is also very dry, and only a slight increase in temperature will result in more of the plants here undergoing water stress. Some models suggest that there may be an increase in snow cover, but most models suggest a drying environment. Increasing temperatures will open much of this terrain to human colonisation as well as increased exposure to mining and oil extraction.

DISTRIBUTION: Cryptic Tundra skirts the northernmost coast of Russia as well as much of coastal and inland Svalbard, Jan Mayen, and Bjørnøya, Norway; and Novaya Zemlya and Vaygach Island, Russia. It exists in limited patches on scree slopes in Iceland, though that habitat is more akin to an extreme NIVAL ROCKY TUNDRA. The tundra borders the POLAR DESERT in the north and in elevated areas. It occurs above ROCKY TUNDRA on high ridges and hills of continental Norway and Russia.

WHERE TO SEE: Svalbard, Norway; Varanger Peninsula, Finnmark, Norway; Novaya Zemlya, Russia.

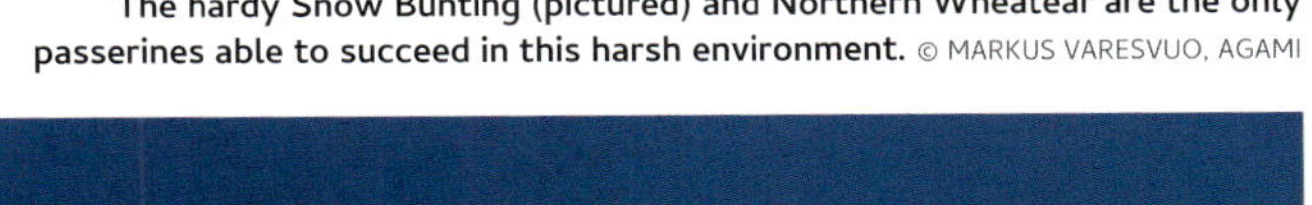

The hardy Snow Bunting (pictured) and Northern Wheatear are the only passerines able to succeed in this harsh environment. © MARKUS VARESVUO, AGAMI

Eu10C EUROPEAN ROCKY TUNDRA

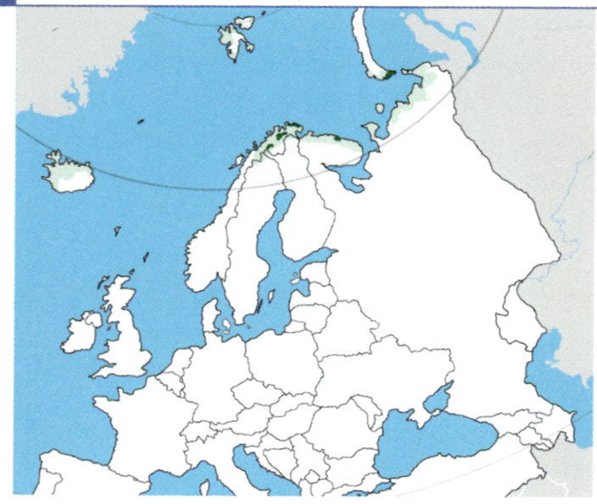

IN A NUTSHELL: The low, dry, or spongy heathlands in Arctic Eurasia that spend three months of the year frozen and in almost complete darkness and three months in full daylight. **Global Habitat Affinities:** NEARCTIC ROCKY TUNDRA; ASIAN ROCKY TUNDRA. **Continental Habitat Affinities:** CRYPTIC TUNDRA; NIVAL ROCKY TUNDRA. **Species Overlap:** CRYPTIC TUNDRA; BOGGY TUNDRA; SHRUBBY TUNDRA.

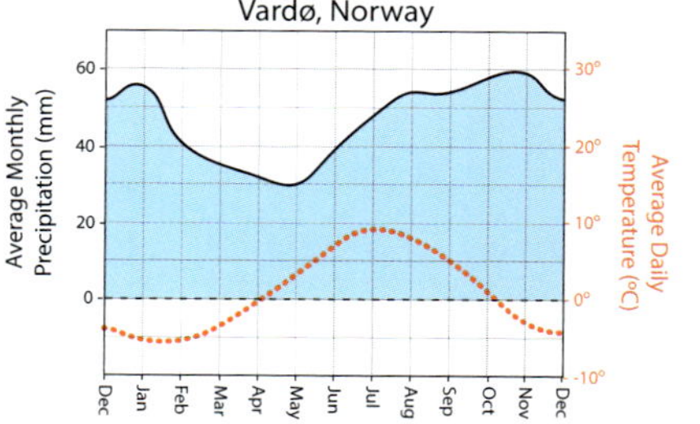

DESCRIPTION: Standing in the tundra in late spring, you see a wide, open landscape with a blend of earthy oranges, olive greens, and browns from the mosses, lichens, and dead growth from the previous year. However, the feel of Rocky Tundra varies markedly through the seasons, and in late May through late June, the landscape is bright green with a low covering of forbs, mosses, and grasses. Rocky Tundra has a very low-lying, two-layered ground cover with few bare patches over rock. There are places where only lichens and mosses grow, but over most of the area where soil has developed, shrubs and a few taller grasses and flowers take hold—though fewer plant species occur here than in more temperate regions. Nevertheless, the dramatic landscapes with uneven snow distribution create many microhabitats, allowing for more biodiversity than might be expected.

Rocky Tundra has sparse vegetation, with 20–50% cover in gullies and snow beds and less on headlands, ridgelines, and steeper scree slopes where this habitat merges with CRYPTIC TUNDRA. In the north of the Rocky Tundra, permafrost thawing is very limited. Vegetation is dominated by lichens such as Grey Reindeer Lichen (*Cladonia rangiferina*), mosses such as Golden Fuzzy Fen Moss (*Tomentypnum nitens*), and sedges such as Rock Sedge (*Carex rupestris*), Short-leaved Sedge (*Carex fuliginosa*), and Nard Sedge (*Carex nardina*). In other, slightly better-drained snow beds, the vegetation is dominated by Arctic Willow (*Salix arctica*) and Dwarf Birch (*Betula nana*) groves. The canopy, ranging from a mere 5 cm (2 in.) to as much as 60 cm (24 in.) high, is mixed with flowers such as Eight-petal Mountain-Avens (*Dryas octopetala*), Moss Campion (*Silene acaulis*), Scheuchzer's Cottongrass (*Eriophorum scheuchzeri*), Purple Saxifrage (*Saxifraga oppositifolia*), Alpine Azalea (*Kalmia procumbens*), and Arctic Dandelion (*Taraxacum arcticum*).

The permafrost thaws down to 50 cm (20 in.) in the southerly regions of Rocky Tundra. These somewhat milder conditions mean vascular plants are more common, and peat formation is possible. Perennial plants dominate the vegetation but are rarely higher than 30 cm (12 in.) above the ground. Dwarf shrubs such as Arctic Bell-Heather (*Cassiope tetragona*), along with Lingonberry (*Vaccinium vitis-idaea*), Marsh Labrador Tea (*Rhododendron tomentosum*), and Black Crowberry (*Empetrum nigrum*), dominate and are complemented by mosses, lichens, and Bigelow's Sedge (*Carex bigelowii*).

Above and below: **Dwarf shrubs dominate the vegetation of this Rocky Tundra in Varanger, Norway, and are complemented by mosses, lichens, and sedges.** © IAIN CAMPBELL, TROPICAL BIRDING

A vast expanse of well-vegetated Rocky Tundra in Varanger, Norway, with Cryptic Tundra in the higher, most exposed areas in the background. © DALE FORBES

The Rocky Tundra lies north of the 10°C (50°F) summer isotherm, and most of it is restricted to areas of permafrost, so the growing environment of this habitat is extremely harsh. With winter average highs of −2 to 3°C (27–28°F), average monthly temperatures of −4 to 10°C (25–50°F), and up to three months of night, three of day, and much of the year in twilight, growth is limited to around half of the year. At these high latitudes, growing periods are cool, with average summer high temperatures between 2 and 12°C (36–53°F). Rocky Tundra should be very arid with only 300–600 mm (12–24 in.) of precipitation per year. Nevertheless, with such low temperatures, the low evapotranspiration creates a (seemingly) humid environment in areas protected from desiccating winds, and surface water is abundant in early summer. Some areas may be snow-free for only a month of the year, allowing vegetation to start growing only at the end of July after the snowbanks have melted.

The weathering in these harsh environments is much more mechanical than chemical, resulting in lithosols with limited humic (organic-matter-containing) layers. The high importance of soil parent material in these immature soils means that differences in underlying rock chemistry from acidic to alkaline play an important role in determining the individual plants that grow there. Nevertheless, it is not as important as in CRYPTIC TUNDRA, because in these Rocky Tundras many more nutrients are derived from the defecation of birds and mammals—generally absent in CRYPTIC TUNDRA.

WILDLIFE: You can find some fascinating insects in the Rocky Tundra in summer, including a staggering array of flies, bees and wasps, butterflies and moths, and some beetles. It is always worth keeping an eye out for the four European Arctic bumblebee species: Alpine Bumblebee (*Bombus alpinus*), Lapland Bumblebee (*Bombus lapponicus*), Golden-belted Bumblebee (*Bombus*

The burst of insect life in spring induces vast numbers of birds to head to the tundra to breed, including millions of shorebirds, such as this European Golden-Plover. © IAIN CAMPBELL, TROPICAL BIRDING

balteatus), and Eurasian Arctic Bumblebee (*Bombus pyrrhopygus*), all of which are restricted to the tundra and surrounding areas. Some exciting, highly localised butterfly species to keep a look out for include Arctic, Polaris, and Dingy Fritillaries (*Boloria chariclea*, *B. polaris*, and *B. improba*); Dewy Ringlet (*Erebia pandrose*); and White-veined Arctic (*Oeneis bore*). Notably, beetles account for over 40% of global insects but only 13% of Rocky Tundra insect species. But as anyone who has spent time in the Arctic in summer can attest, midges are everywhere. Around half of the insect species of the Rocky Tundra are flies and mosquitoes (Diptera); there are nearly 800 species of them in the combined tundras! Even more incredibly, midges and mosquitoes likely make up around half of the tundra insect biomass.

It is the burst of insect life in spring that induces vast numbers of birds to head to the tundra to breed and gorge themselves on the astounding hatches of insects. These include millions of shorebirds, including Common Ringed Plover, Dunlin, Purple Sandpiper, Bar-tailed Godwit, and European Golden-Plover. Ruff is a spectacular shorebird that nests in particularly soggy, grassy patches of Rocky Tundra, avoiding the most open areas. Its communal leks are filled with dancing and leaping males of hundreds of colour variations, all vying for space and the attention of the duller reeves (females). Eurasian Dotterel prefers the driest and highest areas of Rocky Tundra as well as CRYPTIC TUNDRA where it occurs in continental Europe.

Gyrfalcon is the iconic raptor of the Rocky Tundra and one of the species wildlife enthusiasts most want to see when visiting the Arctic. Most European Gyrfalcons stay in the tundra all year round, and males even regularly stay in their breeding territory year-round. Golden Eagle occurs rarely, while White-tailed Eagle is more common,

The powerful Gyrfalcon, the largest falcon in the world, spends much of the year on or near Rocky Tundra. © MARKUS VARESVUO, AGAMI

Skuas and jaegers, such as this Parasitic Jaeger (Arctic Skua), spend most of their lives at sea, harassing other seabirds for their food. In summer, when on land breeding, they become land-based hunters. © DANI LÓPEZ-VELASCO, AGAMI

especially along the coast, where it sits like a giant as it is harassed by Arctic Terns and Common Gulls. Parasitic Jaeger (Arctic Skua) and Long-tailed Jaeger (Long-tailed Skua) are pelagic seabirds through most of the year, but when on land breeding, they change feeding habitats and become land-based hunters. Snowy Owl, rare in Europe, is a Rocky Tundra specialist, often hunting the same prey as the skuas. Rock Ptarmigan is also a tundra specialist. Incredibly, a few of these land birds are even able to eke out an existence in Rocky Tundra in winter. They also happen to be the stars of the monochromatic colour palette: Rock Ptarmigan, Gyrfalcon, and Snowy Owl, as well as Common (Northern) Raven. The only regular migrant passerine (songbird) to Svalbard, Norway is the Snow Bunting, which can be very common in much of the Rocky Tundra. In Norway and Russia, it is joined by other passerines such as Northern Wheatear, Redpoll, and Horned (Shore) Lark, as well as Meadow, Rock, and Red-throated Pipits. Lapland Longspur can be common in the summer months, calling incessantly.

Arctic regions are too frigid in winter to support reptiles or amphibians. Most mammals found in Rocky Tundra are unable to migrate and have had to find ways of dealing with this environment for the eight months of the year when it is inhospitable. This habitat extended over much of Europe during the Pleistocene, and almost all the charismatic larger mammals of the mammoth steppe—a vast, highly productive, dry, cold grassland habitat—went extinct in the past 20,000 years. The most famous of these were the Woolly Rhinoceros, Steppe Bison, and Woolly Mammoth, while the Muskox survived and has subsequently been reintroduced into Norway (see Sidebar 4: Prehistoric Europe, p.208). Today, the largest mammals over most of the European Rocky Tundra are the three subspecies of Reindeer (Caribou): the Svalbard Reindeer on Svalbard, Wild Forest Reindeer in Finnish Lapland and Russia, and Mountain Reindeer in peninsular Norway and Iceland. The Svalbard Reindeer, only about half the size of the continental Reindeer, is the only large forager on Svalbard. Reindeer and Muskox do not hibernate but instead rely on insulation from a thick layer of fat and two layers of fur, the coarser outer fur layer and, beneath it, a much finer, denser undercoat that traps body heat. In the summer months, these large mammals moult their fur for a much cooler coat to prevent overheating when temperatures are milder. Another Rocky Tundra mammal, Arctic Fox, is notable in this habitat, in that it is mostly a coastal species. While it has become rare in continental Europe, where it competes with Red Fox, it is still relatively common, and much easier to find, in Svalbard and n. Russia.

The abundance of many smaller mammals, such as Mountain Hare, Norway Lemming, and Tundra Vole, relates to the number of snowbanks during winter. Areas with limited snow

Rock Ptarmigan is a tundra specialist. It relies upon its cryptic plumage for camouflage during the breeding season and in winter turns completely white to match the snow (see p.310). © VINCENT LEGRAND, AGAMI

Arctic Fox spends much of its time along the coast, where potential prey is most common. © HAN BOUWMEESTER, AGAMI

and snowbanks are generally depauperate in smaller mammals, because they provide little protection against bitter winter temperatures. These small mammals spend the winter in snowbanks, where they can seek protection from the frigid winds, but do not hibernate. Rather, they continue to search for food throughout the winter, and some species store food in preparation for harder times. Both Tundra Vole and Norway Lemming have fluctuating populations; predators control Tundra Vole numbers, whereas Norway Lemming numbers are controlled by food supply. Voles eat mainly fast-growing grasses, which continue to be replenished throughout the summer, and their populations rise and fall with predation. Lemmings feed mainly on mosses, and there is evidence to suggest that lemming numbers rise a little faster than vole numbers in areas where moss is abundant. The lemmings subsequently overgraze, exhausting the moss supply, and their population drops suddenly. The population fluctuations of voles and lemmings directly impact predator populations, such as those of Arctic Fox, Long-tailed and Pomarine Jaegers (Skuas), and Snowy Owl, because they are their staple food source. These fluctuations create cascading effects throughout the ecosystem, affecting not only the predator populations but other animals in the ecosystem, such as nesting shorebirds, that may be secondary food sources for the predators.

CONSERVATION: Rocky Tundra was a dominant habitat over Europe during the last glacial maximum (~20,000 YA). Throughout the Pleistocene there were many ice ages, and at a shorter timescale, colder (stadial) periods and warmer (interstadial) periods within the ice ages. Each of these events profoundly affected the distribution of mammals within the Rocky Tundra, where extinctions created the opportunity for expansion and evolution of surviving species. Even within the glacial periods, there were many, sometimes rapid, minor climate fluctuations. An example is the Younger Dryas mini ice age of 12,000 YA. Average temperatures dropped by between 5 and 10°C (9–18°F) in a couple of decades, causing localised extinction events in Europe. The species that survived the multiple cooling and warming events in the earth's recent history did so by moving southwards during glacial times and northwards during the interstadials. With the current rising planetary temperatures, the rapid speed of warming is having a similar effect of potential extinction bottlenecks.

While increasing temperature should result in more plant growth in humid environments, because precipitation and temperatures are both low, much of the Rocky Tundra has the illusion of humidity. A minor rise in temperatures of a few degrees without a corresponding increase in precipitation will greatly increase plant stress and spur a likely change to a more steppe-like environment. Where there is sufficient water, shrubs will likely increase in dominance, and the Rocky Tundra is already being encroached upon by SHRUBBY TUNDRA from the south, with shrubs replacing many of the herbs and forbs. Much of the Rocky Tundra habitat seems doomed due to increasing temperatures, regardless of the water regime.

DISTRIBUTION: Rocky Tundra skirts the northernmost coasts of Russia (from Murmansk to the Urals) and Norway (from Harstad to the Varanger Peninsula). It occurs on much of coastal and inland Iceland; Svalbard, Jan Mayen, and Bjørnøya, Norway; and Novaya Zemlya and Vaygach Island, Russia. It is widespread throughout Iceland, but on most other islands at higher latitudes, it exists as pockets within areas protected from strong desiccating winds and is surrounded by CRYPTIC TUNDRA. Over most of the continental distribution, it exists as a mosaic with BOGGY TUNDRA between the northern coast and SHRUBBY TUNDRA, SUBARCTIC RIPARIAN WOODLAND, or TUNDRA TAIGA to the south.

WHERE TO SEE: Varanger Peninsula, Finnmark, Norway; Longyearbyen, Svalbard, Norway.

Eu10D EUROPEAN SHRUBBY TUNDRA

IN A NUTSHELL: This low, shrubby, and mossy habitat with patches of taller shrubs spends most of the year under snow but has a spectacular burst of insects and birdlife in summer. **Global Habitat Affinities:** ASIAN SHRUBBY TUNDRA; NEARCTIC SHRUB TUNDRA. **Continental Habitat Affinities:** ROCKY TUNDRA; ALPINE TUNDRA. **Species Overlap:** ROCKY TUNDRA; SUBARCTIC RIPARIAN WOODLAND.

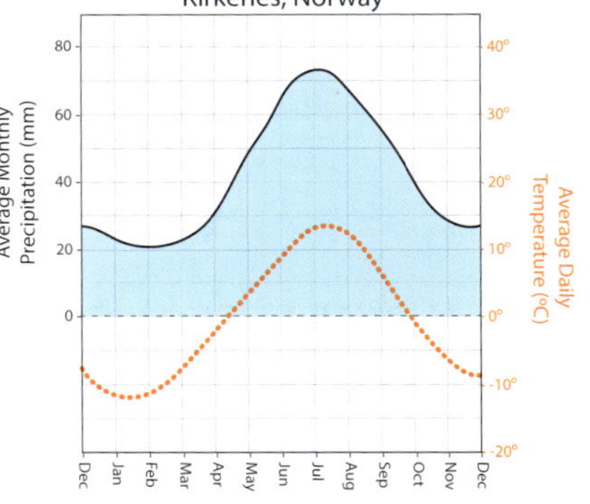

DESCRIPTION: Shrubby Tundra is found in the windswept, treeless barrens of the Arctic where small bushes are just able to eke out an existence. These shrubs can grow several feet high (30–120 cm/1–4 ft.) and are generally taller versions of the same plant species found in the more exposed, shorter ROCKY TUNDRA, such as Common Bilberry (*Vaccinium myrtillus*), Lingonberry (*Vaccinium vitis-idaea*), Bog Bilberry (*Vaccinium uliginosum*), Dwarf Birch (*Betula nana*), Tea-leaved Willow (*Salix phylicifolia*), and Least Willow (*Salix herbacea*). Among these, you will find rushes, such as Highland Rush (*Oreojuncus trifidus*); grasses, such as Viviparous Sheep's Fescue (*Festuca vivipara*); and flowers, such as European Globeflower (*Trollius europaeus*), Swedish Cornel (*Cornus suecica*), Alpine Cinquefoil (*Potentilla crantzii*), and Alpine Milkvetch (*Astragalus alpinus*).

Rocks are almost completely covered by a wide variety of mosses and lichens, including Dusky Fork-Moss (*Dicranum fuscescens*), Woolly Fringe-Moss (*Racomitrium lanuginosum*), Curled Snow Lichen (*Flavocetraria cucullata*), and Iceland Lichen (*Cetraria islandica*). All this growth gives the Shrubby Tundra a much more thickly vegetated and taller appearance than that of the surrounding ROCKY TUNDRA.

Compared with CRYPTIC and ROCKY TUNDRAS, Shrubby Tundra develops in better-protected, thicker soils (in areas with permafrost) or in the milder climate somewhat farther south in the tundra (where there is no permafrost). The growing season is only four months per year, with up to 24 hours of sunlight. During the rest of the year, the habitat remains dormant and is buried under snow cover for about 200 days (which protects the plants from desiccating winds). Perennials and shrubs tend to flower early in the growing season, while annuals or plants without substantial biomass in their root systems flower and seed later in the season before withering away and overwintering as seeds.

Shrubby Tundra has a much more thickly vegetated and taller appearance than the shorter Rocky Tundra. © DALE FORBES

Rather than simply being resistant to extremely cold conditions, the plants of this habitat are adapted to a very short growing season with long periods of daylight and also to withstand intense desiccation and winds in winter, particularly when there is no snow cover. Temperature alone would intuitively seem to be the main factor determining vegetation limitations of this habitat, but that is not the case; temperatures in SPRUCE-FIR TAIGA can be much colder than those of Shrubby Tundra. However, Shrubby Tundra can be very windy, and when coupled with extremely cold temperatures, these winds cause rapid transpiration and desiccation. Plants are not able to replenish this loss, as all water is frozen. So, the drying winds rather than temperature create the microenvironments in the northern tundras. Shrubby

In Shrubby Tundra (shown here in Varanger, Norway), plants can grow several feet high (30–120 cm/1–4 ft.); they are generally taller versions of the same species found in the more exposed, shorter Rocky Tundra. © IAIN CAMPBELL, TROPICAL BIRDING

Boom and bust fluctuations in populations of lemmings, such as this Norway Lemming, have a profound effect on the populations of many Arctic birds. © KARI EISCHER, AGAMI

Tundra takes hold in more protected areas, surrounded by the more exposed, shrubless ROCKY TUNDRA. Farther south, in regions such as coastal Norway and the islands north of Scotland, the milder climate and lack of permafrost mean that Shrubby Tundra is found only on the most brutal, exposed islands and the tops of plateaus and ridgelines. TUNDRA TAIGA grows in the more protected areas.

WILDLIFE: Most of the mammals found in Shrubby Tundra cannot migrate and have had to find ways of dealing with this environment for the six months of the year when it is inhospitable. Reindeer (Caribou) do not hibernate (nor did the Woolly Mammoth or Woolly Rhinoceros before them), but a thick layer of fat helps to insulate them, along with two layers of fur; beneath the coarser outer fur layer is a much finer, denser undercoat that traps body heat. Much of this fur is moulted in the summer months to prevent overheating when temperatures are milder. Grey Wolf also occurs in Shrubby Tundra in Europe, although not in the high densities seen in the NEARCTIC SHRUB TUNDRA of North America. European Shrubby Tundra is home to plenty of smaller mammals, such as Norway Lemming and Tundra Vole. These smaller mammals do not hibernate but spend the winter in snowbanks, where they seek protection from the bitter winds.

The biggest seasonal change in animal numbers comes with the invertebrate ephemeral breeders such as mosquitoes and midges, which burst into life in early summer, have phenomenal growth over a very short time, and provide the food source for the bulk of migratory birds. Many shorebirds migrate north to exploit this source with its 24-hour feeding opportunities, regularly using both the open, exposed ROCKY TUNDRA and the thicker Shrubby Tundra. The ornate male Ruff is particularly conspicuous and makes easy prey, so it will spend a lot of time hiding and feeding among the low shrubs, coming out in the open only to display.

The Whimbrel is among several species of shorebirds that breed in this habitat. © DANIELE OCCHIATO, AGAMI

Whimbrel also tends to nest in or very close to the Shrubby Tundra rather than in the very exposed ROCKY TUNDRA nearby. There are few passerine species this far north, but passerines do make up a big proportion of the bird assemblage in this habitat. A few species, like Snow Bunting, Redpoll, and Lapland Longspur, can be common. Fieldfare and Redwing, both thrushes, can be found in most Shrubby Tundra. Willow Warblers sing incessantly through June and July in most shrubs over 50 cm (20 in.) tall, and their lovely cascading song becomes the background sound to a summer visit to Shrubby Tundra. Bluethroat and Arctic Warbler use the thicker and taller Shrubby Tundra at the southern edge of this habitat, where the willows and birches surpass 1 m (3 ft.) tall.

CONSERVATION: Shrubby Tundra is well protected from farming because of its extreme environment. With warming temperatures, it is expanding north of its range at the expense of the ROCKY TUNDRA. Nevertheless, climate change does threaten the Shrubby Tundra as TUNDRA TAIGA, SPRUCE-FIR TAIGA, and PINE TAIGA encroach from the south.

DISTRIBUTION: Shrubby Tundra is circumpolar, found in Europe, Greenland, the Nearctic (North America), and the Asian Arctic. In Europe, it is found between 71°N and 65°N, from Iceland to Norway, Sweden, and Finland, and across the top of Russia to the Urals.

WHERE TO SEE: Varanger Peninsula, Finnmark, Norway; Flókalundur, Westfjords, Iceland.

Lapland Longspur (pictured) occupies shrubbier areas than its close relative the Snow Bunting.

The Red-spotted form of the wonderful Bluethroat is a common summer visitor to this habitat.

Eu10E EUROPEAN BOGGY TUNDRA

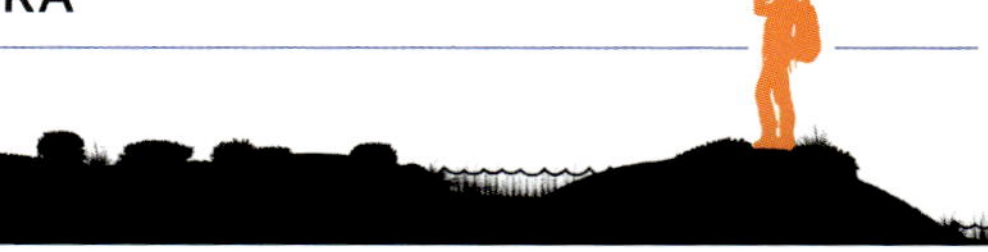

IN A NUTSHELL: A low, marshy, bog-like tundra with scattered meltwater pools. **Global Habitat Affinities:** NEARCTIC BOGGY TUNDRA; ASIAN BOGGY TUNDRA. **Continental Habitat Affinities:** TEMPERATE PEATLAND. **Species Overlap:** ROCKY TUNDRA; TEMPERATE PEATLAND.

DESCRIPTION: Boggy Tundra is a fascinating, ever-changing world: one moment dark, covered in deep snows, and seemingly supremely inhospitable, and just a few short weeks later the setting of a truly unforgettable wildlife spectacle, as myriad diverse Ruffs dance and leap about to the tune of displaying Whimbrels.

At first look, this habitat may look similar to a temperate wetland, but it is much more closely associated with ROCKY TUNDRA, occurring in the same zones with the same tundra climate (Köppen **ET**). Winters are bitterly cold (av. low temperature −11°C/13°F), and summers are cool (av. high 8°C/47°F). Annual precipitation

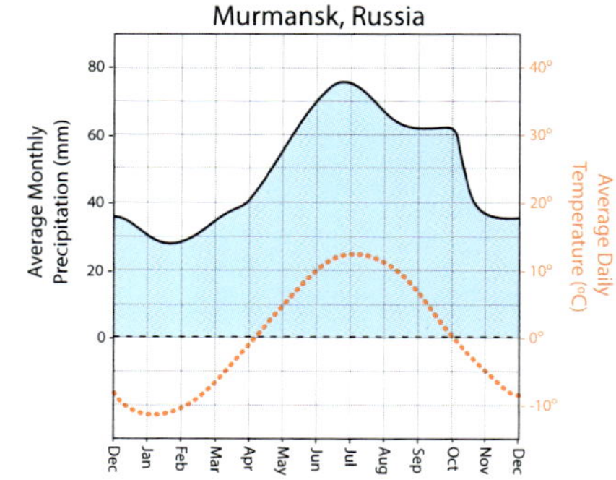

Melting snows and permafrost turn vast areas of the tundra into the ever-changing marshes of the Boggy Tundra. © IAIN CAMPBELL, TROPICAL BIRDING

is around 80 mm (11 in.), often occurring as snowfall in the winter months. The big difference between Boggy and Rocky Tundras is drainage.

Contrary to what initial impressions in early spring may suggest, the rolling terrain of the Boggy Tundra is fascinating, its very irregular drainage patterns revealed only after snowmelt. In late May, most of the terrain is covered in snow, with only scattered snow-free mounds (pingos and palsas). In early June, the Arctic Ocean is still frozen, but on the tundra the snow begins to melt, forming ephemeral lakes that may exist for only a week before they dry out. When visiting Boggy Tundra, a naturalist may find an area with a foot of water and hundreds of ducks one day, and the same area dry and replete with shorebirds starting to breed the next. As the snowmelt continues, the permanent lakes start to thaw. By the end of June, the terrain has revealed uplands with the driest tundra (ROCKY TUNDRA), gentle slopes with extensive sphagnum moss, and marshlands (Boggy Tundra).

Palsa mounds (or just palsas) are raised areas of the mire formed in areas where gradual accumulation of ice in the permafrost causes the ground to swell and rise above the surrounding terrain (see Sidebar 6: A Brief Overview of Europe's Diverse Peatlands, p.332). They are usually elevated only about 1 m (3 ft.) but can be up to 8 m (25 ft.) high. Palsa mounds can also form on the sides of hills where solifluction (freeze-thaw activity moving soils downslope) causes bands of soil ridges and depressions perpendicular to the prevailing slope. These ridges trap snowmelt water and end up resembling a series of rice paddies, complete with rushes like the Highland Rush (*Oreojuncus trifidus*).

By contrast, the raised areas can be windblown and desiccated in the winter, resulting in plants more typical of ROCKY TUNDRA, such as Grey Reindeer Lichen (*Cladonia rangiferina*) and myriad sedges (*Carex* spp.). In any case, it is a thick blanket of mosses that insulates the frozen permafrost heart of the palsa mounds in summer. Peat-forming sphagnum mosses, such as Brown Peatmoss (*Sphagnum fuscum*) and Narrowleaf Peatmoss (*S. angustifolium*), are particularly important, along with a variety of other mosses, such as Broom Fork-Moss (*Dicranum scoparium*), Red-stemmed Feather-Moss (*Pleurozium schreberi*), and Nodding Thread-Moss (*Pohlia nutans*).

On the sides of the palsa mounds, and especially where snowbanks form in winter, the grasses and similar plants (graminoids) are thicker, dominated by Lesser Tussock Sedge (*Carex diandra*), Woolly-fruited Sedge (*Carex lasiocarpa*), and Mud Sedge (*Carex limosa*), and accompanied by other plants, such as Arctic Dandelion (*Taraxacum arcticum*), Eight-petal Mountain-Avens (*Dryas octopetala*), and Bog Cranberry (*Vaccinium oxycoccos*). In the most protected and best-drained areas, small groves of shrubs less than 1.2 m (4 ft.) tall establish with species such as Common Bilberry (*Vaccinium myrtillus*), Cloudberry (*Rubus chamaemorus*), Wild Rosemary (*Andromeda polifolia*), Dwarf Birch (*Betula nana*), and Least Willow (*Salix herbacea*).

Ice-wedge polygons are like palsas, in many respects, but develop when the climate is even more extreme, forming large, geometric forms through the landscape (see Sidebar 6: A Brief Overview of Europe's Diverse Peatlands, p.332). But the most extreme form of Arctic mound is the pingo. Pingos develop in the same general areas as ice-wedge polygons but are not peat structures. Great hydrostatic pressure forms at the base of valleys (invariably Boggy Tundra), forcing water and ice into the permafrost system to grow the mound (an open-system pingo). The mounds can be truly enormous, reaching heights over 40 m (130 ft.). Most of Europe's pingos are found in Svalbard, Norway, where there are 136 of them, averaging about 10 m (33 ft.) high.

WILDLIFE: These boggy and marshy areas are rich in nesting shorebirds and other waterbirds. Waterbirds that use the deeper ponds include King and Steller's Eiders, Arctic Loon (Black-throated Loon or Diver), Red-throated Loon (Diver), and Yellow-billed Loon (White-billed Diver). Waterfowl typical of more temperate areas also come here to breed, including Common Scoter, Long-tailed Duck, Greater Scaup, Smew, and Northern Shoveler.

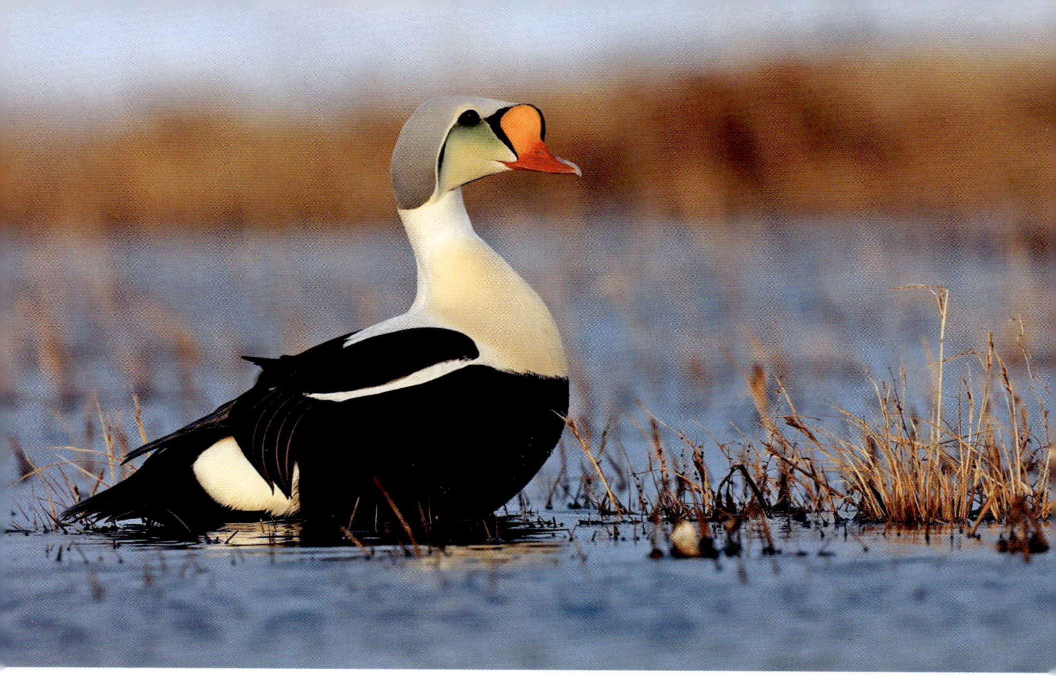

The wonderful King Eider spends most of its time at sea but comes to tundra pools to breed.
© AURÉLIEN AUDEVARD, AGAMI

Shorebirds dominate the bird assemblage in the breeding season. Typical species include Purple Sandpiper, Ruff, Dunlin, European Golden-Plover, Common Redshank, Temminck's Stint, Wood Sandpiper, Bar-tailed Godwit, and Whimbrel. Red-necked and Red Phalaropes both nest in Boggy Tundra but, unusually for shorebirds, readily feed by swimming in deeper waters, taking tiny

Many hundreds of different colour variants have been identified in Ruffs. © DANIELE OCCHIATO, AGAMI

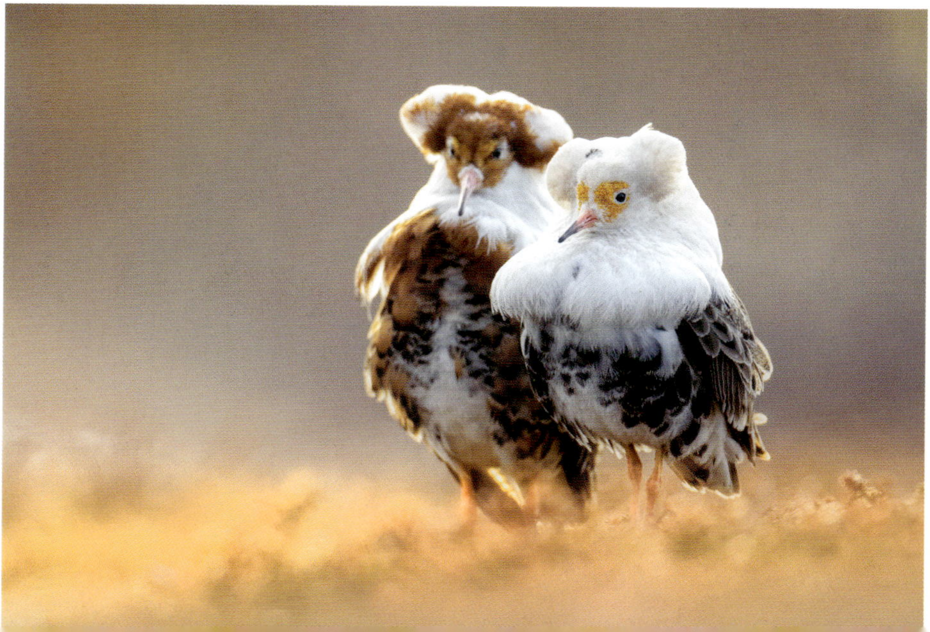

The remarkable Ruff, with its complex lekking display, is Europe's most ornate shorebird. © DANIELE OCCHIATO, AGAMI

insects from the water's surface. Passerines that feed and breed around the mire edge include Meadow Pipit, Lapland Longspur, and Western Yellow Wagtail. Red-throated Pipit breeds almost exclusively in Boggy Tundra. Parasitic Jaeger (Arctic Skua) breeds on Boggy Tundra, even far inland, and can feel omnipresent. Long-tailed Jaeger (Skua) and Great Skua are also relatively

The delightful Red-necked Phalarope breeds on small pools in the tundra. Remarkably, some w. European populations of this tiny bird have been shown to migrate right across the Atlantic and over the Isthmus of Panama to spend the winter in the Pacific Ocean! © JARI PELTOMÄKI, AGAMI

common as they scour the tundra for food, while it is always worth keeping an eye out for the occasional Pomarine Jaeger (Skua), which is concentrated in the Boggy Tundra while breeding.

Very few mammals live in this marshy environment, because it is productive for only a short time each year. Arctic Fox wanders into it from ROCKY TUNDRA to predate nesting birds, and Polar Bears roam here in summer but do not den in this marshy environment. European Common Frog (*Rana temporaria*) is the only amphibian regularly found in Boggy Tundra. No reptiles are found here.

Freija Fritillary (*Boloria freija*) is a Boggy Tundra habitat specialist, while Frigga Fritillary (*Boloria frigga*), White-veined Arctic (*Oeneis bore*), and Norse Grayling (*Oeneis norna*) occur here but will also move into other surrounding habitats.

CONSERVATION: The Boggy Tundra is in extreme risk of a future complete collapse due to global warming. Modelling of the Köppen climate of Fennoscandia in 2100 (see fig. 5) predicts that the area that currently has permafrost will be greatly reduced, and the melting of the permafrost will create thermokarst (melt) ponds in the resulting hollows. The increased temperatures will also change the balance from a humid environment with slowly melting snowfall to a drier one that better promotes the growth of SHRUBBY TUNDRA, PINE TAIGA, and even TEMPERATE OAK FOREST. With the drying out of these Arctic mires, the future of the Arctic-breeding shorebirds looks dire at best.

DISTRIBUTION: The broad distribution of this habitat follows that of the ROCKY TUNDRA, with which it is invariably found in a mosaic. It is found only in the High Arctic, farther north than the taiga forests. It is more common closer to coastlines, where it can be found on Arctic islands and on the mainland from Arctic Norway across the northern coast of Russia to the Urals.

WHERE TO SEE: Varanger Peninsula, Finnmark, Norway.

Red-throated Pipit is a long-distance migrant that takes advantage of the abundant insect life in the tundra.
© MARKUS VARESVUO, AGAMI

Eu10F EUROPEAN ALPINE TUNDRA

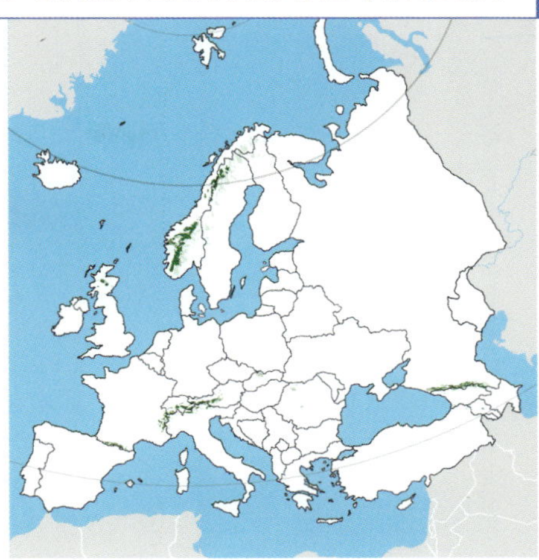

IN A NUTSHELL: The open grasslands and heathlands above the tree line in the alpine zone of Europe's mountains. **Global Habitat Affinities:** NEARCTIC ALPINE TUNDRA; ASIAN ALPINE TUNDRA; AUSTRALIAN ALPINE TUNDRA; AFROPARAMO; ANDEAN HUMID PARAMO. **Continental Habitat Affinities:** NIVAL ROCKY TUNDRA; SHRUBBY TUNDRA; ROCKY TUNDRA. **Species Overlap:** SUBALPINE TIMBERLINE WOODLAND; NIVAL ROCKY TUNDRA.

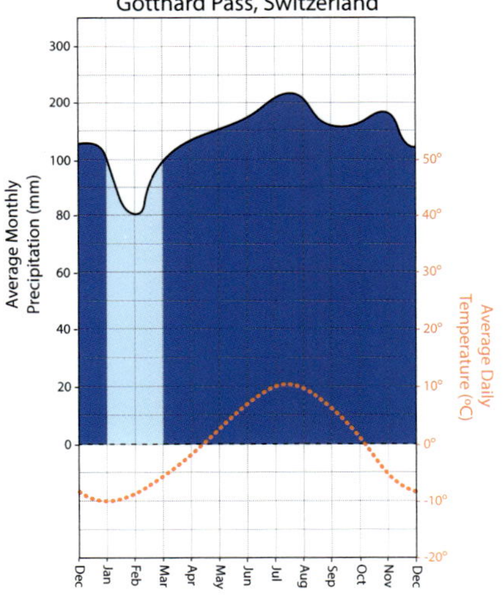

DESCRIPTION: Once you have ascended through the montane forests, you are greeted by the alpine zone—a breathtaking open, treeless landscape of grasses and subshrubs, realm of the Alpine Ibex. Tundra, found above the tree line, starts at a staggering 2600 m (8500 ft.) above sea level in parts of the Pyrenees, Alps, and s. Carpathians but almost at sea level in northernmost latitudes. The plant communities of Alpine Tundra are much like those of Arctic tundra, and they even share many of the same species. However, Alpine Tundra boasts a far greater floral diversity, having served as a crucial refuge for tundra plants during the Pleistocene ice ages.

The climate of Alpine Tundra is even harsher than that of Arctic tundra, with a low median annual temperature, brutal winters (lows to −40°C/−40°F), and cool summers (up to 21°C/70°F; Köppen **Dfd** and **ET**). In the higher reaches, the growing season is only about 4–10 weeks. The Arctic tundra might be similarly cold, but its months of 24-hour daylight during the growing season allow the plants (and animals) to maximise growth during that brief period. By contrast, even in midsummer, nights in the Alpine Tundra can drop below freezing, exposing plants to large temperature fluctuations. Harsh daily freeze-thaw cycles are particularly common when insulating snows are absent in spring and autumn. Nevertheless, snow blankets much of the landscape in winter, insulating the vegetation from strong, desiccating winds and solar radiation. This benefit does, however, mean that the growing season can only start later in the spring, after the snow has melted and the plants can receive sunlight.

The typically sloped terrain presents a unique challenge to vegetation, regularly subjecting it to wet slab avalanches, especially in springtime as snows are melting. These heavy, sliding sheets

The views in the Alpine Tundra are often stunning, taking in Subalpine Timberline Woodland below and Nival Rocky Tundra above. In between, there is great habitat for Northern Wheatear, Alpine Accentor, White-winged Snowfinch, and Rock Ptarmigan, each in its own, specific microhabitat. © DALE FORBES

of snow tear at the vegetation beneath it; consequently, the habitat is most favourable to low-growing vegetation tolerant of the abrasion and resulting damage. The vegetation of the warmer south-facing slopes is dominated by grasses, because the snow layers slide easily over them, frequently opening patches to daylight, even in the dead of winter. These patches are important refuges for Alpine Ibex—the majestic goat of the Alpine Tundra—which takes advantage of the abundant food before returning to cliffs, on which little snow accumulates, to search for small tussocks of grass or moss, or cliff-hanging shrubs. The ibex moves on to the meadows of thick grass and heath when the snows melt.

Vegetation in the Alpine Tundra is typically dense, with mats of grass and small or stunted shrubs. Deeper, raw, humus-rich meadow soils develop, as low temperatures slow decomposition, even leading to mossy, peaty areas. The accumulated organic matter blackens the upper soil layers, so the soil can warm quickly in direct sun. Freeze-thaw processes—particularly in spring and autumn, when insulating snows can be lacking—tend to mix soils, reducing clear soil layering. Soils tend to be shallower on steeper slopes, with erosion moving material downslope to collect in depressions and flatter areas. These flatter areas can form spongy, mossy, boggy areas reminiscent of the BOGGY TUNDRA of the Arctic.

Alpenroses and other *Rhododendron* species cloak many an alpine hillside in pink in the spring and early summer, making for spectacular hikes. The alpenroses can, however, form such extensive, thick mats that the microhabitat heterogeneity can be quite low. Consequently, walks through alpenrose-clad slopes can be rather quiet, with only Water Pipits displaying overhead. There is considerably more wildlife when boulders, small cliffs, and sections of varied micro-topography break up these fields, providing microhabitats for diverse plant species that support Northern Wheatear, Rufous-tailed Rock-Thrush, and Black Redstart.

A fascinatingly diverse heathland mixture of mosses, lichens, and stunted woody plants develops in areas where grasses or rhododendrons do not dominate. Lingonberry (*Vaccinium vitis-idaea*), Common Bilberry (*V. myrtillus*), and Bog Bilberry (*V. uliginosum*) offer delightful snacks for hikers in late summer and wonderful colours in autumn. Scattered Mountain Juniper (*Juniperus communis* var. *saxatilis*), various dwarf willows (e.g., *Salix herbacea*, *S. retusa*, and *S. reticulata*), Alpine Azalea (*Kalmia procumbens*), Common Heather (*Calluna vulgaris*), Spring Heath (*Erica carnea*), and myriad other plants fill in the gaps. The Alpine Tundra is a delight for wildflower enthusiasts, supporting a staggering variety of beautiful species, including Edelweiss (*Leontopodium nivale*), Dark Vanilla Orchid (*Gymnadenia rhellicani*), Frog Orchid (*Dactylorhiza viridis*), Fringe-flowered Gentian (*Gentianopsis ciliata*), and Spotted Gentian (*Gentiana punctata*).

Rock Partridge favours steep, warm (mostly south-facing), grassy slopes with boulders and other rocky material. © DALE FORBES

For much of the year, tundra plants often appear reddish, due to anthocyanins, fascinating chemicals that help protect plants from extreme conditions by filtering out damaging ultraviolet light and protecting them from oxidative and cold stress. The reddish hues of the tundra are subsumed by greens during the short growing season as chlorophyll-rich tissue shines through.

Gravelly and very rocky areas in the alpine zone are tough growing sites for plants. Stable, moister areas allow small succulents and cushion plants to establish, including Moss Campion (*Silene acaulis*), Purple Saxifrage (*Saxifraga oppositifolia*), Alpine Rock-Jasmine (*Androsace alpina*), Swiss Rock-Jasmine (*Androsace helvetica*), Rolling Hen-and-Chicks (*Sempervivum globiferum*), and Mountain Houseleek (*Sempervivum montanum*). The knee-high perennial shrubs and forbs store energy in their roots, ready to shoot up as soon as possible after the snows retreat. This gives them an advantage over annuals, and even though annuals might look quite common when they flower in the summer, they often account for less than 5% of the plant cover. Shrubs from the SUBALPINE KRUMMHOLZ—especially Green Alder (*Alnus alnobetula*)—reach up into the Alpine Tundra in avalanche chutes and drainage lines.

Cows and sheep are seemingly omnipresent throughout much of the Alpine Tundra. With their low-intensity grazing, they are likely an important replacement for the wildlife we have lost (see Sidebar 4: Prehistoric Europe, p.208) and help create a matrix of microhabitats within the Alpine Tundra.

Above: **Alpine Ibex favours warm, sunny, grassy slopes in the Alpine Tundra.** © DALE FORBES

Right: **Alpine Marmot is common in much of Europe's Alpine Tundra and an important prey item of Golden Eagle.** © DALE FORBES

Opposite: **Spring-blooming alpine flowers, such as this Spotted Gentian, are of great interest to botanists.** © DALE FORBES

WILDLIFE: Alpine Ibex, Northern Chamois, Pyrenean Chamois, West Caucasian Tur, and East Caucasian Tur—all large mountain goats—spend much of the summer in Alpine Tundra before retreating to montane forests or steeper cliffs when snow starts to build up. Mountain Hare does something similar, moving into the grassy tundra in summer (when its fur is brown) before returning to the Dwarf Mountain Pine (*Pinus mugo*) thickets of the SUBALPINE KRUMMHOLZ in winter (when its fur is white). Red Fox is ubiquitous, while Brown Bear and Grey Wolf roam this habitat in wilder parts of Europe. Alpine Marmot, a specialist of the Alpine Tundra, is common in many of Europe's mountains and is an important prey item of the

Bearded Vulture (Lammergeier) patrols the Alpine Tundra looking for carcasses. It specialises in feeding on bones and marrow, not meat. © CHRIS VAN RIJSWIJK, AGAMI

Golden Eagle. The marmot's high-pitched warning whistle is heard on many a European high-mountain hike. European Snow Vole sticks to the scree slopes and areas with lots of boulders.

Bearded Vulture (Lammergeier) is slowly making a comeback in the Alps and is most often encountered as it cruises low across mountainsides looking for picked-clean bones. It is, surprisingly, a bone eater, not a meat eater, dropping the bones from great heights to shatter on rocks, making it easier to swallow them and extract the marrow. Sadly, a tragic misconception about its diet drove the vulture's persecution and extinction in much of Europe, as people thought it ate their lambs (*Lämmergeier* means 'lamb vulture' in German). In contrast to the bone eater, Common (Northern) Raven, Golden Eagle—and even Eurasian Griffon in summer—may be seen looking for somewhat fresher carrion and prey. Flocks of loud Yellow-billed Choughs are common in most of Europe's Alpine Tundra but are noticeably absent in the north (Scotland, Norway, and Sweden). Red-billed Chough uses the Alpine Tundra in a similar way in the Pyrenees, sw. Alps, and Caucasus.

Water Pipit is the most common bird in many areas, setting up territories in early spring even before the snows have melted. White-winged Snowfinch and Rock Ptarmigan breed mainly in the high alpine

Water Pipits are ubiquitous in the Alpine Tundra. © DALE FORBES

Alpine Accentor is one of the classic hardy alpine passerines, favouring rough, craggy slopes. © RALPH MARTIN, AGAMI

and nival zones. In winter, the snowfinches will often gather in large flocks of many hundreds, roaming through the Alpine Tundra and often congregating around high-elevation ski huts with bird-feeding stations. They only rarely descend to the SUBALPINE TIMBERLINE WOODLAND. Northern Wheatear is often encountered breeding in this habitat, especially where large boulders are strewn through slightly flatter areas. Black Redstart will be anywhere with large boulders and cliffs, while Alpine Accentor is even more closely tied to sloping, jagged cliffs (but typically not grassy, boulder-strewn slopes or vertical cliffs). Rufous-tailed Rock-Thrush is best found on steeper south-facing slopes with enough lookout posts—in the form of large boulders or small cliff faces, or suitable avalanche barriers, fence posts, or other artificial structures added to the landscape. Similarly, Rock Partridge favours steep, warm, grassy slopes (mostly south-facing) with many boulders and rocky material. Being off trail in good Rock Partridge habitat often feels foolhardy, with unsure, slippery footing and the imminent danger of falling boulders. To make these ventures even more challenging, the partridge tends to be very shy, and even on pleasant spring mornings, when it is most vocal, it can remain silent for hours after it has spotted a person or been disturbed.

Rock Partridge is an elusive denizen of rocky areas in Alpine Tundra. © DALE FORBES

Eurasian Dotterel is a fascinating wader and an incredibly rare breeder in Alpine Tundra. © DALE FORBES

As its name suggests, the Alpine Blue is found at high elevations. It favours habitat similar to that of the Rock Partridge. © IOLENTE NAVARRO, AGAMI

The High Arctic tundra abounds with breeding shorebirds. Alpine Tundra and NIVAL ROCKY TUNDRA, by contrast, are devoid of shorebirds, with one exception: Eurasian Dotterel, an exceptionally rare breeding bird in c. European mountains. It favours flattish, open areas of hilltops and plateaus in classic Alpine Tundra with lichens, short grasses, mosses, and few large obstructions. The dotterel tends to be very reclusive in summer but is significantly easier to see in the Alpine Tundra when on migration, revisiting specific stopover sites season after season.

The wealth of plant species and microhabitats and the sheer age of this habitat mean that butterfly diversity can be truly stunning. Some special species include Mountain Ringlet (*Erebia epiphron*), Lesser Mountain Ringlet (*Erebia melampus*), De Prunner's Ringlet (*Erebia triarius*), Geranium Argus (*Eumedonia eumedon*), Carline Skipper (*Pyrgus carlinae*), Broad-bordered White Underwing (*Anarta melanopa*), Mountain Clouded Yellow (*Colias phicomone*), Shepherd's Fritillary (*Boloria pales*), and Eros Blue (*Polyommatus eros*). Alpine Blue (*Agriades orbitulus*) favours habitat similar to that of Rock Partridge.

CONSERVATION: The tundras are arguably the habitats most affected by climate change. Ecosystem management—particularly the clearing of stones and shrubs—for skiing areas is also having a dramatic effect on this habitat in many alpine areas.

DISTRIBUTION: Alpine Tundra is found in all of Europe's high mountain ranges, including the Alps, Pyrenees, Caucasus, and Carpathians, as well as the highest reaches of Scotland, Norway, and Sweden.

WHERE TO SEE: Hohe Tauern National Park, Austria; Kaunergrat Nature Park, Tyrol, Austria; Zermatt, Valais, Switzerland; Pyrénées Catalanes Regional Nature Park, Pyrénées-Orientales, France; Cairngorms, Scotland, UK; Stepantsminda, Mtskheta-Mtianeti, Georgia.

Eu10G EUROPEAN NIVAL ROCKY TUNDRA

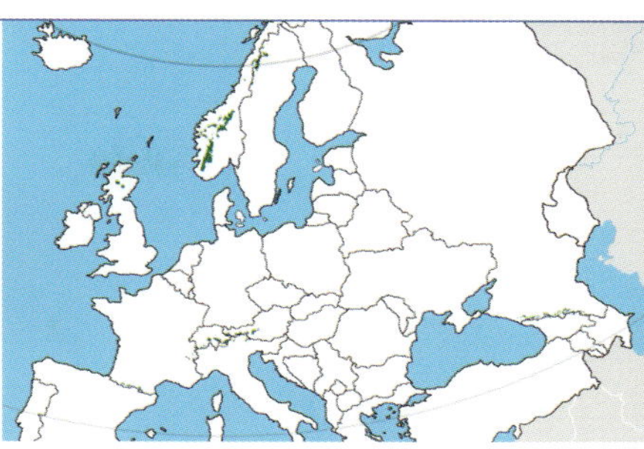

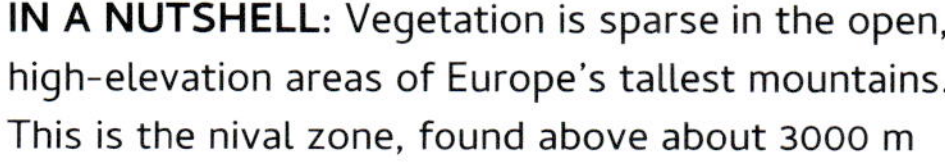

IN A NUTSHELL: Vegetation is sparse in the open, high-elevation areas of Europe's tallest mountains. This is the nival zone, found above about 3000 m (10,000 ft.)—a harsh land of rock and ice. **Global Habitat Affinities:** NEARCTIC POLAR DESERT; NEARCTIC CRYPTIC TUNDRA. **Continental Habitat Affinities:** POLAR DESERT; CRYPTIC TUNDRA; ROCKY TUNDRA. **Species Overlap:** CRYPTIC TUNDRA; ROCKY TUNDRA; ALPINE TUNDRA.

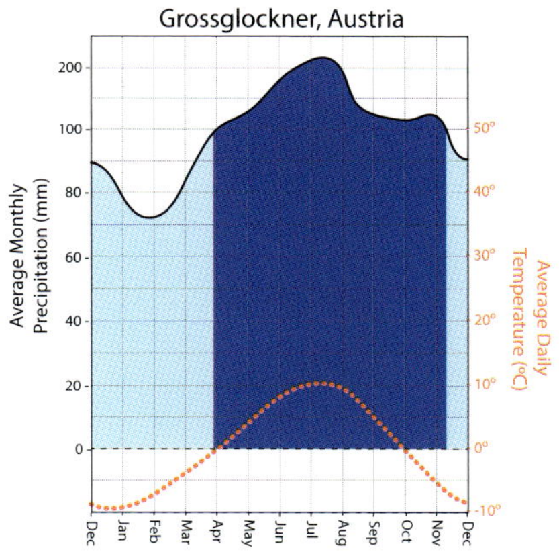

DESCRIPTION: The Nival Rocky Tundra is a quiet place, disturbed only by the chirps of a flock of Yellow-billed Choughs or the occasional bounce of pebbles dislodged by Northern Chamois. Golden Eagles soar by in the vast nothingness, soaking up the breathtaking view. This is Europe's highest habitat, a hidden gem found only on the upper reaches of the tallest mountain ranges. Growing conditions are extremely challenging, with biting winds, icy temperatures, short growing seasons, high solar radiation, and steep, unstable ground. Plants are scarce, but as you look down the mountainside, you will see how growing conditions get progressively easier. There is a lot of open and rocky ground in the nival (snow) zone, but by the time you descend to the alpine zone, grasses and dwarf shrubs blanket most of the landscape. The lower reaches of the Nival Rocky Tundra intertwine with the highest ALPINE TUNDRA as exposure, rockfalls, and avalanches create a mosaic of growing conditions and microclimates.

The topography of Nival Rocky Tundra is typically steep. Low temperatures mean that there is little chemical weathering to form clays or iron-oxides, so soils are mainly shallow regosols. Snow crannies and avalanche chutes are somewhat more protected, aiding chemical weathering and the development of soils.

In the highest regions of Europe's largest mountains, the extreme temperatures, solar radiation, and desiccating winds thin the vegetation to sparse crustose and fruticose lichens, reminiscent of the flora of CRYPTIC TUNDRA or even POLAR DESERT (all three Köppen **ET**). Nevertheless, you might come across the occasional ALPINE TUNDRA plant that has established itself in the nival zone. Purple Saxifrage (*Saxifraga oppositifolia*) has been found at almost 4500 m (15,000 ft.) and is the highest-growing flowering plant known in Europe. Glacier Crowfoot (*Ranunculus glacialis*) and Curvy Sedge (*Carex curvula*) can be found in the siliceous (silica-rich) Nival Rocky Tundra. By contrast, Carnation Grass (*Carex firma*) and Eight-petal Mountain-Avens (*Dryas octopetala*) are

Nival Rocky Tundra in the high, rocky reaches above grassy Alpine Tundra and shrubby Subalpine Krummholz. © DALE FORBES

Nival Rocky Tundra has scant vegetation, with lichen, mosses, and a few plants clinging to the rocks. © DALE FORBES

The views in Nival Rocky Tundra are simply spectacular.
© STEFAN AUFSCHNAITER

associated with calcareous (calcium-carbonate-rich) tundra. Iceland Lichen (*Cetraria islandica*) and Whiteworm Lichen (*Thamnolia vermicularis*) form mats in protected areas, becoming progressively more abundant farther downslope in the sub-nival and alpine zones. The beautiful crustose Yellow Map Lichen (*Rhizocarpon geographicum*) is common on older siliceous rocks, slowly spreading over their surfaces over the course of millennia. In fact, the size of lichen patches is regularly used as a dating method: the annual growth rate of patches indicates the minimum amount of time the rock has been exposed in a moraine or after an ancient rockfall.

Glaciers and persistent snowpack reach through the Nival Rocky Tundra, greatly influencing the wildlife and local climate. A fascinating alga can grow on these summer snows: commonly referred to as Watermelon Snow or *Blutschnee* (blood snow), *Chlamydomonas nivalis* can blanket large snow areas in watermelon pink. It might look and smell great, but it is a toxic laxative for people, so best not to ingest it. The alga's reddish colour comes from secondary carotenoids that help to protect it from ultraviolet radiation through the intense summer months (although a thick cell wall helps too). Fascinatingly, this alga is green in spring and swims through the snow to the

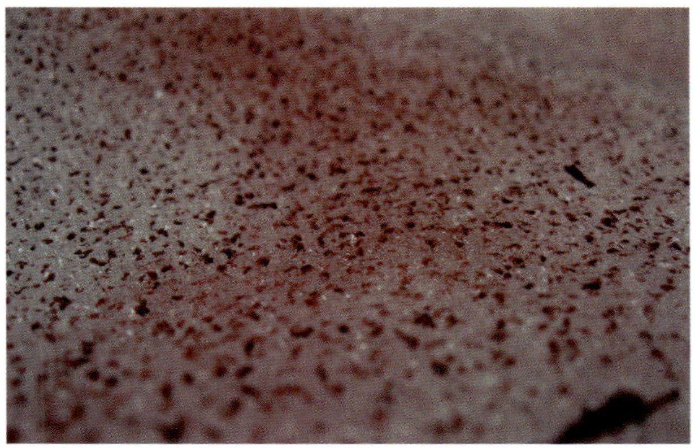

Watermelon Snow (an alga) peppers glacial snow in summer.
© DALE FORBES

Above: **A male Rock Ptarmigan demonstrates why its plumage turns white in winter—the perfect camouflage!** © MARKUS VARESVUO, AGAMI

Left: **White-winged Snowfinch is one of Europe's hardiest passerines, usually seen buzzing quickly across a hillside with flashes of white wings and tail. It spends the entire year in the nival and alpine zones.** © RALPH MARTIN, AGAMI

Below: **Caspian Snowcock emits its far-carrying, curlew-like whistles from prominent locations.** © EDUARD SANGSTER, AGAMI

position with optimal light, water, and nutrient conditions for growth and asexual reproduction. The reddish stages are the result of sexual reproduction.

WILDLIFE: Foggy, drizzly early-summer mornings in the Nival Rocky Tundra are haunted by the eerie call of Rock Ptarmigan. This normally secretive bird flies unseen through the mists, displaying and defending territories. It seems particularly vocal and active when the weather is uncomfortable (for us), though finding a displaying bird in the first rays of a sunny dawn is arguably a more visually impressive experience. At other times of the year, one typically needs more luck to stumble upon a family of ptarmigan scurrying across a hilltop or flushing away from a mountain climber. Incidentally, the name 'ptarmigan' is derived from the Scottish Gaelic for 'croaker', referring to the croaking call we just heard in the early-summer mists.

Caucasian and Caspian Snowcocks are the other grouse specialists of Nival Rocky Tundra. While Rock Partridge, Caucasian Grouse, and Black Grouse can all make it into or close to this habitat, they tend to be more common in the alpine or subalpine zones.

One of the hallmarks of Nival Rocky Tundra is White-winged Snowfinch—usually seen buzzing quickly across a hillside with white flashes of wings and tail. It spends the entire year in the nival and alpine zones, sometimes gathering in the hundreds at winter sunflower-seed bird feeders associated with skiing resorts in the Alps.

Rocks, cliff faces, and scree form an integral part of this habitat, helping to create myriad ecosystems within the tundra. European Snow Vole needs a lot of scree or boulders and is even found above 4000 m (13,000 ft.) in the Alps. Caucasian and Robert's Snow Voles use the same habitat in the mountains of far e. Europe. Sheer cliffs are important winter refuges for Alpine Ibex and Northern Chamois and favoured nesting

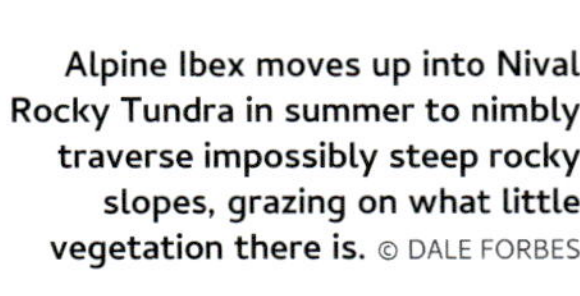

Alpine Ibex moves up into Nival Rocky Tundra in summer to nimbly traverse impossibly steep rocky slopes, grazing on what little vegetation there is. © DALE FORBES

Golden Eagle is frequently seen perched on or flying over the highest mountain ridges. © SAVERIO GATTO, AGAMI

sites of Golden Eagle, Bearded Vulture, Common (Northern) Raven, and Yellow-billed Chough. The astonishing 'butterfly bird', the Wallcreeper, plies these sheer rock faces for small invertebrates.

In summer, Great Rosefinch (Caucasus), White-winged Redstart (Caucasus), and Alpine Accentor (most European tundras) are found in the nival and upper alpine zones. The latter two favour steep rock- and cliff-filled slopes but avoid sheer vertical cliffs.

CONSERVATION: Nival Rocky Tundra, a delicate ecosystem, is under threat from climate change. Ongoing research modelling climate change in the Alps and other nival zones reveals the extent of this threat. Rising temperatures could raise the elevation of the nival zone by hundreds of metres, significantly reducing the land area covered by Nival Rocky Tundra. This would lead to further isolation of nival plant and wildlife communities, creating small islands in the sky.

DISTRIBUTION: Nival Rocky Tundra is found only in the glacial zone of Europe's highest mountain ranges, particularly the Alps, Caucasus, Pyrenees, and the highest reaches of the spine running between Norway and Sweden.

WHERE TO SEE: Hohe Tauern National Park, Austria; Ordesa y Monte Perdido National Park, Spain; Zermatt, Valais, Switzerland; Mt. Kazbek, Stepantsminda, Mtskheta-Mtianeti, Georgia; Folgefonna National Park, Vestland, Norway.

The striking White-winged Redstart moves to the highest rocky slopes in the Caucasus to breed in summer. © RALPH MARTIN, AGAMI

Great Rosefinch is found only in the high Caucasus within Europe. © RALPH MARTIN, AGAMI

FRESHWATER HABITATS

Eu11A EUROPEAN SHALLOW FRESHWATER MARSH

IN A NUTSHELL: Wetlands occurring throughout much of lowland Europe and characterised by shallow water and abundant aquatic vegetation. Many of these wetlands are seasonal. **Global Habitat Affinities:** NEARCTIC SEDGE AND GRASSLAND MARSHES; AUSTRALIAN TEMPERATE WETLAND; ASIAN TEMPERATE MARSH. **Continental Habitat Affinities:** WET GRASSLAND; TEMPERATE PEATLAND. **Species Overlap:** WET GRASSLAND; REEDBED; TEMPERATE PEATLAND.

DESCRIPTION: As the fine veil of mist begins to lift from the water, and the dew on the sedges and spider webs reflects the rising sun, a chorus of Sedge, Common Reed, and Common Grasshopper Warblers fills the air. A Common Cuckoo calls, and a Eurasian Bittern booms in the distance, competing with the loud croaks of Marsh and Edible Frogs emanating from nearby. As the early rays of the sun warm the air, Black-tailed Skimmer and Blue Emperor dragonflies patrol their territories, and an attractive Old World Swallowtail sips nectar from a nearby thistle. Overhead,

A classic freshwater marsh scene in summer, with colourful Purple Loosestrife dominating the vegetation. © MENNO VAN DUIJN, AGAMI

Barn Swallows, Bank Swallows (Sand Martins), and Common Swifts swoop down, attracted by the abundant small invertebrates present, while nearby, a Eurasian Hobby keeps a careful watch from a dead tree, ready to dash over and catch its first prey of the day. A spring morning at a Shallow Freshwater Marsh can provide an absorbing and rewarding experience.

Shallow Freshwater Marsh is a dynamic, wildlife-rich ecosystem, characterised by waterlogged soils and abundant aquatic vegetation. The plants play a crucial role in stabilising the soil, by reducing water erosion. It is a widespread but fragmented habitat, with small pockets occurring frequently along the margins of other water bodies. This habitat appears wetter and more open in the winter months, and it becomes lushly vegetated, often with little or no visible standing water, in the summer months. Some marshes display a tussocky nature, with small, shallow wet areas hidden beneath the visible vegetation. Many of the original areas of this habitat have been destroyed by human modification, with much land having been drained for agricultural purposes, and many of the remaining areas are diminishing.

Shallow Freshwater Marsh typically forms at the margins of larger water bodies, and its vegetation is typically rather short, mostly under 1 m (3 ft.) tall (in contrast to the much taller REEDBED). At the edges of some areas of standing water, such as slow-flowing rivers, areas just above the mean water mark are periodically flooded, creating temporary standing water. The resultant permanently saturated soils are colonised by sedges, forming sedge beds, which are species-poor and often dominated by a single species. The dominant species varies geographically and depending on climate and substrate, but example species are Slender Tufted-Sedge (*Carex acuta*), Brown Sedge (*Carex disticha*), and Greater Pond Sedge (*Carex riparia*). Other characteristic plants of such areas include Reed Canary Grass (*Phalaris arundinacea*), the attractive Purple Loosestrife (*Lythrum salicaria*), the almond-scented Meadowsweet (*Filipendula ulmaria*), Marsh Marigold (*Caltha palustris*), and Creeping Buttercup (*Ranunculus repens*). These plants often grow in a mosaic in the tussocky terrain, with small pools remaining between the tussocks. In wetter situations, such as at the shallow littoral areas of wetlands, where water levels can be variable, other communities of amphibious plants dominate and may include species like Cutleaf Water Parsnip (*Berula erecta*), European Water Plantain (*Alisma plantago-aquatica*), Amphibious Yellowcress (*Rorippa amphibia*), Water Mint (*Mentha aquatica*), and Arrowhead (*Sagittaria sagittifolia*).

WILDLIFE: In areas of permanent water, fish populations thrive. However, much of the shallow and temporary standing water in Shallow Freshwater Marsh is free from fish and, as a result, provides an excellent refuge for amphibians and dragonflies, which can breed successfully without fish predation. A good variety of amphibians occurs across the region, with characteristic species including Pool, Marsh, and Edible Frogs (*Pelophylax lessonae*, *P. ridibundus*, and *P. esculentus*); Yellow-bellied Toad (*Bombina variegata*); and Smooth Newt (*Lissotriton vulgaris*).

Pool Frog and other closely related species frequently can be heard croaking away in shallow pools. It has recently been established that The Pool Frog is native to the UK.

© THEO DOUMA, AGAMI

Nomad (Red-veined Darter) is one among a large variety of odonates that frequent this habitat. © WALTER SOESTBERGEN, AGAMI

Dragonflies are equally well represented, by widely distributed species such as Blue Emperor (*Anax imperator*), Hairy Dragonfly (Hairy Hawker, *Brachytron pratense*), Black-tailed Skimmer (*Orthetrum cancellatum*), and Keeled Skimmer (*O. coerulescens*), as well as by Common Darter (*Sympetrum striolatum*), Ruddy Darter (*S. sanguineum*), and Nomad (Red-veined Darter, *S. fonscolombii*). A wide range of damselfly species are also invariably present, including various bluets (*Enallagma* and *Coenagrion* spp.) and spreadwings (*Lestes* spp.). Invertebrate life is generally rich, with a good diversity of moths and butterflies, including Old World Swallowtail (*Papilio machaon*), attracted to the flowering plants. These invertebrates in turn provide ample food for birds and other predators.

In summer, a rich array of breeding bird species takes advantage of this wetland habitat. Intercontinental migrants, such as Marsh, Common Reed, Sedge, River, and Common Grasshopper Warblers (this habitat is particularly attractive to

Common Grasshopper Warbler is so named because its reeling song strongly resembles the stridulations of a grasshopper. Surprisingly, it often sings through the night. © MARKUS VARESVUO, AGAMI

Above: **Black-tailed Godwit often breeds around the margins of freshwater marshes. This one is keeping an eye out, ready to noisily chase away any potential predators.** © DALE FORBES

Right: **Herons and egrets are frequently found in freshwater marshes, stealthily looking for fish, frogs, large insects, and even small mammals. This Little Egret has developed the long plumes that signify it is in breeding plumage.** © DANIELE OCCHIATO, AGAMI

Acrocephalus and *Locustella* warblers), seek refuge in the dense vegetation, attracting the charismatic Common Cuckoo, the classic brood parasite. Terrestrial species such as Eurasian Moorhen, Eurasian Coot, Water Rail, and the rare Corn Crake use the wetland edges and dense vegetation. Where more extensive areas of Shallow Freshwater Marsh occur, wildfowl such as Northern Shoveler, Gadwall, Mallard, Green-winged Teal, and Garganey and wading birds such as Common Redshank, Northern Lapwing, Common Snipe, and Black-tailed Godwit may breed. Heron species such as Grey and Purple Herons, Eurasian (Great) and Little Bitterns, Great and Little Egrets, and Western Cattle-Egret feed in the wetter areas. Common Kingfisher may be found fishing in areas of open water. Aerial feeders take advantage

Whiskered Tern can often be seen hawking low over the marsh in search of insects. © MARC GUYT, AGAMI

of the abundant insect life too, with swallows and swifts being the most obvious, though these may be joined by dazzling European Bee-eaters, flocks of marsh terns (White-winged, Black, and Whiskered Terns), Collared Pratincole, and the predatory Eurasian Hobby. Overall, shallow marshes can be very rich environments for breeding birds. During the winter, the avifauna is typically dominated more by wildfowl and wading birds, such as Eurasian Wigeon, Green-winged Teal, and Northern Lapwing, with more extensive areas sometimes holding high numbers.

Mammals are not common or conspicuous in this habitat, though wetland specialists such as water voles, water shrews, and Eurasian Otter may all be found in suitable areas.

CONSERVATION: Areas of Shallow Freshwater Marsh are crucial for biodiversity conservation. They act as natural water filters, improving water quality, and provide natural flood protection. However, as is the case for so many habitats, especially in lowlands, this habitat is under increasing threat. Wetlands in Europe have been under intense pressure for centuries. Many areas have been drained for agricultural use, and many more are under imminent threat. Human alterations to natural watercourses, the gradual lowering of the groundwater table through activities such as large-scale irrigation, and pollution from agricultural runoff and industrial spillages also pose significant threats. Some w. European countries lost as much as half of their remaining wetlands just in the latter half of the 20th century! Climate change is also predicted to be an ever more prevalent threat, as rainfall patterns and temperature increases are likely to result in more wetland areas drying out. Thankfully, many of the best remaining wetland areas have designated conservation status and legal protection and are actively managed and protected by conservation organisations. On a more positive note, in some areas, wetlands have been successfully restored and even recreated, in some cases as part of rewilding projects on former agricultural land, such as at Knepp, in s. England (see Sidebar 2: Rewilding Europe, p.164).

DISTRIBUTION: Shallow Freshwater Marsh occurs sporadically throughout the European lowlands but is most prevalent away from the warmer southern region and is absent in the n. Arctic regions.

WHERE TO SEE: Norfolk Broads (such as Hickling Broad), England, UK; Minsmere-Walberswick Marshes, Suffolk, England, UK; Biebrza Marshes, Poland; Danube delta, Romania; Hortobágy, Hungary.

Eu11B EUROPEAN MOUNTAIN STREAMS AND RIVERS

IN A NUTSHELL: Fast-running, cold waters flowing between boulders and a coarse substrate but sometimes slowing in smaller pools and lakes that allow finer sediment to accumulate. **Global Habitat Affinities:** NEARCTIC UPLAND RIVERS; NEOTROPICAL MOUNTAIN STREAMS. **Continental Habitat Affinities:** TEMPERATE RIPARIAN FOREST; ALPINE TUNDRA; MONTANE SPRUCE-FIR FOREST; MONTANE MIXED FOREST. **Species Overlap:** TEMPERATE RIPARIAN FOREST.

DESCRIPTION: Water tumbling down a mountainside can create a noisy environment while also filling the air with a delightful freshness. White faecal spots peppering boulders in rushing mountain streams are often the first giveaway of White-throated Dipper activity. Listen for a high-pitched *tzeet* as the bird buzzes past, just above the water's surface, then stops suddenly on a boulder and scurries down to the water's edge. There it dives in and swims about, picking up larvae of small mayflies (order Ephemeroptera), caddisflies (Trichoptera), stoneflies (Plecoptera), and other insects. Just how it finds or sees anything in the bubbling current boggles the mind.

A wider river running through Montane Mixed Forest in which the landscape vegetation reaches the water's edge with very little obvious, separate riparian vegetation. This river is at the lower elevational limit of Mountain Streams and Rivers habitat, and just a slightly lower elevation or milder climate will allow for the development of Temperate Riparian Forest. © DALE FORBES

A high-elevation stream with little obvious riparian vegetation. © DALE FORBES

Grey Wagtail is often the most frequently encountered species along mountain streams. © DANIELE OCCHIATO, AGAMI

High in the ALPINE TUNDRA (Köppen **Dfd** and **ET**), rainwater and snowmelt seep down into depressions in the landscape, forming marshy, mossy patches of cottongrasses (*Eriophorum* spp.), Marsh Marigold (*Caltha palustris*), primroses (*Primula* spp.), Hairy Kidney-Wort (*Micranthes stellaris*), Water Avens (*Geum rivale*), Dwarf Buttercup (*Ranunculus pygmaeus*), Dwarf Snowbell (*Soldanella pusilla*), and other plants. Small, frigid lakes are relatively rare, thanks to the steep terrain, but they pepper the ALPINE and NIVAL ROCKY TUNDRAS, typically forming behind moraines. These glacial lakes lack higher plants, but some algae and other organisms can establish (mainly cyanoprokaryotes, diatoms, and green algae). The lakes can be picturesque milky blues and greens and are real highlights of summer hikes. Lakes at slightly less dizzying elevations can be equally breathtaking, both for their scenic nature and for the water temperature, but start to support more varied life. Besides algae, various grasses (Poaceae) and sedges (*Carex* spp.) grow on the shores, while Alpine Emerald dragonflies (*Somatochlora*

alpestris) buzz back and forth. The sward can be tightly cropped and low if grazing pressure is high (the usual case) but can grow to around 60 cm (24 in.) high with lower livestock pressure.

Water tumbles down the mountainsides, slowly creating ever-larger streams. In summer, as snow melts and rains filter into the earth, the mountains are filled with innumerable rivulets. Loud cascades and stunning waterfalls invariably form in every valley.

Tongues of bushy Green Alders (*Alnus alnobetula*) reach up into the Alpine Tundra along avalanche chutes and moist channels. Such little depressions and gullies are moist and somewhat sheltered from the elements, allowing the woody plant to establish and flourish. Destructive avalanches regularly scrape away larger vegetation and trees, but the Green Alder is readily able to reestablish from broken stumps and roots. Small Green Alder forests can develop lower downslope, nearer the valley floors, where regular avalanches and landslides cause scree to accumulate and periodically clear most other trees and vegetation.

The continual rush of water slowly erodes the valleys. Large glaciers form U-shaped valleys, while rivers tend to form V-shaped ones. In addition, tight ravines form in small side valleys with relatively stable bedrock that saw limited glacial activity in the last ice age. Centuries of land use in Europe's montane valley floors means that much of the riparian vegetation has been removed or at least altered. Downy Birch (*Betula pubescens*) and Green Alder readily establish along montane watercourses. In forested areas, the streams may run directly through the surrounding MONTANE SPRUCE-FIR FOREST or MONTANE MIXED FOREST. European Aspen (*Populus tremula*) becomes more common as the streams get larger at lower elevations, as the habitat slowly transitions to TEMPERATE RIPARIAN FOREST.

WILDLIFE: The elegant lemon-tinged Grey Wagtail bobs up and down along mountain streams, slowly working the shores for food. Its behaviour is something of a contrast to the frantic nature of the White-throated Dipper buzzing back and forth. Dense Green Alder thickets attract

White-throated Dipper is the only European passerine that forages underwater. © MARKUS VARESVUO, AGAMI

The attractive Hazel Grouse can be found in montane forest, especially in thickets along watercourses. © KARI EISCHER, AGAMI

Hazel Grouse, Lesser Whitethroat, Redpoll, Dunnock, Eurasian Wren, and the occasional Citril Finch (when there are open pastures nearby).

The cliffs of the ravines and canyons in Europe's montane zone are typically the best places to find one of the continent's most incredible birds, the beautiful Wallcreeper. This little cloud-grey bird frantically works its way along cliffs. Its crimson wings flash continuously, startling well-camouflaged arthropods and making it easier for the Wallcreeper to pick out prey on the desolate walls. The low food density means that home ranges of individual Wallcreepers are surprisingly large, so the birds are invariably few and far between. These ravines and canyons are also home to breeding Black Redstart, Eurasian Crag-Martin, and Eurasian Eagle-Owl.

Eurasian Treecreeper can be found in the forests along watercourses in the montane zone; it is typically replaced by Short-toed Treecreeper in the willow-poplar TEMPERATE RIPARIAN FORESTS at lower elevations.

European Common Frog (*Rana temporaria*) and European Toad (*Bufo bufo*) breed in lakes and streams in both the alpine and the montane zones, but it is the fascinating Alpine Newt (*Ichthyosaura alpestris*) that really stands out. It spends much of the year in the forest, returning to clear mountain streams and pools to breed. This is invariably the best place to see the newts as they hang out near the shore—sometimes just sitting on the floor of a clear pool and at other times chasing each other about. The males are quite fetching with their dark blue backs and orange bellies.

Deep-cut canyons and gorges are great habitat for Wallcreepers. © DALE FORBES

The various *Phoxinus* minnows are the classic small fish of Mountain Streams and Rivers, and different species are found in Europe's major montane watersheds. The Adour Minnow (*P. bigerri*) is found in the Pyrenees, the Languedoc Minnow (*P. septimaniae*) in the greater Rhône basin in the w. Alps and e. Pyrenees (France, Switzerland), the Danubian Minnow (*P. csikii*) in the Danube basin (Switzerland, Germany, Austria), the Balkan Italic Minnow (*P. lumaireul*) in the

Alpine Newts survive at very high elevations, laying their eggs in various alpine water bodies. © ALAIN GHIGNONE, AGAMI

Downy Emerald can be seen patrolling watercourses. © FAZAL SARDAR, AGAMI

s. Alps of the Po basin (Italy, Austria, Croatia), and the Marsili's Minnow (*Phoxinus marsilii*) in the Carpathians (Poland, Slovakia, Ukraine, Romania, Hungary). These small minnows and the camouflaged little European Bullhead (*Cottus gobio*) are often food for the larger predatory fish that also favour clear, fast-flowing, cold streams. Of these predators, European Grayling (*Thymallus thymallus*) and Brown Trout (*Salmo trutta*) are widespread and can be abundant, but non-native Rainbow Trout (*Oncorhynchus mykiss*), Brook Trout (*Salvelinus fontinalis*), and others are also well established in the region.

A wide variety of dragonflies and damselflies use the somewhat more free-flowing waters of the montane and alpine zones, including Small Whiteface (*Leucorrhinia dubia*), Downy Emerald (*Cordulia aenea*), and Sedge Darner (Moorland Hawker, *Aeshna juncea*). Alpine Emerald is restricted to Europe's Mountain Streams and Rivers and the bogs (see TEMPERATE PEATLAND) of the montane zone. Common Spreadwing (*Lestes sponsa*) prefers slow-moving mountain waterways.

CONSERVATION: The greatest conservation challenges in the mountains of Europe are likely pollution from livestock and the removal of vegetation to maximise pasture and hay meadows. At lower elevations, mountain streams are often dammed to construct small hydroelectric power plants, stopping the free movement of fish such as the various *Phoxinus* minnows. Climate change is altering precipitation patterns and playing havoc with this habitat as well.

DISTRIBUTION: Found in all of Europe's mountainous regions above around 600 m (2000 ft.) elevation.

WHERE TO SEE: Rosengartenschlucht, Tyrol, Austria; Karersee, South Tyrol, Italy; Partschinser Waterfall, South Tyrol, Italy; Partnach Gorge, Bavaria, Germany; Lac de Gaube, Occitania, France; Estany de Sant Maurici, Catalonia, Spain.

Eu11C EUROPEAN REEDBED

IN A NUTSHELL: Tall reedbeds found along watercourses and surrounding lakes and flooded patches. **Global Habitat Affinities:** NEARCTIC REEDBED MARSHES; ASIAN TEMPERATE MARSH; AUSTRALASIAN TEMPERATE WETLAND. **Continental Habitat Affinities:** SODA PAN AND INLAND SALT MARSH; FRESHWATER LAKES, DAMS, AND PONDS. **Species Overlap:** FRESHWATER LAKES, DAMS, AND PONDS; SHALLOW FRESHWATER MARSH.

DESCRIPTION: Reedbeds, crucial components of wetland systems, develop in standing or slow-moving water on the edges of lakes, rivers, estuaries, drainage ditches, and many other water bodies. The density of plant growth in these reedbeds slows water movement, leading to surprisingly little water exchange between the reedbeds and the main water body. Over time, organic matter builds up, and—at its extreme—a tight-knit reedbed can even detach from the substrate and start to float. These vast floating reed mats can sometimes drift and move extensively through water bodies and wetland systems.

Reedbeds are highly productive ecosystems, with plants growing incredibly quickly in spring, effectively outcompeting most other species and resulting in fairly uniform 2–4 m

A Reedbed in winter, wedged between Temperate Riparian Forest and open water. © HANS GEBUIS, AGAMI

(6.5–13 ft.) tall, species-poor plant communities. The dominant plant species at any one site is influenced by various factors, such as water depth, flooding regime, climate, substrate, grazing intensity, nutrification, and direct human impact. The most typical species found in European Reedbed is Common Reed (*Phragmites australis*). In other areas, bulrushes (*Schoenoplectus* spp., *Bolboschoenus* spp., or *Scirpus* spp.), cattails (*Typha* spp.), Reed Canary Grass (*Phalaris arundinacea*), or other species can form dense stands. Broad-leaved shrubs and herbs, such as Water Dock (*Rumex hydrolapathum*) and Cowbane (*Cicuta virosa*), can be scattered sporadically through healthy reedbeds. However, where fertilisers and nitrification are a problem, more diverse broad-leaved plants can invade the reedbeds. Siltation and the buildup of organic material over decades can slowly raise the reedbed, allowing a broader range of plant species to colonise. This process can successively morph the wetland into a fen (TEMPERATE PEATLAND), a more diverse (shorter) SHALLOW FRESHWATER MARSH, or even a TEMPERATE RIPARIAN FOREST. Slightly raised islands develop small woody communities, adding to the structural heterogeneity of the reedbed and attracting interesting birds and other wildlife.

Reedbeds are hard to access, their saturated, dense stands covering large areas. This makes it difficult to appreciate or get a sense of what is happening within them. Their naturally uniform nature can give a false sense of monotony, but the stem, root, and rhizome systems create a wonderfully complex structure for wildlife. Myriad insects, amphibians, and small fish use the underwater nooks and crannies for feeding and shelter. They, in turn, feed a wonderful diversity of birds and small mammals.

Systems of boardwalks and hides in some wetland reserves afford the wildlife enthusiast a window into the secrets of the reedbeds. In some places, small towers allow one to look over the reedbeds and—with any luck—find a group of Bearded Reedlings as they bob about and express themselves with their iconic *tiuu* call. The call of a Water Rail, hidden in the reeds, explodes over the booming voice of the reclusive Eurasian (Great) Bittern. While Water Rail will inhabit many types of wetlands, Eurasian Bittern is quite specific in its habitat requirements, needing at least 20 ha (50 ac.) of reedbed and preferring areas with about 20–30 cm (8–12 in.) of standing water in the reedbed as well as some open pools. Unstable water conditions, disturbance, and improper reed harvesting can negatively affect bittern populations. Nevertheless, the smart harvesting of reeds (no more than 20–30% of the reed area) can create a useful matrix of reeds of various ages, benefitting bitterns and many other reedbed inhabitants.

The secretive Spotted Crake breeds at some sites without ever being seen! Indeed, its loud whiplash call is often the only sign that it is present.

WILDLIFE: Reedbeds are the magical realm of cryptic species. Little Crake, Spotted Crake, and Water Rail skulk down near the water. Eurasian Bittern is also mostly low down, but the smaller Little Bittern will often climb up the reeds into the domain

Little Bittern visits European Reedbed to breed in summer. It can be very secretive, though it often makes regular flights to and from its nest. © CHRIS VAN RIJSWIJK, AGAMI

of the warblers. Great Reed, Common Reed, Sedge, Moustached, Cetti's, Paddyfield, and Savi's Warblers are just some of the species found in reedbeds. Reed Bunting and Bearded Reedling are invariably found in this habitat. Western Marsh Harrier hunts and breeds in reedbeds alongside Purple and Grey Herons, Pygmy and Great Cormorants, Great and Little Egrets, and Eurasian Spoonbill. Ferruginous and White-headed Ducks favour a complex of reeds and smaller pools, frequenting these alongside Great Crested and Little Grebes, Eurasian Coot, and Eurasian Moorhen. Swallows and martins readily feed on flying insects over reedbeds and use them to roost. Phenomenal numbers of starlings can roost together in reedbeds during winter.

Mammals associated with reedbeds include Eurasian Otter, European Water Vole, and Eurasian Water Shrew. European Elk (Moose) and Western Roe Deer regularly feed in Reedbed and associated WET GRASSLAND.

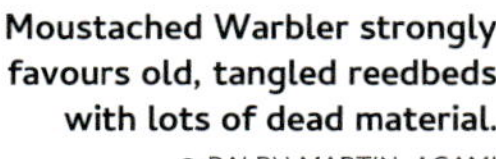

Moustached Warbler strongly favours old, tangled reedbeds with lots of dead material. © RALPH MARTIN, AGAMI

A wide variety of invertebrates use reedbeds; some interesting habitat specialists include the rare Reed Yellow-face Bee (*Hylaeus pectoralis*), Reed Leopard moth (*Phragmataecia castaneae*), Reed Leafhopper (*Paralimnus phragmitis*), and the uncommon beetle *Demetrias imperialis*. Dragonflies and damselflies abound as both aquatic larvae and flying adults. Keep a look out for Red-eyed Damselfly (Large Redeye, *Erythromma najas*) as well as the similar Azure Damselfly (Azure Bluet, *Coenagrion puella*) and Common Blue Damselfly (Common Bluet, *Enallagma cyathigerum*). Migrant Hawker (*Aeshna mixta*), Hairy Dragonfly (Hairy Hawker, *Brachytron pratense*), Four-spotted

Left: **Bearded Reedling, a true Reedbed specialist, is of great interest to global birders, as it is now placed in its own unique family.** © MARKUS VARESVUO, AGAMI

Below: **Western Marsh Harrier (a male is pictured) is the default breeding raptor in Reedbeds.** © MARKUS VARESVUO, AGAMI

Red-eyed Damselfly (Large Redeye) is often found on vegetation floating on the water's surface. © FAZAL SARDAR, AGAMI

Skimmer (Chaser, *Libellula quadrimaculata*), and the large Blue Emperor (*Anax imperator*) are also associated with reedbeds and interlaced pools.

Amphibians are abundant in Reedbeds, including European Common Frog (*Rana temporaria*), Edible Frog (*Pelophylax esculentus*), European Toad (*Bufo bufo*), and European Fire-bellied Toad (*Bombina bombina*). They provide ample food for the *Natrix* water snakes that hunt them (e.g., Grass Snake, *N. natrix*; and Viperine Snake, *N. maura*).

CONSERVATION: Reed has been harvested for millennia, typically in wintertime, and then dried for use as thatch. When reed harvesting is too extensive or incorrectly managed, it can have dire consequences on breeding populations of Purple Heron, Eurasian Bittern, and other species. Common Reed Warbler and Sedge Warbler both nest at a greater density in older reedbeds than in freshly regrown reed, and Moustached Warbler strongly favours old, tangled reedbeds with lots of dead material, so even in the best of cases, reed harvesting is not without its consequences.

Fresh spring and summer growth is also grazed with livestock in many areas, and if managed carefully, it can be done sustainably and support the regional balance between Reedbeds and other habitats. Reedbeds also play an incredibly important filtering role in cleaning water and are often used in open wastewater treatment pools during the final cleaning stages.

DISTRIBUTION: Found throughout Europe from the boreal zone to the Mediterranean but not in the Arctic or higher mountains, Reedbeds can range from small ribbons along drainage ditches to huge expanses covering many thousands of hectares (acres) in fresh or slightly brackish water.

WHERE TO SEE: Danube delta, Romania (the world's largest reedbed); Ebro delta, Catalonia, Spain; RSPB Minsmere, Suffolk, England, UK; Camargue, Bouches-du-Rhône, France; Oostvaardersplassen, Flevoland, Netherlands; Lake Neusiedl, Austria and Hungary.

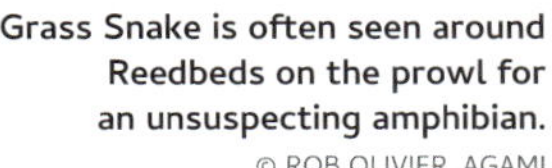

Grass Snake is often seen around Reedbeds on the prowl for an unsuspecting amphibian. © ROB OLIVIER, AGAMI

Eu11D EUROPEAN TEMPERATE PEATLAND

IN A NUTSHELL: The soggy, peat-forming wetlands of Europe's temperate zone, mostly treeless with small pools of standing water. **Global Habitat Affinities:** NEARCTIC BOREAL BOG AND FEN; AUSTRALIAN ALPINE BOG AND FEN. **Continental Habitat Affinities:** BOGGY TUNDRA; SHALLOW FRESHWATER MARSH. **Species Overlap:** BOGGY TUNDRA; SHALLOW FRESHWATER MARSH.

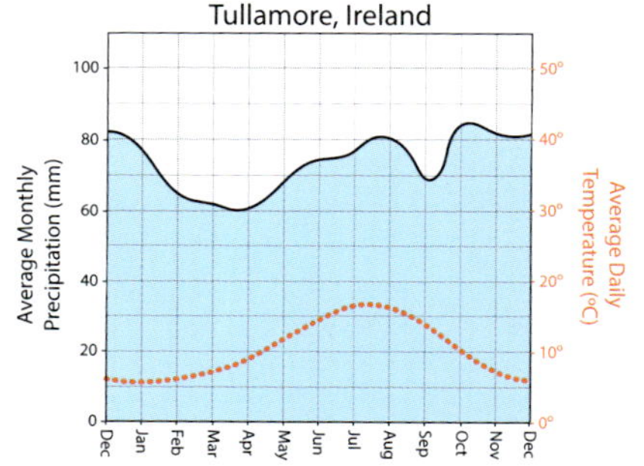

DESCRIPTION: Peatlands are wetland habitats where semi-decomposed organic matter has accumulated to form peat. In Europe, they are soggy, flattish places with low vegetation of mosses, grasses, sedges, wildflowers, and fascinating carnivorous plants. Insects abound, attracting myriad insectivorous birds and other small predators, making them fascinating places for

A bog in s. Germany showing dark heathers, lighter grasses, and birches that managed to establish in slightly drier locations. © DALE FORBES

wildlife-watchers. Humans have a profound, primal connection with peatlands, which have been a vital source of heat and cooking fuel for eons. They also have been unsettling places of purgatory made real: foggy, treacherous haunts of clawing mud, unspeakable mystical dangers, witches, beasts, and ogres.

Peatlands that are actively accumulating peat are known as mires. Europe's mires can be divided in myriad ways, but perhaps the most critical dividing feature is their source of water. Fens are mires that are regularly supplied with groundwater (minerotrophic). In contrast, bogs have risen above the water table and receive moisture only from direct precipitation (ombrotrophic). Separating peatland types based on water sources may seem arbitrary, but the distinction is remarkably ecologically significant. Groundwater picks up minerals from the surrounding rocks and soils. This keeps the pH higher, flushes fertility through a fen, and results in a much more diverse ecosystem of sedges, flowers, grasses, shrubs, mosses, and even some trees. By contrast, the rainwater and meltwater in bogs are almost completely devoid of nutrients, and sphagnum mosses dominate these acidic peatlands. Europe's mires exist on a continuum from rich fens through poor fens to bogs, and dozens of habitat subtypes have been described to reflect the diversity of mires throughout the region.

The most biodiverse peatlands are **rich fens**. These form around springs and drainage channels distant from streams and lakes, allowing groundwater to accumulate basic minerals from calcium-rich bedrock. These cations keep the pH of rich fens close to neutral by balancing out the acidity produced by the brown mosses (mostly of the family Amblystegiaceae) and organic decomposition in a waterlogged environment. Plant communities are rich with sedges (e.g., Long-stalked Yellow-Sedge, *Carex lepidocarpa*; Yellow-green Sedge, *Carex flava*; and Few-flower Spikerush, *Eleocharis quinqueflora*), grasses (e.g., Broad-leaved Cottongrass, *Eriophorum latifolium*; Purple Moor Grass, *Molinia caerulea*; and Common Reed, *Phragmites australis*), and diverse brown mosses (e.g., Yellow Starry Fen Moss, *Campylium stellatum*), as well as a broad range of broad-leaved plants

Bog, Wooldse Veen, Netherlands. © MENNO VAN DUIJN, AGAMI

(such as Hemp Agrimony, *Eupatorium cannabinum*; Bird's-eye Primrose, *Primula farinosa*; and the carnivorous Common Butterwort, *Pinguicula vulgaris*). Specialist species are most associated with Europe's larger mountain ranges, with additional latitude, temperature, and precipitation gradients affecting plant community composition.

SIDEBAR 6 A BRIEF OVERVIEW OF EUROPE'S DIVERSE PEATLANDS

A fascinating diversity of mire subtypes is found across Europe, with climate, hydrology, and geology driving much of this diversity.

Ice-wedge polygon mires are common in lowland Arctic tundra (Köppen ET) on poorly drained soils. Repeated freeze-thaw cycles of the permafrost result in growing ice wedges that force soil upwards (with discrete ice and peat/soil elements). Plant growth is sluggish in the Arctic, but so is decomposition, resulting in the slow growth of peat on top of the raised ridges. This peat layer, 65–100 cm (25–40 in.) thick, insulates the frozen ground during the summer months. Polygon mires typically create honeycomb-like structures with almost straight lines. The cells are 15–30 m (50–100 ft.) across and can create fascinating geometrically shaped ridges and valleys across the landscape.

Palsa mounds develop in the lower Arctic (Köppen ET) and subarctic zones (Dfd, Dfc), where average annual temperatures are still well below freezing. These large, dry permafrost ridges or mounds (palsas), 3 m (10 ft.) high or more, develop in a similar way to the ice-wedge polygons. Low winter snow cover (often because it is windblown) allows for deeper melting and freezing of the permafrost and peat. The subsequent injection of ice intrusions into the peat causes the palsa to slowly grow over time. Unique plant communities grow at the base, sides, and tops of the palsas (see BOGGY TUNDRA).

Farther south, patterned *aapa mires* develop in snow-rich taiga areas (mostly Köppen Dfb). Rapid snowmelt in spring floods the mires and washes downhill to be caught in pools (flarks) by the characteristic elongated mounds (strings) that run across the slope. Forested mires also develop in the same general climatic zone (Dfb), either with a natural succession on raised hummocks that slowly dry out patches of the mire enough for pines and spruces to establish, or because a bog has been drained for peat harvesting, allowing pines and birches to establish (see CONIFEROUS PEAT WOODLAND).

Quaking mires form around productive water bodies where peat can slowly build in sheltered areas and spread out as a raft from the sides. This encroachment can even cover the entire pool or grow to a raised bog where the mire is no longer in contact with groundwater but gets moisture from precipitation (ombrotrophic), and a unique bog plant community develops. *Blanket bogs* form in cool, wet climates with low evaporation (Köppen Cfb), ideal for sphagnum moss growth. Over millennia, the bog grows up and out and can cover vast areas of entire landscapes. This type is particularly widespread in Ireland and Scotland, where the peat traditionally has been cut and dried for winter fuel. *Continental fens and bogs* develop in Europe's temperate regions (Cfb, Dfb), where drainage patterns and climate determine whether a groundwater-fed fen or a rainwater-fed bog develops.

Some (simplified) definitions:

- *PEATLAND*. Wetland habitat in which peat has accumulated.
- *MIRE*. A living peatland in which peat continues to accumulate.
- *BOG*. A mire above the water table and cut off from groundwater.
- *FEN*. A mire that is regularly fed with groundwater.

Poor fens develop in more acidic areas. This can be because the bedrock is not as alkaline—or the groundwater has had less time to accumulate basic minerals—or the peat layer has built up to such an extent that it has started to restrict the amount of groundwater that can move through the fen. Plant communities in poor fens tend to be less diverse and a subset of those found in rich fens, but they generally still include species like Beaked Sedge (*Carex rostrata*), Devil's-bit Scabious (*Succisa pratensis*), Common Cottongrass (*Eriophorum angustifolium*), and Marsh Cinquefoil (*Comarum palustre*).

Fens exist on a spectrum from rich to poor. The **sedge fens** of e. Europe are mesotrophic (somewhere between the two extremes) and are the breeding habitat of the endangered Aquatic Warbler (see Sidebar 7: Saving the Aquatic Warbler, p.336). These sedge fens typically have 1–10 cm (0.5–4 in.) of standing water and are dominated by a variety of sedges and grasses, such as Tufted-Sedge (*Carex elata*), Lesser Tussock Sedge (*Carex diandra*), Beaked Sedge, and Swamp Sawgrass (*Cladium mariscus*).

Right: **Everything in bogs revolves around the unassuming sphagnum moss.** © WIL LEURS, AGAMI

Below: **A bog in Fochteloërveen, Netherlands, showing the clear pools associated with this habitat.** © WIL LEURS, AGAMI

The peat layer in fens is relatively thin—from 2.5 cm (1 in.) to 2 m (6ft.). Thicker layers progressively raise the mire above the water table and away from a constant supply of basic minerals and flushing of acidity. While the brown mosses characteristic of fens acidify their environment much as sphagnum mosses do, the latter are more tolerant of acidity. Consequently, as the peat layer grows, the moss communities shift from brown to sphagnum mosses, with poor fens being intermediate between the two extremes.

Bogs are the realm of sphagnum—unassuming but fascinatingly diverse mosses with an incredible capacity to hold water. Specially adapted hyaline cells allow them to hold 25 times more water than the weight of the dry plant! This allows the sphagnum to store rainwater and engineer its own ultra-moist environment independent of groundwater.

Acidic bog pools develop in the sphagnum mats, while the slightly raised islands (hummocks) are just a little drier. This allows plants like Tussock Cottongrass (*Eriophorum vaginatum*), Bog Cranberry (*Vaccinium oxycoccos*), Lingonberry (*Vaccinium vitis-idaea*), Common Heather (*Calluna vulgaris*), Common Bilberry (*Vaccinium myrtillus*), Bog Bilberry (*Vaccinium uliginosum*), and Dwarf Birch (*Betula nana*) to establish amidst the sphagnum. Even trees like Downy Birch (*Betula pubescens*) and Scots Pine (*Pinus sylvestris*) can eke out an existence on the hummocks of some bogs.

Bogs, being nutrient-poor environments, pose a challenge for plant growth, and nitrogen (essential for building proteins) is in particularly short supply. Sundews (*Drosera* spp.), however, have found an innovative solution. These little insectivores have leaves covered in red tentacles that produce sticky, sugary droplets. The sweet scent attracts insects, which get trapped among the tentacles. More tentacles then actively move towards the insect to increase the hold on it, and some sundews even roll a leaf over the insect over the course of many hours or days. The prey eventually succumbs to exhaustion or suffocation from the droplets. The plant then secretes enzymes to digest the insect and extract amino acids and other nutrients. The prey can be as small as flies or as large as damselflies, butterflies, and other larger arthropods. Common Butterwort and bladderworts (*Utricularia* spp.) have similar techniques to capture insects to compensate for the shortage of nitrogen, with the bladderworts using an elaborate underwater trap to capture their prey.

As the sphagnum and other bog plants grow upwards, their lower, shaded parts die and start to decompose, but the environmental acidity and lack of oxygen halt that process. Peat can take many decades to form after the plant has died. The peat is lighter brown on the upper layers and darkens downwards to a rich black caused by humification. Primary production in bogs is significantly higher (200%) and decomposition slower (25%) than in fens, resulting in a quicker accumulation of peat. Nevertheless, even in bogs, peat forms only at about 1–3 mm (0.04–0.12 in.) per year.

Sphagnum mosses are not the only life-forms to die and be preserved in bogs. Hundreds of human 'bog bodies' have been found in Europe, the oldest (known as Koelbjerg Man) is around 10,000 years old. Some of these corpses are incredibly well preserved and provide an amazing window into another time.

WILDLIFE: The avian poster child of mires is the Aquatic Warbler, Europe's most endangered bird species. It breeds on sedge fens (mainly) in Poland, Belarus, Ukraine, and Lithuania, but drainage for agriculture has dramatically reduced and deteriorated its breeding habitat (see Sidebar 7: Saving the Aquatic Warbler, p.336). Snipes are classic mire birds. Common Snipe, Jack Snipe, and the magnificent Great

Opposite: **Cranberry Blue and Cranberry Fritillary butterflies are both named for their host plant, Bog Cranberry (pictured), which itself is an indicator of coniferous mires.** © WIL LEURS, AGAMI

Inset: **The Oblong-leaved Sundew is one of many carnivorous bog plants. They catch insects, such as this spreadwing damselfly, on the sticky barbs.** © THEO DOUMA, AGAMI

Snipe have amazingly diverse display strategies, with brilliant aerial displays and incredible otherworldly sounds, and in the case of Great Snipe, nocturnal lekking, with males flashing white tail feathers in the gloomy moonlight. The critical importance of fens for breeding birds is nowhere as obvious as on the boreal palsa mounds (see Sidebar 6: A Brief Overview of Europe's Diverse Peatlands, p.332), which often have the highest abundance of breeding birds in a local region. Even out of the boreal zone, mires attract a wide range of breeding birds, and the high density of insects (especially craneflies) offers plentiful food. Shorebirds (especially Black-tailed Godwit), harriers, Western Yellow Wagtail, Common Crane, Western Barn Owl, Short-eared Owl, and many more species regularly nest on fens. In addition, blanket and raised bogs farther north attract breeding European Golden-Plovers, Dunlins, and Eurasian Curlews.

Mammals are not particularly obvious in mires, with water voles and harvest mice being hard to see. Nevertheless, so many bodies of an extinct giant deer were found in Irish bogs that the species was even called the Irish Deer. In modern times, fens in the UK are regularly used by the non-native Water Deer. Open mire pools and waterways can attract the acrobatic Daubenton's Bat, while pipistrelles and other bats pick up midges, moths, craneflies, and other flying insects over the mires.

Insect diversity is awe-inspiring in mires, with several habitat specialists co-evolving with the unique plants found in fens and bogs. Cranberry Blue (*Agriades optilete*) and Cranberry

SIDEBAR 7 SAVING THE AQUATIC WARBLER

The Aquatic Warbler is an extreme habitat specialist and one of the most threatened bird species in Europe. Its survival depends on ongoing restoration efforts of its wetland habitat.

Spending the winter in w. African wetlands, the Aquatic Warbler breeds in open sedge fens in e. Europe. Unfortunately, virtually all fens used by the Aquatic Warbler have been destroyed or heavily degraded by agricultural drainage. Many sites where the water table had been lowered were maintained through hay making, but the collapse of Soviet-era agriculture meant that this management was largely abandoned. Once cutting stops, the habitat is rapidly colonised by Common Reed (*Phragmites australis*), Common Alder (*Alnus glutinosa*), or willows (*Salix* spp.) and is lost to the Aquatic Warbler and other specialist species. The warbler has consequently disappeared from most of its range. In recent decades, it has been lost from Hungary and w. Siberia and has undergone massive declines in Ukraine and Belarus. It is just about hanging on in e. Germany.

Conservation efforts started in the early 1990s with the establishment of the Aquatic Warbler Working Group and support from the Royal Society for the Protection of Birds, Swarovski Optik, and many others. An enormous boost came in the mid-2000s when EU LIFE funding allowed BirdLife International Partners in Poland (OTOP), Belarus (APB, now dissolved on government orders), Lithuania (LOD), and others to dramatically increase their on-the-ground conservation efforts. The first priority was the restoration and protection of key habitat by managing water levels and reinstating traditional agricultural practices, including mowing, the cutting of shrubs and trees, and controlled burning. Seeding was used to encourage the growth of key plant species in rehabilitated fens, while some smaller Aquatic Warbler populations were boosted with individuals translocated from larger colonies.

Snipes are the classic mire birds. Common Snipe, Jack Snipe, and the magnificent Great Snipe (pictured) have amazingly diverse display strategies, with brilliant aerial displays and, in the case of Great Snipe, nocturnal lekking. © MARKUS VARESVUO, AGAMI

Large-scale habitat restoration in e. Poland has led to a fantastic recovery from fewer than 3000 male Aquatic Warblers in 1997 to 4000–5000 since 2015. Similarly, in Lithuania, populations increased from about 50 males in 2013 to 208–316 males since 2020. Some of the emblematic sites where the Aquatic Warbler is bouncing back are the Biebrza Marshes and Chełm Marshes in Poland, Zvaniec Mire in Belarus, and Žuvintas Mire complex in Lithuania.

Protecting the Aquatic Warbler's unique fen breeding habitat also helps to protect a whole host of other, less prominent species of animals and plants. Specialist species like Fen Orchid (*Liparis loeselii*), Flea Sedge (*Carex pulicaris*), and Varnished Hook-Moss (*Hamatocaulis vernicosus*) are all highly dependent on the same habitat. In addition, protecting this habitat also brings with it a host of other ecosystem services, such as carbon storage and sequestration, nutrient retention, groundwater storage, evapotranspiration cooling, flood protection, and many more diverse provisioning, regulating, and cultural services.

While the future of the charming Aquatic Warbler is still far from secure, the successes of recent conservation action do give us hope for our special habitats and specialist species.

Aquatic Warbler in a sedge fen. © RALPH MARTIN, AGAMI

The attractive Bog Fritillary favours this habitat. © WIL LEURS, AGAMI

Fritillary (*Boloria aquilonaris*) butterflies are both named for their host plant, Bog Cranberry—which itself is an indicator of coniferous mires. Other mire specialists include Moorland Clouded Yellow (*Colias palaeno*), Large Heath (*Coenonympha tullia*), Marsh Carpet moth (*Gagitodes sagittata*), and Bog Fritillary (*Boloria eunomia*). Abundant craneflies of the family Tipulidae (e.g., *Molophilus ater*, *Limonia dilutior*, *Molophilus ater*, *Tipula subnodicornis*, and *Tipula serrulifera*) form the dietary backbone of many breeding and passage bird species, especially in bogs. March flies (family Bibionidae) in willow bog edge habitats feed the breeding European Golden-Plovers in Scandinavia. Eurasian Drone Fly (*Eristalis arbustorum*) can be common in Temperate Peatland.

The pretty Small Whiteface is a characteristic dragonfly of peat bogs. © WIL LEURS, AGAMI

The Fen Raft Spider is a peatland specialist that can be looked for in small fen ponds.
© THEO DOUMA, AGAMI

Mires typically have very few fish, especially in acidic bog waters. The reduced predatory pressure makes them an ideal environment for dragonflies, including several species strongly associated with mires: Northern Emerald (*Somatochlora arctica*), Alpine Emerald (*Somatochlora alpestris*), Small Whiteface (*Leucorrhinia dubia*), and Norfolk Hawker (Green-eyed Hawker, *Isoaeschna isoceles*). The gorgeous, metallic Tansy Beetle (*Chrysolina graminis*) and the semiaquatic Fen Raft Spider (*Dolomedes plantarius*) are also associated with mires.

Many of Europe's amphibians inhabit mires, and the beautifully blue Moor Frog (*Rana arvalis*) stands out in particular, because of its ability to tolerate the low pH waters of bogs and poor fens.

CONSERVATION: Half of all European peatlands have been lost. For eons, people have been harvesting peat to fuel their stoves, heat their houses, supplement planting soils, and even generate electricity. This destruction is worrying, as up to 20% of global soil carbon is contained in peatlands, and the release of that carbon would have dramatic consequences for our climate and the planet. In addition, peatlands have been drained for agriculture and grazing, exposing them to oxygen and fuelling the decomposition process. These degraded peatlands are significant sources of atmospheric greenhouse gasses. Rewetting peatlands has shown optimistic results in recently drained and weakly disturbed areas, but ominously, this is not the case for areas that have been more heavily disturbed. Mineralisation of peat, fertilisers from agriculture, and greater availability of phosphorus when rewetted dramatically change the plant species in 'rehabilitated' peatlands, and because the drained peat settles and starts to denature, its porosity and ability to store water are significantly altered. This changes the hydrology of the peatland and can result in periodic peaks in methane release. Our climate desperately needs continued innovation and effort to recover disturbed sites in addition to the strict protection of intact mires.

DISTRIBUTION: Temperate Peatlands are found across Europe, with climate and geology determining the types of mires found across broad regions. Freeze-thaw cycles create the polygon, palsa, and aapa mires of the boreal zone, while a broad swath of raised and blanket bogs occurs farther south. Europe's mountain ranges have complex systems of varied peatland types, with topography, elevation, geology, aspect, and latitude all playing roles in determining the kind of system that develops in any location.

WHERE TO SEE: Clara Bog, Offaly, Ireland; Wicken Fen, Cambridgeshire, England, UK; Forsinard Flows, Scotland, UK; Großes Torfmoor, North Rhine-Westphalia, Germany; Biebrza National Park, Poland.

Eu11E EUROPEAN FRESHWATER LAKES, DAMS, AND PONDS

IN A NUTSHELL: Open water bodies from Scandinavia's innumerable clear, frigid lakes to the turbid dams of Iberia and the duck pond in your local park. **Global Habitat Affinities:** NEARCTIC OPEN WATER; ASIAN OPEN WATER. **Continental Habitat Affinities:** SODA PAN AND INLAND SALT MARSH; MOUNTAIN STREAMS AND RIVERS. **Species Overlap:** SODA PAN AND INLAND SALT MARSH; MOUNTAIN STREAMS AND RIVERS.

DESCRIPTION: Europe is blessed with a wide range of open freshwater habitats—the go-to habitats for anyone looking for waterfowl and fish-eating birds. One could easily define dozens of different habitat types based on water pH, clarity, nutrients, vegetation, and myriad other factors. Nevertheless, from a wildlife-watcher's perspective, the most important factors are the water body's size, location, vegetation growth, fish stocks, and latitude.

In arid areas, even the smallest of ponds can become a hub of activity, attracting a variety of wildfowl and other birds, especially during migration, when inclement weather forces night-migrating waterbirds to fly low. These birds, including Garganey, Green-winged Teal, Black Tern, and others, descend upon the water body, joining the resident Mallards until the weather

Lake Constance in c. Europe hosts tens of thousands of ducks, swans, and grebes in winter, when quiet, sheltered bays and large areas of ice-free water provide good refuge. This makes for some great birding. © DALE FORBES

Mallard is the most common and widespread European duck, and for that reason, its good looks are generally ignored. In spring, males are incredibly active and aggressive in their pursuit of mates. © DANIELE OCCHIATO, AGAMI

improves. Larger natural lakes with diverse vegetation communities around their shores provide a year-round home for significant wildfowl populations. The importance of these lakes shifts with the seasons, with those farther north being crucial for breeding, while those farther south play a vital role in overwintering and moulting.

Reservoirs and dams tend to be rather sterile environments with low structural diversity, rather 'clean' shores, low plant diversity, and consequently poor fish stocks. They also tend to be less interesting for birds. The obvious exceptions are artificial fish ponds, salt production lakes, sewage settling ponds, and larger lakes used by overwintering wildfowl.

Sprinkled through the taiga forests of n. Europe are innumerable oligotrophic lakes with low nutrient content and (refreshingly) cool water. The last ice age (~20,000 YA) was critical in forming these lakes, typically on mineral-poor bedrock or sandy plains. The water is generally clear but can be stained dark by tannins from decomposing leaves (in dystrophic lakes associated with TEMPERATE PEATLAND). Plant diversity is relatively limited in the lakes. Still, European White Water Lily (*Nymphaea alba*), Yellow Water Lily (*Nuphar lutea*), and pondweeds (*Potamogeton* spp.) often add to the appeal of these picturesque bodies of water. Breeding Arctic Loon (Black-throated Diver), Greater Scaup, Tufted Duck, and Whooper Swan ply the waters before Eurasian Beaver and European Elk (Moose) take the night shift. Many of these lakes freeze in winter, forcing their inhabitants into hibernation or migration. Wildfowl will largely overwinter and moult on lakes farther south in c. Europe.

On the borders between Austria, Switzerland, and Germany, Lake Constance hosts tens of thousands of ducks, swans, and grebes in winter, its quiet, sheltered bays and large areas of ice-free water providing good refuge. In springtime, most wildfowl depart for the north to breed, joined by additional migrants from farther south. The delicate flight of Little Gulls and marsh terns, stopping over for a few days while on passage, is a delight for any birder. Raucous colonies of Great Cormorant, Black-headed Gull, Yellow-legged Gull, Caspian Gull, Common Tern, and others dominate the lakeshore soundscape in the breeding season.

Winter rainfall in the Mediterranean climate zone of s. Europe forms temporary lakes and ponds that typically last into the spring and support a unique plant community. Rushes (*Juncus* spp.), loosestrifes (*Lythrum* spp.), waterworts (*Elatine* spp.), and a variety of beautiful tongue orchids (*Serapias* spp.) shoot up in the wet season, flowering when conditions start to dry out. These water bodies are important for overwintering Common Cranes and large numbers of shorebirds, larger wading birds, and waterfowl. Dragonflies and damselflies breed early in the year to take advantage of these habitats before they dry up later in the spring and summer.

Overleaf: **Freshwater Lakes, Dams and Ponds are important for overwintering Common Cranes (pictured) and large numbers of shorebirds, larger wading birds, and waterfowl.** © BENCE MÁTÉ, AGAMI

In winter, many species of wildfowls, such as these Tufted Ducks, gather in flocks on ice-free lakes and reservoirs. © MENNO VAN DUIJN, AGAMI

White-headed Duck, a scarce species found in s. and e. Europe, favours complexes of smaller ponds and reedbeds. © RALPH MARTIN, AGAMI

Few mammals are found in European freshwater lakes, but Eurasian Otter (pictured), Eurasian Beaver, and European Elk (Moose) can be locally common. © DALE FORBES

WILDLIFE: European Freshwater Lakes, Dams, and Ponds are of great importance to wildfowl, such as Northern Shoveler, Garganey, Gadwall, Greater Scaup, Tufted Duck, Whooper Swan, and White-headed Duck. They are also critical for large piscivores, such as Osprey, Great Cormorant, Pygmy Cormorant, Common Merganser (Goosander), Smew, Great Crested Grebe, marsh terns, Common Tern, Caspian Gull, Dalmatian Pelican, and many others.

Few mammals are found in European freshwater lakes, but Eurasian Otter, Eurasian Beaver, and European Elk (Moose) can be locally common. The native European Pond Turtle (*Emys*

Our native European Pond Turtle (pictured) is largely restricted to Freshwater Lakes, Dams, and Ponds in c. and s. Europe but faces stiff competition from the invasive Pond Slider. © NICOLAS BASTIDE, AGAMI

Grass Snake is as at home in the water as it is on land and frequently can be seen in marshes hunting amphibians. © DALE FORBES

orbicularis) is largely restricted to Freshwater Lakes, Dams, and Ponds in c. and s. Europe but faces stiff competition from the invasive Pond Slider (*Trachemys scripta*). Cars, roads, and other infrastructure have also heavily affected the turtle's populations. Europe's various grass snakes (*Natrix* spp.) are strongly associated with this habitat, feeding on the myriad frogs, toads, and newts found here.

Over 500 fish species are found in European waterways, but unfortunately 200 are endangered. Wels Catfish (*Silurus glanis*) and critically endangered Beluga Sturgeon (*Huso huso*) are both enormous fish of large rivers, growing to over 3 m (10 ft.) in length. At the other end of the spectrum, the diminutive European Bitterling (*Rhodeus amarus*) (10 cm/4 in.) lives in slow-moving streams and pools and has a fascinating breeding relationship with mussels. The female bitterling's ovipositor is adapted to lay eggs within the gills of mussels while mussel larvae stick to the belly of the fish, to be taxied about and deposited to other parts of the waterway. The male bitterling deposits sperm in the mussel's siphon, and the fish's spawn and larvae develop within the mussel until they are ready to emerge after about a month.

CONSERVATION: Eutrophication—the overaccumulation of nutrients caused by large quantities of fertilisers as well as animal and human waste products entering our water systems—is arguably the greatest threat to Europe's water bodies. This upsets the delicate nutrient balance and allows a few, specific organisms to proliferate (especially algae), subsequently causing a partial or complete collapse of the ecosystem. Water removal is particularly perilous in drier areas of Europe, resulting in critical changes to water flow and the drying out of many water bodies.

DISTRIBUTION: Freshwater lakes, dams, and ponds, with great diversity in appearance, are found throughout the region.

WHERE TO SEE: Lake Tisza, Heves, Hungary; Lake Constance, Austria, Switzerland, and Germany; Lake Der-Chantecoq, Champagne-Ardenne, France; Rutland Water, East Midlands, England, UK; Lake Rogen, Härjedalen, Sweden; Trøndelag, Norway.

Eu12A EUROPEAN ARCTIC AND TEMPERATE ROCKY COASTLINE

IN A NUTSHELL: The rocky coasts and headlands of the Arctic Ocean, Baltic Sea, North Sea, and Atlantic Ocean. **Global Habitat Affinities:** NEARCTIC ROCKY COASTLINE; ASIAN ROCKY COASTLINE. **Continental Habitat Affinities:** MEDITERRANEAN TO CASPIAN ROCKY COASTLINE. **Species Overlap:** ARCTIC AND TEMPERATE PELAGIC WATERS.

DESCRIPTION: In the crisp ocean air, the rich smell of guano wafting up from the squabbling Northern Gannet colony below and the charming sounds of Black-legged Kittiwakes filling the air, you stand mesmerised by the action unfolding in front of you. Gannets sail along the cliffs, a cheeky Atlantic Puffin crash-lands in a gloriously pink patch of Sea Thrift (*Armeria maritima*) by its burrow and looks confused, while a pair of Razorbills take off from their ledge as if in a synchronised, slow-motion flying contest. As they disappear from view below you, you dare not look down. From the top of these towering cliffs, it's a long way down to the unforgiving ocean! This is the Arctic and Temperate Rocky Coastline at its absolute best.

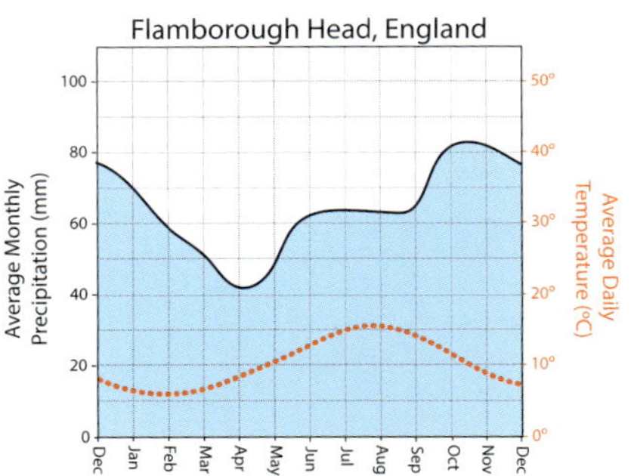

Black-legged Kittiwake is a gull species that has adapted to nesting on cliffs. The name 'kittiwake' is derived from its distinctive call.

Arctic and Temperate Rocky Coastline. © IAIN CAMPBELL, TROPICAL BIRDING

This habitat consists of a narrow strip of usually eroding rocky coast, of varying substrates, ranging from low rock platforms to towering cliffs. Stretches of rocky coastline are interspersed with areas of SANDY SHORE AND DUNE and TIDAL FLAT AND ESTUARY. The harsh, exposed, and eroding nature of rocky coastline, lacking in topsoil, coupled with the inundation of salt spray make it a harsh environment for plants to colonise. Consequently, vegetation is sparse. The remote and inaccessible nature of much of the habitat renders it a favoured nesting habitat for many seabirds, and some spectacular colonies exist. These coastlines are also some of our most picturesque landscapes and seascapes.

Arctic and Temperate Rocky Coastline may seem similar to MEDITERRANEAN TO CASPIAN ROCKY COASTLINE, but it differs in its formation processes. During the last major glaciation, which peaked around 20,000 YA, much of n. Europe was covered by ice sheets; they were 2500–3000 m (8200–9800 ft.) thick in Norway and 1000–1500 m (3300–4900 ft.) thick in Scotland. The weight put onto the underlying landscape was a massive 2250 tonnes per square metre (208,882 tons/sq. ft.). These ice sheets carved out massive, steep-walled, U-shaped valleys, which later flooded to form fjords such as Sognefjord in Norway and Loch Torridon in Scotland. As the ice sheets melted, the massive pressure of the sheets was removed, and the landscape rebounded through isostatic readjustment. For example, the Varanger Peninsula of n. Norway has uplifted 100–150 m (330–500 ft.), and along the Scottish coastline, Islay has uplifted about 120 m (400 ft.). Along with the land rise, the melting ice caused a rise in sea level of 120–130 m (400–430 ft.); counterintuitively, even some areas that were below sea level were raised above it after the glacial melt and rebound. Other areas, such as the English Channel, did not have the isostatic rebound so were flooded with the rising sea levels.

The fjord lands and Arctic coastline have been subjected to the ocean for less than 18,000 years so have not had much time to weather (break down) and erode (be removed). The underlying bedrock, therefore, has had less influence on the headland shape than it has in the warmer areas where coastal erosion began long before and continued through the ice ages. In these temperate and Arctic regions, chemical weathering is limited because of the cold temperatures, and mechanical weathering becomes far more important. Some rocks, such as granite, gneiss, and sandstone, are more resistant to erosion than other rocks, such as shale and siltstones. Headlands usually consist of the harder material, but the distinction is relative, in that if there are two hard rocks in a region, one will still weather and erode faster than the other; the headland just needs to be more resistant to the relentless mechanical beating of waves than the surrounding rocks. Sea cliffs are most pronounced where there is layering or jointing (fractures), such as with columnar basalts or shists, and least likely to form where the rock is a very homogeneous one such as granite; granite headlands tend to be more rounded than steep.

A vast majority of the Arctic and Temperate Rocky Coastline habitat is exposed bedrock with very little vegetation cover. Erosion of bedrock at sea level causes upper areas of the cliff face to fall, keeping a very steep aspect to the habitat. Sea cliffs range in height from a few metres to a dizzying 300 m (1000 ft.) or more, with extremes of around 400 m (1300 ft.) in Iceland and around 600 m (2000 ft.) in w. Ireland. Along the Baltic coast, glacial abrasion left many of the shoreline's rocky habitats lower and smoother.

On Arctic and Temperate Rocky Coastline formed from hard bedrock, lower areas of the cliffs (above the high-tide mark but in the supralittoral or splash zone) are exposed to constant wave action and salt spray. Little is able to grow other than some algae and lichens clinging to the rock face. Moving up, the middle regions of the cliff are still heavily influenced by the actions of the sea and frequently windy conditions. This, coupled with the almost total absence of topsoil, means that very few vascular plants are able to colonise, and where plants can colonise, little or no succession takes place. Specialist species that have adapted to this zone, such as the fern Sea Spleenwort (*Asplenium marinum*), need to be salt tolerant (halophytic). Higher up, towards the top of the cliff, older and more established cracks and crevices appear, some of which allow colonisation by pioneer plants. In these crevices, over time, a small amount of shallow topsoil may gather and form, allowing colonisation by more species. Widespread examples of the flora occupying these areas include Sea Thrift (*Armeria maritima*), which is responsible for many of the glorious pink blooms along clifftops; the edible succulent Rock Samphire (*Crithmum maritimum*); Buck's-horn and Sea Plantains (*Plantago coronopus* and *P. maritima*); and the attractive Sea Campion (*Silene uniflora*). On the clifftop, grass species may take over, with typical species including Creeping Bent (*Agrostis stolonifera*) and Red Fescue (*Festuca rubra*). These sometimes form pockets of maritime grassland on less dramatic slopes. Above the top of the cliff, the transition into adjacent habitats will depend on a number of factors, including grazing and other human land uses, but is often grassland and scrub. Few, if any, larger plants or trees are able to survive on Arctic and Temperate Rocky Coastline.

As with most habitats, the exact composition of the flora depends on the location, and the species composition changes as one moves farther north or south. In the Arctic, such as around Spitsbergen, Norway, additional characteristic colonisers of the cliffs include Alpine Sorrel (*Oxyria digyna*), the attractive Northern Golden-Saxifrage (*Chrysosplenium tetrandrum*), Alpine Foxtail (*Alopecurus magellanicus*), and Arctic Dandelion (*Taraxacum arcticum*). Along Europe's North Atlantic coast, species may include Scottish Scurvygrass (*Cochlearia scotica*), Purple Saxifrage (*Saxifraga oppositifolia*), Roseroot (*Rhodiola rosea*), and Moss Campion (*Silene acaulis*), while farther south in more temperate waters, typical colonisers include Sea Fern-Grass (*Catapodium marinum*), Sea Pearlwort (*Sagina maritima*), Sea Carrot (*Daucus carota* ssp. *gummifer*), Portland Spurge (*Euphorbia portlandica*), the succulent Golden Samphire (*Inula crithmoides*), Rock Sea-Spurrey (*Spergularia rupicola*), and Sea Heath (*Frankenia laevis*).

Areas of less stable rocky coastlines with softer bedrock are far more restricted, occurring extensively only along the Baltic coast. Due to their unstable nature, they are of less value to wildlife, largely lacking seabird colonies, but they can have a more extensive and varied flora, particularly on the upper slopes. In good examples, a variety of microhabitats form through erosion, landslides, and water seepage. Most species that colonise these areas are common and widespread pioneer and ephemeral species able to adapt to the changing conditions. Some of the species found on harder bedrock cliffs, such as Sea Thrift and Buck's-horn and Sea Plantains, can also take advantage of softer eroding cliffs, growing alongside species such as Wild Cabbage (*Brassica oleracea*); Common Butterbur (*Petasites hybridus*), which frequents wetter areas; catchflies (*Silene* spp.); Colt's-foot (*Tussilago farfara*); Bushgrass (*Calamagrostis epigejos*); Field Horsetail (*Equisetum arvense*); and Umbellate Hawkweed (*Hieracium umbellatum*).

WILDLIFE: Arctic and Temperate Rocky Coastline is extremely seasonal in its value to wildlife. During the wild winters, when fierce storms batter the coastline, this habitat can seem almost devoid of wildlife. A few wading species, including Arctic-breeding Purple Sandpiper and Ruddy Turnstone, eke out an existence on the rocky shoreline alongside Eurasian Oystercatcher—with the specially adapted bill that enables it to eat shellfish. A few Common Eiders forage offshore, and some rock platforms give sanctuary to roosting waders and gulls. Come spring, this habitat, in some areas at least, is completely transformed. A whole suite of seabirds utilises the safety of the cliffs as a secure breeding habitat. Perhaps most charismatic are the auks, the Northern Hemisphere's flying penguins. Widespread Common Murre (Common Guillemot), Razorbill, and, farther north, Thick-billed Murre (Brünnich's Guillemot) fill ledges and crevices, carefully guarding their vulnerable eggs. As with many seabirds, these are at their most vulnerable when they come to land, and they have developed various breeding strategies to overcome this danger. The chicks of these birds are forced to take a remarkable leap of faith soon after hatching, making a kamikaze dive off the cliff face, from the ledge upon which they have just hatched, to the ocean far below. If they survive, they are shepherded out to pelagic waters, away from the predatory gulls that would decimate them if they remained within reach, and they spend the next couple of months being reared at sea. Atlantic Puffin, on the other hand, burrows into soft soil at the top of the cliffs and raises its chicks away from predators in the sanctuary of a burrow; after flying off in search of food, the adult puffin returns with its colourful beak full of sand eels for its hungry young. Around rocky coastlines in the west and north, Black Guillemot seeks shelter in crevices in boulder fields, while in the Arctic, tiny Little Auk (Dovekie) also uses crevices.

This habitat is also important for tubenoses (order Procellariiformes). The widespread Northern Fulmar is at home on cliff ledges and even dry-stone walls. Vulnerable on land, it protects itself by projectile-vomiting foul, fishy stomach contents over any unwanted intruders. This is so

Above: **Little Auk (Dovekie) can be found in dense colonies along Svalbard's rocky coast.** © MARC GUYT, AGAMI

Left: **Razorbill lays its eggs in narrow crevices in steep cliff faces. Once hatched, the chicks throw themselves into the sea in a great leap of faith and, if they survive, swim out to sea, away from predators.** © MARKUS VARESVUO, AGAMI

Below: **The comical Atlantic Puffin nests in a burrow, often at the top of a cliff, where it can rear its young in some safety.** © DANNY GREEN, AGAMI

Northern Gannets breed in huge colonies on rocky headlands and islands. The tightly packed nature of the breeding grounds has, sadly, allowed the rapid spread of bird flu in some areas. © DANNY GREEN, AGAMI

pungent that it is almost impossible to remove from clothing, or indeed feathers, and consequently the fulmars are left well alone! Other tubenoses, including European and Leach's Storm-Petrels and Manx Shearwater, avoid predation by nesting in rocky crevices and burrows (some farther inland, away from sea cliffs), coming ashore only under cover of darkness, and leaving again before first light.

This is also the realm of the Northern Gannet, some huge colonies of which nest on some of the impressive rock stacks around our coasts. Another classic cliff-nester is the attractive European Shag, and in some areas, Great Cormorant can also be found nesting on cliffs. Black-legged Kittiwake is the classic cliff-nesting gull, though other, larger species, including European Herring Gull, Great Black-backed Gull, and, farther south, Yellow-legged Gull, also nest along coastal cliffs.

Around many seabird colonies in the north of the region, skuas can be seen harassing the nesting birds to gain a meal to feed their own chicks. The cliffs also offer secure breeding sites for raptors. Peregrine Falcon frequently uses sea cliffs, as does White-tailed Eagle, and in some areas, such as Islay, in Scotland, Golden Eagle even nests on sea cliffs. Other bird species taking advantage of this habitat include Rock Dove (the wild ancestor of the widespread Feral Pigeon), Rock Pipit, and, in some areas, Red-billed Chough and Common (Northern) Raven. Other passerines use this habitat during migration, including Black Redstart and Northern Wheatear.

Mammals are less common on these rocky coastlines. Rabbits graze right up to the cliff edges, and in some areas Arctic Fox frequents this realm, predating the seabird colonies. By the sea, various seal species, including Harbour Seal and Grey Seal, use the rocky coast to haul out, and a few cetaceans feed close inshore, including Harbour Porpoise. Where good populations of smaller sea mammals are present, Orcas are sometimes enticed right into the rocks as they hunt seals.

The emerald eye of a European Shag, a species of rocky coastlines. © SAVERIO GATTO, AGAMI

Few insects specialise in this harsh realm, though one species of note is the tiny Thrift Clearwing (*Pyropteron muscaeformis*), a moth that lives along western coasts. On a warm summer morning, with a keen eye, you can sometimes spot one atop a Sea Thrift flower head.

In certain areas, as the tide drops, attractive rock pools form a fascinating habitat to investigate. These tidal pools, with their variety of crabs, lobsters, shrimps, sea anemones, and small fish, are popular with marine biologists and can also provide a fascinating few hours of exploration for inquisitive children.

CONSERVATION: Rocky coastlines are, by their very nature, rather inaccessible, so direct human disturbance is limited. Nevertheless, humans are responsible for the greatest threats to these habitats, which include direct disturbance, such as trampling and disturbance to seabird colonies and sea mammals; agricultural runoff and pesticide contamination; and the effects of rising sea levels through climate change. All these threats have a detrimental effect on Arctic and Temperate Rocky Coastline. Fortunately, many areas of this habitat are remote, difficult to reach, and safe from most pressures.

The indirect effects of rising sea levels, as well as changing rainfall patterns, temperatures, and storms, are potential threats.

DISTRIBUTION: Arctic and Temperate Rocky Coastline is found intermittently around the coastline of the Arctic Ocean, Baltic Sea, North Sea, and Atlantic Ocean as far south as c. Portugal, where it is replaced by MEDITERRANEAN TO CASPIAN ROCKY COASTLINE.

WHERE TO SEE: Bempton Cliffs, Yorkshire, England, UK; Hermaness, Shetland, Scotland, UK; Látrabjarg, Westfjords, Iceland; Hornøya, Vardø, Norway; various cliffs around Spitsbergen, Norway, accessible on boat trips and cruises from Longyearbyen, Svalbard.

Orcas can sometimes be seen close to shore, where they will hunt seals and porpoises along rocky coastlines. © VINCENT LEGRAND, AGAMI

Eu12B MEDITERRANEAN TO CASPIAN ROCKY COASTLINE

IN A NUTSHELL: Rocky coastlines and headlands occurring intermittently from the central coast of Portugal all the way around the Mediterranean coast, as well as along the coasts of the Black and Caspian Seas. **Global Habitat Affinities:** NEARCTIC ROCKY COASTLINE; AFRICAN ROCKY SHORELINE. **Continental Habitat Affinities:** ARCTIC AND TEMPERATE ROCKY COASTLINE. **Species Overlap:** EUROPEAN TIDAL FLAT AND ESTUARY; ARCTIC AND TEMPERATE PELAGIC WATERS; MEDITERRANEAN TO CASPIAN PELAGIC WATERS.

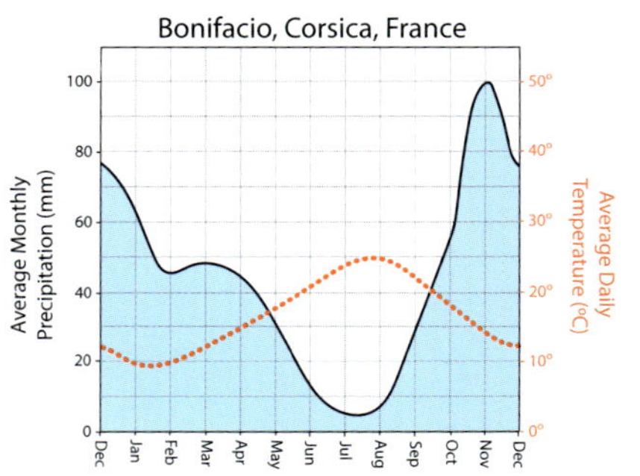

DESCRIPTION: When people think of the Mediterranean coast, they may picture sandy beaches packed with sun loungers, sunshades, and throngs of holidaymakers. There is, however, a more diverse and interesting side to the coastline, if you know where to look. In some places, you can stand atop magnificent cliffs, peering out at the silver-sheened sea below. Scopoli's Shearwaters flap lazily below the cliffs, and a Blue Rock-Thrush gives his melodic song. Alpine and Pallid Swifts flash by, and numerous Yellow-legged Gulls cry out loudly from an adjacent stack. Careful scrutiny reveals the presence of the rare Audouin's Gull too, and with luck, a menacing Eleonora's Falcon will flash by, surely one of the continent's most graceful flyers. Away from all the hustle and bustle, the Mediterranean coast has plenty to offer the wildlife enthusiast.

The Mediterranean to Caspian Rocky Coastline is interspersed with areas of SANDY SHORE AND DUNE and TIDAL FLAT AND ESTUARY. It comprises narrow strips of usually eroding rocky coast, of varying substrates, ranging from low rock platforms to towering cliffs. The harsh, exposed, and eroding nature of the habitat and the lack of topsoil, coupled with the inundation of salt spray, make it a difficult environment for plants to colonise, and consequently vegetation is sparse. The remote and inaccessible nature of much of the habitat renders it a favoured nesting habitat for several species of rare seabirds, especially on the Mediterranean islands. It also encompasses some of our most breathtaking landscapes and seascapes.

Typically, Mediterranean to Caspian Rocky Coastline is formed when bedrock is exposed and eroded by the actions of the sea. In areas where the bedrock is hard (such as basalt lava, granite, sandstone, limestone, or marble), this can lead to the formation of steep and sometimes high cliffs. Rocky coastlines are the result of weathering (breakdown) and erosion (removal) of bedrock by the sea, part of a long but important process. Initially, rocks have to be uplifted by tectonic plates to create elevated areas along coastlines. Some rocks, such as granite, gneiss, or sandstone, are more resistant to erosion than other rocks, such as shale and siltstones. Headlands usually consist of the harder material, but the distinction is relative, in that if there are two hard rocks in a region, one will still weather and erode faster than the other; similarly, there are many coastlines with weak limestone cliffs that are only marginally more resistant to erosion than the surrounding shales. To become a headland, the uplifted material just needs to be more resistant than the surrounding rocks to the relentless mechanical beating of waves and the chemical attack of salt.

When the rocks are flat, such as tilted sedimentary rocks, the headlands tend to be flat and the bays wide. When the rocks are intruded with volcanics or are very tilted, such as vertical

Above: **The beautiful Eleonora's Falcon breeds in discrete colonies on rocky headlands around the Mediterranean coast, especially on islands. It breeds late in the summer, which coincides with the autumn migration of birds from n. Eurasia to their wintering grounds in Africa, ensuring a plentiful supply of food.** © DANIELE OCCHIATO, AGAMI

Right: **This stretch of classic Mediterranean to Caspian Rocky Coastline on Sardinia is wonderful for Eleonora's Falcons in the summer months.** © DALE FORBES

sediments, the differential weathering and erosion can be much more pronounced, with many bays and islands in a very rugged coastline. Multiple geomorphological features become very important for vegetation and wildlife. The most obvious are sea cliffs on the seaward side of the headland, where wave action steepens the bluff. The very steep cliffs are most pronounced where there is layering or jointing (fractures), such as with columnar basalts or shists, and least likely to form where the rock is a very homogeneous type, such as granite. These granite headlands tend to be more rounded than steep. Erosion can lead to the formation of sea caves at the base of cliffs. If these caves erode through a headland, they can create natural arches. When these arches collapse, they leave isolated pillars of rock (sea stacks), which are usually incredibly rugged and so inhospitable as to be predator-free, therefore providing prime nesting sites for birds such as auks, puffins, and guillemots (family Alcidae).

The local climatic and topographic conditions affecting the coastline, along with regional climatic variations, help to determine the vegetation present, and a number of endemic plant species characterise this habitat. In areas with softer bedrock, such as clays, shales or loamy sands, erosion occurs much more quickly, not just by the actions of the sea but through storms and water running down the cliffs, which may cause landslides, creating a shallower profile and more unstable ground.

In the Mediterranean and Black Seas, cliffs range in height from a few metres to 394 m (1300 ft.) at Cap Canaille, on the s. French coast. This is a harsh environment, and the vegetation able to colonise the exposed bedrock is heavily affected by salt spray. At lower levels in the supralittoral zone (above the normal high-tide line), diverse lichen communities may develop, with such species as Common Sunburst Lichen (*Xanthoria parietina*), Orange Sea Lichen (*Flavoplaca marina*), and Black-eye Lichen (*Tephromela atra*). The greater the area of rock affected by sea spray (as in areas with higher winds and higher waves), the wider the band of lichen dominance. Above the lichens, higher on the cliffs, in areas with less direct maritime influence, salt-tolerant plants are able to colonise, especially in small cracks and crevices, while towards the clifftops, salt-tolerant grassland often prevails, characterised by species such as Sea Fern-Grass (*Catapodium marinum*), Sickle Grass (*Parapholis incurva*), timothy grasses (*Phleum* spp.), and Bristletail Grass (*Psilurus incurvus*). Many of the species adapted to this environment are perennials, although a few annuals do occur, and the species composition is heavily influenced by the bedrock substrate. Species composition includes many widespread pioneer and nitrophilous species as well as a number of rare and endemic species. Rock Samphire (*Crithmum maritimum*) is one of the most widespread and characteristic species of this habitat, but perhaps most notable is the array of sea-lavenders (*Limonium* spp.) present around

Balearic Shearwater is restricted to the w. Mediterranean as a breeding species and is one of Europe's most threatened endemic birds, listed by BirdLife International/IUCN as Critically Endangered. At the current rate of decline, the species may have less than 40 years to extinction, driven mainly by accidental fisheries bycatch and predation by introduced predators (especially cats and rats). © OSCAR DÍEZ, AGAMI

the region, many species of which are restricted to very small ranges and consequently are highly threatened: *Limonium strictissimum* is found on Corsica, and *Limonium remotispiculum* in s. Italy. The variety of vascular plants can provide a riot of colour; typical plants include Sea Thrift (*Armeria maritima*), brooms (*Genista* spp.), groundsels (*Senecio* spp.), catchflies (*Silene* spp.), and several species of sea heaths (*Frankenia* spp.) and everlastings (*Helichrysum* spp.). The lower herbaceous layer may be diverse and include species such as Gold Coin (*Pallenis maritima*), Common Chicory (*Cichorium intybus*), Grey Bird's-foot Trefoil (*Lotus cytisoides*), and brighteyes (*Reichardia* spp.).

Less stable rocky coastlines with softer bedrock are far more restricted and occur mostly along the Black Sea coast. Due to their unstable nature, they are of less interest to wildlife, largely lacking seabird colonies, but they can have a more extensive and varied flora, particularly on the upper slopes. In good examples, a variety of microhabitats form through erosion, landslides, and water seepage. Most species that colonise these areas are common and widespread ruderal and ephemeral species that can adapt to the changing conditions, including Cultivated Liquorice (*Glycyrrhiza glabra*), Spreading Bedstraw (*Galium humifusum*), Saline Wormwood (*Artemisia santonicum*), and Stranglewort (*Cynanchum acutum*).

WILDLIFE: The Mediterranean to Caspian Rocky Coastline rarely provides the wildlife spectacle associated with the seabird colonies on the ARCTIC AND TEMPERATE ROCKY COASTLINE farther north. Nevertheless, it forms vital habitats for a number of very important species. It is seasonal in its value to wildlife, and during winter, when frequent storms sweep through the region, it seems almost devoid of wildlife. A few wading species, including Ruddy Turnstone, eke out an existence on the rocky shoreline, and some rock platforms give sanctuary to roosting birds, particularly gulls. A few passerines, such as Black Redstart, may be found on the rocky cliffs. Come the spring, this habitat, in some areas at least, is completely transformed.

A whole suite of seabirds utilises the cliffs and the crevices within them as secure breeding habitat. The auks and Northern Gannets from farther north are absent, and the tubenoses (order Procellariiformes) using the habitat are nocturnal in their movements, coming ashore to their concealed burrows only under cover of darkness, to avoid predation. In the Mediterranean, important breeding species of tubenoses include Balearic, Yelkouan, and Scopoli's Shearwaters (some of these nest in crevices and burrows in the cliffs; others find similar habitat further inland). The entire world population of these three species breeds in this realm, as does the Mediterranean form of European Storm-Petrel. Balearic and Yelkouan Shearwaters are closely related; the two were formerly regarded as conspecific, and it is likely they will be lumped together again in the future. Diurnal seabirds to be found on the cliffs include colonies of the uncommon European Shag (Mediterranean form, *Gulosus aristotelis desmarestii*), Yellow-legged Gull, and the attractive and threatened Audouin's Gull.

The beautiful Audouin's Gull is restricted mostly to Mediterranean coasts. © RALPH MARTIN, AGAMI

A sweet, melodious flurry may signal the presence of a Blue Rock-Thrush, a cliff-loving species regularly found along the Mediterranean to Caspian Rocky Coastline. © DALE FORBES

Raptors also take advantage of cliffs as breeding sites. Eleanora's Falcon is always stunning to watch as it cruises slowly in the upwind along a cliff edge or swoops with dizzying speed in pursuit of prey. Peregrine Falcon also nests on the cliffs, and in some areas, such as Cyprus, Eurasian Griffon comes right down to coastal cliffs. The many nooks and crannies provide nesting habitat for Common, Pallid, and Alpine Swifts, and in some areas, colonies of Western House-Martins may be found. A sweet, melodious flurry may signal the presence of a Blue Rock-Thrush, another cliff-loving species. Other species may be found along the clifftops as well; though not restricted to the Mediterranean to Caspian Rocky Coastline habitat, Eurasian Hoopoe, wheatears, Tawny Pipit, and others make forays into this realm.

Few seabirds breed along the Black Sea coast, though a handful of Yelkouan Shearwaters do, and there are colonies of European Shag and Yellow-legged and Caspian Gulls. The Caspian Sea, being landlocked, is less diverse still in its seabird species, though Caspian Gull (named for the sea) and Great Cormorant nest

The chunky Yellow-legged Gull is common and widespread throughout this habitat. As a successful scavenger, it has adapted well to humans. © RALPH MARTIN, AGAMI

along the coast. The nomadic Rosy (Rose-coloured) Starling, a colonial cliff-nester, sometimes uses cliffs along coasts of the Black and Caspian Seas. There are few finer sights than a busy colony of pink-and-black Rosy Starlings as they twist and turn along the cliffs in spectacular flocks.

Mammals are few and far between on the Mediterranean to Caspian Rocky Coastline. Rabbits graze on the clifftops, sometimes right up to the edge. The rare Mediterranean Monk Seal, numbering just a few hundred individuals, has notable populations in the Aegean Sea and on the Madeiran coast. It utilises secluded coves and caves along the rocky shore. This is the last remaining sanctuary for the species, as beaches it would have used historically are now completely unsuitable, due to heavy human disturbance. In the Caspian Sea, the iconic mammal is the small, endemic Caspian Seal, which lives along the rocky coastline and islands. A century ago, the population was estimated at 1.5 million, but numbers have been declining by 3–4% per year, and fewer than 68,000 seals remain.

No truly pelagic species of bird occurs in the Caspian Sea, though a variety of ducks, geese, grebes, loons (divers), gulls, and terns use the sea at times.

Few notable invertebrates exclusively specialise in this habitat, though a number of attractive moths and butterflies occur in the adjacent grasslands and MAQUIS and will consume nectar on available clifftop flowers where the habitats meet. The tiny Italian Sea Slater (*Ligia italica*), an isopod (sea louse), is a characteristic species just above the littoral zone, and in the same area, Small Periwinkle (*Melarhaphe neritoides*) can be seen clinging to rocks at low tide.

CONSERVATION: Rocky coastlines are, by their very nature, rather inaccessible, so direct human disturbance is limited. The indirect effects of rising sea levels as well as changing rainfall patterns, temperatures, and storms are potential threats.

DISTRIBUTION: Mediterranean to Caspian Rocky Coastline is found along the Mediterranean, Black, and Caspian Seas but is also intermittently present on Portugal's s. Atlantic coastline.

WHERE TO SEE: Formentor cliffs, Mallorca, Spain; Bonifacio coastline, Corsica, France; Capo Montesanto, Sardinia, Italy; Kensington cliffs, Cyprus; Deserta Grande, Madeira.

The diminutive Caspian Seal, as the name suggests, is endemic to the Caspian Sea. Its population has plummeted over the past century by more than 90%, and sadly, the population continues to shrink annually, due to various incompatible human activities. © EDWIN WINKEL, AGAMI

Eu12C EUROPEAN SANDY SHORE AND DUNE

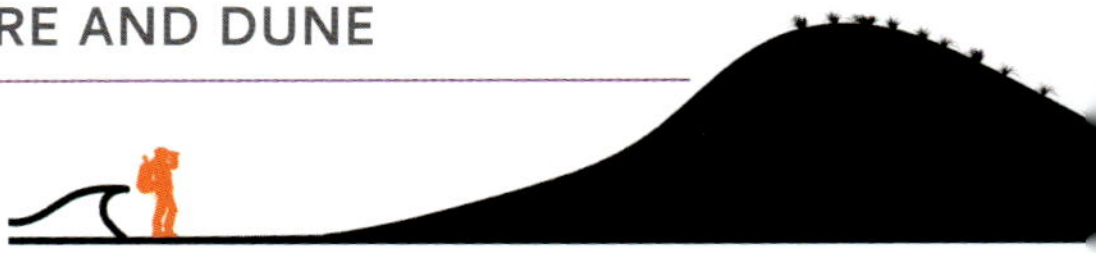

IN A NUTSHELL: Sandy shores are scattered around Europe's coastline; persistent wind blowing these sands inland creates a unique, ever-changing habitat of moving, arid dunes and more stable depressions known as dune slacks. **Global Habitat Affinities:** NEARCTIC SANDY BEACH AND DUNES; AUSTRALIAN SANDY BEACH. **Continental Habitat Affinities:** LOWLAND HEATH; TEMPERATE GRASSLAND AND SAVANNA. **Species Overlap:** LOWLAND HEATH; TEMPERATE GRASSLAND AND SAVANNA.

DESCRIPTION: Watching a flock of Sanderlings race up the beach away from a wave, while the sounds of cawing gulls and whistling wind fill the air, is delightfully meditative. The wave retreats, and the Sanderlings chase the receding water, picking up little crustaceans and molluscs. It is easy to watch their antics for hours.

Change is a constant on sandy shores. Ocean currents churn up sand and pebbles, while wave action, tides, and storms deposit them on beaches along many of our coastlines. This can be a steady process but is often most dramatic during major storms when entire beaches are deposited or removed in a matter of hours. The dynamic nature of sandy and shingle shores means that the types of feeding opportunities and living spaces they provide wildlife also change through time. Twice a day, at high tide, water floods the beaches, and twice a day, at low tide, the beaches are left exposed. This effect is extreme in the Severn estuary, between England and Wales, and in

Undisturbed beaches are used by a variety of waterbirds. Here, a mixed group of gulls loaf on the sand and feed in the adjacent shallows. © MENNO VAN DUIJN, AGAMI

Sanderlings are the classic shorebird of sandy beaches. They run along at great speed, following each wave as it comes in and recedes, like comical clockwork toys. © MENNO VAN DUIJN, AGAMI

the Mont-Saint-Michel Bay, in France, where high tides are regularly 15 m (50 ft.) higher than low tides. By contrast, tidal ranges in the Mediterranean, Baltic, and Black Seas are negligible, less than 60 cm (24 in.).

Sanderlings take advantage of direct wave action, but receding tides leave all sorts of deposits that birds and other wildlife can feed on. Eurasian Oystercatchers, Ruddy Turnstones, and Common Greenshanks regularly search for exposed molluscs and crustaceans or probe the sands for food. A wide variety of gulls and terns roost on sandy and shingle beaches. While the terns mainly feed offshore or in estuaries, the gulls readily scour the beaches for food washed up by the tide.

Grasses are well adapted to the ever-changing, mobile Sandy Shore and Dune environments, and their roots and rhizomes begin the process of stabilising and building a dune. © DALE FORBES

Short-eared Owl abundance is very much tied to the abundance of voles. In good years, the owls can be quite common, but when voles are scarce, the owls can be completely absent.
© ARNOLD MEIJER, AGAMI

Relentless winds over millennia have blown sands from the beaches farther inland, creating sand dunes. They typically form successive lines parallel with the coast, the dunes often many metres higher than the depressions between them (dune slacks). The most salt-tolerant and hardy plants establish just behind the high-tide line. Grasses such as European Marram Grass (*Calamagrostis arenaria*) and Lyme Grass (*Leymus arenarius*) are well adapted to these ever-changing and mobile environments, and their roots and rhizomes begin the process of stabilising and building a dune. These grasses are fascinatingly resistant to being buried by sand, and their wax-coated leaves help to reduce the loss of precious water in these parched and windy environments.

Dune vegetation around the Mediterranean can be closely related to the Maquis and Garrigue found in the surrounding area.
© DALE FORBES

Migrating birds will often rest in dune vegetation after a tiring passage over the sea or in preparation for a longer flight. This can attract a great variety of predators, including Peregrine Falcon (pictured), one of the world's fastest and most capable hunters. © ARIE OUWERKERK, AGAMI

The dunes are more stable farther from the shore, where plants like Sea Bindweed (*Calystegia soldanella*), Sea Spurge (*Euphorbia paralias*), Viper's-Bugloss (*Echium vulgare*), Saltwort (*Salsola kali*), and Sea Daffodil (*Pancratium maritimum*) establish. Heathlands—like LOWLAND HEATH or MAQUIS—establish on the more stable acidic sands even farther back. Rich, biodiverse TEMPERATE GRASSLAND AND SAVANNA develops on alkaline and shell-filled soils. Pine (*Pinus* spp.) woodlands and forests often establish or are planted on these somewhat more stable dune sands. Creeping Willow (*Salix repens*) is a classic species of dune slacks—the wetlands formed in the depressions between dunes where the water table can be particularly high.

WILDLIFE: Heathland birds like European Stonechat and various small warblers, especially Dartford Warbler, are common at many dune sites. Eurasian Skylark and Meadow Pipit often dominate the soundscape with their songs, competing with the pervasive sounds of wind and waves. Western Barn Owl, Short-eared Owl, Eurasian Nightjar, and Montagu's Harrier are highlights, but unfortunately, all are rather localised, needing sites where they are protected from disturbance and persecution. Eurasian (Common) Kestrel, Peregrine Falcon, and Eurasian Hobby regularly hunt over dunes. Common Ringed Plover uses sheltered dunes for breeding while feeding on sandy beaches and in dune slacks.

Seals use sandy and rocky beaches for resting and breeding. Grey Seal and Harbour Seal are the most widespread, while Ringed Seal (Baltic Sea), Mediterranean Monk Seal (Greece and Türkiye), and Caspian Seal (Caspian Sea) have localised populations. European Rabbit is the most important herbivore in most of the region's dune ecosystems, where the soft, sandy soils are ideal

Grey Seal spends much of its time at sea or hauled out along rocky coasts, but in late autumn and winter it comes ashore to pup on secluded beaches and dunes. © RALPH MARTIN, AGAMI

for burrowing. Red Fox can be common, especially where rabbit populations are high.

The sandy environments and protected wetlands in dune slacks can be wonderfully diverse and a real delight for plant, invertebrate, and herp enthusiasts. Natterjack Toad (*Epidalea calamita*) and Great Crested Newt (*Triturus cristatus*) will readily use dune slacks to breed, as they need fish-free water bodies (the pools dry out seasonally, meaning that fish populations are invariably low). Various other crested newts (*Triturus* spp.) replace the Great Crested Newt in Iberia, the Mediterranean, and the Black Sea. The warm, open sand environment is excellent for a wide range of reptiles. Sand Lizard (*Lacerta agilis*), Common Lizard (*Zootoca vivipara*), all the *Natrix* grass snakes, Common Slowworm (*Anguis fragilis*), and Adder (*Vipera berus*) can be relatively common. A range of more localised reptiles are also found in dune habitats.

Red Fox can be abundant in the dunes, especially when rabbits are common. © HAN BOUWMEESTER, AGAMI

Above: **Natterjack Toad (pictured) and crested newts need fish-free waters to breed, and they find these in the seasonal pools of dune slacks.**
© NICOLAS BASTIDE, AGAMI

Right: **Blue-tailed Damselfly (Common Bluetail) is one of several generalist odonates found in dune systems.**
© DALE FORBES

The fish-free pools of the dune slacks are great habitat for the beautiful, crimson Ruddy Darter (*Sympetrum sanguineum*) as well as a host of other dragonfly and damselfly species, including Blue-tailed Damselfly (Common Bluetail, *Ischnura elegans*) and Nomad (Red-veined Darter, *Sympetrum fonscolombii*).

The habitat's warm soils with open patches provide perfect conditions for many ant species. Blue butterflies (and others in the family Lycaenidae) take advantage of the abundant ants in various mutualistic, parasitic, and predatory ways. For example, the caterpillars of the Silver-studded Blue (*Plebejus argus*) spend the day in ant nests—rewarding the ants with an amino-acid-rich sweet liquid—before emerging at night to feed. Even the eggs are protected by *Lasius* ants. Grayling (*Hipparchia*

The gorgeous Silver-studded Blue, which needs warmer locations with sandy soils, is one of several species of blues that have a fascinating symbiotic relationship with ants. © WIL LEURS, AGAMI

semele) is a classic butterfly of dunes and sandy heaths and often lives alongside Grey Bush-Cricket (*Platycleis albopunctata*) and Green Tiger Beetle (*Cicindela campestris*). Red-belted Sand Wasp (*Ammophila sabulosa*) specialises in hairless caterpillars (especially those of geometer and owlet moths), catching large caterpillars and paralysing them with stings to their underside before burying them alive in soft sand with a single egg laid in the burrow. The large Convolvulus Hawkmoth (*Agrius convolvuli*) pollinates the Sea Daffodil's beautiful, tubular white flowers. However, this evidently happens only when there is no wind—no mean feat in such a windy habitat.

CONSERVATION: Moving sand is critical for dunes to remain healthy and biodiverse. Stabilisation through planting trees and building sea walls or other structures sounds a death knell for the ecosystem, as the dunes successively become more stable. In addition, our coastal habitats are being squeezed into increasingly smaller patches, as settlements and recreational land use push ever closer to the coast. Changing deposition through dredging, silt from river systems, and (human-induced) changes in ocean currents can have catastrophic effects on the health of sandy and shingle beaches.

DISTRIBUTION: Sandy Shore and Dune habitat is scattered along all of Europe's coasts but is particularly extensive in Portugal, France's Bay of Biscay, the Netherlands, Denmark, and Poland.

WHERE TO SEE: Dunes of Texel National Park, Netherlands; Magilligan Point Nature Reserve, Northern Ireland, UK; Morrich More, Dornoch Firth, Scotland, UK; Landes, Nouvelle-Aquitaine, France; Canche Bay National Nature Reserve, Hauts-de-France, France; Doñana National Park, Andalusia, Spain; Slovincian National Park, Pomeranian Voivodeship, Poland; Circeo National Park, Lazio, Italy.

Eu12D EUROPEAN COASTAL SALT MARSH

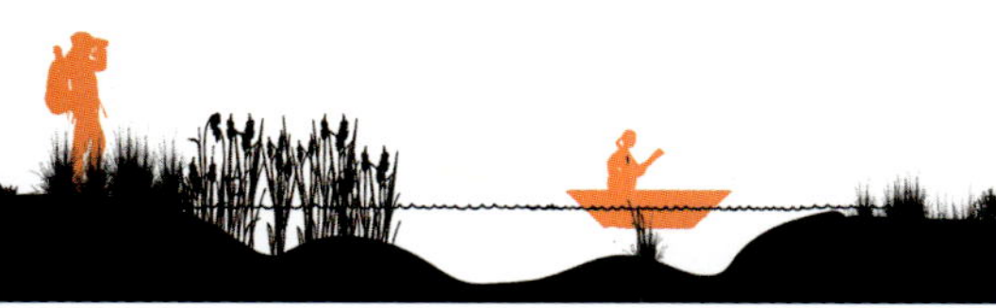

IN A NUTSHELL: Wetland ecosystems on sheltered shores and estuaries around Europe, where regular tidal saltwater flooding creates a unique plant species mix and a complex, ever-changing matrix of microhabitats for wildlife. **Global Habitat Affinities:** NEARCTIC SALT MARSH; ASIAN COASTAL SALT MARSH; AFRICAN SALT MARSH. **Continental Habitat Affinities:** SODA PAN AND INLAND SALT MARSH. **Species Overlap:** TIDAL FLAT AND ESTUARY.

DESCRIPTION: Coastal Salt Marsh, a testament to nature's resilience, is a truly fascinating habitat formed where gentle seas meet the coast. Over millennia, fine silt, clay, and organic sediments slowly accumulate and settle within estuaries and protected bays, creating expanses of flat land. At low tide, most of the habitat is exposed. As the tide rises, salt and brackish water streams up rivulets and channels, ultimately flooding or saturating the surrounding lands. Lower parts of the Coastal Salt Marsh are typically flooded twice a day, while the upper reaches are flooded only with the extremes of neap and spring tides.

An aerial view of a salt marsh showing the complexity of the channels running through it. Salt-resistant plants help to collect sediment, slowly raising the ground level and allowing further plants to colonise, creating the main salt-marsh platform. These raised areas are crisscrossed by venous channels that form the major conduits for tidal water to stream into and out of the marsh. © MARC GUYT, AGAMI

The low-growing, highly salt-tolerant pickleweeds, such as Common Glasswort (pictured), have a unique ability to store excess salt in small chambers (vacuoles). As the vacuoles fill, the plants turn a beautiful reddish colour, giving the salt marsh its distinctive hue. Northern Lapwing (in the distance) prefers these areas of short vegetation.
© RALPH MARTIN, AGAMI

Even slight variations in land elevation can significantly influence salt-marsh plant communities. Areas that are almost always submerged in water give rise to tidal mudflats, devoid of vegetation, where fine silt, clay, and organic particles settle out of the water column and accumulate (see TIDAL FLAT AND ESTUARY). In contrast, only the coarsest particles settle if currents are stronger or there is regular wave action, leading to the formation of sandy beaches (see SANDY SHORE AND DUNE).

Vegetation starts to take hold in areas raised ever so slightly above the tidal mudflats, with the species composition changing according to the extent of flooding and the resulting substrate. The first plants encountered in the low marsh are the highly salt-tolerant pickleweeds, like Common Glasswort (*Salicornia europaea*), which grow in low mats less than 30 cm (12 in.) high. These curious succulents, with their unique ability to store excess salt in small chambers (vacuoles) in their stem tips, are not only edible but also play a crucial role in the ecosystem's balance. As the vacuoles fill, they turn a beautiful reddish colour, giving salt marshes their distinctive hue, particularly evident in autumn. The plants ultimately shed the saturated segments, thereby ridding themselves of the salt.

Higher in the upper marsh, above the level of daily inundation, other salt-resistant plants take root in the somewhat firmer and drier mud behind the pickleweeds. These can include sea-lavenders (*Limonium* spp.), Sea-Purslane (*Atriplex portulacoides*), Sea Aster (*Tripolium pannonicum*), rushes (*Juncus* spp.), and various cordgrasses (*Sporobolus* spp.), which additionally help to collect sediment, slowly raising the ground level and allowing further plants to colonise, creating the main salt-marsh deck. These raised areas, however, continue to be crisscrossed by venous channels that form the major conduits for tidal water to stream in and out of the marsh. If tidal fluctuations are stopped or limited—for example, when a river's mouth is blocked, or a sea wall is built—these channels slowly fill with colonising plants. Eventually, the habitat develops into a freshwater marsh or dryland habitat.

Soils are typically sandier in the highest, inland reaches and on natural, raised levees through the salt marsh (and are muddier in lower parts). Plants in this zone are adapted to salt spray with the occasional flooding, and many will have mechanisms to cope with desiccation (such as having waxy leaves), as the well-drained sandy soils do not hold moisture for long. In some areas, small islands of dryland vegetation—including trees—can develop in a sea of salt marsh.

Species in salt marshes need to cope with ever-changing conditions. Tides, salinity, rainfall, oxygen levels, temperature, and sunlight fluctuate enormously. Spring high tides flood the highest parts of the salt marsh, bringing nutrients and sediment flooding through. They also increase the salinity on the marsh platform. By contrast, neap tides and heavy rainfall create periods of much lower salinity, with lots of standing fresh water.

The heavy clays, organic sediments, and shallow, relatively warm waters result in extremely low available oxygen levels. Some bacteria, algae, and fungi are specialised for these anoxic environments and can use sulphates from the water in anaerobic respiration. One of the by-products is hydrogen sulphide, which gives the salt marshes their distinctive rotten-egg smell. This might be unappealing to delicate noses, but hydrogen sulphide is an important contributor to the base of the detritus-based food web, as various worms, shrimps, clams, mud snails, periwinkle snails, and fiddler crabs (among myriad other invertebrates) feed on the abundant soil microbes. Bird activity is greatest during rising and dropping tides, when the water movement exposes and disturbs fresh prey. When tides are relatively high, and the mudflats and channels are flooded, shorebirds and wading birds move onto the marsh platform. Sandpipers probe the soils to the depths that their beaks allow, and egrets scour the vegetation for swimming and crawling prey.

Coastal Salt Marsh is found along all of Europe's coastlines, especially around the Atlantic Ocean and North Sea and the Mediterranean. However, there are stark regional differences, with climate, tidal amplitude, and sedimentation type being the most important factors influencing community composition.

The open cordgrass grasslands of **Atlantic Ocean and North Sea Salt Marsh** have been grazed for centuries, and livestock play an important part in the species assemblages in them, from the plants and invertebrates to the birds and mammals. About half of Britain's Common Redshanks nest on salt marshes, and they appear to benefit from the structural diversity that grazing brings. However, their breeding success plummets when livestock density is too high or grazing is in particularly sensitive periods. Flowering Common Sea-Lavender (*Limonium vulgare*) turns Atlantic salt marshes a beautiful pink in late summer and autumn. In the winter, the relatively high salinity means that the salt marshes are often the last water bodies to freeze over, thus providing important refuges for waterbirds such as Brant (Brent Goose), Eurasian Wigeon, Green-winged Teal, Common Snipe, Black-bellied (Grey) Plover, Dunlin, and Black-tailed Godwit. Ungrazed upper areas of the Atlantic salt marshes are of importance to voles, mice, and shrews.

Some secretive species, such as Common Snipe, readily utilise salt marsh and can be extremely hard to detect. However, during a big spring tide, many of these shy denizens are flushed out from their cover. © ONNO WILDSCHUT, AGAMI

The n. Atlantic salt marshes slowly transition to **Arctic Salt Marsh**, found mainly in Iceland, far n. Norway, Russia, and Svalbard. These marshes tend to be rather small. Most plant species are related to those in the Atlantic salt marshes, but a few Arctic species are to be found. The habitat is important to shorebirds and waterfowl that breed in the High Arctic before they move to more southerly marshes with the onset of winter.

Mediterranean Salt Marsh occurs in areas with hot, dry summers that result in high soil salinity, creating conditions favourable to drought-tolerant plants. These marshes tend to develop very diverse communities of shrubby halophytes, with regional differences in climate, sediment, and disturbance determining the local vegetation. The complex nature of environmental conditions—changing quickly within the marsh from one metre to the next—means that upper marshes tend to develop an intertwined mosaic of plant communities under good (natural) conditions. Typical plants include tall rushes, sea-lavenders, wormwoods (*Artemisia* spp.), sea heaths (*Frankenia* spp.), plantains (*Plantago* spp.), Grand Statice (*Limoniastrum monopetalum*), Jointed Glasswort (*Halocnemum strobilaceum*) and Herbaceous Seepweed (*Suaeda maritima*). Somewhat higher areas may allow salt-resilient tamarisks (*Tamarix* spp.) to establish as small trees. At the other end, in the lowest parts of the marsh, the extreme saline environments will support more pickleweeds (*Salicornia* spp.). The complex nature of Mediterranean Coastal Salt Marsh creates innumerable microhabitats for wildlife.

In **Baltic Salt Marsh**, the flora is related to that of the Atlantic, North Sea, and Arctic, but the topography is quite distinct. Insignificant tidal changes in the Baltic Sea mean that rains, winds, snows, and ice buildup have greater influence on the water level, yet even these effects are minor. As a consequence, salt marshes that form in large, sheltered, clay-filled bays are extremely flat, without the structures we see in more tidal areas—no channels, no levees, no small islands, just flat meadows. Salinity varies significantly through the Baltic Sea, naturally influencing the vegetation found in any one location, with the salt concentration being the greatest nearest the North Sea. The plant communities in the wettest and most saline areas may support Common Arrowgrass (*Triglochin maritima*), Sea Plantain (*Plantago maritima*), and Saltmarsh Sand-Spurrey (*Spergularia salina*). Occasionally, pickleweeds are also to be found. Somewhat higher areas will have species like Saltmeadow Rush (*Juncus gerardi*) and more cosmopolitan meadow species that are able to survive minor levels of salt exposure.

Black Sea Salt Marsh is less diverse than salt marshes in other parts of Europe. The smaller tidal range and less extreme salinity difference within the marsh lead to more constant environmental conditions with fewer micro-niches. Plant communities are related to those found in the Mediterranean but tend to be species-poor and can resemble the low, spreading heathlands of SODA PAN AND INLAND SALT MARSH. Nevertheless, the marshes are extremely important for a wide range of wildlife, especially migrating shorebirds.

Salt marshes contribute a range of ecosystem services, many of which we have only recently started to acknowledge. They protect our coasts from storm surges and coastal erosion and capture an estimated 2–20 tonnes of carbon per hectare (1–8 tons/ac.) per year. This carbon is locked in the growing plants and subsequently in the substrate in a similar way to equally anaerobic peat bogs. Salt marshes also have an important cleaning function, contributing to water quality and general ecosystem health. Many of the world's commercial and recreational fisheries depend on these ecosystems functioning well—not to mention the nursery function they provide to countless economically valuable species. Salt marshes have also been modified for millennia for the production of sea salt, and some of Europe's most well-known salt-marsh birding areas, like the Salina di Comacchio (Po delta, Italy) and the Salin d'Aigues-Mortes (Camargue, France) are associated with salt production.

Bar-tailed Godwit can frequently be found feeding in the muddy channels running through salt marshes and may use the marshes as roosts at high tide. © RALPH MARTIN, AGAMI

WILDLIFE: Salt marshes are highly productive ecosystems with active detritus- and plant-based food webs. This makes for a dazzling array and abundance of invertebrates, which in turn draw an amazing diversity of birds. Salt marshes are some of the most loved habitats by birders in Europe.

Coastal Salt Marshes are particularly important for a wide range of shorebirds, especially when the mudflats are flooded at high tide. These include Dunlin, Common Redshank, Black-bellied (Grey) Plover, Northern Lapwing, Red Knot, Bar-tailed Godwit, Black-tailed Godwit, Black-winged Stilt, and—in more open areas—Kentish Plover. Sandwich Tern, Gull-billed Tern, Common Tern, and the very localised Elegant Tern all breed in Coastal Salt Marsh. Mediterranean salt marshes

In the areas above the high-water mark, and where there is protection from human disturbance and predation, colonies of gulls and terns may form. The red-billed Elegant Tern (middle left) is a very rare salt-marsh breeder, here nesting alongside black-billed Sandwich Terns (middle right and foreground) and a Mediterranean Gull (far left) in Valencia, Spain. © DAVID MONTICELLI, AGAMI

Above: **Barnacle Geese overwinter on Coastal Salt Marshes, wet pastures, and surrounding croplands.** © MENNO VAN DUIJN, AGAMI

Opposite: **Black-winged Stilt is a noisy and aggressive inhabitant of this habitat in the south of the continent, fearlessly chasing away any intruder.** © DANIELE OCCHIATO, AGAMI

are important for breeding Mediterranean Short-toed Lark and Spectacled Warbler. Atlantic salt marshes can attract awe-inspiring numbers of wintering wildfowl, including Eurasian Wigeon, Green-winged Teal, Brant (Brent Goose), Barnacle Goose, and Pink-footed Goose. Salt marshes are also important wintering habitats for Merlin, Twite, Meadow Pipit, and Eurasian Skylark. The abundance of birds and other prey in salt marshes invariably attracts the attention of Peregrine Falcon, Eurasian Hobby, various harriers, and many other raptors.

In natural, functioning systems, some of the channels snaking through the salt marsh may remain flooded at low tide, forming important retreats for aquatic wildlife such as fish and more mobile crustaceans. Many of these species spawn in estuaries. Tides then carry the larvae and young up the channels into the salt marshes, where food is abundant, and they are relatively safe from predators. The spawn of many species often have a higher tolerance for the low-oxygen environments found in salt marshes than adults, and the shallows additionally exclude larger water-based predators. This affords them some level of protection. Nevertheless, their presence also draws in otters and wading birds like herons and egrets that exploit the concentrated food supply.

High-salinity pans and lakes can develop in some salt marshes, forming a matrix of open water and various plant communities. These slightly deeper (semi-)permanent waters can develop high

Greater Flamingo breeds on salt marshes and feeds in the surrounding salt pans. Its diet of tiny crustaceans gives the bird its pink colouration. © DANIELE OCCHIATO, AGAMI

concentrations of crustaceans and are the favoured habitat of the Greater Flamingo. European Eel (*Anguilla anguilla*) also does well in these ecosystems, drawing in both hundreds of fishermen and thousands of Great and Pygmy Cormorants (the latter in the Mediterranean and Black Sea).

CONSERVATION: Unfortunately, salt marshes are highly threatened ecosystems. Rising sea levels will change the cycles of flooding, salinity, sunlight, and sedimentation, dramatically affecting salt-marsh plant communities. In many cases, salt marshes cannot adapt by extending farther inland, as the habitat is boxed in by human development and structures 'defending' settlements and farmland from seawater surges. Salt marshes are additionally drained for agriculture and settlement. In response to the increasing frequency and severity of storm surges, sea walls are being built on many coastlines. Such obstructions ultimately cut off salt marshes from their lifeline, tidal flow. Nutrient enrichment from farmland fertilisation and coastal sewage disposal are also changing the dynamics of sensitive salt marshes and putting additional pressure on their environmental health, as are overgrazing and pollution. Over 18% of Europe's salt-marsh habitat has been lost in the past 50 years, and a good proportion of the remaining habitat is either degraded or threatened.

DISTRIBUTION: Coastal Salt Marsh habitat is found throughout coastal Europe but is most prevalent along the Atlantic, North Sea, and Mediterranean coastlines. It is less widespread in the Baltic Sea, Black Sea, and Arctic.

WHERE TO SEE: Mont Saint-Michel, Normandy, France; Camargue, Bouches-du-Rhône, France; North Norfolk coast, England, UK; Salina di Comacchio, Emilia-Romagna, Italy; Ses Salines, Ibiza, Spain.

Eu12E EUROPEAN SODA PAN AND INLAND SALT MARSH

IN A NUTSHELL: Seasonal inland shallow-water pans, lakes, and marshes with a high concentration of alkaline salts, typically flooded in spring and drier through summer. **Global Habitat Affinities:** ASIAN SALT PAN; NORTH AMERICAN PLAYAS; AFRICAN SALT PANS AND LAKES. **Continental Habitat Affinities:** COASTAL SALT MARSH. **Species Overlap:** PUSZTA AND PONTIC STEPPE; COASTAL SALT MARSH.

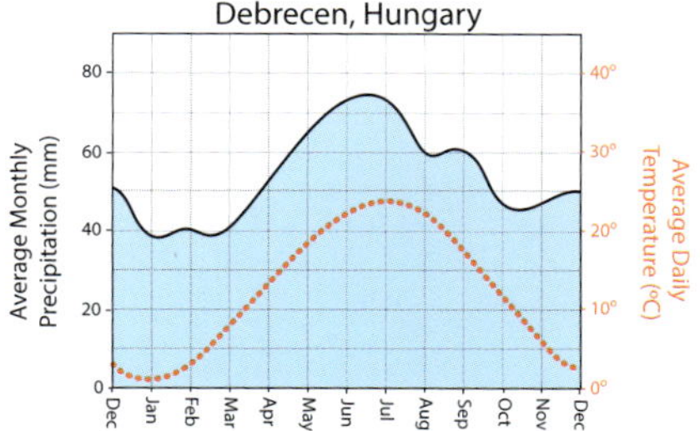

DESCRIPTION: Soda Pan and Inland Salt Marsh is a rare but ecologically distinct habitat, scattered across Europe in areas with fossil salt deposits or saline groundwater. Many of these inland salt-marsh systems, particularly those found in Iberia, France, Germany, and Poland, are dominated by

Many of the ephemeral Soda Pans scattered through the Puszta are tiny. If the natural hydrology is disturbed and salts are flushed away from the surface (rather than continuing to accumulate), the Soda Pan will transform to steppe or may be converted to cropland. © LEANDER KHIL

When the waters retreat in Soda Pans, salts and clays collect at the surface and form a hard, white crust. © LEANDER KHIL

sodium chloride and other salts that were deposited in ancient seas during the late Palaeozoic and Mesozoic eras (mostly 300–145 MYA). As these fossil salts leached out, they created marshes, pans, and lakes with brackish or saline water and halophytic vegetation such as Saltmeadow Rush (*Juncus gerardi*), Common Glasswort (*Salicornia europaea*), Sea Clubrush (*Bolboschoenus maritimus*), and Narrow-leaf Bird's-foot Trefoil (*Lotus tenuis*).

The vast majority of Soda Pans and Inland Salt Marshes are found in Hungary and the neighbouring countries of the Pannonian Basin, where seasonal Soda Pans pepper the alkaline PUSZTA AND PONTIC STEPPE. These saline lakes and smaller water bodies transform dramatically with the seasons. They flood in late winter and spring with snowmelt and rainfall, creating a breathtaking sight, and slowly dry through the summer as the shallow surface waters evaporate in the humid continental climate (Köppen **Dfa** and **Dfb**). These unique ecosystems, with their fascinating ecology and species composition, are a testament to the wonders of nature. They are also of immense importance to shorebirds migrating north in preparation for the spring breeding season, adding to their allure.

Soda Pan and Inland Salt Marsh systems are superficially like the classic saltwater COASTAL SALT MARSH and brackish wetlands. However, the salts of the Pannonian Soda Pans tend to be alkaline soda salts like sodium bicarbonate or sodium carbonate, as opposed to the sodium chloride (table salt) of marine saltwater ecosystems. The exact salt composition and its concentration vary widely seasonally and from pan to pan.

The mechanisms behind the formation of a Soda Pan are diverse, as a complex interplay of geological, hydrological, geomorphological, and climatic factors determines the pan's location, physical structure, salt composition, salt concentration, and ultimate species composition.

Groundwater, flowing from major rivers and the surrounding landscape, accumulates salts from Quaternary feldspar and carbonate-rich loess, and the now alkaline water additionally dissolves silicates from the soils. Prehistoric riverbeds and other subterranean relief formations can result in deep upflow zones, with the groundwater flowing closer to the surface. This becomes particularly relevant when natural land depressions on the surface collect precipitation that cannot wash away, creating a capillary pump. As surface water evaporates, the concentration of salts increases and draws groundwater to the surface through capillary action. The desiccating summer sun and winds leave many pans dry by autumn, with the salts accumulating in and on the soil surface. The formation of these Soda Pans started at least by the latter part of the last ice age (~20,000 YA), and millennia of capillary salt pumping have resulted in the alkaline environments we see today.

The size, depth, hydrology, seasonality, salinity, and vegetation of these water bodies vary greatly. They range from large, shallow lakes like Lake Neusiedl/Fertő, on the Austria-Hungary border, through shallow (seasonal) pans like Zicklacke, Austria and Kelemenszék, Hungary, to the thousands of small wetlands and impermanent water bodies scattered through the Pannonian Basin of Hungary and surrounding countries. While the salt concentrations in these soda systems vary widely through the year and between water bodies, their average salinity is low (hyposaline) compared to other saltwater systems. However, it is still significant enough to dictate the vegetation and create a unique ecosystem.

Typical plants of Soda Pan habitat include Pannonian Seepweed (*Suaeda pannonica*), the beautiful mauve-flowering Sea Aster (*Tripolium pannonicum*), Perennial-jointed Glasswort (*Salicornia prostrata*), sand-spurries (*Spergularia* spp.), saltgrasses (*Puccinellia* spp.), and Sharp-leaved Grass (*Sporobolus aculeatus*). A unique community of species like Dwarf Heliotrope (*Heliotropium supinum*) and Procumbent Vervain (*Verbena supina*) forms in the lake beds when they have dried out in the summer. In addition, many species associated with wetland ecosystems or the surrounding PUSZTA AND PONTIC STEPPE can also be found in Soda Pan and Inland Salt Marsh.

WILDLIFE: Soda Pans are some of the greatest birding habitats in Europe, attracting thousands of interesting migrating and resident birds. They are particularly important for shorebirds and waterbirds migrating north in spring, when myriad pans offer diverse water conditions and depths as well as mudflats and vegetated shoreline habitats. Conditions in these water bodies can change rapidly, opening new feeding niches and opportunities, with birds flowing between water bodies as conditions improve or deteriorate for that species. Ruff, Dunlin, Common Greenshank, Common Redshank, Spotted Redshank, Wood Sandpiper, and

Many migrant shorebirds, such as this stunning Spotted Redshank in breeding plumage, use Soda Pan and Inland Salt Marsh habitat as a stop-off on their long migration to and from breeding grounds.
© DANIELE OCCHIATO, AGAMI

A male Kentish Plover blends into his surroundings. This is one of the few species able to succeed on the sparsely vegetated flats in this harsh environment. © MENNO VAN DUIJN, AGAMI

Black-tailed Godwit, among others, are all to be expected in relatively large numbers. They are joined by the somewhat more unusual Broad-billed, Terek, Marsh, and Curlew Sandpipers; Red-necked Phalarope; and Collared Pratincoles. Marsh terns, Little Gull, Common Crane, wagtails, pipits, and large numbers of wildfowl use the Soda Pans on migration, adding to the cacophonic spectacle of these systems during the season.

The breeding Kentish Plover is strongly associated with open soda mudflats and sparsely vegetated zones. Other characteristic breeders are Black-headed, Yellow-legged, and Caspian Gulls (and the occasional Mediterranean Gull), as well as White-winged and Whiskered Terns, Pied Avocet, Black-winged Stilt, Common Redshank, Northern Lapwing, and Black-tailed Godwit. Inland Salt Marsh and the surrounding salt-laden IBERIAN STEPPE are the prime habitats of the Mediterranean Short-toed Lark in Iberia.

The attractive White-tailed Skimmer is one of several salt-tolerant dragonflies and damselflies that can be found in this habitat. © ROB DE JONG, AGAMI

White-winged Tern feeds in Soda Pan and Inland Salt Marsh habitat and may form colonies in suitable areas around its margins, though it does not necessarily breed in the same areas from one year to the next. © RALPH MARTIN, AGAMI

Larger Soda Pans play a very significant role for roosting waterfowl in winter, with tens of thousands of geese roosting in some areas. A few of the cute Lesser White-fronted Geese and gorgeous Red-breasted Geese are sprinkled among the large numbers of Greylag and Greater White-fronted Geese and Tundra Bean-Geese. Besides roosting on the water, the geese and other wildfowl also feed on the halophytic vegetation of the Soda Pan.

In spring, large numbers of birds feed on the abundant salt-loving fairy shrimps (especially *Branchinecta orientalis* and *Arctodiaptomus spinosus*). Later in spring, a wide variety of salt-tolerant damselflies and dragonflies can be found, including various spreadwings (*Lestes* spp.), Blue-tailed Damselfly (Common Bluetail, *Ischnura elegans*), Scarce Blue-tailed Damselfly (Small Bluetail, *Ischnura pumilio*), Ruddy Darter (*Sympetrum sanguineum*), Southern Darter (*Sympetrum meridionale*), White-tailed Skimmer (*Orthetrum albistylum*), Southern Migrant Hawker (Blue-eyed Hawker, *Aeshna affinis*), and the gorgeous Broad Scarlet (*Crocothemis erythraea*). Steppe Tarantula (*Lycosa singoriensis*) is a stunning, large hunting spider that favours the open areas around Soda Pans for its burrows, coming out at night to hunt.

High salinity and water turbidity limit amphibian distribution in Soda Pans, but several species common in the wet PUSZTA STEPPE will also enter this habitat. These include European Fire-bellied

High salinity and water turbidity limit amphibian distribution in Soda Pans, but several species common in the wet Puszta also enter this habitat. The colourful European Fire-bellied Toad is first detected by its eerie bubbling calls as it tries to attract a mate. © ROB DE JONG, AGAMI

Toad (*Bombina bombina*), Common Spadefoot (*Pelobates fuscus*), water frogs (*Rana* spp.), and potentially Danube Crested Newt (*Triturus dobrogicus*) in wetter years and less saline conditions. Grass snakes (*Natrix* spp.) are ubiquitous, and European Pond Turtle (*Emys orbicularis*) can be common, especially in larger, less saline water bodies.

CONSERVATION: The Soda Pan and Inland Salt Marsh ecosystem, a treasure trove of biodiversity, is under threat. It is disappearing quickly as drainage and melioration transform these systems into alkaline steppes, meadows, or agricultural land. The indirect effects of changes to the water table are likely to be the more significant and ominous drivers of the deterioration and loss of this habitat. Increased water extraction for irrigation and direct human consumption is causing changes to the height of the water table, but also to how the underground waters flow, leading to a reduction in surface water and the breaking down of the all-important capillary pump systems that have built and maintained the Soda Pans. The usual suspects of agriculture, human settlement, pollution, and general exploitation are also driving forces for deterioration in and around Soda Pans. The time for action is now.

DISTRIBUTION: Ninety percent of European Soda Pan and Inland Salt Marsh habitat is found in a mosaic within the PUSZTA STEPPE of the Pannonian Basin, with the bulk in Hungary. Soda Pans are almost non-existent elsewhere in Europe. Inland Salt Marshes are also relatively rare but can form where relict seawater is present or on fossil salt. Examples are mainly in Iberia, France, Germany, and Poland.

WHERE TO SEE: Kiskunság National Park, Hungary; Neusiedler See-Seewinkel National Park, Austria; Ráczovo Jazierko, Slovakia; Esperstedter Ried, Thuringia, Germany; Pasturefields Salt Marsh, Staffordshire, England, UK.

Eu12F MEDITERRANEAN TO CASPIAN PELAGIC WATERS

IN A NUTSHELL: Deepwater marine environments in the Mediterranean and Caspian Seas. **Global Habitat Affinities:** AFRICAN PELAGIC WATERS; NEARCTIC PELAGIC WATERS. **Continental Habitat Affinities:** ARCTIC AND TEMPERATE PELAGIC WATERS. **Species Overlap:** ARCTIC AND TEMPERATE PELAGIC WATERS; MEDITERRANEAN TO CASPIAN ROCKY COASTLINE.

DESCRIPTION: When thinking of the Mediterranean, many conjure up images of sun, sea, sand, and holidaymakers. Offshore, in the open sea (aka the pelagic zone), it is quite a different picture, especially on a cold, wild, windy winter day. Nevertheless, the Mediterranean Sea is, on the whole, relatively warm year-round (av. 20°C/67°F), with average surface temperatures in summer of 25°C (77°F) and in winter of 15°C (59°F). The Mediterranean occupies an area of about 2.5 million km^2 (970,000 sq. mi.), has an average depth of 1500 m (4900 ft.), and is almost completely enclosed by land. In the east, the Mediterranean connects to the Black Sea through the narrow Turkish straits, which are only 700 m (2300 ft.) wide at the narrowest point. In the west, it is connected to the colder, more nutrient-rich Atlantic Ocean at the Strait of Gibraltar, where only 13 km (8 mi.) separates Europe from Africa. This gap opened up only about 5 MYA. Before that, the entire

Sailing the Mediterranean is a wonderful way to explore this habitat. © KAJETAN FUISZ

Mediterranean basin was dry for about 600,000 years. Consequently, the marine life that colonised the Mediterranean has had to evolve and adapt to these differing conditions in the time since the basin was reflooded. Being virtually landlocked, the Mediterranean Sea experiences far more regular and stable currents than the adjacent ARCTIC AND TEMPERATE PELAGIC WATERS, though, as with that habitat, the greatest diversity of pelagic species is found around continental shelves and areas of upwelling.

The Black Sea occupies about 450,000 km^2 (170,000 sq. mi.) and has a maximum depth of 2200 m (7250 ft.). Surface temperatures are warm in summer (25°C/77°F) and cold in winter (7°C/45°F). Almost 75% of the fresh water entering the sea comes from the Danube River, and this brings with it large quantities of mud and silt. Consequently, the Black Sea has a large, shallow shelf in the northwest.

The Caspian Sea is situated between Europe and Asia and is the world's largest inland water body (371,000 km^2/143,000 sq. mi.). It is an endorheic basin, in which the river network supplying the sea is completely isolated from all the world's oceans. This means that the water salinity is only about one-third that of average seawater. Surface water temperatures are warm in summer (25°C/77°F) but much colder in winter, when the average surface temperature drops to below 5°C (40°F) in the north and 12°C (54°F) in the south.

WILDLIFE: The pelagic waters of the Mediterranean, Black, and Caspian Seas are rich in sea mammals, though less rich and diverse in pelagic seabirds than the adjacent ARCTIC AND

The Mediterranean Sea is inhabited by a diverse selection of cetaceans. Common Dolphin is one of the showiest and most acrobatic. © VINCENT LEGRAND, AGAMI

TEMPERATE PELAGIC WATERS. The pelagic area is largely used in the summer months by the handful of seabird species that have adapted to breeding and feeding within the Mediterranean Sea; because most pelagic species avoid crossing the narrow Strait of Gibraltar, few enter the Mediterranean from the Atlantic.

Many marine mammal species occur in these seas; there are at least 12 regularly occurring species plus several rare or vagrant species. Numbers and diversity are higher in the western parts of the Mediterranean, and here, if out on a boat, it is not uncommon to encounter a pod of playful Long-finned Pilot Whales, Common Bottlenose Dolphins, or even Orcas. Dolphins include Common Dolphin, Risso's Dolphin, and Striped Dolphin, while the scarce Rough-toothed Dolphin prefers deep water. Small numbers of elusive Cuvier's Beaked Whales occur where the sea depth is greater than 1000 m (3300 ft.). Sperm and Fin Whales are both more common in the w. and c. Mediterranean than in the e. Mediterranean, with the Liguro-Provençal Basin (between Sardinia, Menorca, and the s. French coast) being among the best areas to look for them. The Mediterranean Monk Seal, the world's rarest pinniped, still survives in small numbers, largely in the eastern part of the Mediterranean, particularly around the Aegean Sea, where a population in the low hundreds still survives. Historically, this species was more common and widespread, even pupping on beaches, but human pressure has forced it to become far more reclusive, and it now pups in remote coves and caves.

The prehistoric-looking Sperm Whale is the largest of the toothed whales and still has a population in the Mediterranean, though it is not found in the Black Sea. This species typically feeds in deep water and can dive for up to two hours, though 35–60 minutes is more typical. © VINCENT LEGRAND, AGAMI

Scopoli's Shearwater, a close relative of Cory's Shearwater, is confined to the Mediterranean as a breeding species but ventures farther afield when foraging. © JACOB GARVELINK, AGAMI

The Mediterranean Sea has a vast number of islands, and the region's seabirds use these as breeding grounds, especially islands without high numbers of introduced predators (particularly domestic cats and rats). Scopoli's and Yelkouan Shearwaters breed on islands in the Mediterranean and spend most of their time foraging in the pelagic zone. In certain areas, such as s. Corsica, both species may be seen from land, particularly early and late in the day, when the lazy flight of the larger Scopoli's Shearwater easily distinguishes it from the much faster-flying, smaller Yelkouan Shearwater. Elsewhere these species may be encountered on ferry rides between islands. A particularly exciting spectacle is watching fast-moving flocks of Yelkouan Shearwaters passing swiftly through the Bosporus (one of the Turkish straits) as they head from the Sea of Marmora to rich feeding areas in the Black Sea and back again. Their larger relative seldom undertakes this feat, presumably to avoid predation. In the winter months, Scopoli's Shearwater moves west, out of the Mediterranean, and heads south to warmer parts of the Atlantic, while numerous Yelkouan Shearwaters stay in the e. Mediterranean, many taking advantage of feeding opportunities in the Black Sea. The Mediterranean form of European Storm-Petrel is also restricted to this habitat in summer, though it too heads into warmer s. Atlantic waters in the winter, where it is lost (to us, at least!) among the nominate birds. Another important species that forages in the pelagic zone of the Mediterranean is the rare and range-restricted Audouin's Gull. At the western end of the Mediterranean, a few Balearic Shearwaters, a Critically Endangered species, may be found. In winter, a small number of more northerly breeding species move into the Mediterranean, including Northern Gannet and, in the western areas, Atlantic Puffin.

Distinct endemic subspecies of three cetaceans are found in the Black Sea: Common Dolphin, Common Bottlenose Dolphin, and Harbour Porpoise. All three subspecies, unfortunately, are under

The Yelkouan Shearwater is restricted to the c. and e. Mediterranean Sea and the Black Sea. Its constant passage through the narrow Bosporus strait is a true ornithological wonder. © DANIELE OCCHIATO, AGAMI

threat from human activities. The Caspian Sea is home to the small, endemic Caspian Seal. Evidence suggests that seals probably colonised the Caspian Sea via rivers that flowed south from the Arctic Ocean. When these connecting rivers disappeared during the Pleistocene ice ages, the seal populations were isolated. They subsequently adapted and evolved into the endemic species present today. A century ago, there were an estimated 1.5 million Caspian Seals, but by 2005 only about 104,000 remained. The most recent population estimate is 68,000, and the number is most likely still declining.

No truly pelagic species of birds occur in the Caspian Sea, though it is on a major migration route used by millions. A variety of ducks, geese, grebes, loons (divers), gulls, and terns use the sea at times. In addition, some individuals of a handful of Arctic breeding species, such as Parasitic Jaeger (Arctic Skua), take an overland shortcut from breeding grounds to wintering areas in the Mediterranean Sea, Arabian Sea, and Indian Ocean. Some of these individuals stage in the Black, Caspian, or Mediterranean Sea, where the Parasitic Jaeger feeds by harassing the local gulls and terns and forcing them to regurgitate their stomach contents. Once refuelled, the birds are fit to continue their journey south. Below the surface, the Caspian Sea has developed a high level of species endemism and has significant populations of various sturgeons (family Acipenseridae).

CONSERVATION: Overfishing has significantly reduced fish stocks across the Mediterranean, Black, and Caspian Seas. This has caused cataclysmic ripples through the entire food web, but large predators (like cetaceans and birds) have been particularly hard hit. Accidental bycatch is also a serious issue for marine mammals and seabirds of the region. Pollution through toxic chemicals, fertilisers, and plastics is having dire effects on the oceanic environment, while heavy boat and ship traffic is impacting marine mammal populations throughout the region.

DISTRIBUTION: The deeper, offshore waters of the Mediterranean, Black, and Caspian Seas.

WHERE TO SEE: There are few opportunities to explore the pelagic areas of this region. Commercial pelagic trips operate from Tarifa, Spain, into the Strait of Gibraltar, allowing for some good views of cetaceans and a variety of Mediterranean seabirds. Cetacean-watching trips are also available from San Remo, Italy, and from other holiday destinations around the Mediterranean. Various ferry routes offer good opportunities to see pelagic species, and of course, if you are fortunate enough, it is difficult to beat sailing your own boat around the Balearic Islands, Corsica, the Tuscan islands, or the Greek islands.

Eu12G ARCTIC AND TEMPERATE PELAGIC WATERS

IN A NUTSHELL: Deepwater marine environments in Europe's more northerly, colder waters. **Global Habitat Affinities:** NEARCTIC PELAGIC WATERS; ASIAN TEMPERATE PELAGIC WATERS. **Continental Habitat Affinities:** MEDITERRANEAN TO CASPIAN PELAGIC WATERS. **Species Overlap:** MEDITERRANEAN TO CASPIAN PELAGIC WATERS; ARCTIC AND TEMPERATE ROCKY COASTLINE.

DESCRIPTION: The cold, wild, and windy Arctic and North Atlantic Oceans, with huge swells and horizontal spray whipping off white-capped waves, are a far cry from the warm and serene rolling waves of summer along the Portuguese coast. Such are the changing scenes in the vast areas covered by this habitat. Exploring the depths of this habitat in the deep pelagic waters off the continental shelf is no mean feat either, often requiring a long journey far from land on a small vessel. High levels of endurance and the ability to cope with discomfort are certainly beneficial, as you are buffeted up and down and side to side by the waves, and your binoculars and other equipment are constantly covered in sea spray. However, the seldom-seen treasures that inhabit this realm make it all worthwhile. Amazing experiences include witnessing pods of bow-riding dolphins, a blow from a Fin Whale, a breaching Humpback Whale, or being immersed in a huge feeding flock of shearwaters, all after the same bait fish that schools of the incredible Yellowfin Tuna are chasing. Be warned, though: many hours may be spent staring at very little. But this just makes the action even more exciting and appreciated when it happens.

Europe is surrounded to the north by the Barents Sea and the Arctic Ocean and to the west by the Atlantic Ocean. The location of the deep waters of the pelagic zone varies widely; in some areas, deep water is situated relatively close inshore, while in other areas, the continental shelf extends far out, and shallow seas extend for well over 160 km (100 mi.) offshore.

Acrobatic White-beaked Dolphin is among the regularly occurring species in more northerly pelagic areas. It is often seen in quite large pods. © W. J. STRIETMAN, AGAMI

While vast areas of pelagic waters can appear devoid of life, other areas are rich in food and can support large numbers of feeding cetaceans along with flocks of thousands of seabirds. What looks like a homogeneous habitat from above the water is a very complex environment under the water, where the distribution of marine life is determined by such factors as water temperature, sea depth, complex and ever-changing currents, and the presence of oceanic upwellings. Upwellings typically occur around deep troughs and seamounts and are caused by winds blowing across the surface of the ocean, pushing water away and in turn pulling colder and nutrient-rich deep water to the surface. This provides nutrients at the surface, providing food for fish and other marine life. This ultimately attracts the associated predators, in the form of larger fish, cetaceans, and seabirds. Finding a good upwelling is the holy grail when out on a pelagic boat trip, though the presence of this phenomenon is not entirely predictable, due to such factors as currents and wind speed and direction. Heading to waters over seamounts and underwater canyons is thus common practice when seeking pelagic life, though it produces variable results.

The Gulf Stream current brings warm water from the Gulf of Mexico up the eastern side of North America and across the Atlantic towards nw. Europe. These waters are highly productive and important for feeding cetaceans and seabirds. The bountiful feeding opportunities also make it an important migration route for birds, marine mammals, and fish. The Gulf Stream is also incredibly important to Europe's climate, keeping much of the continent relatively mild and providing a steady stream of moisture-laden winds drifting in from the west and falling as rain or snow.

WILDLIFE: The marine life of Arctic and Temperate Pelagic Waters changes radically from the cold waters of the north to the warmer, more temperate waters from the Gulf Stream to the south. The distribution of species also changes seasonally, as many species move north in summer to take advantage of the increased food availability. A wealth of large whale species can be found in the region, including Humpback, Common Minke, Fin, and Sperm Whales. They typically move to higher latitudes in the summer months to feed, returning to warmer water in the south in winter to breed. Dolphins are widespread in these seas, the most common invariably being Common Bottlenose, Common, and White-beaked Dolphins, while Orca and Long-finned Pilot Whale (both dolphins despite their names) are seen regularly.

In the colder Arctic Ocean, specialist cetaceans include such near-mythical species as Narwhal, Beluga, Bowhead Whale, and the extremely rare North Atlantic Right Whale. The amazing Walrus and the Bearded, Harp, and Ribbon Seals are also found in these Arctic waters. When pack ice is present, Polar Bears may be found hunting these species, surely one of the most iconic sights of the region. Sadly, climate change is leading to a year-on-year reduction in pack ice, threatening the very existence of some bear populations.

In the boreal summer, many seabirds move north to breed and take advantage of the increased food availability in the pelagic waters in which they feed. These include huge numbers of auks—Atlantic Puffin, Little Auk (Dovekie), Common and Thick-billed Murres (Common and Brünnich's Guillemots), and Razorbill—as well as Northern Fulmars, Northern Gannets, and Black-legged Kittiwakes, which often form huge mixed colonies on coastal cliffs. Other breeding birds in the region include Arctic Terns; Great Skuas; and Long-tailed, Parasitic (Arctic), and Pomarine Jaegers (Skuas). Scarce Arctic specialists such as Yellow-billed Loon (White-billed Diver) and Sabine's, Ross's, and Ivory Gulls are the stuff of dreams for most birders—you can never see too many of any of them! Great and Sooty Shearwaters breed in the Southern Hemisphere and migrate north during the European summer to take advantage of the food-rich waters alongside local breeding species like Manx Shearwater and European and Leach's Storm-Petrels. With the onset of winter, the vast majority of these birds move south into more temperate waters.

The warmer waters farther south, from Portugal towards the Azores, have a different species composition. A much richer diversity of cetaceans occurs, with additional species such as Sei Whale, Bryde's Whale, Cuvier's Beaked Whale (and a few other rare species of beaked whales), Short-finned Pilot Whale, Striped Dolphin, and Atlantic Spotted Dolphin. The Azores, in particular, are a hotspot for whale diversity. In the southern parts of this habitat, as the seas become warmer, the numbers of auks and other northern species diminish, and species with more southerly distributions become more prominent. Shearwaters (both breeding and migrant species) become much more numerous, as Cory's and Scopoli's Shearwaters (breeding in the Atlantic and on Mediterranean islands, respectively), Manx Shearwater, Balearic Shearwater, and the rare

Sabine's Gull breeds in the High Arctic but migrates through our region, especially in autumn, on its way to the s. Atlantic, where it spends the winter. © SYLVAIN REYT, AGAMI

A Sei Whale powers through the ocean. The Gulf Stream current brings warm water from the Gulf of Mexico up the eastern side of North America and across the Atlantic towards nw. Europe. These waters are highly productive and important for feeding cetaceans and seabirds. © MARC GUYT, AGAMI

Above: **Cory's Shearwater has large breeding populations in the Azores and Madeira but also breeds nearer the Portuguese mainland on the Berlengas archipelago. It spends the European winter farther south in the Atlantic.** © SYLVAIN REYT, AGAMI

Barolo Shearwater all range as far north as the Gulf Stream. Sooty and Great Shearwaters can be abundant in places. Joining these feeding throngs are European Storm-Petrels, Monteiro's Storm-Petrels, and migrant Wilson's Storm-Petrels, as well as Bulwer's Petrels and small numbers of the rare Fea's (Desertas) and Zino's Petrels, two species that breed in Madeira (these three latter species tend to stay a little farther south, seldom venturing north of the Bay of Biscay). In autumn, large numbers of migrants from farther north also take advantage of these waters, including Red-necked and Red Phalaropes, skuas, and Sabine's Gulls, and a pelagic boat trip at this time of year, combining the late-summer-feeding shearwaters and the migrant skuas and others, can be a highlight of a birding year, if not a lifetime. These warm-water species largely vacate the area in winter, heading to seas south of the equator, and are replaced by a mix of more northerly breeding species, including Northern Fulmar, Northern Gannet, auks, and loons (divers).

CONSERVATION: Overfishing and bycatch are major threats to pelagic wildlife. Much of the sea area covered by this habitat is designated as international waters, falling outside the jurisdiction of national territorial waters. The Convention for the Protection of the Marine Environment of the North-East Atlantic (OSPAR) was set up in 1992 in an attempt to protect marine life in international waters in the ne. Atlantic. In 2021, approximately 600,000 km^2 (230,000 sq. mi.) of a high-seas region of the Atlantic was established as the North Atlantic Current and Evlanov Sea (NACES) Marine Protected Area. The designated area aims to protect vitally important feeding areas for seabirds, though policing the area and responding to human impacts are far from straightforward.

During a period of intensive whaling in the 17th and 18th centuries, many larger species of cetaceans were driven towards extinction. Thankfully, whaling has largely, though not completely, ceased. Cetacean populations have rebounded in the past few decades, dramatically increasing

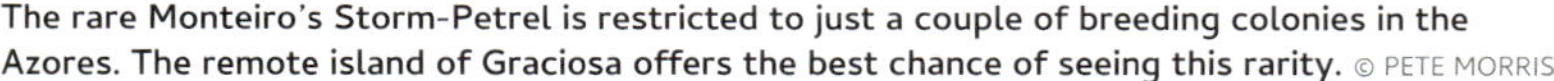

The rare Monteiro's Storm-Petrel is restricted to just a couple of breeding colonies in the Azores. The remote island of Graciosa offers the best chance of seeing this rarity. © PETE MORRIS

the chances of seeing a blowing Blue Whale, a breaching Common Minke Whale, or a fluking Humpback Whale.

Global oscillations in sea temperatures and sea-current distributions (affected by phenomena such as El Niño and La Niña) can have a strong effect on the distribution of marine life. In recent years, average ocean surface temperatures have risen dramatically, causing a northwards shift in the distributions of many species and a lack of available food in sea areas that were historically rich feeding grounds. Indeed, some studies have suggested that human impact through climate change is having a rapid and profound effect on the established ocean currents. Current predictions are that the critical circulatory currents—especially the Atlantic Meridional Overturning Circulation (AMOC) and its component the Gulf Stream—are likely to collapse by the middle of the 21st century. This will undoubtedly have a catastrophic effect on marine wildlife—and indeed all life on earth. Without the Gulf Stream as we know it, Europe will be very significantly drier and colder, with more extreme weather events and storms.

DISTRIBUTION: Arctic and Temperate Pelagic Waters are found all the way around the northern and western coasts of Europe, including the Atlantic Ocean, Bay of Biscay, North Sea, Baltic Sea, Norwegian Sea, Barents Sea, and Arctic Ocean.

WHERE TO SEE: Pelagic areas are difficult to access generally. Pelagic boat trips are available into the Bay of Biscay from n. Spain, and commercial ferries cross this rich area and are frequently billed by the ferry companies as 'pelagic cruises'. Pelagic trips are also available from the Isles of Scilly, UK; Madeira; and Graciosa in the Azores. In the Arctic, the best ways to access pelagic waters are on commercial tours around Spitsbergen, Norway, and on pelagic trips from Iceland.

The magnificent Fea's (Desertas) Petrel breeds in Madeira and tends to stay in Europe's warmer pelagic waters, seldom venturing north of the Bay of Biscay. © PETE MORRIS

Eu12H EUROPEAN TIDAL FLAT AND ESTUARY

IN A NUTSHELL: This habitat occurs intermittently along the coasts of the Arctic Ocean, Baltic Sea, North Sea, Irish Sea, Atlantic Ocean, and Mediterranean Sea. **Global Habitat Affinities:** NEARCTIC TIDAL MUDFLATS; AUSTRALASIAN MUDFLAT; ASIAN TEMPERATE TIDAL FLAT. **Continental Habitat Affinities:** SANDY SHORE AND DUNE; COASTAL SALT MARSH. **Species Overlap:** SANDY SHORE AND DUNE; SHALLOW FRESHWATER MARSH; COASTAL SALT MARSH.

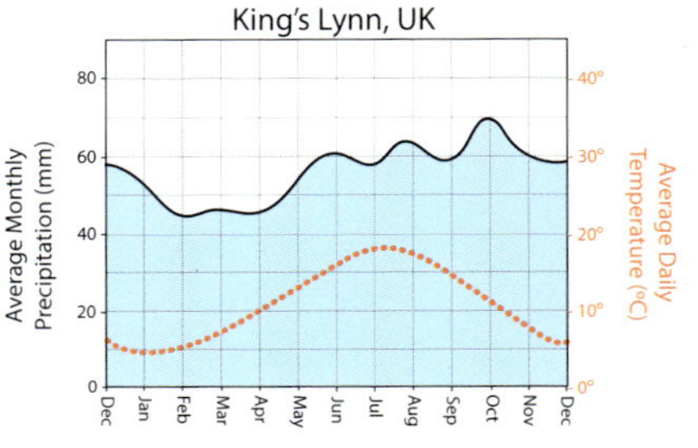

DESCRIPTION: Wandering along a sea wall, buffeted by the cool breeze that whips across barren and seemingly endless mudflats, you could be forgiven for thinking that you are staring at an empty and desolate wasteland. Only the distant bubbling calls of Eurasian Curlews and the piping of Eurasian Oystercatchers give any indication of life. Then the most incredible transformation takes place. Waves from the barely visible ocean race across the mudflats, pushing with them hordes of hungry wading birds that just minutes before were the tiniest of specks in the distance. Within no time at all, the tide has raced in. Countless Sanderlings, Red Knots, and Dunlins jostle along the tide line, desperately finding their last meal before the whole of the flats is covered. Bar-tailed Godwits, Eurasian Curlews, and Common Redshanks exploit the shallow waters, but every minute or two,

Estuary scene at low tide in Portugal showing the complexity of the environment. © MENNO VAN DUIJN, AGAMI

As the tide rises, the flocks are pushed into denser and denser congregations as they take advantage of the last minutes of available feeding time. Here, the Red Knots have been pushed off, while the Eurasian Oystercatchers scamper for drier ground. © DALE FORBES

flocks are forced to move farther in by the relentless tidal surge. Groups of plovers, oystercatchers, gulls, and terns choose higher sandbars to rest on, but these too are soon covered as high tide approaches. Huge swirling masses of birds seek sanctuary and a safe place to roost near to the high-tide mark, where they wait for the tide to drop and expose their food source again. But there is little rest in this food-rich but harsh environment. As the feeding is a daily event, it is quite literally an avian buffet for predators. Harriers hunt along the fringes, and as the feeding birds try to settle, Peregrine Falcons stoop down, flushing everything, filling the sky once more with shorebird murmurations, flashing silver and white as they twist and turn in a synchronised escape flight before they finally settle to roost. On a good day, especially during spring tides, witnessing an incoming tide at a bird-rich estuary can provide a mind-boggling spectacle—a truly incredible experience.

Tidal Flat and Estuary is an extensive coastal ecosystem composed of largely non-vegetated areas of coastline that are exposed and subsequently re-covered by tidal cycles. The geomorphology of the coastline determines the distribution of tidal flats.

Mudflats provide abundant food for millions of hungry shorebirds. The variety of bill shapes among the shorebirds allows them to take advantage of the variety of foods available. © WIL LEURS, AGAMI

As the tide drops, shorebirds quickly leave their roosts to feed, as not only is this often the most productive time, but the birds are hungry after roosting during high tide. © ROB RIEMER, AGAMI

A sheltered, calm area with a gently sloping coastal shelf and the presence of rivers are key factors. These factors allow the deposition and buildup of the sediments that form the flats. Tides are then the fundamental driver that determines the extent of the habitat. Where tidal range (the difference between low and high tide) is high, large areas are exposed at low tide, forming extensive tidal flats, while in areas with a smaller tidal range, such as the Mediterranean, tidal flats are far less extensive. Tidal flats consist of fine sediments transported to the area by rivers, coastal currents, and wave action. They experience regular cycles of submersion and exposure, which create gradients of moisture, salinity, and temperature. The sediment composition can vary, forming sand flats from coarser components, such as sand and gravel, or mudflats from finer sediments, such as silts, mud, and clay. Sand flats are more permeable and oxygenated, while mudflats are more compact, anoxic, and organically rich. Flats are a constantly changing environment, with sediment being moved around and re-deposited by each and every tidal cycle. Other events such as heavy rain can lead to increased soil erosion and thus bigger volumes of sediment being transported downriver and deposited. Situated between the sea and landward habitats, tidal flats act as natural buffers, reducing wave energy and thus protecting shorelines from wave erosion.

Areas of Tidal Flat and Estuary are interspersed with SANDY SHORE AND DUNE and ARCTIC AND TEMPERATE ROCKY COASTLINE habitats. Tidal Flats typically form in sheltered intertidal zones where low tides expose large expanses of mud and silt, or sandy substrates, such as along the estuaries of major rivers. The area exposed is determined by how gently the aspect slopes and by the tidal range. While little can grow on Tidal Flats, other than a few colonising plants along the strandline (an area that spring tides only occasionally flood), they are teeming with life below the surface, providing an important feeding habitat for fish and birds.

WILDLIFE: Tidal Flats can, at first glance, appear to be fairly devoid of life. However, the constant wetting and drying cycles along with the rich organic material, especially in mudflats, create an environment suited to a variety of specialised organisms. Microorganisms on the surface of the mud photosynthesise and generate organic matter that supports the food chain. This in turn supports a diverse benthic community of invertebrates dominated by animals such as polychaete worms (class Polychaeta), bivalves (such as cockles and mussels; class Bivalvia), and crustaceans (such as amphipods and crabs; subphylum Crustacea). These invertebrates play a critical role in bioturbation, the process of reworking sediments, which enhances nutrient availability and sediment aeration. Species such as the Blow Lugworm (*Arenicola marina*) create burrows, oxygenating the sediment and facilitating microbial activity.

In this environment, few plants can exist. At the strandline, where there is only occasional flooding by the highest of spring tides, a few species of salt-tolerant plants, or halophytes, such as *Spartina* spp. and *Salicornia* spp., are able to colonise, helping to trap sediments, prevent erosion, and slowly establish COASTAL SALT MARSH. In some sheltered sandier intertidal areas, beds of Eelgrass (*Zostera marina*) provide another important habitat. Persisting in shallow seas as far as 10 m (33 ft.) below the high-tide mark, this species can form dense seagrass meadows. These meadows provide refuge for an array of species, such as seahorses and pipefish, as well as providing important nursery habitat for a variety of fish and invertebrates. They also provide important feeding grounds for species such as Brant (Brent Goose) and Common Shelduck. Macroalgae such as sea lettuces (*Ulva* spp.) can also be found in some lower intertidal areas, providing additional habitat and food for invertebrates and wildfowl.

The real wildlife stars of the Tidal Flat and Estuary are the birds, and at certain times of year, some sites can support hundreds of thousands of shorebirds as well as a smaller number of ducks, geese, herons, gulls, and terns. Usage by these species is highest during spring and autumn migration and during winter, though some species utilise the habitat during the breeding season in low numbers. Many species are entirely dependent upon this habitat during winter and on migration, landing at tidal-flat stopover sites for essential refuelling during energy-costly migration flights. Conspicuous species using this habitat include Red Knot, Bar-tailed Godwit, Eurasian Oystercatcher, Black-bellied (Grey) Plover, Eurasian Curlew, Common Redshank, and Dunlin, while sandier substrates are favoured by Common Ringed and Kentish Plovers, Common Greenshank, and Sanderling, the last of which scuttles across the sand like a clockwork toy. Brant uses Eelgrass beds (though the availability of agricultural feeding sites makes this habitat less crucial to them), Common Shelduck forages widely, and Little Egret and Grey Heron may be found fishing along the small tidal creeks that intersperse the tidal flats. These tidal creeks also attract the skilful Osprey, on the look out for a European

There's safety in numbers, and consequently feeding shorebirds often gather in big flocks. This group largely comprises Bar-tailed Godwits and Red Knots, two species very dependent on mudflats. © DALE FORBES

Flounder (*Platichthys flesus*) or Sea Mullet (Flathead Grey Mullet, *Mugil cephalus*). Falling and rising tides attract the most frenzied feeding concentrations, and individuals and flocks often roam over large areas, particularly when disturbance levels are high. The high numbers of birds using mudflats inevitably attracts predators, such as harrier species and Merlin, though the real menace for the feeding birds at many locations is the extremely fast and powerful Peregrine.

CONSERVATION: You may think that such inhospitable and often remote habitats would have few threats, but sadly, this is not the case. Land reclamation has taken many areas, especially in the Low Countries, reducing the amount of habitat available. In a few areas, there are ongoing efforts to recreate and restore some of the habitat that was reclaimed for agricultural purposes, by allowing the sea to breach the sea wall, but the net loss is still great. The recently built Cardiff Bay Barrage removed a large area of intertidal flats in Cardiff Bay, Wales, and has been demonstrated to have had a severely detrimental effect on the populations of birds formerly using the site. Such human pressures are only likely to intensify. Global warming and the inevitable sea-level rises will also reduce the area of intertidal areas, as sea defences will prevent the natural inland creep of the intertidal areas, effectively removing the strandline area and diminishing the area that is exposed at low tide and the amount of time suitable feeding areas are exposed. Human disturbance to wildlife is also increasing rapidly, and direct disturbance to fragile populations of shorebirds is increasing exponentially. Such activities as unregulated dog walking and jet ski and sailboard use frequently cause high disturbance levels to both roosting and feeding congregations of shorebirds and others. Pollution from industrial spills and agricultural runoff into rivers also detrimentally affects the quality of the tidal flats.

To complicate matters further, many bird species require a whole series of sites to survive, comprising breeding and wintering grounds and migratory stopover sites. Europe's Tidal Flat and Estuary habitat is part of two major flyways: the East Atlantic Flyway and the Eurasian–African Flyway. These two major migration routes are used by shorebirds and other waterbirds that breed in the Arctic and migrate to and from wintering areas in nw. Europe and areas farther south in w. and s. Africa. The flyways, formed by a series of separate areas, are best regarded as interconnected systems that form a unit, and habitat loss or disturbance to just one part of the flyway may result in serious damage to a species' or group of species' survival rates, demonstrating the need for an international approach to conservation of such ecosystems.

DISTRIBUTION: Tidal Flat and Estuary is found intermittently around the coastline of the Arctic Ocean, Baltic Sea, North Sea, Irish Sea, Atlantic Ocean, and, to a lesser extent, Mediterranean Sea. Due to the absence of significant tides in the Mediterranean Sea, there are few tidal flats, though some more extensive areas occur in the Gulf of Gabes, in s. Tunisia. This habitat is all but absent in the landlocked Caspian Sea, as no real tides occur. Although the habitat is relatively widespread, not all sites are the same, and some are far more important to wildlife than others, particularly for migratory and wintering shorebirds. The Wadden Sea, a UNESCO site stretching along the coasts of Germany, the Netherlands, and Denmark, is one of the largest and most well-studied tidal-flat ecosystems in Europe. It is characterised by extensive mudflats and sandbanks, supporting an estimated 12 million birds per year from the East Atlantic and Eurasian–African Flyways, many of which are short-term migrants and wintering birds. The Wash, on the east coast of England, is another vast site, holding internationally important numbers of no fewer than 16 species of birds, with up to 500,000 individual birds using the site at one time. Other tidal flats of major importance include Morecambe Bay and the Severn Estuary, between Wales and England.

WHERE TO SEE: The Wash, England, UK (best seen at Snettisham RSPB reserve); Heysham, Morecambe Bay, England, UK; Wadden Sea, Netherlands, Germany, and Denmark.

ANTHROPOGENIC HABITATS

Eu13A EUROPEAN CROPLAND

IN A NUTSHELL: The vast, diverse croplands that feed Europe's people and have been adopted by animal species that evolved in open landscapes. **Global Habitat Affinities:** NORTH AMERICAN CROPLAND; NORTH AFRICAN TEMPERATE CULTIVATION. **Continental Habitat Affinities:** OAK DEHESA; IBERIAN STEPPE; TEMPERATE GRASSLAND AND SAVANNA; PUSZTA AND PONTIC STEPPE. **Species Overlap:** OAK DEHESA; IBERIAN STEPPE; TEMPERATE GRASSLAND AND SAVANNA; PUSZTA AND PONTIC STEPPE; WET GRASSLAND.

DESCRIPTION: Agriculture has been widespread in Europe for at least 5000 years, and it is so integrally tied to our lives and survival that it is almost impossible to imagine a Europe without extensive croplands. Many of us have a wildly romanticised view of this habitat, a sentiment captured in the heart-tugging images of a gladiator striding pensively through a field of golden wheat in a recent Hollywood blockbuster.

Orchards, such as this cherry grove, provide cover and food for many birds, though farmers do whatever they can to protect their crops. © MARC GUYT, AGAMI

Ploughing and other mechanical applications expose insects, seeds, and other food sources, which are quickly taken advantage of by a variety of birds, like this large flock of Black-headed Gulls. © MENNO VAN DUIJN, AGAMI

Cropland covers almost half of Europe's land area (42% of the EU), and half of our bird species use these agricultural lands. This is not a surprise, given that, structurally, croplands somewhat resemble the open habitats that have dominated Europe for the past 2.5 million years (the Pleistocene). The cropland communities are, then, naturally a subset of the open habitat communities of the region. Unfortunately, bird abundance in croplands has plummeted in the past few decades, with populations now at least 36% lower than in 1990. The intensification of agriculture has been the primary driver.

Fertilisers dramatically increase plant growth rates and help produce greater quantities of food faster. Unfortunately, the greater growth rates also mean that the habitat changes more quickly, crops are harvested sooner, and fields can be replanted almost immediately. This leaves precious little time for birds and other wildlife to breed. In addition, fertiliser runoff enriches surrounding water bodies, causing algal blooms (through eutrophication) and, ultimately, the collapse of the ecosystem. Herbicides decrease plant diversity, meaning fewer seed and sprout types are available for birds to eat. They also eliminate plants—both weeds and nontarget species—that help to create a wider range of micro-niches for invertebrates. Pesticide use also decreases the availability of smaller animals, with a knock-on effect throughout the food chain.

Landscape heterogeneity makes a huge difference to birds: many microhabitats in a small area mean that birds (and other animals) can easily move between areas to fill all their requirements (diverse shelter, feeding, temperature, etc.). Non-cultivated edge habitat is critical for farmland birds and other wildlife. Hedgerows, trees, streams, field edges, patches of 'weeds', and fallow land were common in traditional small-plot agriculture. A bird's home range could easily encompass sprouting crops, more mature crops, ploughed land, single bushes, and forest scrub. One fascinating example of this are the *åkerholmar* of Scandinavia: over centuries, glacial stones were painstakingly removed from arable fields and collected in piles. These developed into islands of natural vegetation,

Grey Partridge is a classic farmland bird, but it disappears when the regime becomes too intensive and edge habitats are removed. © RAN SCHOLS, AGAMI

significantly contributing to the diversity and health of the ecosystem. By contrast, large farms of monocultures with little edge habitat or variation and no 'weeds' are metaphoric deserts for most animals. This is compounded by intensive insecticide and other chemical use.

Wheat is the most extensive crop in Europe, covering a staggering 35 million ha (86 million ac.), excluding Russia. Barley, oats, and rye are grown on an additional 20 million ha (50 million ac.). Traditionally, most of our cereals were planted in spring, and the sprouting crops then provided a long period for grassland birds to feed and nest before the crops became too dense and tall. After the harvest, cereal stubble fields were left open and were very important for various granivorous birds over winter. Most of our cereals are now planted in autumn, so there are fewer stubble fields available in winter. These winter cereals grow quickly in the spring, offering a very short window of opportunity for breeding birds like the Eurasian Skylark, which cannot effectively use tall, dense croplands. In addition, heavy use of insecticides means that adults struggle to find invertebrate food for their nestlings.

Maize (17 million ha/40 million ac.) and rapeseed (7 million ha/17 million ac.) fields typically have a greater invertebrate density than wheat, but the structure of the crops is far from ideal for feeding and breeding birds. Consequently, they are only really used near the edges of the planted fields. Fallow land and patches of more natural habitat can significantly improve the extent to which birds and other wildlife can use the landscape. This is also true for sunflower fields (12 million ha/ 30 million ac.), where birds can cause severe crop losses, especially near trees and patches of natural habitat. Stubble fields of many crops are extremely important for many of our farmland birds in winter, especially Eurasian Skylark, Yellowhammer, Northern Lapwing, Stock Dove, Eurasian Linnet, Meadow Pipit, Pin-tailed Sandgrouse, Black-bellied Sandgrouse, and Great Bustard.

Rice is typically produced in flooded paddies that, unsurprisingly, emulate natural WET GRASSLAND and similar ecosystems for various wetland bird and other wildlife species. In many regions in the greater Mediterranean, rice paddies are the only suitable wetland habitats remaining. They are particularly important during the autumn migration and early winter, when invertebrate biomass is at its greatest and temporary wetlands in the landscape are dry. Bird diversity can be wonderfully high, including Eurasian (Great) Bittern, Squacco Heron, Glossy Ibis, Purple Heron, Northern Lapwing, Curlew Sandpiper, Jack Snipe, Black-headed Gull, Gull-billed Tern, and Whiskered Tern. This diversity is supported by farmers who favour organic agriculture and allow some scattered patches of weeds to grow, especially along ditches. The Reserva Natural Riet Vell, in Spain's Ebro delta, is a prime example of how rice and other crops can be grown successfully while providing very significant benefits for wildlife.

Traditional olive groves emulate the natural savannas of the Mediterranean, and the wildlife is consequently related to that of OAK DEHESA. Cirl Buntings and Rufous-tailed Scrub-Robins trill to the drumbeat of the Eurasian Hoopoe while Eurasian Blackcaps provide the melody. Olive-tree Warbler even tells you where to find it in its name. As in other agricultural settings, landscape heterogeneity, lower chemical use, and lower crop density yield a more natural ecosystem with a more diverse wildlife community.

Forestry plantations cover mind-bogglingly vast swaths of Europe, and much of our forest area is managed for timber production. As with other croplands, management intensity has enormous consequences for wildlife communities. Lightly managed forests hold communities reminiscent of natural forests (and are treated in the forest chapters). By contrast, heavily managed plantations in neat, sterile rows with no structural heterogeneity provide precious few microhabitats for invertebrates, birds, and other wildlife. They are also largely devoid of fun for the avid wildlife-watcher. We can choose neatness or nature, not both.

WILDLIFE: The wildlife communities of European Cropland are subsets of the region's natural open habitat communities. Cereal fields attract grassland species, while savanna-like olive groves are filled with species from the OAK DEHESA, and rice paddies with wetland species.

Below: **Traditionally, most cereals were planted in spring, and the sprouting crops provided a long period for grassland birds to feed and nest before the plants became too dense and tall. A wide variety of grassland and savanna birds were able to take advantage of such lower-intensity croplands, including Western Yellow Wagtail (pictured), Yellowhammer, Eurasian Skylark, and Whinchat.** © JACOB SCHUT, AGAMI

Below right: **Rough edges around agricultural fields often have high densities of small mammals and create perfect hunting grounds for Eurasian (Common) Kestrel. Sadly, modern agricultural practice is minimising and eliminating such rough ground.** © DANIELE OCCHIATO, AGAMI

Opposite right: **Western Roe Deer does best in mixed landscapes, feeding in cereal fields at night and resting in tall maize fields or woodlots during the day.** © JACOB SCHUT, AGAMI

Eurasian Skylark prefers open habitats devoid of larger bushes and trees, so it can do well in low-intensity croplands. Landscape heterogeneity is important to the skylarks, with breeding birds preferring territories with a mixture of different crop heights, including covered and open areas. By leaving small patches of winter wheat unplanted, farmers can create 'skylark patches', relatively open areas for skylarks to land and feed, significantly affecting local skylark populations. Unsurprisingly, they do not do well with extensive use of pesticides or fertilisers. In addition to Eurasian Skylark, Calandra Lark and many other lark species will use croplands, particularly cereals.

Common Quail readily uses clover and cereal croplands. It has driven many a birder crazy trying to locate the *wet-my-lips* call in the dense cover of a lush wheat field. Western Yellow Wagtail readily breeds in winter cereals, provided adequate feeding areas are available nearby. It uses potato fields heavily later in the breeding season. Eurasian Tree Sparrow, Spanish Sparrow, Eurasian Linnet, Common Chaffinch, European Goldfinch, and many other finches will readily feed in cereal and other croplands. Cereals and stubble are important for Grey Partridge. Eurasian (Common) Kestrel is invariably the most common raptor, although Common Buzzard can also be very abundant in places.

Corn Bunting favours wide-open, dense grasslands and cereal fields with a relatively high abundance of weeds. Yellowhammer, Ortolan Bunting, and Cirl Bunting are savanna species and readily use croplands, provided hedgerows or trees are available as song posts. Ortolan Bunting is particularly dependent on croplands but requires high landscape heterogeneity with smaller patches of cereals, potatoes, and wooded patches (as in the *åkerholmar*). Western Roe Deer does best in mixed landscapes, feeding in cereal fields at night and resting in tall maize fields or woodlots during the day.

Cranes, egrets, storks, waterfowl, and myriad shorebirds use rice paddies, particularly in autumn and early winter.

CONSERVATION: Croplands are critically important for European wildlife, but they can continue to play this role only if managed wisely. This will need to involve some fallow land, rotational crop systems, careful use of chemicals and fertilisers, and a general awareness of the needs of local wildlife.

DISTRIBUTION: Cropland is found across Europe and carved out of almost every natural habitat except for the most extreme (e.g., tundra).

WHERE TO SEE: Likely within walking distance of wherever you are right now.

Eu13B EUROPEAN URBAN ENVIRONMENTS

IN A NUTSHELL: A wide range of birds and other wildlife have adopted urban areas and human settlements. **Global Habitat Affinities:** NORTH AMERICAN URBAN AND SUBURBAN ENVIRONMENTS; AUSTRALIAN URBAN AREAS. **Habitat Affinities:** TEMPERATE RIPARIAN FOREST; TEMPERATE GRASSLAND AND SAVANNA; FRESHWATER LAKES, DAMS, AND PONDS. **Species Overlap:** TEMPERATE RIPARIAN FOREST; TEMPERATE GRASSLAND AND SAVANNA; FRESHWATER LAKES, DAMS, AND PONDS.

DESCRIPTION AND WILDLIFE: For most of us, our first and most common encounters with wildlife are in towns and cities. Most of Europe's woodland and forest species are generalists and quite adaptable, typically looking for a habitat structure that somewhat resembles their natural habitat. TEMPERATE RIPARIAN FORESTS run through towns, while parks and gardens often resemble open woodlands and savannas, and buildings and bridges are akin to cliffs.

Cities can have large areas that are almost like rocky desert in their lack of vegetation and dominance of rock (concrete). Few animals can eke out an existence in this barren, stark landscape. The Feral Pigeon has flourished in the built urban environment. Its wild ancestor—Rock Dove—evolved to breed and live on cliffs. Millennia of domestication have created a species that is very comfortable around people and adaptable enough to thrive in the heart of cities. Pigeons are supreme scavengers, surviving on human scraps and somewhat natural food sources

Feral Pigeons descended from the Rock Dove. They have been extremely successful and are present in almost all cities throughout Europe. © WIL LEURS, AGAMI

Rose-ringed Parakeet is an introduced species that has been very successful in many cities. Sadly, it outcompetes many native species, such as starlings, for nesting cavities.
© SYLVAIN REYT, AGAMI

in parks. Some cities have found that they can quickly reduce the population just by prohibiting the feeding of pigeons.

Abundant Feral Pigeons, along with Rose-ringed Parakeets and European Starlings, have attracted Peregrine Falcons, which now nest in the pseudo-cliff landscape of many European cities. Some Peregrine Falcons have even learned to hunt at night, rising high in the sky to use the city lights to backlight passing migrant birds as they fly over the city.

Other bird species that use the urban landscape as artificial cliffs include Black Redstart, Wallcreeper, Western House-Martin, and Common Swift. Dawn is the best time to listen for Black Redstarts moving around quiet city centres, so 'look up!' (as David Lindo, the Urban Birder, would say). They are surprisingly common in many of Europe's cities, but they tend to be unassuming and stay on roofs and higher ledges, where they are harder to spot. Wallcreepers overwinter in their mountainous breeding range (even above 2000 m/6500 ft. in the Alps), but there is also significant dispersal, and the odd bird invariably ends up on an ancient cathedral in a city somewhere. Common Swifts spend only about 100 days each year in Europe but can be wonderfully abundant in historical city centres. Both Common and Pallid Swifts are colonial breeders and have used the nooks and crannies of churches and other old buildings as breeding sites for centuries. The steady modernisation of façades and sealing of crevices have dramatically limited swift nest sites. Using swift bricks—artificial nest boxes for swifts—can go a long way to keeping swifts in our cities and towns.

Many European cities and towns are set along larger rivers. Bridges spanning these rivers are readily used as breeding sites by Eurasian Crag-Martin in c. and s. Europe. Some bridges can even

Everyone's favourite, the European Robin, has adapted well to urban environments and is present in many gardens in w. Europe. © MARC GUYT, AGAMI

hold large colonies of Western House-Martin. Both martins and various gulls can regularly be seen feeding up and down the rivers.

Many of these watercourses also have adjacent green spaces and parks. While far from being pristine TEMPERATE RIPARIAN FORESTS, they still represent valuable wildlife habitats. They are relatively safe conduits for species moving through urban areas and provide refuge for numerous breeding species. European Robin, various thrushes and tits, Common Chiffchaff, European Greenfinch, Common Chaffinch, House Sparrow, Eurasian Wren, and many more passerines are found in abundance in these green spaces. These species are also regularly seen in other parks and gardens of our urban spaces, where they are invariably joined by diversely coloured feral and wild Mallards as well as Mute Swans and Eurasian Moorhens. These parks and their duck ponds can also be interesting migrant traps for birds dazzled by city lights at night while seeking refuge in the somewhat darker green spaces. In the morning, you may find a Northern Shoveler has joined the Mallards, and a Wood Warbler is feeding alongside Eurasian Blue Tits.

The savanna-like nature of many of our parks and gardens would theoretically be great for Eurasian Hoopoe. Unfortunately, it does not stand a chance against domestic cats. Parks and gardens are also important for Eurasian Sparrowhawk and Eurasian (Common) Kestrel, both of which readily use the urban environment. Vienna even has a considerably higher density of kestrels than the surrounding non-urbanised landscape. This small falcon typically feeds mainly on small mammals (especially Common Vole), but its prey can be as much as 50% birds in an urban setting. Some individuals have even become adept at hunting Feral Pigeon, a prey item that is at least as heavy as the kestrel itself.

The domestic cat runs riot in urban habitats. A top predator, present in unnatural densities, it is responsible for the deaths of millions upon millions of birds and small mammals. © ROB OLIVIER, AGAMI

Green spaces with diverse feeding options are typically the most productive for finding wildlife. Open lawns and wildflower meadows are important for savanna-adapted species like Eurasian Blackbird, Fieldfare, Stock Dove, and Common Chaffinch. Large trees, such as London Plane (*Platanus* × *hispanica*), Silver Birch (*Betula pendula*), Sycamore Maple (*Acer pseudoplatanus*), and English Oak (*Quercus robur*), provide space for Great Spotted Woodpecker, Eurasian Nuthatch, Tawny Owl, Eurasian

Many species have adapted to urbanised environments, including Common Hedgehog (pictured), which seeks refuge in suitable gardens and parks. © ROY DE HAAS, AGAMI

Eurasian Red Squirrel happily survives in parks and gardens except in areas where it has been outcompeted and extirpated by the introduced North American Eastern Grey Squirrel. © SYLVAIN REYT, AGAMI

Red Squirrel, and the invasive Eastern Grey Squirrel. Fruiting plants like European Black Elderberry (*Sambucus nigra*), Guelder-Rose (*Viburnum opulus*), Common Ivy (*Hedera helix*), and European Mountain Ash (*Sorbus aucuparia*) are important wildlife food sources. Bird feeders are common in Europe's gardens and parks, though approaches to feeding birds differ somewhat from country to country. Mixed seeds and fat (suet) balls are likely the most common throughout the region, particularly in winter. Garden bird feeders are a wonderful way for people to experience Eurasian Blackbirds, Eurasian Tree Sparrows, European Greenfinches, Eurasian Blue Tits, Great Tits, and a wealth of other species up close and personal. For many people, this is their entry into the fascinating world of birds.

CONSERVATION: A surprisingly wide range of wildlife uses urban settlements, particularly where parks and gardens offer a diversity of niches and opportunities for feeding, resting, and breeding. Domestic cats kill an estimated 200 million animals each year in the UK alone, and roughly 100 million birds die annually after colliding with windows in Germany. The consequences for wildlife across Europe are enormous. Recent developments encouraging wildflower meadows and more structurally diverse 'untidy' gardening have certainly helped foster the biodiversity in our urban areas.

DISTRIBUTION: Urban settlements and cities throughout Europe.

WHERE TO SEE: Hyde Park and Kensington Gardens, London, England, UK; Bois de Boulogne, Paris, France; Vondelpark, Amsterdam, Netherlands; Englischer Garten, Munich, Germany; Großer Tiergarten, Berlin, Germany.

APPENDIX

SOIL GROUPS AND HABITATS

There are numerous soil classification systems, all with different names for the various soil types. The global soil reference is the World Reference Base for Soil Resources (WRB). The American system is the USDA's Soil Taxonomy (perhaps better described as 'Soil Typology', because, although it is hierarchical, it does not have an evolutionary direction, and soils can change from one type to another). In this book, we usually use the WRB system and clarify it with more specific names when needed. Although a direct walk-through between the two soil systems is difficult, because the USDA system has 12 types, while the WRB system has over twice that number, we can do a rough comparison with biomes, USDA order, and their WRB equivalents where they exist (see figure on p.408).

The most globally widespread of the soils in the WRB classification are as follows:

Acrisols, though not widespread in Europe, are the dominant soil type in older, stable landscapes such as in sub-Saharan Africa, Australia, non-Amazonian Brazil, and India. They are highly weathered, with a subsurface horizon of clay accumulation, and usually have a very high iron and aluminium-oxide concentration at the soil surface. Because they form in environments with strong seasonal rainfall (monsoonal regions) and fluctuating water tables, they promote the development of MIDDLE EASTERN SAVANNA.

Andosols are formed in volcanic ash and other volcanic materials. They chemically weather very quickly in tropical humid terrains so are very fertile and generally retain water well; for these reasons, they tend to promote growth of rainforests, but they are also found in other environments in Iceland, Greece, and Italy.

Calcisols are characterised by precipitation and accumulation of calcium carbonate (calcrete). They differ from the calcrete durisol in that they don't form a hardpan within the soil. They are found mainly in Mediterranean and semi-arid habitats such as EUROPEAN GARRIGUE or EUROPEAN MAQUIS.

Cambisols are a slightly more developed version of regosols, with minimal horizon development. They are widespread, can be found in a variety of environments, and don't have a strong relationship with any vegetation type.

Chernozems are soils rich in organic matter that have a thick, dark surface horizon. They are associated mainly with temperate grasslands such as EUROPEAN FOREST STEPPE.

Cryosols are the soils that develop over permafrost that is close to the surface in polar regions. Because leaching is impeded by the ice, and decomposition is so slow, they usually develop organic-rich surface horizons. They are minimally affected by the chemistry of the inorganic matter, because chemical weathering of the underlying rock is so limited. They are typical of EUROPEAN ROCKY TUNDRA.

Durisols are soils characterised by a hardpan layer of silica (silcrete), calcium (calcrete), iron (ferricrete), or gypsum (gypcrete), which limits root penetration and water movement. They typically form in warm arid or monsoonal environments such as deserts and savannas.

Ferralsols are the highly weathered soils found in tropical humid environments with fairly uniform rainfall. They are characterised by low fertility, due to intense leaching over time, but can be fertile if formed on mafic (iron and magnesium) igneous rocks such as basalt. They are very localised in Europe but may exist as palaeosols (soils in sync with the existing environment).

Gleysols form in waterlogged areas and obtain a mid-grey colour through leaching and anaerobic conditions. With drying, they will form into one of the other soil groups and generally do not determine vegetation type.

Histosols are soils found in areas of impeded drainage and seasonal or permanent flooding. They undergo little soil development, are usually composed of organic materials, and can form peat. They are found mainly in marshes or flooded forests such as TEMPERATE RIPARIAN FOREST.

Leptosols are young soils that form over stony or gravelly material. They are generally well drained and show little profile development. They are very poor for agriculture, so they are often left as scrubland.

Luvisols are moderately leached soils that have a subsurface horizon of clay accumulation. They are fertile and found mainly in temperate forests such as EUROPEAN BEECH FOREST.

Podzols are acidic soils under coniferous forests in cool, moist environments, such as EUROPEAN SPRUCE-FIR TAIGA. The intense leaching of nutrients caused by the highly acidic waters removes organic material and most minerals from the surface, leaving it white-coloured, and deposits them in a dark iron- and organic-rich horizon within 2 m (6 ft.) of the surface.

Regosols are young soils commonly found in areas of recent sediment deposition, colluvial slopes, and alluvial plains after massive flooding. They can also be dry soils typical of deserts such as CASPIAN WORMWOOD DESERT and CAUCASIAN SHRUB DESERT. They can show evidence of soil horizon development but have limited organic matter, due to limited vegetation cover.

Solonchaks have many salts either at the surface as crust or within the profile. They are generally found in poor drainage of arid and semi-arid climates where evaporation exceeds precipitation. Vegetation that grows in these soils tends to be halophytic (salt tolerant). Solonchak is found in habitats such as CAUCASIAN SHRUB DESERT.

Biome	USDA Soil Group	WORLD (WRB)
Conifer Forests	Spodosol	Podzol
Deserts and Arid Scrubs	Aridisol	Durisol Regosol
Temperate Deciduous Forests	Alfisol Spodosol (weak)	Luvisol Podzol (weak)
Tropical Humid Forests	Oxisol Andisol	Ferralsol Andosol
Dry Deciduous Forests	Oxisol Inceptisol	Ferralsol Cambisol
Savanna Habitats	Ultisol Entisol	Acrisol Leptosol
Grasslands and Steppes	Mollisol Vertisol	Chernozem Vertisol
Mediterranean Habitats	Mollisol Aridisol	Chernozem Calcisol
Tundras	Gelisol	Cryosol
Freshwater Wetlands	Histosol	Histosol Gleysol
Saline Habitats	Histosol	Solonchak

Vertisols are clayey soils that swell when wet and shrink when dry, causing deep cracks during dry periods and sometimes making it difficult for large trees to grow. They form in PUSZTA AND PONTIC STEPPE, but they can underlie a variety of other grasslands or low scrub habitats.

It is a general understanding that soil is determined by underlying geology and hydrology, and that it greatly influences vegetation type. Changes in hydrology affect the soil type; typical examples would be the impeding of drainage over a chernozem in the grasslands and the resulting formation of a histosol. Vegetation can also influence soil type, such as when desertification occurs or, as is well documented, when plantations of spruce or pine replace TEMPERATE OAK FOREST, and the increase in acidity of the waters percolating from the decomposing conifer needles changes the soils from chernozem to podzol.

COMMON CANOPY LEAF TYPES AND THE FORESTS WHERE YOU MAY FIND THEM

This table presents the most common leaf types used in describing different types of forest canopy and some of the habitats where they are prominent. This does not take into account the many types of leaves of understorey plants such as grasses, sedges, ferns, and euphorbias.

PLANT GROUP	LEAF SHAPE	LEAF NAME	HABITATS
GYMNOSPERMS		**Conifer Lobe** Flat, lobed, evergreen.	Temperate forests, mixed conifer/ broadleaf forests
		Conifer Needle Thin linear leaves. Usually evergreen.	Boreal conifer forests, dry conifer forests
ANGIOSPERMS		**Deciduous Broadleaf** Broad, thin leaves that grow quickly and last one season.	Temperate deciduous forests, wet/dry deciduous forests
		Evergreen Broadleaf Broad, thin, often with drip tips. They last a long time.	Rainforests, cloud forests
		Sclerophyllous Evergreen Thick, leathery leaves that resist transpiration and fires.	Eucalypt forests, sclerophyll forests, heathlands, Maquis, fynbos, mallee, Mulga, matorral, cerrado
		Microphyllous Small leaves that resist transpiration.	Acacia savanna, thornscrub, Chaco seco, desert scrubs

INDEX

Habitats are worded **in full** in the index beginning with the word European, where relevant. The word 'European' has been dropped from references to habitats within the *actual* text, e.g., 'Montane Spruce-Fir Forest' refers to *European* Montane Spruce-Fir Forest (*see page 10*).

Page numbers in **bold** indicate photographs.